EUROPEANS IN THE WORLD
Volume One

Sources on Cultural Contact from Antiquity to 1700

James R. Lehning
University of Utah

and

Megan Armstrong
University of Utah

Prentice Hall

Upper Saddle River, New Jersey 07458

Library of Congress Cataloging-in-Publication Data

Europeans in the world; sources on cultural contact/[compiled] by Meagan Armstrong and
James R. Lehning.
   p.cm.
  Includes bibliographical references.
  Contents: v. 1. From antiquity to 1700 –v. 2. From 1650 to the present.
  ISBN 0-13-091269-7 (v. 1) –ISBN 0-13-091260-3 (v. 2)
   1. Civilization, Western. 2. Europe–Civilization. 3. Europe–Intellectual life. 4.
  Europe–History. I. Armstrong, Megan II. Lehning, James R.
  CB245.#75 2002
  909'.09821–dc21

2001037443

VP, Editorial Director: Charlyce Jones-Owen
Senior Acquisitions Editor: Charles Cavaliere
Editorial Assistant: Adrienne Paul
Senior Managing Editor: Jan Stephan
Production Liaison: Fran Russello
Project Manager: Russell Jones (Pine Tree Composition)
Prepress and Manufacturing Buyer: Tricia Kenny
Art Director: Jayne Conte
Cover Designer: Kiwi Design
Cover Image: Tapestries of Catherine de Medici: Assault of a turreted elephant.
Copyright © Scala/Art Resource, NY; Uffizi, Florence, Italy
Marketing Manager: Claire Rehwinkel

Cartography in this book configured by Maryland Cartographics, Oxford, Maryland
This book was set in 10/12 Baskerville by Pine Tree Composition
and was printed and bound by Courier Companies, Inc.
The cover was printed by Phoenix Color Corp.

 © 2002 by Pearson Education, Inc.
Upper Saddle River, New Jersey 07458

Printed in the United States of America

10 9 8 7 6 5 4 3 2 1

ISBN 0-13-091269-7

Pearson Education Limited, *London*
Pearson Education Australia, Pte. Limited, *Sydney*
Pearson Education Singapore, Pte. Ltd.
Pearson Education North Asia Ltd., *Hong Kong*
Pearson Education Canada, Ltd., *Toronto*
Pearson Educación de Mexico, S.A. de C.V.
Pearson Education—Japan, *Tokyo*
Pearson Education Malaysia, Pte. Ltd.
Pearson Education, Upper Saddle River, *New Jersey*

for
Noreen and Jack

CONTENTS

Chapter 14 The Plantation Complex and the Slave Trade, 1650–1800 A.D.   303

Credits   321

ACKNOWLEDGEMENTS

The authors would like to acknowledge friends and colleagues who helped in the completion of this work. In particular, we would like to thank Faith Childress, Elizabeth Clement, Nadja Durbach, Ipek Giencel Sezgin, Ray Gunn, Eric Hinderaker, Rebecca Horn, Isabel Moreira, Bradley Parker, Luise Poulton, Richard Raiswell, Wes Sasaki-Uemura, Janet Theiss, Peter Von Sivers, and Anand Yang for their advice and assistance.

We would also like to thank Charles Cavaliere of Prentice Hall for his support and advice throughout this project, and the staff at Prentice Hall for helping produce the book.

No acknowledgment would be complete without mentioning our colleagues who were gracious enough to review these volumes. They are: Jack M. Balcer, Ohio State University; Sara E. Chapman, Oakland University; Carol E. Harrison, Kent State University; and Larissa J. Taylor, Colby College. We thank them for their efforts in fulfilling this critical responsibility.

PREFACE

In the last generation, undergraduate history curricula in North American colleges and universities have increasingly become concerned with teaching national, thematic, and continental histories in a global context. There has been a growing recognition that civilizations are not airtight containers, as they have been thought of in the past, but rather that contact between civilizations is an important aspect of historical processes. Journals that focus on the history of European interaction with the rest of the globe, such as the *Journal of World History* and *Itinerario: The European Journal of Overseas History,* have been developed and become normal reading for historians—no matter what their specific interests. These changes have affected many of the staple courses in the curriculum, such as Western Civilization; have led to new courses, such as World Civilization; and have also led to more specialized courses on topics such as Travel, Exploration, Imperialism, and Colonialism.

At the same time, more and more college and university teachers attempt to use primary sources in their classes. Theses sources act as a way of teaching the craft of the historian through exposure to the words and phrases of people who lived in the past, as well as allowing the student to see the raw material from which historical accounts are developed, which makes those accounts more meaningful.

Europeans in the World is primary source reader which focuses on the relations between European civilization and the rest of the world and covers chronologically, in two volumes, the period from antiquity to the late twentieth century. It presents excerpts from primary source texts, both written documents and visual images, which where possible, express multiple voices about the ways in which European civilization interacted with the civilizations of other parts of the world. The texts presented here cover themes such as politics, gender, religion, and ethnicity in non-European parts of the world. The readings not only include such standard accounts as J. A. Hobson's *Imperialism,* but also accounts by Catholic religious men and women such as Marie de l'Incarnation (*Letters*) and Matteo Ricci (*Journals*), unusual European travelers such as Mary Kingsley (*Travels in West Africa*), and by colonial subjects such as Mohandas K. Gandhi (*Hind Swaraj*).

Because textbooks typically treat the subject sparingly, each volume begins with a schematic account of European contact with the rest of the world which is aimed at providing a context for the selected documents. The volume introductions also include a suggestion of the the themes that may be found in the documents, as well as a guide to the student on how to read them. The documents themselves are divided into topical chapters arranged in roughly chronological order. Each of these chapters begins with a discussion of the specific events and themes that mark the chapter, and there are brief introductions to each document that provides background information about the author and about the document itself. At the end of each chapter are suggestions for further reading, recommended Web sites, and study questions to assist the student in further exploring the topic.

Europeans in the World therefore presents college and university teachers of history with materials that can be used to increase the sense in their students of the importance of contact throughout its history between the West and the rest of the world. It allows and understanding that this contact at times not only imposed Western institutions and values on those parts of the world, but also affected the development of Western Civilization.

James R. Lehning
Megan Armstrong

INTRODUCTION

Cultural interaction has always been one of the most important forces in shaping Western culture. The documents selected for this volume focus attention on different facets of cultural interaction of the earliest civilizations to the end of the Early Modern period. They shed light in particular on the cultural impact of conquest and trade on European and non-European societies, the rise of imperial powers and colonization, and the influence of Eastern intellectual and spiritual traditions upon Western philosophy, theology, legal systems, science, and literature. They raise questions about Western assumptions about human nature and human society, specifically with regard to gender roles, spirituality, and race. To give students some appreciation for the richness and variety of historical sources, we include travel accounts, chronicles, memoirs, legal codes, economic records, correspondence, plays, and poems. Most of the documents in this reader were written by European men. Whenever possible, however, we have included accounts written by non-Europeans, by both European and non-European women, and by individuals of different socioeconomic status, so that students can compare and contrast differing perspectives on cultural interaction. The documents are arranged both chronologically and thematically. The Ancient World covers the period 3,000 B.C. to the end of the Roman Empire (ca. 500 A.D.). The Medieval period (early, middle, late) begins in 500 A.D. and continues to the end of the fourteenth century, and the Early Modern period extends from the Italian Renaissance of the fourteenth century, including the period of the Reformation and overseas expansion of the sixteenth and seventeenth centuries.

ANCIENT WORLD (*3000 B.C.–500 A.D.*)

It was during the Bronze Age (ca, 3000 B.C.) that we find the earliest evidence of complex human societies. These societies first appeared in the Middle East in the region known as Mesopotamia. The fertile character of the "land between two rivers" attracted migrating peoples from the Arabian and Syrian deserts of the northwest to settle along the shores of the Tigris and Euphrates rivers. During the early dynastic period (2900–2350 B.C.), conquest and trade fueled the emergence of larger urbanized societies which showed evidence of what scholars term "civilization"—in other words, polities suggesting signs of political centralization, systematic cultivation of the land through irrigation, the organization of large labor forces, sophisticated temple-based religious systems, extensive trade networks, and writing systems (chapter 1). The first great empire was established by Sargon, leader of the Akkadians, around 2300 B.C. The Akkadians admired the sophisticated culture of the conquered Sumerians who were based in the southern part of Mesopotamia. They absorbed Sumerian central-ized political and economic structures, religious deities, and the Sumerian writing sys-tem which to this day remains the first known writing system in the world. The later empires of the Babylonians, Kassites, and Assyrians similarly absorbed and trans-formed elements of preceding cultures in the region, and spread this new culture throughout their respective empires. By the time King Hammurabi united virtually all of Mesopotamia under his rule (ca. 1792–1750 B.C.), historians were able to talk about the emergence of a distinct "mesopotamian" culture.

Trade however, was as important as conquest for spreading Mesopotamian culture not only throughout Mesopotamia but also into Egypt, Palestine, and other Mediter-ranean regions. Mesopotamian societies were trading societies, and they were in regular contact with other peoples from the period of Sargon onward. During the height of the Neo-Babylonian Empire (612–539 B.C.), for example, merchants from Arabia and Africa were a regular presence in the markets of the bustling metropolis of Babylon.

The spread of Mesopotamian culture is also suggested by the vital bronze age Mi-noan culture which developed on the island of Crete in the Mediterranean Sea after 2900 BC. Here we find evidence of a lively artistic and intellectual life; complex social, economic, and political structures; a sophisticated polytheistic religious system; and three writing systems. The more warlike culture of Mycenae, which emerged after 1600 B.C. on the mainland of modern day Greece, similarly shows evidence of a complex soci-ety, but both in the case of Mycenaean and Minoan culture, their distinctive character owed as much to their location in the Aegean as it did to Mesopotamian influence. Prox-imity to the sea and constant interactions between these societies and other peoples who began to establish settlements along the rugged, mountainous coastline of the Aegean laid the basis for the emergence of an entirely new and distinctive culture by 700 B.C.

It was here in ancient Greece that an intellectual culture emerges which to this day has profoundly shaped European perspectives on human nature and human rela-tions to the physical environment (chapter 2). Greek culture spread throughout much of the Mediterranean during the height of Athenian power around 450 B.C., and it penetrated more deeply into Asia Minor following the campaigns of Alexander the Great against the Persian empire. It was through the agency of merchants as well as in the Greek communities established by Alexander in the East (many of which were called Alexandria) that Greek culture encountered Eastern intellectual, spiri-tual, and artistic traditions. By the end of the campaigns of Alexander, Eastern mys-tery cults were making their way across the Mediterranean to Greece, and Eastern works on astronomy, medicine and philosophy attracted the attention of Greek thinkers. The rise of the Roman Empire by 300 B.C. further encouraged cultural ex-change between the northern Mediterranean lands, North Africa, and Asia Minor. Greek learning in particular spread because the Romans admired it enormously, espe-cially in the realms of philosophy and literature. The Romans were also attracted to Eastern and Greek religions. Romans transformed Greek deities into Roman ones by Latinizing their names and including them alongside their own collection of spiritual authorities. Eastern cults such as the Phyrigian cult of Cybele and the Egyptian cult of Isis were also popular among the Roman populace at varying times in the history of the empire, even though they were not officially recognized by Roman authority. The militaristic Mithraic cult, for example, appealed enormously to Roman soldiers.

Greek culture continued to spread to new regions as the Roman Empire grew to include by 200 A.D. not only much of Asia Minor and the regions around the

Mediterranean but also parts of the modern day British Isles, France, Spain, and Germany. Roman admiration for Greek learning, however, cannot overshadow the remarkable contribution made by Roman society to the cultural development of the West as well. The practical Romans were superb engineers, administrators, law-makers and warriors. Long after the Roman empire fell (fifth century A.D.), Europeans continued to use Roman roads, baths, and theaters. They also maintained certain Roman civil administrative structures such as the "diocese" and the office of "count" (comites). After disappearing for a few hundred years, Roman law reemerged in Western Europe in the eleventh century to form the basis of European civil and canon law codes. Roman society also brought Christianity to the farthest reaches of the Empire, first clandestinely by preachers using Roman roads to spread the Word, and later officially, following the legal recognition of the cult in 313 A.D. by Emperor Constantine.

MEDIEVAL WORLD (500 A.D.–1300 A.D.)

During the last days of the Roman Empire, new cultural forces emerged to shape western society. These forces were the Germanic tribes who came to settle in the western parts of the Roman Empire during the fourth and fifth centuries. First peacefully and later by conquest, these peoples gradually established their own kingdoms: the Ostrogoths in Italy, the Visigoths in Spain, the Allemans in modern day Germany, and the Franks in Gaul. These new societies mixed Roman, regional, and Germanic cultural traditions, and in doing so lay the foundation for the modern day nations of France, Germany and Spain (chapter 3). Germanic influence is seen in particular in the emergence of a new political system in these regions known as feudalism which was based on a personal relationship between a king, the chief warrior and lawgiver, and a warrior elite who governed and protected society in his name. Germanic influence is also evident in marriage and inheritance customs, social structures, and in the development of a literature that reflected the values of these new societies. This literature reflected the warrior values of the military elite, and the culture's absorption of Christian beliefs, practices, and institutions. It was during the early Medieval period (500–900) that Eastern monasticism took root in the West and that the monastery became the center of Christian learning, as well as piety.

These new cultures of Western Europe developed largely in isolation from the political, economic, and cultural changes taking place in the East until the eleventh century when the kings of Europe in conjunction with the papacy, the head of the Christian Church in the West, united to combat Muslim authority in the East. The rise of Islam in the sixth century sparked the emergence of new and powerful political forces, as well as spiritual forces in the East, and by the tenth century, much of Asia Minor, North Africa, and Spain were under the jurisdiction of the Islamic peoples. The defeat of the Byzantine Empire in 1071 by the Seljuk Turks and their takeover of the Holy Land of Palestine convinced many Christian Europeans that these Islamic people were poised for westward expansion. This fear justified a series of "holy wars" (Crusades) beginning in 1099.

The cultural influence of these wars upon the formation of Western societies cannot be exaggerated (chapter 4). The Crusades stimulated Christian piety and cultural intolerance in the West because it presented western Christians with an easily identifiable spiritual enemy: the Muslim "infidel." The Crusades also contributed to the ever-rising authority of the pope in Europe as the political as well as spiritual leader. The pope was already considered a powerful figure in Europe by this time because he was the only truly universal authority in all of Western Europe. By the eleventh century, the pope presided over a vast and varied religious organization which included both a large parochial religious structure (parish priest, bishop) and numerous rule-bound communities of religious men and women (monks, friars, nuns). The Crusades not only enhanced the reputation and authority of the pope in the West as a spiritual leader but also offered him an opportunity to spread his authority farther eastward into Asia Minor. The Crusades, however, were not the only means of contact between Western Europe and the East during this period. By the tenth century, trade between the East and West was already expanding as Europeans developed a taste for such Eastern luxury goods as textiles (silk) and perfumes and spices (cloves, pepper). Increasing trade between East and West further stimulated local economies, which were already growing in response to the rising population of Europe, and contributed to the emergence of more urban centers. Italian cities such as Venice and Genoa in particular became enormously wealthy and powerful political entities because of their control of trade with the East. These cities were also remarkably cosmopolitan by the standards of twelfth-century Europe. Merchants from all around the Mediterranean and beyond came to the Italian port cities; this cultural interaction further stimulated European interest in Eastern culture, as well as Eastern products.

Interest in Eastern culture was in fact one of the most important reasons for the development of the university in Italy during this time. European traders were awestruck by the intellectual and cultural sophistication of Eastern societies such as the Christian city of Constantinople and the Muslim centers of Alexandria in Egypt, Medina, and Baghdad. Byzantine and Arabic texts on mathematics, astronomy, medicine, and philosophy began pouring into European markets because they were highly valued by European scholars. What these scholars also eagerly sought from the East, however, were Greek and Roman texts (chapter 5). The disappearance of classical texts was one of the results of the disintegration of the Roman Empire in the West after 400 A.D.; but many of these were preserved in the East, especially in Constantinople. Particularly valued during the twelfth century were classical philosophical, scientific, and legal texts. Roman law made its way to the city of Bologna where Gratian and other scholars used it to develop a more systematic approach to the study of law. Students and professors alike quickly saw the possibilities in Roman law for rationalizing existing legal codes to suit the needs of the larger, more urbanized, and politically centralized societies which were beginning to take shape in Europe. Monarchies, the papacy, and municipal governments were all developing more complex bureaucracies by this time. By the end of the twelfth century, the prestige of Bologne as a center of legal studies attracted students from across Europe and gave rise to the emergence of one of the earliest universities in Europe—the University of Bologna. The single greatest influence on the formation of the European university, however, was the Greek philosopher Aristotle. Aristotle was known before the eleventh century but heightened contact with Byzantine and Arabic scholars brought more of his manuscripts to the attention of Europeans. By the end of the twelfth century, most of his corpus of work was known to the West. Aristotle's work influenced every field of study from science, philosophy, and religion to law and politics. So highly was he respected by contemporaries that he was often simply called "the philosopher."

EARLY MODERN PERIOD (*1300* A.D.–*1750* A.D.)

Cultural interaction with the East continued into the Early Modern period as trade further fueled the Western demand for Eastern goods and its appetite for travel stories of the exotic East. One of the most significant effects of this East-West interaction, however, was the emergence of the Renaissance in Italy (chapter 6). The term Renaissance (renascimento) appears in the writings of certain fourteenth-century Italians who believed that they were restoring classical culture to Italy. It was being "reborn." The recovery of long-lost classical texts, which began during the twelfth century, grew enormously in subsequent centuries as European thirst for this literature continued unabated. This fascination with classical literature was particularly strong in the urban centers of Italy and above all in Florence. As members of a newly formed republic governed by a wealthy, politically active, and cosmopolitan mercantile elite, Florentines felt more of a rapport with the urban societies of Athens and Rome than they did with the noble-dominated society of medieval Europe. The Florentines were captivated, in particular, by classical perceptions of the individual as a rational creature who, through the exercise of reason, could pursue a virtuous life on earth. In contrast to medieval thinkers who associated secular society with moral corruption, Cicero and fellow philosopher-statesmen insisted that true virtue lay in active participation in the political and cultural life of the state and not in withdrawal from it. The new intellectual and spiritual culture which took hold of Florence in the fourteenth-century adapted classical values to the needs of an urban Christian society and in the process created a new definition of the virtuous life. Writers such as Francesco Petrarch, Giovanni Boccaccio, Leonardo Bruni, and later on Marsilio Ficino and Pico della Mirandola celebrated the individual not only as a rational creature but also as a glorious creation of God. Practitioners of the "new learning" also developed a classically based educational program known as the studia humanitatis to mold Europeans into active, virtuous members of the secular state. This educational system quickly spread throughout Europe.

The new culture of the Renaissance transformed not only the way in which Europeans viewed human nature and human society but also the way in which they viewed and experienced the natural world. In doing so, the Renaissance paved the way for another important cultural development of the Early Modern period: European exploration. By the fifteenth century, Europeans became more interested in examining the earth because it, like humankind, was a glorious creation of God. True, the earliest European explorers such as Vasco da Gama and Christopher Columbus did not set out to challenge the existing knowledge of the world. These men expected to find the known, not the unknown. Like their contemporaries, they believed that all knowledge of the physical world already lay in the ancient Greek and Roman texts. Columbus, for example, brought with him on his first voyage in 1492 a well-thumbed copy of Pierre d'Ailly's Imago Mundi, a popular work which relied heavily on Ptolemy's Geographia. Even when his own eyes proved otherwise, Columbus was reluctant to accept that he was off the coast of a continent which was not marked on any Greek or European map. Columbus could not prevent later explorers, however, from concluding that classical knowledge of the world was deficient to that of Early Modern Europeans. Observation and experience, they argued, were teaching Europeans more about the world than was every known before, and these men reveled in every new discovery.

As influential as European desire to learn was in inspiring exploration of the Atlantic, we cannot deny that profit was the greater motive (chapter 7). Columbus, Vasco da Gama, and later venturers crossed the Atlantic in search of a faster, and safer route to the Indies. By the middle of the fifteenth century, the rising maritime powers of Spain and Portugal wanted a share in the lucrative Eastern trade which was then dominated by Italian merchants and the new Muslim power in the East, the Ottoman Turks. Rather than challenging the Turks on the Mediterranean Sea, the Portuguese and Spanish sought new routes to India by venturing into the Atlantic Ocean. The Portuguese were convinced that a route could by found by traveling around the western coast of Africa. After several attempts, the Portuguese reached Calcutta in India in 1498 under the helm of Vasco da Gama. Six years earlier, Christopher Columbus's search for a new route to the East brought him directly across the Atlantic Ocean to the shores of a world largely unknown to Europeans before this time: the Americas. Within the next three decades, the continents of Africa and North and South America were explored by European adventurers eager to find profit in these new lands. Gold and silver from Peru and Mexico began flowing into Spanish coffers by the middle of the sixteenth century, making it the most powerful nation in Europe at the time. Other products that quickly found a lucrative niche in the European market by the end of the sixteenth century included timber and fur. Foods from the new lands also began to make an impression on the European diet, in particular the tomato, red peppers, maize for cattle, and, much later, the potato. Tobacco was first planted as a crop for European markets in 1611 in Virginia, and its market grew enormously within the next few decades. Sugar cane also became an extremely important crop from the Caribbean. First introduced in the mid-1540s, by 1630 production of sugar cane was up to more than 20,000 tons, about ten times that of any other sugar colony.

To protect their trade in these products, European powers established political administrations in the conquered lands and sent out European settlers to rule the region, as well as cultivate the land (chapter 9). By the middle of the seventeenth century, Europeans had established settlements all along the coast of Northern and Southern America, the western coast of Africa, and the islands of the Caribbean. European administrators usually attracted colonists to these new regions by promising land. The English, for example, offered the new colonists of Virginia 50 acres of land upon arrival (the headright system); this land distribution system further stimulated the development of tobacco cultivation in the region. The flow of European and African peoples to the New World stimulated the growth of larger trading and agricultural settlements. In consequence, more goods flowed to Europe. The Atlantic trade transformed European economies virtually overnight. Trading companies such as the Dutch East Indies Company, the Levant Company, and the Hudson's Bay Company emerged to direct growing trade, and they in turn sponsored further exploration of the new lands. These companies became very powerful in the newly colonized regions, at times even exercising political and judicial, as well as economic authority, over the land.

Continuing exploration also had a profound effect on the intellectual development of European society, stimulating in particular the expansion of European knowledge of the physical world (chapter 11). New maps and geographic texts reflecting the new discoveries and travel accounts, and describing previously unknown lands and cultures, increasingly convinced Europeans that travel was an avenue to knowledge, as well as adventure. European encounters with the very different societies of the new lands stimulated enormous discussion in particular about human nature and what constituted human society (chapter 8). The cultures of the New World varied enormously, ranging from small communities practicing a hunting-gathering economy to the complex imperial Mayan, Aztec, and Inca kingdoms of Mexico and Peru. These cultures were very different from the societies that Europeans knew in both Europe and the East, and European encounters with them raised important questions about classical conceptions of "civilization," religion, ethnicity, and gender. Interactions with these cultures also inspired Early Modern moralists to use fictional "utopic" lands and characters as vehicles for examining and satirizing the moral state of European society (chapter 12).

Needless to say, Europeans usually fared the best in their evaluations of cultural sophistication. This assumption of cultural superiority became a useful justification for the subsequent economic and political exploitation of other peoples. A significant part of this justification lay in the European conviction that Christianity was the only true religion (chapter 10). For this reason it is not surprising that fast upon the heels of the European merchant adventurers and colonists were Catholic missionaries. The first missionaries were members of the great Catholic missionary orders—Franciscans, Dominicans, Augustinians, Carmelites, and Jesuits. Their purpose was to bring people into the Catholic Church whether they were members of an ancient and complex society such as that of China, which had long had contact with the Christian West, or the New World cultures that had never heard of Christianity. Strongly encouraging these missionary activities was the Renaissance papacy, an institution which was eager by the end of the fifteenth century to regain its once substantial political and spiritual authority in Europe after over a century of decline. The papacy viewed the missionary orders as effective agents of spiritual reform among the New World cultures because these clerics were comfortable working in different cultural environments and were zealous in their cause. Catholics, however, were not the only ones to see the spiritual possibilities offered by travel to the New World. The division of the Catholic Church after 1521 in the wake of Martin Luther's public advocacy of a new faith unleashed massive defection from the Catholic Church and the emergence of numerous different "protesting" churches. By the end of the sixteenth century, Lutheran, Calvinist, Zwinglian, and Anabaptist communities dotted the religious canvas of Europe. Religious intolerance and a desire for land led many of the new Protestant faiths to establish themselves in the Americas where they hoped to practice their faith in relative freedom. Here they could establish their own godly communities much in the way that Calvin did in Geneva.

This flow of new religious sects continued over the course of the next two centuries. Historians have pointed out that they contributed enormously to the vibrant and varied religious mixture found in the Americas, and also played no small role in the development of American political views on human liberty. What these migrants also contributed, however, was continuing European subjugation of the peoples of the new lands throughout the Early Modern period and after. European political and legal institutions persisted in viewing indigenous peoples as inferior to Europeans, and this view permeated European administration of justice in the colonies, as well as the distribution of land among settlers. European culture and religious beliefs were frequently forced upon the peoples in the New World, in many cases forever shattering the unique cultures. The experiences of women in the colonies provide a unique perspective on the effects of European exploitation of other cultures. Women were always among the most vulnerable members of European society and their treatment by Europeans and aboriginal peoples is revealing about Early Modern perceptions of women (chapter 13). By far the most traumatic effect of European exploitation of the new lands, however, was its introduction of large-scale slavery (chapter 14). The high mortality caused after contact among the indigenous populations by exposure to European disease, and the difficulties of providing labor through the system of indentured service, made it difficult for the colonizers to find adequate labor for these crops, either among the native population or new migrants from Europe. Portuguese, and later Dutch, trading posts on the coast of West Africa provided the solution through the development of the slave trade. With its existing colonies on the African coast, Portugal was able to draw on slavery as a source for a growing plantation system in Brazil and slave ships from other European countries were also soon plying the Atlantic. Slavery was particularly predominant between Brazil and the middle Atlantic colonies in North America, and on the Caribbean islands. In Saint Domingue, for example, 82 percent of the population was slave by 1740. This forced removal of so many Africans undeniably caused enormous cultural dislocation both in Africa and the New World, and one of its most significant legacies to this day is a history of poor race relations in these regions.

THEMATIC ISSUES IN THE STUDY OF EUROPEAN CONTACT WITH THE WORLD

The documents presented in this volume describe very specific instances of the relationship between Europeans and the peoples who lived in other parts of the world. They are the evidence from which historian's accounts are constructed. Understanding what they have to say is the basic purpose of reading them critically. Such a reading involves understanding the specific context of the document with regard to its creation in time and place. The introductions to each document are designed to provide the information required to achieve this understanding: They will tell you who the author of the document was (individual or institution), when the document was created, and what the circumstances were that led to its creation. This information should be kept in mind as you read and discuss the document. The documents themselves express different kinds of information about the relationship between Europeans and the rest of the world. Drawing the full meaning from them, therefore, means examining them in terms of the following themes.

As Europeans and non-Europeans met each other, they noticed different physical characteristics about each other and about the places in which they met. These characteristics helped to define the similarities and the differences between the participants in contact, and over time became important aspects of the ongoing interactions between Europeans and non-Europeans. Skin color, facial features, and stature helped these groups distinguish themselves from each other. Similarly, the ships on which the Europeans arrived, the military camps and churches that they established, or the trading caravans in which they moved became cultural spaces in which Europeans attempted to control the extent and nature of the transactions between themselves and the indigenous peoples of the lands they visited. Rivers, forests, sacred places, and native villages, on the other hand, were places in which these relations might be reversed, and Europeans would become dependent on those peoples for assistance and protection. How these characteristics were defined, therefore, is a significant part of the process of cultural contact.

The documents presented here virtually always express in some way the relationships of power between Europe and the rest of the world. This might be in terms of the obvious diplomatic or institutional aspects of politics, but they also express less formal aspects of politics. Contact between Europeans and non-Europeans involved assumptions each party made about their ability to influence each other. The document may be explicit about these assumptions, but many of them only imply the relations of power. The documents also describe the agency of the European and of the non-European, another aspect of a political relationship. Describing Europeans as capable of great feats, where as non-Europeans are either invisible or passive, is a further way of expressing these relationships.

The documents also describe economic relationships between Europeans and non-Europeans. Although Europeans thought about and traveled to other parts of the world for a wide range of reasons, they often saw the non-European in economic terms, whether as a potential market for European goods, as a source of raw materials for European industry, as a potential destination for emigration from Europe, or as a source of commodities that Europeans desired for their own consumption. When Europeans traveled to other parts of the world, they purchased or simply seized goods, services, and even people for their own use. Indigenous peoples often did the same. Such transactions could be crucial to the way in which relations between non-Europeans and Europeans developed, and paying attention to them is an important part of understanding these documents.

Economics undeniably played an important role in shaping European interactions with other cultures but no more so than social status and religion. The European and non-European societies discussed in this volume were far from egalitarian. For these peoples, inequality was almost always a necessary foundation of a stable political and social structure. Even in "democratic" Athens and Republican Rome, most political, economic, and social authority lay in the hands of a small elite—and male— sector of society. Differences in social status among Europeans and non-Europeans therefore not surprisingly colored the expectations that individuals had of each other, as well as their understanding of other cultures. Religion also undeniably shaped cultural interactions between Europeans and non-Europeans in a fundamental way. Medieval and Early Modern Europeans, for example, were convinced that their faith, Christianity, was the true religion. Religion justified the massacre of Jewish and Muslim populations because such people were considered as willful disbelievers and enemies of the Christian God. Christianity also justified the enforced conversion of New World peoples and their political and economic subjugation to Christian European powers. Aztec religious beliefs also explain to some extent Montezuma's willingness to cooperate with the Spanish conquistador Fernando Cortes. We cannot ignore the fact that these documents were all produced by believers of one religious faith or another and that the authors could not help but examine other cultures through the filter of their own spiritual conceptions.

The documents here also express assumptions about gender. In both European and non-European societies, men and women had differing roles, privileges, and powers, and these are reflected in the interactions between the two groups and in the ways the documents describe those interactions. That many of the documents were written by men is therefore an important aspect. The rare women who traveled outside of Europe, or who were able to leave behind a record of their reactions to the Europeans who visited them, are important witnesses to the process of interaction and brought their own perspective, determined to some extent by their sex, to the process. But even if the documents do not explicitly discuss women, and even if they were not written by women, they do often describe the actions by men and women that were considered appropriate, the ways in which relationships between the sexes were supposed to be carried out, and the reactions of observers to these actions. These are all therefore indicators of the way in which gender operates in these encounters. Gender also acts as a convenient and powerful metaphor by which Europeans and non-Europeans alike could express their own interpretation of their interactions through intimations of the masculinity or femininity of the participants in the encounter. Assumptions about gender therefore provided a way in which Europeans and non-Europeans alike could describe their version of the relationship.

Finally, the documents presented in this volume speak about the interaction of two and sometimes more cultures. This interaction could be as fundamental as language, but there was more to contacts between Europeans and non-Europeans than just trying to learn each other's languages. Europeans, whether they traveled to other parts of the world or merely speculated about them did so using a set of assumptions, drawn from European culture, about human beings and about how they were supposed to act. The non-Europeans who offered assistance to the New England pilgrims, acted as guides to European explorers or interacted with colonial administration were similarly influenced by their own cultural assumptions. In the descriptions of interaction that are given in these documents, these differing assumptions played out as each party attempted to communicate their own thoughts and and feelings about the nature of the interaction. Not surprisingly, European and non-European accounts of a cultural interaction rarely mirror one another because their perception of the interaction was shaped by their own distinctive cultural framework.

Megan Armstrong
University of Utah

1

Ancient Near East
3000 B.C.–700 B.C.

TEXTS

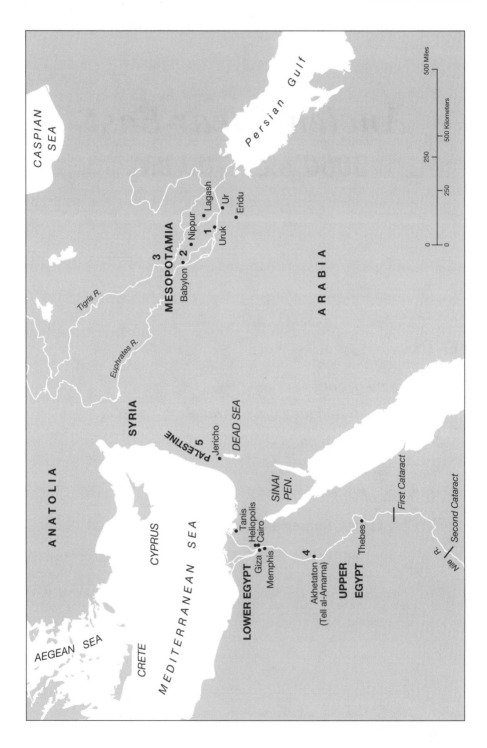

The origins of Western civilization lay not in the Mediterranean but in Mesopotamia, the lands located between the Tigris and Euphrates rivers. Here and in the nearby regions of modern Iraq and Syria, archaeologists have found evidence of permanent human settlements from as early as the Ubaid period (5000–4000 B.C.). By the early dynastic period (2900–2350 B.C.), larger urbanized cultures appeared, showing evidence of what scholars term "civilization," that is, political centralization, systematic cultivation of the land through irrigation, the organization of large labor forces, sophisticated temple-based religious systems, extensive trade networks, and writing. Although a desire to control and tame the land was clearly an important factor in the emergence of these cultures, another that was also of enormous importance was immigration. A constant flow of peoples from the deserts of Syria and the Arabian peninsula into the fertile crescent of the Tigris-Euphrates Valley fueled the development of larger settled communities and encouraged the mixing of cultures. Many of the great civilizations that emerged in the region during this period were in fact the product of these migrations.

The Sumerians (pre-2200 B.C.), the first great culture in Mesopotamia, were clearly from a distant land because their language system bears no resemblance to any known linguistic group in the region. With regard to the development of Mesopotamian civilization, their legacy, however, cannot be overstated. In addition to providing a model of centralized political, social, and economic organization, which was imitated by their conquerors, the Akkadians and later empires, Sumerian deities were also absorbed into the Akkadian religious system. The Sumerians also developed the first known writing system, an adaptation of cuneiform ("wedge-shaped" representations) which was used as early as 3000 B.C. for bookkeeping. The change from literal to symbolic signs gave the language greater flexibility, a flexibility that was increased further when the Semitic-speaking Akkadians adapted Sumerian to their own syllabic linguistic structure. From this time forward, Akkadian became the language of choice in Mesopotamia.

Cultural exchange and assimilation through the mingling of peoples remained an important force both for change and continuity in Mesopotamian civilizations long after the time of the Sumerians and Akkadians. The emergence of codified law during the reign of Hammurabi, king of Babylon (1728–1686 B.C.), for example, reflected the demands of an empire which for the first time united the entire region of Mesopotamia under one rule. The Hammurabi law code was designed to systematize and standardize human relations within a state composed of numerous different cultures, and it laid the basis for subsequent Mesopotamian law codes. The later kingdoms of the Kassites and Assyrians similarly show the influence of cultural continuity, as well as change, preserving facets of Mesopotamian civilization which would later find a home in the West. The transfer of civilization from the fertile crescent to the Mediterranean, however, did not happen overnight but rather over a period of centuries, as trade and war brought this region into greater contact with other parts of the world. During the neo-Babylonian Empire (605–539 B.C.), caravans from India, Africa, and South Arabia made their way to the markets of the region and carried back with them not only regional goods but also Babylonian science and learning. The Persian defeat of Babylonia in 539 B.C. ended the last great Mesopotamian Empire. However, the wars of Alexander the Great in the fourth century B.C. brought Near Eastern cultures to the attention of Greece and eventually Rome.

The documents used in this section highlight political, economic, and cultural interaction between the different societies in Mesopotamia, as well as between these societies and their powerful neighbors. *Enmerkar and the Lord of Aratta* [2] is the oldest of the texts followed by the *Legend of Sargon* [1]. Both literary tales reflect societies that were accustomed to regular contact and conflict with their neighbors. However, whereas the *Legend of Sargon* celebrates the rise of a great warrior ruler and the creation of an empire through war, *Enmerkar* pays tribute to cunning and peaceful resolutions to societal conflicts. The *Laws of Eshnunna* [3] was one of the early Mesopotamian law codes. It sheds light on Mesopotamian culture of the eighteenth century B.C., and it also reflects the emergence of conceptions of justice and rulership in Mesopotamia in the wake of imperial expansion. The *Amarna Letters* [4] and the *Book of Isaiah* [5] both shed light on Mesopotamian interaction with other cultures beyond the Fertile Crescent. The *Amarna Letters* reflect Egyptian governance at the peak of its power as an empire and its relations with Mesopotamian rulers. In contrast, the *Book of Isaiah* portrays Jerusalem under siege by Assyrian forces.

1. The Legend of Sargon

The Akkadian Empire (2296–2105 B.C.) was one of the earliest and greatest of the Mesopotamian Empires; under its rule the Sumerian political, economic, and religious institutions and cuneiform writing system spread throughout Mesopotamia. One of the most significant legacies of Akkadian culture to Mesopotamia was a flourishing literary tradition largely devoted to tales of mighty military leaders and kings. Akkadian rulers were admired enormously by later imperial powers, and the town of Akkade became a pilgrimage site for those interested in visiting the tombs of these legendary figures. As the founder of the Akkadian Empire, Sargon I (2340–2284 B.C.) was, not surprisingly, one of the most revered of the Akkadian rulers. Under his leadership the empire grew to encompass the entire region between modern day Syria and Iran and enjoyed diplomatic and trading relations with even more distant regions. His rule also set the model for later imperial powers in Mesopotamia through its reconceptualization of the nature of kingship. Akkadian art, architecture, and literature portrayed the king not simply as a political leader but as the ideological embodiment of the state. Sargon's reputation as a great ruler was such that the later Assyrian monarch Sargon II (721–705 B.C.) took his name. The *Legend of Sargon* recounts the birth and life of Sargon. This tale is one of a series of literary compositions known as *narû* which imitated the form of inscriptions on Akkadian stone memorials (stele). The truth of Sargon's tale is much disputed, but what cannot be denied is the similarity between several elements of this tale and that of the story of the birth of Moses. These similarities point to the spread of Mesopotamian culture into the regions of Egypt and Palestine by 1000 B.C.

The Legend of Sargon

Sargon, the mighty king, king of Agade, am I.
My mother was a *changeling,* my father I knew not.
The brother(s) of my father *loved* the hills.
My city is Azupiranu, which is situated on the banks of the Euphrates.
My *changeling* mother conceived me, in secret she bore me.
She set me in a basket of rushes, with bitumen she sealed my lid.
She cast me into the river which rose not (over) me.
The river bore me up and carried me to Akki, the drawer of water.
Akki, the drawer of water lifted me out as he dipped his e[w]er.
Akki, the drawer of water, [took me] as his son (and) reared me.
Akki, the drawer of water, appointed me as his gardener.
While I was a gardener, Ishtar granted me (her) love,
And for four and [. . .] years I exercised kingship.
The black-headed [people] I ruled, I gov[erned];
Mighty [moun]tains with chip-axes of bronze I conquered,
The upper ranges I scaled,
The lower ranges I [trav]ersed,
The sea *[lan]ds* three times I circled.
Dilmun my [hand] cap[tured],
[To] the great Der I [went up], I [. . .],
[. . .] I altered and [. . .].
Whatever king may come up after me,
[. . .],
Let him r[ule, let him govern] the black-headed [peo]ple;
[Let him conquer] mighty [mountains] with chip-axe[s of bronze],
[Let] him scale the upper ranges,
[Let him traverse the lower ranges],
Let him circle the sea *[lan]ds* three times!
[Dilmun let his hand capture],
Let him go up [to] the great Der and [. . .]!
[. . .] from my city, Aga[de . . .]
[. . .] . . . [. . .].

(Remainder broken away.)

2. Enmerkar and the Lord of Aratta

Sumerian civilization first emerged in the southern part of Mesopotamia during the fourth millennium B.C. and flourished for several hundred years before it was conquered by the Akkadians (ca. 2300 B.C.). Impressed by the sophistication of Sumerian society, the Akkadians adopted its political, economic, and religious institutions. Perhaps the greatest single contribution of the Sumerians to the evolution of Mesopotamian culture, however, was its system of writing. The Sumerians were the first society in Mesopotamia to develop a complex writing system capable of supporting a broad literary culture. This writing system involved wedge-shaped impressions (cuneiform) made by a reed stylus on a clay tablet, and it was used not only for legal, economic, and administrative documents but also for religious and literary texts. Under Akkadian rule, this writing system spread more widely in Mesopotamia. Sumerians wrote both in narrative and verse form, and surviving literature from the Sumerian period suggests that epic tales and hymns in praise of a ruler or a god were preferred literary forms. *Enmerkar and the Lord of Aratta* is one of the most famous of the Sumerian verse texts. It dates to the Third Dynasty of Ur (2112–2004 B.C.), the period from which we have the greatest body of Sumerian literature. The story of *Enmerkar,* however, is situated in the distant past, long before the invention of writing. Enmerkar, the king of Ur, wants the Lord of Aratta and his people to give him gold so that he can decorate the temples of the goddess Inanna, the patron goddess of Ur. As Inanna's favorite son, Enmerkar agrees to withhold rain from the land of Aratta, another kingdom under her care, in order to pressure the lord to send the gold. The Lord of Aratta is not easily pressured, however, and the poem is as much a study in the art of rulership as it is a study of religion. Intelligence and might were necessary to save the people of Aratta. Both men are so effective as rulers that in the end they create trade between their two lands, making each city-state more prosperous than ever before. The following excerpt describes two of three tasks set by Aratta to foil Enmerkar. These tasks are historically significant because they represent two inventions important to the people of Ur: malt and writing.

Enmerkar and the Lord of Aratta

FIRST TEST: GRAIN FOR ARATTA
"Meanwhile,
 as to the relief grain due us,
 let him not load it
 into carts,
let him not take it
 by portage into the mountains,

and when he has cut it,
   let him not place it
   in (carrying) yokes,
but if,
   having filled it
   into carrying-nets,
loaded it onto packasses,
and provided spare asses
   beside them,
he piles it up
   in Aratta's courtyard,
then *he* says true,
   and (Inanna),
   the power of rain,
   the granary's delight,
(will have flung Aratta),
   the placer of beacons on all mountains,
   well suited for settlements,
adorned with seven city walls—
then he says true: the queen,
   the warrior fit for battle,
Inanna, the warrior all set
   to vie in dusty battle,
in Inanna's dance,
will have flung from the hand
   Aratta
as were it a dog-cadaver plant.
On *that* day I on my part
   shall bow to *him,*
I, on my part, shall,
   like the city,
   submit as the lesser one
   say unto him!"

After thus he had been telling him,
the Lord of Aratta
   had the envoy
reproduce with his mouth
   his words.

REQUEST REPORTED
Like a wild bull
   he slept on his haunches,
resting like a sandfly,
   at dawn he was ready to go.
Into brickbuilt Kullab
   he joyously set foot.

Into the main courtyard,
   the courtyard of the council,
   the envoy made his way
and to his master,
   the lord of Kullab,
he reported
   in the manner of his message,
bellowed it at him
   like a bull,
and he—like the oxdriver—
   paid attention.

The king turned his right side
   to the fire,
turned his left side
   back to it.
"He says true!
   Aratta must know
   that (divine) instructions were given!"
   he said.

MORNING RITUAL
The day dawned,
   and unto Utu,
   who had risen,
it made the country's
   "Utu," (the king)
   lift up the head.
The king matched
   Tigris (water) with Euphrates (water),
matched Euphrates (water) with Tigris (water)
set up the great jars
   unto An,
leaned the little jars
   against their sides
   like hungry lambs,
and stood An's shiny jars
   beside them.
The king, Enmerkar, Utu's son
   was hurrying up
to the gold inwrought
   eshda chalice—

INSPIRATION FROM GRAIN GODDESS
That day did she
   who is (like) shining brass,
   the refulgent reedstalk,

the aureate shape,
   born on a propitious day,
borne. . . . .
   by green Nanibgal,
Nidaba,
   the lady of vast intelligence,
open for him
   her "Nidaba's holy house
   of understanding,"
and entering An's palace
   he was paying heed.
The lord opened the door
   to his huge granary
and set on the ground
   his huge standard measure.
The king took out from the grain
   his old grain,
soaked with water
   the malt spread on the ground,
and its lips locked together
   like *sassatu* and *hirinnu* weed.
On the carrying-nets
   he reduced in size the meshes,
and the stewards filled the grain
   of the grain piles into them;
   and the stewards
   added to it for the birds.

FIRST TEST PASSED
When he had loaded up
   the packasses,
and placed spare asses
   at their sides,
did the king of vast intelligence,
the lord of Uruk,
   the lord of Kullab,
direct them
   unto the road to Aratta;
and the people,
   like ants of the cracks
   in the ground,
wended their way by themselves
   to Aratta.

VASSAL SCEPTER FOR ARATTA
The lord gave the envoy
   going to the highland

a further message for Aratta
   (saying:)
"Envoy, when you have spoken
   to the Lord of Aratta,
   and elaborated thereon
   for him, (say:)
'The base of my scepter
   is in the sacred office
   of princedom,
its crown gives shade
   for Kullab,
under its ever-branching crown
   does the Eanna-close—
does holy Inanna—
   cool off.
When he has cut from it a scepter,
   may he carry it,
may it be in his hand
   as were it (one of)
   carnelian sections
   and lapis lazuli sections,
and may the lord of Aratta
   bring it before me!'
   say to him."
After thus he had been telling him,
the envoy going to Aratta
plunged his foot
   into the dust of the road,
sent rattling the little stones
   of the mountain ranges,
like a basilisk prowling its desert,
   he had none opposing him.

ARATTA RELIEVED
To the envoy,
   when he had neared Aratta,
came Aratta's people
to admire the packasses.
In Aratta's courtyard
   the envoy
had the stewards fill the grain
   into grain bins,
   had the stewards
   add to it for the birds.
As if there had been
   rains of heaven and storms,
abundance filled Aratta,
as if the gods
   had returned to their abodes,

the Arattans' hunger
abated by and by.
The people of Aratta
sowed the fields
with his water-soaked malt.

THE LETTER INVENTED
That day the words
of the lord [. . . . .]
seated on [. . . .,]
the seed of princes,
[a *mēsu* tree (?)]
grown up singly,
were difficult,
their meaning not to fathom,
and, his words being difficult,
the envoy
was unable to render them.
Since the envoy
—his words being difficult—
was unable to render them,
the lord of Kullab
smoothed clay with the hand
and set down the words on it
in the manner of a tablet.
While up to then
there had been no one
setting down words on clay,
now, on that day,
under that sun,
thus it verily
came to be;
the lord of Kullab
set down wo[rds on clay,]
thus it verily
came to be!

The envoy, like a bird,
was beating the wings,
like a wolf
closing in on a buck
he was hurrying
to the kill.
Five mountain ranges,
six mountain ranges,
seven mountain ranges,
he crossed over,
lifted up the eyes,
he was approaching Aratta;

and joyfully he set foot
    in Aratta's courtyard.

His master's preeminence
    he proclaimed,
and was decorously speaking
    the words he had by heart,
the envoy was translating them
    for the Lord of Aratta:
"It being that your father,
    [my] master,
    has sent me [to you,]
it being that the lord of Uruk,
    and lord of Kullab,
    has sent me to you. . . ."

THE LORD OF ARATTA INTERRUPTS
"What is to me
    your master's wo[rds?]
    What is to me
    what he said further?"

"My master—[what] did he say?
    what did he say further?
My master,
    [des]cendant (?) of Enlil,
grown as high as . . [. ,]
abutting [. . . . ,]
the [. . . . of. . . . ,]
who is outstanding
    in lordship and kingship,
Enmerkar, son of Utu,
    has given me a tablet.
When the Lord of Aratta
    has looked at the clay,
    and understood from it
    the meaning of the words,
and you have told me
    what you have to say to me
    about it.

3. THE LAWS OF ESHNUNNA

The invention of writing facilitated the emergence of yet another facet of
Mesopotamian civilization that would come to shape Western culture: the law
code. Several law codes emerged in Mesopotamia between 2000 and

500 B.C., including the most famous of all, the Code of Hammurabi. The majority of these codes little resemble modern understanding of the genre. None are comprehensive, and in many cases there is little evidence to suggest that these codes were routinely used by the societies that produced them. That being said, these law codes tell us a great deal about Mesopotamian value systems. The *Laws of Eshnunna* (ca. 1770 B.C.) reflect economic and social relations in the kingdom of Eshnunna during the eighteenth century B.C. Eshnunna was a powerful kingdom during the Old Babylonian period; its influence spread as far as Assyria in the north and Babylonia in the south. The *Laws* were written during the reign of King Dadusha, a contemporary of the Babylonian monarch, Hammurabi. Comprising only sixty articles, this code governs such matters as trade, marriage, inheritance, war, and social hierarchy. Above all, this and other law codes tell us about the Mesopotamian conceptions of justice and the practice of rulership.

Eshnunna

[. . .] day 21 [. . .] of the gods Enlil and Ninazu, [when Dadusha ascended to] the kingship of the city of Eshnunna [and entered] into the house of his father, [when] he conquered with mighty weapons within one year the cities Supur-Shamash [and . . . on] the far bank of the Tigris River [. . .].

Laws

¶ **1** 300 silas of barley (can be purchased) for 1 shekel of silver. 3 silas of fine oil—for 1 shekel of silver. 12 silas of oil—for 1 shekel of silver. 15 silas of lard—for 1 shekel of silver. 40 silas of bitumen—for 1 shekel of silver. 360 shekels of wool—for 1 shekel of silver. 600 silas of salt—for 1 shekel of silver. 300 silas of potash—for 1 shekel of silver. 180 shekels of copper—for 1 shekel of silver. 120 shekels of wrought copper—for 1 shekel of silver.

¶ **2** 1 sila of oil, extract(?)—30 silas is its grain equivalent. 1 sila of lard, extract(?)—25 silas is its grain equivalent. 1 sila of bitumen, extract(?)—8 silas is its grain equivalent.

¶ **3** A wagon together with its oxen and its driver—100 silas of grain is its hire; if (paid in) silver, ⅓ shekel (i.e., 60 barleycorns) is its hire; he shall drive it for the entire day.

¶ **4** The hire of a boat is, per 300-sila capacity, 2 silas; furthermore, [x] silas is the hire of the boatman; he shall drive it for the entire day.

¶ **5** If the boatman is negligent and causes the boat to sink, he shall restore as much as he caused to sink.

¶ **6** If a man, under fraudulent circumstances, should seize a boat which does not belong to him, he shall weigh and deliver 10 shekels of silver.

¶ **7** 20 silas of grain is the hire of a harvester; if (paid in) silver, 12 barleycorns is his hire.

¶ **8** 10 silas of grain is the hire of a winnower.

¶ **9** A man gave 1 shekel of silver to a workman for harvesting—if he (the workman) does not keep himself available to work and does not harvest for him, he shall weigh and deliver 10 shekels of silver.

¶ **9A** 15 silas is the hire of a sickle, and the broken blade(?) shall revert to its owner.

¶ **10** 10 silas of grain is the hire of a donkey, and 10 silas of grain is the hire of its driver; he shall drive it for the entire day.

¶ **11** The hire of a laborer is 1 shekel of silver, 60 silas of grain is his provender; he shall serve for one month.

¶ **12** A man who is seized in the field of a commoner among the sheaves at midday shall weigh and deliver 10 shekels of silver; he who is seized at night among the sheaves shall die, he will not live.

¶ **13** A man who is seized in the house of a commoner, within the house, at midday, shall weigh and deliver 10 shekels of silver; he who is seized at night within the house shall die, he will not live.

¶ **14** The hire of a fuller, per one garment valued at 5 shekels of silver—1 shekel is his hire; (per one garment) valued at 10 shekels of silver—2 shekels is his hire.

¶ **15** A merchant or a woman innkeeper will not accept silver, grain, wool, oil, or anything else from a male or female slave.

¶ **16** The son of a man who has not yet received his inheritance share or a slave will not be advanced credit.

¶ **17** Should a member of the *awīlu*-class bring the bridewealth to the house of his father-in-law—if either (the groom or bride then) should go to his or her fate, the silver shall revert to its original owner (i.e., the widower or his heir).

¶ **18** If he marries her and she enters his house and then either the groom or the bride goes to his or her fate, he shall not take out all that he had brought, but only its excess shall he take.

¶ **18A** Per 1 shekel (of silver) interest accrues at the rate of 36 barleycorns (= 20%); per 300 silas (of grain) interest accrues at the rate of 100 silas (= 33%).

¶ **19** A man who lends against its corresponding commodity(?) shall collect at the threshing floor.

¶ **20** If a man loans . . . grain . . . and then converts the grain into silver, at the harvest he shall take the grain and the interest on it at (the established rate of 33%, i.e.,) 100 silas per 300 silas.

¶ **21** If a man gives silver for/to his/its . . . , he shall take the silver and the interest on it at (the established rate of 20%, i.e.,) 36 barleycorns per 1 shekel.

¶ **22** If a man has no claim against another man but he nonetheless takes the man's slave woman as a distress, the owner of the slave woman shall swear an oath by the god: "You have no claim against me"; he (the distrainer) shall weigh and deliver silver as much as is the value(?) of the slave woman.

¶ **23** If a man has no claim against another man but he nonetheless takes the man's slave woman as a distress, detains the distress in his house, and causes her death, he shall replace her with two slave women for the owner of the slave woman.

¶ **24** If he has no claim against him but he nonetheless takes the wife of a commoner or the child of a commoner as a distress, detains the distress in his house, and causes her or his death, it is a capital offense—the distrainer who distrained shall die.

¶ **25** If a man comes to claim (his bride) at the house of his father-in-law, but his father-in-law wrongs(?) him and then gives his daughter to [another], the father of the daughter shall return two-fold the bridewealth which he received.

¶ **26** If a man brings the bridewealth for the daughter of a man, but another, without the consent of her father and mother, abducts her and then deflowers her, it is indeed a capital offense—he shall die.

¶ **27** If a man marries the daughter of another man without the consent of her father and mother, and moreover does not conclude the nuptial feast and the contract for(?) her father and mother, should she reside in his house for even one full year, she is not a wife.

¶ **28** If he concludes the contract and the nuptial feast for(?) her father and mother and he marries her, she is indeed a wife; the day she is seized in the lap of another man, she shall die, she will not live.

¶ **29** If a man should be captured or abducted during a raiding expedition or while on patrol(?), even should he reside in a foreign land for a long time, should someone else marry his wife and even should she bear a child, whenever he returns he shall take back his wife.

¶ **30** If a man repudiates his city and his master and then flees, and someone else then marries his wife, whenever he returns he will have no claim to his wife.

¶ **31** If a man should deflower the slave woman of another man, he shall weigh and deliver 20 shekels of silver, but the slave woman remains the property of her master.

¶ **32** If a man gives his child for suckling and for rearing but does not give the food, oil, and clothing rations (to the caregiver) for 3 years, he shall weight and deliver 10 shekels of silver for the cost of the rearing of his child, and he shall take away his child.

¶ **33** If a slave woman acts to defraud and gives her child to a woman of the *awīlu*-class, when he grows up should his master locate him, he shall seize him and take him away.

¶ **34** If a slave woman of the palace should give her son or her daughter to a commoner for rearing, the palace shall remove the son or daughter whom she gave.

¶ **35** However, an adoptor who takes in adoption the child of a slave woman of the palace shall restore (another slave of) equal value for the palace.

¶ **36** If a man gives his goods to a *naptaru* for safekeeping, and he (the *naptaru*) then allows the goods which he gave to him for safekeeping to become lost—without evidence that the house has been broken into, the doorjamb scraped, the window forced—he shall replace his goods for him.

¶ **37** If the man's house has been burglarized, and the owner of the house incurs a loss along with the goods which the depositor gave to him, the owner of the house shall swear an oath to satisfy him at the gate of (the temple of) the god Tishpak: "My goods have been lost along with your goods; I have not committed a fraud or misdeed"; thus shall he swear an oath to satisfy him and he will have no claim against him.

¶ **38** If, in a partnership, one intends to sell his share and his partner wishes to buy, he shall match any outside offer.

¶ **39** If a man becomes impoverished and then sells his house, whenever the buyer offers it for sale, the owner of the house shall have the right to redeem it.

¶ **40** If a man buys a slave, a slave woman, an ox, or any other purchase, but cannot establish the identity of the seller, it is he who is a thief.

¶ **41** If a foreigner, a *naptaru*, or a *mudū* wishes to sell his beer, the woman innkeeper shall sell the beer for him at the current rate.

¶ **42** If a man bites the nose of another man and thus cuts it off, he shall weigh and deliver 60 shekels of silver; an eye—60 shekels; a tooth—30 shekels; an ear—30 shekels; a slap to the cheek—he shall weigh and deliver 10 shekels of silver.

¶ **43** If a man should cut off the finger of another man, he shall weigh and deliver 20 shekels of silver.

¶ **44** If a man knocks down another man in the street(?) and thereby breaks his hand, he shall weigh and deliver 30 shekels of silver.

¶ **45** If he should break his foot, he shall weigh and deliver 30 shekels of silver.

¶ **46** If a man strikes another man and thus breaks his collarbone, he shall weigh and deliver 20 shekels of silver.

¶ **47** If a man should inflict(?) any other injuries(?) on another man in the course of a fray, he shall weigh and deliver 10 shekels of silver.

¶ **47A** If a man, in the course of a brawl, should cause the death of another member of the *awīlu*-class, he shall weigh and deliver 40 shekels of silver.

¶ **48** And for a case involving a penalty of silver in amounts ranging from 20 shekels to 60 shekels, the judges shall determine the case against him; however, a capital case is only for the king.

¶ **49** If a man should be seized with a stolen slave or a stolen slave woman, a slave shall lead a slave, a slave woman shall lead a slave woman.

¶ **50** If a military governor, a governor of the canal system, or any person in a position of authority seizes a fugitive slave, fugitive slave woman, stray ox, or stray donkey belonging either to the palace or to a commoner, and does not lead it to Eshnunna but detains it in his house and allows more than one month to elapse, the palace shall bring a charge of theft against him.

¶ **51** A slave or slave woman belonging to (a resident of) Eshnunna who bears fetters, shackles, or a slave hairlock will not exit through the main city-gate of Eshnunna without his owner.

¶ **52** A slave or slave woman who has entered the main city-gate of Eshnunna in the safekeeping of only a foreign envoy shall be made to bear fetters, shackles, or a slave hairlock and thereby is kept safe for his owner.

¶ **53** If an ox gores another ox and thus causes its death, the two ox-owners shall divide the value of the living ox and the carcass of the dead ox.

¶ **54** If an ox is a gorer and the ward authorities so notify its owner, but he fails to keep his ox in check and it gores a man and thus causes his death, the owner of the ox shall weigh and deliver 40 shekels of silver.

¶ **55** If it gores a slave and thus causes his death, he shall weigh and deliver 15 shekels of silver.

¶ **56** If a dog is vicious and the ward authorities so notify its owner, but he fails to control his dog and it bites a man and thus causes his death, the owner of the dog shall weigh and deliver 40 shekels of silver.

¶ **57** If it bites a slave and thus causes his death, he shall weigh and deliver 15 shekels of silver.

¶ **58** If a wall is buckling and the ward authorities so notify the owner of the wall, but he does not reinforce his wall and the wall collapses and thus causes the death of a member of the *awīlu*-class—it is a capital case, it is decided by a royal decree.

¶ **59** If a man sired children but divorces his wife and then marries another, he shall be expelled from the house and any possessions there may be and he shall depart after the one who . . . , [. . .] the house . . .

¶ **60** [If] a guard is negligent in guarding [a house], and a burglar [breaks into the house], they shall kill the guard of the house that was broken into [. . .], and he shall be buried [at] the breach without a grave.

4. THE AMARNA LETTERS

The Amarna letters were first discovered in the nineteenth century in the city of el-Amarna, once the seat of the Egyptian kingdom during the time of Amenophis IV (1364–1347 B.C.). Amenophis is better known as Akenhaten, the pharoah who briefly banished polytheism from Egypt by replacing it with worship of the sun god Aton. Although the new religion did not long survive his death, the Amarna letters do give us some information on the nature of Egyptian rule and Egyptian interactions with other societies during this period. By the time of Amenophis's rule, Egypt was a powerful empire, and its influence was felt in the numerous city-states of the nearby region of Syro-Palestine in particular. The letters span a period of thirty years during the latter part of his reign. The letters can be divided into two types: between the pharoah of Egypt and other rulers, and between the pharoah and his vassal states in Syro-Palestine. The letters between the pharoah and his vassals concern Eygptian authority in these regions and are informative about contemporary political events. One such example is the letter sent by the vassal Rib-Hadda, the ruler of Gubla, subtitled "a bird in a trap (EA 74)." In contrast to this letter are the two letters sent from two different kings of Karaduniyas (EA 3, EA 8) and the pharaoh to the king of Babylon (EA 1). These three letters are typical of the correspondence between rulers. The kings address one another as brother. Conversation is not about political events but about personal and political relations between the rulers, and, above all, about gift-giving and marriage. Letter EA 8 is unusual because it is the only one that indicates flourishing trading relations between Egypt and another state. At the very least, it suggests that harmonious political relations during this period went hand in hand with trade.

The Amarna Letters
(EA 1)

Say [t]o Kadašman-Enlil, the king of Karadun[i]še, my brother: Thus Nibmuarea, Great King, the king of Egypt, your brother. For me all goes well. For you may all go well. For your household, for your wives, for your sons, for your magnates, your horses, your chariots, for your countries, may all go very well. For me all goes well. For my household, for my wives, for my sons, for my magnates, my horses, the numerous troops, all goes well, and in my countries all goes very well. I have just heard what you wrote me about, saying, "Here you are asking for my daughter in marriage, but my sister whom my father gave you was (already) there with you, and no one has seen her (so as to know) if now she is alive or if she is dead." These are your words that you sent me on your tablet. Did you, however, ever send here a dignitary of yours who knows your sister, who could speak with her and identify her? Suppose he spoke with her. The men whom you sent here are nobodies. One was the [. . .] of Zaqara, [*the ot]her,* an assherder [*fr*]om [. . .] There has been no one among the[m *wh*]o [*knows her, wh*]o was an intimate of your father, and *w*[*ho could identify her*]. Moreover, the messengers [*who*] . . . [. . .] And as for your writing me, "You addressed my me[ssen]gers as your wives were standing gathered in your presence, saying, 'Here is your mistress who stands before you.' But my messengers did not know her, (whether) it was my sister who *was at your side"—about whom* you yourself have now written me, "My messengers did not know her," and (still) you say, "Who is to identify her?"— Why don't you send me a dignitary of yours who can tell you the truth, the well-being of your sister who is here, and then you can believe the one who enters to *see* her quarters and her relationship with the king? And as for your writing me, "Perhaps the one my messengers saw was the daughter of some poor man, or of some Ka(s)kean, or the daughter of some Hanigalbatean, or perhaps someone from Ugarit. Who can believe them? *The one who was at your side* . . . , she did not op[en] her mouth. One cannot believe them at all." These are your words. But if your [sister] were de[ad], what reason would there be for one's concealing *her de[ath, and]* our presenting someone [else]? [*May*] Aman [*be my witness*] . . . [. . .] And as for your writing me, "My daughters who are married to *neigh[bori]ng* kings, if my messengers [*go*] there, they speak with th[em, and they bri]ng me a greeting-gift. *The one with you* [. . . " Th]ese are your words. Undoubtedly *[your neigh]boring* kings are *[ri]ch* (and) mighty. Your daughters can acquire something from them and send (it) to you. But what does she have, your sister who is with me? But should she make some acquisition, I will send (it) to you! It is a fine thing that you give your daughters *in order to acquire a nugget of gold* from your neighbors! As for your writing me the words of my father, never mind! you do not cite his (exact) words. Furthermore, "Establish friendly brotherhood between us"— these are the words that you wrote me. Now, we are brothers, you and I, but I have quarreled because of your messengers, since they report to you saying, "Nothing is given to us who go to Egypt." Those who come to me—has a single one of them ever come [*and not*] received silver, gold, oil, solemn garb, every sort of finery, *[more than i]n* any other country? He does not tell the truth to the one who sends him! The first time the messengers went off to *[y]our f[ather],* and their mouths told lies. The next time they went off [and] they told lies to you. So I said to myself, "Whether I [gi]ve them anything or do not give them anything, they are going to go on te(l)ling [l]i[e]s just the same." So I made up my mind in their regard and I did not *gi[ve t]o them anymore.* And as for your writing me, "You said to my messengers, 'Has your master no troops? The girl he gave to me is not beautiful.'"—these are your words, (but) it is not so! Your messengers keep telling you what is not true, (saying things) like this. Whether soldiers are on hand or not can be found out for me. What reason is there for asking about whether there are troops on hand belonging to you, whether there are horses on hand also belonging to you? Please, do not listen to *them!* Your messengers, of whom the mouths of both groups are untruthful and whom you sent here, I swear that they have not served you, and so they go on t(el)ling lies in order to escape your punishment. As for your saying to me, "He put my chariots among the chariots of the mayors. You did not *review* them *separately.* You *humiliated* them before the country *where you are.* You did not rev(iew) (them) *separately." Whether* the chariots were *here or there, the chariots needed the horses of my [coun]try—all were my horses.* As for your writing me *in order to aggrandize yourself* (and) to put oil on the *h[ea]d* of a girl, you for your part sent me one *pr[es]ent. Are we to laugh?*

(EA 3)

[S]ay [to Nim]u'wareya, the king of Eg[ypt, m]y [brother]: [Thus Kad]ašman-Enlil, the king of Karaduniyaš, your brother. [For me all indeed goes w]ell. For you, your household, your wives, [and for you]r [sons], your country, your chariots, your horses, your [mag]nates may all go very well.

With regard to the girl, my daughter, about whom you wrote to me in view of marriage, she has become a woman; she is nubile. Just send a delegation to fetch her. Previously, my father would send a messenger to you, and you would not detain him for long. You qui[ck]ly sent him off, and you would also send here to my father a beautiful greeting-gift.

But now when I sent a messenger to you, you have detained him for six years, and you have sent me as my greeting-gift, the only thing in six years, 30 minas of gold that *looked like silver.* That gold was melted down in the presence of Kasi, your messenger, and he was a witness. When you celebrated a great festival, you did not send your messenger to me, saying, "Come t[o eat an]d drink." No[r did you send me] my greeting-gift in connection with the festival. It was just 30 minas of gold that you [sent me]. My [gi]ft *[does not amoun]t to what [I have given you] every yea[r].*

I have built a *[ne]w [house]. I[n my house]* I have built a [l]arge [. . .]. Your [mes]sengers have see[n *the house and the . . . , and are pleased. No]w* I am going to hav[e] a house-opening. Come [*yourself*] to [eat an]d drink with me. [*I shall not act a*]s you yourself did. [25 *men* and] 25 women, altogether 50 *i[n my service],* I send [to you *in connection with the house-opening*].

[. . .] for 10 wooden chariots, [and 10 teams of hor]ses I send to you as your greeting-gift.

(EA 8)

Sa[y to] Naphu'rure[ya], the king of Egypt, my brother: Thus Burra-Buriyaš, the king of Kara[duniyaš], your brother. For me all goes well. For you, your country, your household, your wives, yo[ur] sons, your magnates, your horses, your chariots, may all go very well.

My brother and I made a mutual declaration of friendship, and this is what we said: "Just as our fathers were friends with one another, so will we be friends with one another." Now, my merchants who were on their way with Ahu-tabu, were detained in Canaan for business matters. After Ahu-tabu went on to my brother, in Hinnatuna of Canaan, Šum-Adda, the son of Balumme, and Šutatna, the son of Šaratum of Akka, having sent their men, killed my merchants and took away [th]eir money. [I] send [. . .] . . . to y[o]u post[haste]. Inqu[ire from him so] he can inform yo[u. C]anaan is your country, and [*its*] king[s are *your servants*]. In your country I have been despoiled. Bring [them] to account and make compensat[ion] for the money that they took away. Put to death the men who put my servants [to] death, and so avenge their blood. And if you do not put these men to death, they are going to kill again, be it a caravan of mine or your own messengers, and so messengers between us will thereby be cut off. And if they try to deny this to you, Šum-Adda, having blocked the passage of one man of mine, retained him in his company, and another man, having been forced into service by Šutatna of

Akka, is still serving him. These men sh[ould be] brought to you so you can investigate, inquire *[whether they are de]ad,* and thus become informed. [As a greet]ing-gift I send you 1 mina of lapis lazuli. Se[nd off] my [mess]enger immediately so I may kno[w] my brother's [dec]ision. Do not deta[in] my [mess]enger. Let him be off [to me imm]-ediately.

(EA 74)

Rib-Hadda says to [his] lord, king of all countries, Great King, King of Battle: May [the Lady] of Gubla grant power to the king, my lord. I fall at the feet of my lord, my Sun, 7 times and 7 times. May the king, the lord, know that Gubla, the loyal maidservant of the king since the days of his ancestors, is safe and sound. The king, however, has now with-drawn his support of his local city. May the king inspect the tablets of his father's house (for the time) when the ruler in Gubla was not a loyal servant. Do not be negligent of your servant. Behold, the war of the ʿApiru against ‹me› is severe and, as the gods of *y[our]* land *[are ali]ve,* our sons and daughters *(as well as we ourselves)* are gone since they have been sold in the land of Yarimuta for provisions to keep us alive. "For lack of a cultivator, my field is like a woman without a husband." All my villages that are in the mountains : ḫa-ar-ri or along the sea have been joined to the ʿApiru. Left to me are Gubla and two towns. After taking Šigata for himself, ʿAbdi-Aširta said to the men of Ammiya, "Kill your *leader* and then you will be like us and at peace." They were won over, follow-ing his message, and they are like ʿApiru. So now ʿAbdi-Aširta has written to the troops: "Assemble in the temple of NINURTA, and then let us fall upon Gubla. Look, there is no one that will save it from u[s]. Then let us drive out the mayors from the country that the en-tire country be joined to the ʿApiru, ... to the entire country. Then will (our) sons and daughters be at peace forever. Should even so the king come out, the entire country will be against him and what will he do to us?" Accordingly, they have made an alliance among themselves and, accordingly, I am very, very afraid, since [in] fact there is no one will save me from them. Like a bird in a trap : *ki-lu-bi* (cage), so am I in Gubla. Why have you neglected your country? I have written like this to the palace, but you do not heed my words. Look, Amanappa is with you. Ask him. He is the one that knows and has expe-rienced the stra[its] I am in. May the king heed the words of his servant. May he grant provisions for his servant and keep his servant alive so I may guard his [lo]yal [city], *along with our L[ad]y* (and) our gods, *f[or you].* May *[the king] vis[it]* his [land] and *[his servant].* [May he] give thought to his land. *Pac[ify yo]ur [land]!* May it seem go[od] in the sight of the k[ing], my [lo]rd. May he send a *[ma]n* of his to stay this time so I may arri[ve] in the presence of the king, my lord. It is good for me to be with you. What can I do by [my]self? This is what I long for day and night.

5. BOOK OF ISAIAH

One of the most important historical sources for Mesopotamian cultural in-fluence on Western society is the Old Testament. The Old Testament records the religious history of the Jewish people from their settlement in Judah to their movement westward (1000–700 B.C.). During the course of the narrative, however, it also paints a vivid portrait of the complexity and heterogeneity of the Mesopotamian world during this period. Contact was frequent between peoples, whether in the form of war, diplomatic relations, or trade. The following excerpt from the *Book of Isaiah* recounts an Assyrian siege of the Jewish city of Jerusalem by King Sennacherib (704–681 B.C.). The Neo-Assyrian empire (934–610 B.C.) represented the recovery and rapid expansion of Assyrian power in Mesopotamia. Two of its most effective leaders were Tigleth-Pileser III (744–727 B.C.) and Sargon II (721–705 B.C.) who oversaw the spread of Assyrian power throughout much of the Fertile Crescent. Sennerachib spent his reign consolidating the gains of these previous rulers and extending the boundaries of the empire farther into the regions of Anatolia and the southern Levant. The following excerpt describes an Assyrian siege of the city of Jerusalem. Sennerachib sent his representative, the Rabshakeh (chief steward), to the king of the Jews, Hezekiah, who was based at Jerusalem. The speech tells us a great deal about relations between the Assyrians and the Jewish people during this time. The cultural fluidity of this part of the world is nowhere better indicated, however, than in the multilingualism of the Rabshakeh himself.

Isaiah

Now it came to pass in the fourteenth year of king Hezekiah, that Sennacherib king of Assyria came up against all the fortified cities of Judah, and took them. And the king of Assyria sent Rabshakeh from Lachish to Jerusalem unto king Hezekiah with a great army, And he stood by the conduit of the upper pool in the highway of the fuller's field. Then came forth unto him Eliakim the son of Hilkiah, who was over the household, and Shebna the scribe and Joah, the son of Asaph, the recorder.

And Rabshakeh said unto them, Say ye now to Hezekiah, Thus saith the great king, the king of Assyria, What confidence is this wherein thou trustest? I say, *thy* counsel and strength for the war are but vain words: now on whom dost thou trust, that thou hast rebelled against me? Behold, thou trustest upon the staff of this bruised reed, even upon Egypt, whereon if a man lean, it will go into his hand, and pierce it: so is Pharaoh king of Egypt to all that trust on him. But if thou say unto me, We trust in Jehovah our God: is not that he, whose high places and whose altars Hezekiah hath taken away, and hath said to Judah and to Jerusalem, Ye shall worship before this altar? Now therefore, I pray thee, give pledges to my master the king of Assyria, and I will give thee two thousand horses, if thou be able on thy part to set riders upon them. How then canst thou turn away the face of one captain of the least of my master's servants, and put thy trust on Egypt for chariots and for horsemen? And am I now come up without Jehovah against this land to destroy it? Jehovah said unto me, Go up against this land, and destroy it.

Then said Eliakim and Shebna and Joah unto Rabshakeh, Speak, I pray thee, unto thy servants in the Syrian language; for we understand it: and speak not to us in the Jews' language, in the ears of the people that are on the wall. But Rabshakeh said, Hath my master sent me to thy master, and to thee, to speak these words? *hath he* not *sent me* to the men that sit upon the wall, to eat their own dung, and to drink their own water with you?

Then Rabshakeh stood, and cried with a loud voice in the Jews' language and said, Hear ye the words of the great king, the king of Assyria. Thus saith the king, Let not Hezekiah deceive you; for he will not be able to deliver you: neither let Hezekiah make you trust in Jehovah, saying, Jehovah will surely deliver us; this city shall not be given into the hand of the king of Assyria. 16 Hearken not to Hezekiah: for thus saith the king of Assyria, Make your peace with me, and come out to me; and eat ye every one of his vine, and every one of his fig-tree, and drink ye every one the waters of his own cistern; until I come and take you away to a land like your own land, a land of grain and new wine, a land of bread and vineyards. Beware lest Hezekiah persuade you, saying, Jehovah will deliver us. Hath any of the gods of the nations delivered his land out of the hand of the king of Assyria? Where are the gods of Hamath and Arpad? Where are the gods of Sepharvaim? and have they delivered Samaria out of my hand? Who are they among all the gods of these countries, that have delivered their country out of my hand, that Jehovah should deliver Jerusalem out of my hand?

But they held their peace, and answered him not a word; for the king's commandment was saying, Answer him not. Then came Eliakim the son of Hilkiah, that was over the household, and Shebna the scribe, and Joah, the son of Asaph, the recorder, to Hezekiah with their clothes rent, and told him the words of Rabshakeh.

And it came to pass, when king Hezekiah heard it, that he rent his clothes, and covered himself with sackcloth, and went into the house of Jehovah. And he sent Eliakim, who was, over the household, and Shebna the scribe, and the elders of the priests, covered with sackcloth, unto Isaiah the prophet the son of Amoz. And they said unto him, Thus saith Hezekiah, This day is a day of trouble, and of rebuke, and of contumely; for the children are come to the birth, and there is not strength to bring forth. It may be Jehovah thy God will hear the words of Rabshakeh, whom the king of Assyria his master hath sent to defy the living God, and will rebuke the words which Jehovah thy God hath heard: wherefore lift up thy prayer for the remnant that is left.

So the servants of king Hezekiah came to Isaiah. And Isaiah said unto them, Thus shall ye say to your master, Thus saith Jehovah, Be not afraid of the words that thou hast heard, wherewith the servants of the king of Assyria have blasphemed me. Behold, I will put a spirit in him, and he shall hear tidings, and shall return unto his own land; and I will cause him to fall by the sword in his own land.

So Rabshakeh returned, and found the king of Assyria warring against Libnah; for he had heard that he was departed from Lachish. And he heard say concerning Tirhakah king of Ethiopia, He is come out to fight against thee. And when he heard it, he sent messengers to Hezekiah, saying, Thus shall ye speak to Hezekiah king of Judah, saying, Let not thy God in whom thou trustest deceive thee, saying, Jerusalem shall not be given into the hand of the king of Assyria. Behold, thou hast heard what the kings of Assyria have done to all lands, by destroying them utterly: and shalt thou be delivered? Have the gods of the nations delivered them which my fathers have destroyed, Gozan, and Haran, and Rezeph, and the children of Eden that were in Telassar? Where is the king of Hamath, and the king of Arpad, and the king of the city of Sepharvaim, of Hena, and Ivvah?

And Hezekiah received the letter from the hand of the messengers, and read it; and Hezekiah went up unto the house of Jehovah, and spread it before Jehovah. And

Hezekiah prayed unto Jehovah, saying, O Jehovah of hosts, the God of Israel, that sittest *above* the cherubim, thou art the God, even thou alone, of all the kingdoms of the earth; thou hast made heaven and earth. Incline thine ear, O Jehovah, and hear; open thine eyes, O Jehovah, and see; and hear all the words of Sennacherib, who hath sent to defy the living God. Of a truth, Jehovah, the kings of Assyria have laid waste all the countries, and their land, and have cast their gods into the fire: for they were no gods, but the work of men's hands, wood and stone; therefore they have destroyed them. Now therefore, O Jehovah our God, save us from his hand, that all the kingdoms of the earth may know that thou art Jehovah, even thou only.

Then Isaiah the son of Amoz sent unto Hezekiah, saying, Thus saith Jehovah, the God of Israel, Whereas thou hast prayed to me against Sennacherib king of Assyria, this is the word which Jehovah hath spoken concerning him: The virgin daughter of Zion hath despised thee and laughed thee to scorn; the daughter of Jerusalem hath shaken her head at thee. Whom hast thou defied and blasphemed? and against whom hast thou exalted thy voice and lifted up thine eyes on high? *even* against the Holy One of Israel. By thy servants hast thou defied the Lord, and hast said, With the multitude of my chariots am I come up to the height of the mountains, to the innermost parts of Lebanon; and I will cut down the tall cedars thereof, and the choice fir-trees thereof; and I will enter into its farthest height, the forest of its fruitful field; I have digged and drunk water, and with the sole of my feet will I dry up all the rivers of Egypt.

Hast thou not heard how I have done it long ago, and formed it of ancient times? now have I brought it to pass, that it should be thine to lay waste fortified cities into ruinous heaps. Therefore their inhabitants were of small power, they were dismayed and confounded; they were as the grass of the field, and as the green herb, as the grass on the housetops, and as a field *of grain* before it is grown up. But I know thy sitting down, and thy going out, and thy coming in, and thy raging against me. Because of thy raging against me, and because thine arrogancy is come up into mine ears, therefore will I put my hook in thy nose, and my bridle in thy lips, and I will turn thee back by the way by which thou camest.

And this shall be the sign unto thee: ye shall eat this year that which groweth of itself, and in the second year that which springeth of the same; and in the third year sow ye, and reap, and plant vineyards, and eat the fruit thereof. And the remnant that is escaped of the house of Judah shall again take root downward, and bear fruit upward. For out of Jerusalem shall go forth a remnant, and out of mount Zion they that shall escape. The zeal of Jehovah of hosts will perform this.

Therefore thus saith Jehovah concerning the king of Assyria, He shall not come unto this city, nor shoot an arrow there, neither shall he come before it with shield, nor cast up a mound against it. By the way that he came, by the same shall he return, and he shall not come unto this city, saith Jehovah. For I will defend this city to save it, for mine own sake, and for my servant David's sake.

And the angel of Jehovah went forth, and smote in the camp of the Assyrians a hundred and fourscore and five thousand; and when men arose early in the morning, behold, these were all dead bodies. So Sennacherib king of Assyria departed, and went and returned, and dwelt at Nineveh. And it came to pass, as he was worshipping in the house of Nisroch his god, that Adrammelech and Sharezer his sons smote him with the sword; and they escaped into the land of Ararat. And Esar-haddon his son reigned in his stead.

Figure 1.1   Clay tablet. Sumerian. Rare Books Division, J. Willard Marriott
Library, University of Utah.

Study Questions

1. Why was the invention of malt and writing important to the Sumerians who wrote *Enmerkar?*
2. What qualities of Sargon I did the Mesopotamians admire? Why?
3. What were specific concerns of the people who lived in the city-state of Eshnunna? What do these concerns tell us about the structure of their society? Their values?
4. What do the Amarna letters tell us about the nature and character of Egyptian rule?
5. What forms of cultural exchange can one see taking place in all of the documents included in this section? Which ones become particularly important for the formation of Western civilization?

Suggested Readings

Crawford, Harriet. *Sumer and the Sumerians.* Cambridge: Cambridge University Press, 1991.

Kemp, Barry. *Ancient Egypt: Anatomy of a Civilization.* London/New York: Routledge, 1989.

Kuhrt, Amelie. *The Ancient Near East.* 2 vols. London and New York: Routledge, 1995.

Postgate, J. N. *Early Mesopotamia. Society and Economy at the Dawn of History.* London and New York: Routledge, 1992.

Web Sites

1. The Avalon Project, Yale: The Code of Hammurabi

   http://www.yale.edu/lawweb/avalon/hammenu.htm

2. The Epic of Gilgamesh

   http://www.hist.unt.edu/ane-09.htm

3. Sumerian artifacts and writing

   http://www.sumerian.org

2

Classical World
700 B.C.–*500* A.D.

TEXTS

1. Homer, *The Odyssey*
2. Herodotus, *Histories*
3. Pliny the Elder, *Natural History*
4. Egeria, *Diary of a Pilgrimage*
5. Euclid, *Elementa Geometriae*

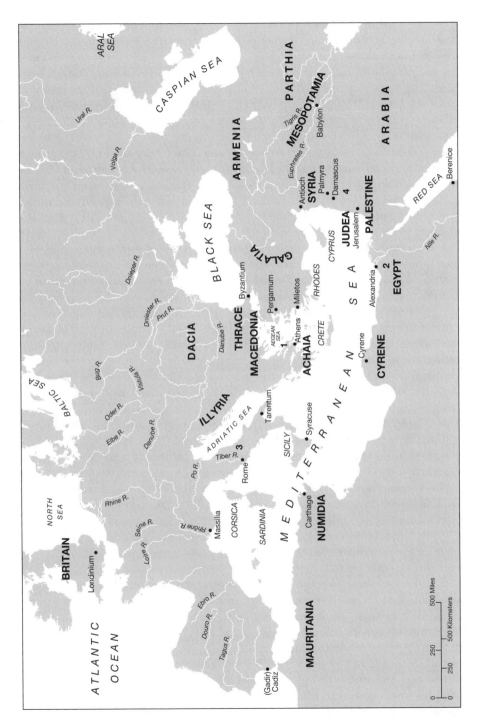

By the end of the second millennium B.C., Mesopotamian culture spread into the Mediterranean and laid the groundwork for the emergence of a new distinct culture, that of ancient Greece. It is on the island of Crete and the mainland of modern day Greece that we find traces of early "Greek" culture. The legacy of the Minoan (2900–1100 B.C.) figurative artistic tradition to Greek art is still visible in the vibrant, colorful figures painted on the walls of the great Minoan palace of Knossos on Crete, also the home to the Greek mythical half-man half-bull Minotaur. During the peak of its power, Minoan society used as many as three writing systems, and its pottery and other crafts were in high demand across the Mediterranean Sea. The Mycenaean civilization, which appeared on mainland Greece by 1600 B.C., influenced the form of Greek culture but its contribution lay less in art than in political, social, and military organization. By 500 B.C., we can see emerging in this region the classical form of Greek culture which came to play such a formative role in the emergence of Western artistic traditions, political and social structures, and intellectual life. Democratic institutions and ideology, the celebration of man as a rational being, [1, 2] and Platonic and Aristotlean conceptions of virtue are among the many legacies of Greek culture to Western society.

Greek culture first began spreading rapidly throughout the Mediterranean during the period 450–300 B.C., but it was the armies of the Macedonian ruler Alexander the Great and later of Rome (200 B.C.–500 A.D.) that brought it to Asia Minor. Alexander's campaigns against the Persian emperor Darius (363–323 B.C.) subjected the once mighty Eastern power to Macedonian rule. Within a few years, 250 Greek cities, colonized by Greek-speaking peoples, sprang up across Asia Minor and implanted Greek culture in the East. These "Hellenist" cities imported Greek political and educational institutions, supported Greek artistic life, and used the Greek language as the language of trade and government. Important as transmitters of Greek culture eastward, the Greek colonies also fostered cultural hybridization. Eastern mystery cults shaped by Egyptian and Greek religions spread throughout the Hellenist world. A new Hellenist intellectual tradition also emerged when Greek culture encountered Eastern mysticism, philosophy, and science.

By the second century A.D., new Eastern-influenced schools of thought such as Epicureanism, Stoicism, and Skepticism appeared in Athens. It was also during this period that Aristotle's student, Aristarchus of Samos (ca. 310–230 B.C.), developed the first heliocentric interpretation of the universe, and mathematics and botany became more fully developed fields of knowledge. By this time, however, Athens was no longer the only important intellectual center in the Hellenist world. Archimedes (ca. 282–212 B.C.) developed many of the most important principles of mechanics and hydrostatics while living in his hometown of Syracuse in Sicily. Pergamum in Asia Minor and Alexandria in Egypt also became great centers of science and philosophy. It was in Alexandria, for example, that Euclid (ca. 300 B.C.) wrote his foundational work the *Elementa Geometriae* and much later in the second century A.D. that Claudius Ptolemy wrote his famous treatise *Geographia*. Alexandria was also famous for its royal library, the single largest collection of Greek manuscripts and other writings in the Hellenist world.

The spread of Roman authority eastward by 300 B.C. further encouraged cultural as well as economic exchange between Mediterranean regions and Asia Minor. Eastern mystery religions began making inroads in Roman society, and the cults of Isis and Mithras in particular became very popular. Roman admiration of Greek culture also ensured that Greek philosophy, religion, and art spread to the farthest reaches of the Roman empire. Roman boys studied Greek literature and Roman authors imitated Greek literary models. [3] As historians (Tacitus, Livy) and poets (Vergil, Juvenal, Catullus), the Romans were worthy successors of the ancient Greeks. It was in the fields of law, engineering, and politics, however, that Rome made its own unique contribution to the development of Western society. The rediscovery of Roman law in the West during the twelfth century A.D. fundamentally transformed European legal systems. To this day, Roman roads are among the main arteries of communication and transportation in Western Europe. Roman aqueducts, sanitation systems, and theaters were used by Europeans long after Roman society itself collapsed. Roman genius for political organization also survived in the West in the administrative structure of the Roman Catholic Church (the diocese). Perhaps the most significant legacy of the Roman empire to the West, however, was Christianity. [4] Long before Christianity was officially recognized by the Roman state in 311 A.D., Christian evangelists such as Paul of Tarsus were plying their message along Roman roads. With Roman support, Christianity moved from being one of many cults to the most powerful religion in the West by the end of the fourth century.

1. HOMER, *THE ODYSSEY*

Little is known about the historical Homer even though his two epic poems, the *Iliad* and the *Odyssey*, remain among the most important literary contributions to the West. Written sometime during the eighth or ninth century B.C., the *Iliad* and the *Odyssey* recount an heroic age when courage in battle and the fraternal bond defined true masculinity, the ideal woman was beautiful and virtuous, and the gods directly intervened in human affairs. The *Iliad* recounts an historic battle between Mycenaean Greeks led by King Agamemnon and the Trojans after the son of the king of the Trojans, Paris, absconded to Troy with Agamemnon's wife, Helen. A sequel to the *Iliad*, the *Odyssey* begins with the return journey of one of the Greek heroes, Odysseus, to his homeland of Ithaca following the destruction of Troy. The *Odyssey* suggests that the homecoming from Troy for the Greeks was as arduous as the battle itself. Many of them died along the route or returned to find their domestic situations substantially altered. The leader of the Greek forces, Agamemnon, returned home in triumph only to be killed by his wife Clytemnestra and her lover. Odysseus was forced to wander the seas for a period of twenty years before setting foot on his beloved Ithaca. To this day, the image of the wandering Odysseus remains an immediately recognizable trope in Western iconography and literature, the model not only for standard adventure tales but also for metaphorical explanations of spiritual and intellectual journeying. Odysseus is also celebrated for his shrewd intelligence because it was his cleverness rather than his physical strength as a warrior that enabled him to survive every dangerous encounter with god, man, and beast. The following excerpt describes Odysseus's encounter with the enchantress Circe. Odysseus's travels took him to many strange, exotic lands and brought him into contact with a host of fascinating individuals, but none are more intriguing than Circe, the Western archetype of the dazzling temptress.

The Odyssey of Homer

"'Followers and friends, attend what I propose:
Ye sad companions of Ulysses' woes!
We know not here what land before us lies,
Or to what quarter now we turn our eyes,
Or where the sun shall set, or where shall rise,
Here let us think (if thinking be not vain)
If any counsel, any hope remain.
Alas! from yonder promontory's brow
I view'd the coast, a region flat and low;
An isle encircled with the boundless flood;
A length of thickets, and entangled wood.
Some smoke I saw amid the forest rise;
And all around it only seas and skies!'
  "With broken hearts my sad companions stood,
Mindful of Cyclops and his human food,
And horrid Læstrygons, the men of blood.
Presaging tears apace began to rain;
But tears in mortal miseries are vain.
In equal parts I straight divide my band,
And name a chief each party to command;
I led the one, and of the other side
Appointed brave Eurylochus the guide.
Then in the brazen helm the lots we throw,
And fortune casts Eurylochus to go;
He march'd with twice eleven in his train;
Pensive they march, and pensive we remain.
  "The palace in a woody vale they found,
High raised of stone; a shaded space around;
Where mountain wolves and brindled lions roam,

(By magic tamed,) familiar to the dome.
With gentle blandishment our men they meet,
And wag their tails, and fawning lick their feet.
As from some feast a man returning late,
His faithful dogs all meet him at the gate,
Rejoicing round, some morsel to receive,
(Such as the good man ever used to give,)
Domestic thus the grisly beasts drew near;
They gaze with wonder not unmix'd with fear.
Now on the threshold of the dome they stood,
And heard a voice resounding through the wood:
Placed at her loom within, the goddess sung;
The vaulted roofs and solid pavement rung.
O'er the fair web the rising figures shine,
Immortal labour! worthy hands divine.
Polites to the rest the question moved
(A gallant leader, and a man I loved):
    "'What voice celestial, chanting to the loom
(Or nymph, or goddess), echoes from the room?
Say, shall we seek access?' With that they call;
And wide unfold the portals of the hall.
    "The goddess, rising, asks her guests to stay,
Who blindly follow where she leads the way.
Eurylochus alone of all the band,
Suspecting fraud, more prudently remain'd.
On thrones around with downy covering graced,
With semblance fair, the unhappy men she placed.
Milk newly press'd, the sacred flour of wheat,
And honey fresh, and Pramnian wines the treat:
But venom'd was the bread, and mix'd the bowl,
With drugs of force to darken all the soul:
Soon in the luscious feast themselves they lost,
And drank oblivion of their native coast.
Instant her circling wand the goddess waves,
To hogs transforms them, and the sty receives.
No more was seen the human form divine;
Head, face, and members, bristle into swine:
Still cursed with sense, their minds remain alone,
And their own voice affrights them when they groan.
Meanwhile the goddess in disdain bestows
The mast and acorn, brutal food! and strows
The fruits and cornel, as their feast, around;
Now prone and grovelling on unsavoury ground.
    "Eurylochus, with pensive steps and slow,
Aghast returns; the messenger of woe,
And bitter fate. To speak he made essay,
In vain essay'd, nor would his tongue obey.
His swelling heart denied the words their way:
But speaking tears the want of words supply,

And the full soul bursts copious from his eye.
Affrighted, anxious for our fellows' faces,
We press to hear what sadly he relates:
  "'We went, Ulysses! (such was thy command)
Through the lone thicket and the desert land.
A palace in a woody vale we found
Brown with dark forests, and with shades around.
A voice celestial echoed through the dome,
Or nymph or goddess, chanting to the loom.
Access we sought, nor was access denied:
Radiant she came: the portals open'd wide:
The goddess mild invites the guests to stay:
They blindly follow where she leads the way.
I only wait behind of all the train:
I waited long, and eyed the doors in vain:
The rest are vanish'd, none repass'd the gate,
And not a man appears to tell their fate.'
  "I heard, and instant o'er my shoulder flung
The belt in which my weighty falchion hung
(A beamy blade): then seized the bended bow,
And bade him guide the way, resolved to go.
He, prostrate falling, with both hands embraced
My knees, and weeping thus his suit address'd:
  "'O king, beloved of Jove, thy servant spare,
And ah, thyself the rash attempt forbear!
Never, alas! thou never shalt return,
Or see the wretched for whose loss we mourn.
With what remains from certain ruin fly,
And save the few not fated yet to die.'
  "I answer'd stern: 'Inglorious then remain,
Here feast and loiter, and desert thy train.
Alone, unfriended, will I tempt my way;
The laws of fate compel, and I obey.'
This said, and scornful turning from the shore
My haughty step, I stalk'd the valley o'er.
Till now approaching nigh the magic bower,
Where dwelt the enchantress skill'd in herbs of power,
A form divine forth issued from the wood
(Immortal Hermes with the golden rod)
In human semblance. On his bloomy face
Youth smiled celestial, with each opening grace.
He seized my hand, and gracious thus began:
'Ah whither roam'st thou, much-enduring man?
O blind to fate! what led thy steps to rove
The horrid mazes of this magic grove?
Each friend you seek in yon enclosure lies,
All lost their form, and habitants of sties.
Think'st thou by wit to model their escape?
Sooner shalt thou, a stranger to thy shape,

Fall prone their equal: first thy danger know,
Then take the antidote the gods bestow.
The plant I give through all the direful bower
Shall guard thee, and avert the evil hour.
Now hear her wicked arts: Before thy eyes
The bowl shall sparkle, and the banquet rise;
Take this, nor from the faithless feast abstain,
For temper'd drugs and poisons shall be vain.
Soon as she strikes her wand, and gives the word,
Draw forth and brandish thy refulgent sword,
And menace death: those menaces shall move
Her alter'd mind to blandishment and love.
Nor shun the blessing proffer'd to thy arms,
Ascend her bed, and taste celestial charms:
So shall thy tedious toils a respite find,
And thy lost friends return to human-kind.
But swear her first by those dread oaths that tie
The powers below, the blessed in the sky;
Lest to thee naked secret fraud he meant,
Or magic bind the cold and impotent.'
    "Thus while he spoke, the sovereign plant he drew
Where on the all-bearing earth unmark'd it grew,
And show'd its nature and its wondrous power:
Black was the root, but milky white the flower;
Moly the name, to mortals hard to find,
But all is easy to the ethereal kind.
This Hermes gave, then, gliding off the glade,
Shot to Olympus from the woodland shade
While, full of thought, revolving fates to come,
I speed my passage to the enchanted dome.
Arrived, before the lofty gates I stay'd;
The lofty gates the goddess wide display'd:
She leads before, and to the feast invites;
I follow sadly to the magic rites.
Radiant with starry studs, a silver seat
Received my limbs; a footstool eased my feet,
She mix'd the potion, fraudulent of soul;
The poison mantled in the golden bowl.
I took, and quaff'd it, confident in heaven.
Then waved the wand, and then the word was given.
'Hence to thy fellows! (dreadful she began:)
Go, be a beast!'—I heard, and yet was man.
    "Then, sudden whirling, like a waving flame,
My beamy falchion, I assault the dame.
Struck with unusual fear, she trembling cries,
She faints, she falls; she lifts her weeping eyes.
    "'What art thou? say! from whence, from whom you came?
O more than human! tell thy race, thy name.
Amazing strength, these poisons to sustain!

Not mortal thou, nor mortal is thy brain.
Or art thou he, the man to come (foretold
By Hermes, powerful with the wand of gold),
The man from Troy, who wander'd ocean round;
The man for wisdom's various arts renown'd,
Ulysses? Oh! thy threatening fury cease;
Sheathe thy bright sword, and join our hands in peace!
Let mutual joys our mutual trust combine,
And love, and love-born confidence, be thine.'
   "'And how, dread Circe! (furious I rejoin)
Can love, and love-born confidence, be mine.
Beneath thy charms when my companions groan,
Transform'd to beasts, with accents not their own?
O thou of fraudful heart, shall I be led
To share thy feast-rites, or ascend thy bed;
That, all unarm'd, thy vengeance may have vent,
And magic bind me, cold and impotent?
Celestial as thou art, yet stand denied;
Or swear that oath by which the gods are tied,
Swear, in thy soul no latent frauds remain,
Swear by the vow which never can be vain.'
   "The goddess swore: then seized my hand, and led
To the sweet transports of the genial bed.
Ministrant to the queen, with busy care
Four faithful handmaids the soft rites prepare;
Nymphs sprung from fountains, or from shady woods,
Or the fair offspring of the sacred floods.
One o'er the couches painted carpets threw,
Whose purple lustre glow'd against the view:
White linen lay beneath. Another placed
The silver stands, with golden flaskets graced:
With dulcet beverage this the beaker crown'd,
Fair in the midst, with gilded cups around:
That in the tripod o'er the kindled pile
The water pours; the bubbling waters boil;
An ample vase receives the smoking wave;
And, in the bath prepared, my limbs I lave:
Reviving sweets repair the mind's decay,
And take the painful sense of toil away.
A vest and tunic o'er me next she threw,
Fresh from the bath, and dropping balmy dew;
Then led and placed me on the sovereign seat,
With carpets spread; a footstool at my feet.
The golden ewer a nymph obsequious brings,
Replenish'd from the cool translucent springs;
With copious water the bright vase supplies
A silver laver of capacious size.
I wash'd. The table in fair order spread,

They heap the glittering canisters with bread:
Viands of various kinds allure the taste,
Of choicest sort and savour, rich repast!
Circe in vain invites the feast to share;
Absent I ponder, and absorb'd in care;
While scenes of woe rose anxious in my breast,
The queen beheld me, and these words address'd:
   "'Why sits Ulysses silent and apart,
Some hoard of grief close harbour'd at his heart
Untouch'd before thee stand the cates divine,
And unregarded laughs the rosy wine.
Can yet a doubt or any dread remain,
When sworn that oath which never can be vain?'
   "I answered: 'Goddess! human is my breast,
By justice sway'd, by tender pity press'd:
Ill fits it me, whose friends are sunk to beasts,
To quaff thy bowls, or riot in thy feasts.
Me would'st thou please? for them thy cares employ,
And them to me restore, and me to joy.'
   "With that she parted: in her potent hand
She bore the virtue of the magic wand.
Then, hastening to the sties, set wide the door,
Urged forth, and drove the bristly herd before;
Unwieldy, out they rush'd with general cry,
Enormous beasts, dishonest to the eye.
Now touch'd by counter-charms they change again,
And stand majestic, and recall'd to men.
Those hairs of late that bristled every part,
Fall off, miraculous effect of art!
Till all the form in full proportion rise,
More young, more large, more graceful to my eyes.
They saw, they knew me, and with eager pace
Clung to their master in a long embrace:
Sad, pleasing sight! with tears each eye ran o'er,
And sobs of joy re-echoed through the bower;
E'en Circe wept, her adamantine heart
Felt pity enter, and sustain'd her part.
   "'Son of Laertes! (then the queen began)
Oh much-enduring, much experienced man!
Haste to thy vessel on the sea-beat shore,
Unload thy treasures, and the galley moor;
Then bring thy friends, secure from future harms,
And in our grottoes stow thy spoils and arms.'
   "She said. Obedient to her high command
I quit the place, and hasten to the strand,
My sad companions on the beach I found,
Their wistful eyes in floods of sorrow drown'd.
   "As from fresh pastures and the dewy field

(When loaded cribs their evening banquet yield)
The lowing herds return; around them throng
With leaps and bounds their late imprison'd young,
Rush to their mothers with unruly joy,
And echoing hills return the tender cry:
So round me press'd, exulting at my sight,
With cries and agonies of wild delight,
The weeping sailors; nor less fierce their joy
Than if return'd to Ithaca from Troy.
'Ah master I ever honour'd, ever dear!
(These tender words on every side I hear)
What other joy can equal thy return?
Not that loved country for whose sight we mourn,
The soil that nursed us, and that gave us breath:
But ah! relate our lost companions' death.'

   "I answer'd cheerful: 'Haste, your galley moor,
And bring our treasures and our arms ashore:
Those in yon hollow caverns let us lay,
Then rise, and follow where I lead the way.
Your fellows live; believe your eyes, and come
To taste the joys of Circe's sacred dome.'

   "With ready speed the joyful crew obey:
Alone Eurylochus persuades their stay.

   "'Whither (he cried), ah whither will ye run?
Seek ye to meet those evils ye should shun?
Will you the terrors of the dome explore,
In swine to grovel, or in lions roar,
Or wolf-like howl away the midnight hour
In dreadful watch around the magic bower?
Remember Cyclops, and his bloody deed;
The leader's rashness made the soldiers bleed.'

   "I heard incensed, and first resolved to speed
My flying falchion at the rebel's head.
Dear as he was, by ties of kindred bound,
This hand had stretch'd him breathless on the ground,
But all at once my interposing train
For mercy pleaded, nor could plead in vain.
'Leave here the man who dares his prince desert,
Leave to repentance and his own sad heart,
To guard the ship. Seek we the sacred shades
Of Circe's palace, where Ulysses leads.'

   "This with one voice declared, the rising train
Left the black vessel by the murmuring main.
Shame touch'd Eurylochus' alter'd breast;
He fear'd my threats, and follow'd with the rest.

   "Meanwhile the goddess, with indulgent cares
And social joys, the late transform'd repairs;
The bath, the feast, their fainting soul renews:

Rich in refulgent robes, and dropping balmy dews:
Brightening with joy, their eager eyes behold,
Each other's face, and each his story told;
Then gushing tears the narrative confound,
And with their sobs the vaulted roof resound.
When hush'd their passion, thus the goddess cries:
'Ulysses, taught by labours to be wise,
Let this short memory of grief suffice.
To me are known the various woes ye bore,
In storms by sea, in perils on the shore;
Forget whatever was in Fortune's power,
And share the pleasures of this genial hour.
Such be your mind as ere ye left your coast,
Or learn'd to sorrow for a country lost.
Exiles and wanderers now, where'er ye go,
Too faithful memory renews your woe:
The cause removed, habitual griefs remain,
And the soul saddens by the use of pain.'
 "Her kind entreaty moved the general breast;
Tired with long toil, we willing sunk to rest.
We plied the banquet, and the bowl we crown'd,
Till the full circle of the year came round.
But when the seasons following in their train,
Brought back the months, the days, and hours again;
As from a lethargy at once they rise,
And urge their chief with animating cries:
 "'Is this, Ulysses, our inglorious lot?
And is the name of Ithaca forgot?
Shall never the dear land in prospect rise,
Or the loved palace glitter in our eyes?'
 "Melting I heard; yet till the sun's decline
Prolong'd the feast, and quaff'd the rosy wine:
But when the shades came on at evening hour,
And all lay slumbering in the dusky bower,
I came a suppliant to fair Circe's bed,
The tender moment seized, and thus I said:
'Be mindful, goddess! of thy promise made;
Must sad Ulysses ever be delay'd?
Around their lord my sad companions mourn,
Each breast beats homeward, anxious to return:
If but a moment parted from thy eyes,
Their tears flow round me, and my heart complies.'
 "'Go then (she cried), ah go! yet think, not I,
Not Circe, but the Fates, your wish deny.
Ah, hope not yet to breathe thy native air!
Far other journey first demands thy care;
To tread the uncomfortable paths beneath,
And view the realms of darkness and of death.

There seek the Theban bard, deprived of sight;
Within, irradiate with prophetic light;
To whom Persephone, entire and whole,
Gave to retain the unseparated soul:
The rest are forms, of empty ether made;
Impassive semblance, and a flitting shade.'
    "Struck at the word, my very heart was dead:
Pensive I sate: my tears bedew'd the bed:
To hate the light and life my soul begun,
And saw that all was grief beneath the sun.
Composed at length the gushing tears suppress'd,
And my toss'd limbs now wearied into rest.
'How shall I tread (I cried), ah, Circe! say,
The dark descent, and who shall guide the way?
Can living eyes behold the realms below?
What bark to waft me, and what wind to blow?'

2. HERODOTUS, *HISTORIES*

Herodotus (ca. 484–420 B.C.) lived during the height of Athenian power, a time
when Hellenist culture was rapidly spreading throughout the Mediterranean
world. Growing up as he did in the Greek city of Halicarnassus on the southwest
coast of Asia Minor, Herodotus was himself a product of Greek expansionism.
It is perhaps because he grew up in this part of the world that the *Histories* focuses a great deal of attention upon North Africa and the regions leading to the
Black Sea. However, we know that Herodotus also traveled widely all over the
Mediterranean and even spent some time in Athens. The following passage describes Egyptian culture. Here we can see why Herodotus's *Histories* remains
one of the most important historical treatises ever produced. Its detailed, rational, almost ethnographic model of analysis and description influenced much
later models of historical and anthropological study. Herodotus discusses not
only social, political, and economic structures and religious beliefs but also the
topography, climate, flora, and fauna of many different cultures. As a Greek by
birth, it is not surprising that Herodotus considers Greek culture the most "civilized" of all those he encounters. Even so, he is clearly impressed by the sophistication of Egyptian society.

Histories

15. If then we choose to adopt the views of the Ionians concerning Egypt, we must come
to the conclusion that the Egyptians had formerly no country at all. For the Ionians say
that nothing is really Egypt but the Delta, which extends along shore from the Watch-
tower of Perseus, as it is called, to the Pelusiac Salt-pans, a distance of forty schœnes, and

stretches inland as far as the city of Cercasôrus, where the Nile divides into the two streams which reach the sea at Pelusium and Canôbus respectively. The rest of what is accounted Egypt belongs, they say, either to Arabia or Libya. But the Delta, as the Egyptians affirm, and as I myself am persuaded, is formed of the deposits of the river, and has only recently, if I may use the expression, come to light. If, then, they had formerly no territory at all, how came they to be so extravagant as to fancy themselves the most ancient race in the world? Surely there was no need of their making the experiment with the children to see what language they would first speak. But in truth I do not believe that the Egyptians came into being at the same time with the Delta, as the Ionians call it; I think they have always existed ever since the human race began; as the land went on increasing, part of the population came down into the new country, part remained in their old settlements. In ancient times the Thebaïs bore the name of Egypt, a district of which the entire circumference is but 6120 furlongs.

16. If, then, my judgment on these matters be right, the Ionians are mistaken in what they say of Egypt. If, on the contrary, it is they who are right, then I undertake to show that neither the Ionians nor any of the other Greeks know how to count. For they all say that the earth is divided into three parts, Europe, Asia, and Libya, whereas they ought to add a fourth part, the Delta of Egypt, since they do not include it either in Asia or Libya. For is it not their theory that the Nile separates Asia from Libya? As the Nile, therefore, splits in two at the apex of the Delta, the Delta itself must be a separate country, not contained in either Asia or Libya.

17. Here I take my leave of the opinions of the Ionians, and proceed to deliver my own sentiments on these subjects. I consider Egypt to be the whole country inhabited by the Egyptians, just as Cilicia is the tract occupied by the Cilicians, and Assyria that possessed by the Assyrians. And I regard the only proper boundary-line between Libya and Asia to be that which is marked out by the Egyptian frontier. For if we take the boundary-line commonly received by the Greeks, we must regard Egypt as divided, along its whole length from Elephantiné and the Cataracts to Cercasôrus, into two parts, each belonging to a different portion of the world, one to Asia, the other to Libya; since the Nile divides Egypt in two from the Cataracts to the sea, running as far as the city of Cercasôrus in a single stream, but at that point separating into three branches, whereof the one which bends eastward is called the Pelusiac mouth, and that which slants to the west, the Canobic. Meanwhile the straight course of the stream, which comes down from the upper country and meets the apex of the Delta, continues on, dividing the Delta down the middle, and empties itself into the sea by a mouth, which is as celebrated, and carries as large a body of water, as most of the others, the mouth called the Sebennytic. Besides these there are two other mouths which run out of the Sebennytic called respectively the Saitic and the Mendesian. The Bolbitine mouth, and the Bucolic, are not natural branches, but channels made by excavation....

77. With respect to the Egyptians themselves, it is to be remarked that those who live in the corn country, devoting themselves, as they do, far more than any other people in the world, to the preservation of the memory of past actions, are the best skilled in history of any men that I have ever met. The following is the mode of life habitual to them:—For three successive days in each month they purge the body by means of emetics and clysters, which is done out of a regard for their health, since they have a persuasion that every disease to which men are liable is occasioned by the substances whereon they feed. Apart from any such precautions, they are, I believe, next to the Libyans, the healthiest people in the world—an effect of their climate, in my opinion,

which has no sudden changes. Diseases almost always attack men when they are exposed to a change, and never more than during changes of the weather. They live on bread made of spelt, which they form into loaves called in their own tongue *cyllēstis*. Their drink is a wine which they obtain from barley, as they have no vines in their country. Many kinds of fish they eat raw, either salted or dried in the sun. Quails also, and ducks and small birds, they eat uncooked, merely first salting them. All other birds and fishes, excepting those which are set apart as sacred, are eaten either roasted or boiled.

78. In social meetings among the rich, when the banquet is ended, a servant carries round to the several guests a coffin, in which there is a wooden image of a corpse, carved and painted to resemble nature as nearly as possible, about a cubit or two cubits in length. As he shows it to each guest in turn, the servant says, "Gaze here, and drink and be merry; for when you die, such will you be."

79. The Egyptians adhere to their own national customs, and adopt no foreign usages. Many of these customs are worthy of note: among others their song, the Linus, which is sung under various names not only in Egypt but in Phœnicia, in Cyprus, and in other places; and which seems to be exactly the same as that in use among the Greeks, and by them called Linus. There were very many things in Egypt which filled me with astonishment, and this was one of them. Whence could the Egyptians have got the Linus? It appears to have been sung by them from the very earliest times. For the Linus in Egyptian is called Manerôs; and they told me that Manerôs was the only son of their first king, and that on his untimely death he was honoured by the Egyptians with these dirgelike strains, and in this way they got their first and only melody.

80. There is another custom in which the Egyptians resemble a particular Greek people, namely the Lacedæmonians. Their young men, when they meet their elders in the streets, give way to them and step aside; and if an elder come in where young men are present, these latter rise from their seats. In a third point they differ entirely from all the nations of Greece. Instead of speaking to each other when they meet in the streets, they make an obeisance, sinking the hand to the knee.

81. They wear a linen tunic fringed about the legs, and called *calasiris;* over this they have a white woollen garment thrown on afterwards. Nothing of woollen, however, is taken into their temples or buried with them, as their religion forbids it. Here their practice resembles the rites called Orphic and Bacchic, but which are in reality Egyptian and Pythagorean; for no one initiated in these mysteries can be buried in a woollen shroud, a religious reason being assigned for the observance.

82. The Egyptians likewise discovered to which of the gods each month and day is sacred, and found out from the day of a man's birth, what he will meet with in the course of his life, and how he will end his days, and what sort of man he will be—discoveries whereof the Greeks engaged in poetry have made a use. The Egyptians have also discovered more prognostics than all the rest of mankind besides. Whenever a prodigy takes place, they watch and record the result; then, if anything similar ever happens again, they expect the same consequences.

83. With respect to divination, they hold that it is a gift which no mortal possesses, but only certain of the gods: thus they have an oracle of Hercules, one of Apollo, of Minerva, of Diana, of Mars, and of Jupiter. Besides these, there is the oracle of Latona at Buto, which is held in much higher repute than any of the rest. The mode of delivering the oracles is not uniform, but varies at the different shrines.

84. Medicine is practised among them on a plan of separation; each physician treats a single disorder, and no more: thus the county swarms with medical practitioners,

some undertaking to cure diseases of the eye, others of the head, others again of the teeth, others of the intestines, and some those which are not local.

85. The following is the way in which they conduct their mournings and their funerals:—On the death in any house of a man of consequence, forthwith the women of the family beplaster their heads, and sometimes even their faces, with mud; and then, leaving the body indoors, sally forth and wander through the city, with their dress fastened by a band, and their bosoms bare, beating themselves as they walk. All the female relations join them and do the same. The men too, similarly begirt, beat their breasts separately. When these ceremonies are over, the body is carried away to be embalmed.

86. There are a set of men in Egypt who practice the art of embalming, and make it their proper business. These persons, when a body is brought to them, show the bearers various models of corpses, made in wood, and painted so as to resemble nature. The most perfect is said to be after the manner of him whom I do not think it religious to name in connection with such a matter; the second sort is inferior to the first, and less costly; the third is the cheapest of all. All this the embalmers explain, and then ask in which way it is wished that the corpse should be prepared. The bearers tell them, and having concluded their bargain, take their departure, while the embalmers, left to themselves, proceed to their task. The mode of embalming, according to the most perfect process, is the following:—They take first a crooked piece of iron, and with it draw out the brain through the nostrils, thus getting rid of a portion, while the skull is cleared of the rest by rinsing with drugs; next they make a cut along the flank with a sharp Ethiopian stone, and take out the whole contents of the abdomen, which they then cleanse, washing it thoroughly with palm wine, and again frequently with an infusion of pounded aromatics. After this they fill the cavity with the purest bruised myrrh, with cassia, and every other sort of spicery except frankincense, and sew up the opening. Then the body is placed in natrum for seventy days, and covered entirely over. After the expiration of that space of time, which must not be exceeded, the body is washed, and wrapped round, from head to foot, with bandages of fine linen cloth, smeared over with gum, which is used generally by the Egyptians in the place of glue, and in this state it is given back to the relations, who enclose it in a wooden case which they have had made for the purpose, shaped into the figure of a man. Then fastening the case, they place it in a sepulchral chamber, upright against the wall. Such is the most costly way of embalming the dead.

87. If persons wish to avoid expense, and choose the second process, the following is the method pursued:—Syringes are filled with oil made from the cedar-tree, which is then, without any incision or disembowelling, injected into the abdomen. The passage by which it might be likely to return is stopped, and the body laid in natrum the prescribed number of days. At the end of the time the cedar-oil is allowed to make its escape; and such is its power that it brings with it the whole stomach and intestines in a liquid state. The natrum meanwhile has dissolved the flesh, and so nothing is left of the dead body but the skin and the bones. It is returned in this condition to the relatives, without any further trouble being bestowed upon it.

88. The third method of embalming, which is practised in the case of the poorer classes, is to clear out the intestines with a clyster, and let the body lie in natrum the seventy days, after which it is at once given to those who come to fetch it away.

89. The wives of men of rank are not given to be embalmed immediately after death, nor indeed are any of the more beautiful and valued women. It is not till they have been dead three or four days that they are carried to the embalmers. This is done

to prevent indignities from being offered them. It is said that once a case of this kind occurred: the man was detected by the information of his fellow-workman.

90. Whensoever any one, Egyptian or foreigner, has lost his life by falling a prey to a crocodile, or by drowning in the river, the law compels the inhabitants of the city near which the body is cast up to have it embalmed, and to bury it in one of the sacred repositories with all possible magnificence. No one may touch the corpse, not even any of the friends or relatives, but only the priests of the Nile, who prepare it for burial with their own hands—regarding it as something more than the mere body of a man—and themselves lay it in the tomb.

3. PLINY THE ELDER, *NATURAL HISTORY*

Greek and Roman scholars were as fascinated with the natural world as they were with the human mind because the world was the habitat of humankind. They were convinced that an essential unity bound individual and cosmos, and that understanding of universal truth could be found through the examination of the physical environment. The Greek philosopher Aristotle (384–322 B.C.) is perhaps the best known ancient investigator of the natural world, and he wrote numerous treatises that touched on everything from human biology to plant life. One of the most comprehensive and influential ancient texts on the natural world until the end of the early modern period, however, was the *Natural History* of Pliny the Elder (23–79 A.D.). The Gaul-born Caius Plinius Secundus was a high-ranking official in the Roman army who in his leisure time wrote numerous treatises on a wide variety of subjects. Only his *Historia Naturalis* (Natural History) has survived to this day. The *Natural History* is an encyclopedic account of all ancient knowledge on the natural world, including the work of Aristotle. Comprising thirty-seven books, Pliny discusses the nature of the cosmos, the geography of the known world, and plant and animal life. The book also discusses human nature and human society. The following excerpt from Book VII of the *Natural History* discusses the biological origins of men and women.

Man, His Birth, His Organization, and the Invention of the Arts

Such then is the present state of the world, and of the countries, nations, more remarkable seas, islands, and cities which it contains. The nature of the animated beings which exist upon it, is hardly in any degree less worthy of our contemplation than its other features; if, indeed, the human mind is able to embrace the whole of so diversified a subject. Our first attention is justly due to Man, for whose sake all other things appear to have been produced by Nature; though, on the other hand, with so great and so severe penalties for the enjoyment of her bounteous gifts, that it is far from easy to determine, whether she has proved to him a kind parent, or a merciless step-mother.

In the first place, she obliges him alone, of all animated beings, to clothe himself with the spoils of the others; while, to all the rest, she has given various kinds of coverings, such as shells, crusts, spines, hides, furs, bristles, hair, down, feathers, scales, and fleeces. The very trunks of the trees even, she has protected against the effects of heat and cold by a bark, which is, in some cases, twofold. Man alone, at the very moment of his birth cast naked upon the naked earth, does she abandon to cries, to lamentations, and, a thing that is the case with no other animal whatever, to tears: this, too, from the very moment that he enters upon existence. But as for laughter, why, by Hercules!—to laugh, if but for an instant only, has never been granted to man before the fortieth day from his birth, and then it is looked upon as a miracle of precocity. Introduced thus to the light, man has fetters and swathings instantly put upon all his limbs, a thing that falls to the lot of none of the brutes even that are born among us. Born to such singular good fortune, there lies the animal, which is destined to command all the others, lies, fast bound hand and foot, and weeping aloud! such being the penalty which he has to pay on beginning life, and that for the sole fault of having been born. Alas! for the folly of those who can think after such a beginning as this, that they have been born for the display of vanity!

The earliest presage of future strength, the earliest bounty of time, confers upon him nought but the resemblance to a quadruped. How soon does man gain the power of walking? How soon does he gain the faculty of speech? How soon is his mouth fitted for mastication? How long are the pulsations of the crown of his head to proclaim him the weakest of all animated beings? And then, the diseases to which he is subject, the numerous remedies which he is obliged to devise against his maladies, and those thwarted every now and then by new forms and features of disease. While other animals have an instinctive knowledge of their natural powers; some, of their swiftness of pace, some of their rapidity of flight, and some again of their power of swimming; man is the only one that knows nothing, that can learn nothing without being taught; he can neither speak, nor walk, nor eat, and, in short, he can do nothing, at the prompting of nature only, but weep. For this it is, that many have been of opinion, that it were better not to have been born, or if born, to have been annihilated at the earliest possible moment.

To man alone, of all animated beings, has it been given, to grieve, to him alone to be guilty of luxury and excess; and that in modes innumerable, and in every part of his body. Man is the only being that is a prey to ambition, to avarice, to an immoderate desire of life, to superstition,—he is the only one that troubles himself about his burial, and even what is to become of him after death. By none is life held on a tenure more frail; none are more influenced by unbridled desires for all things; none are sensible of fears more bewildering; none are actuated by rage more frantic and violent. Other animals, in fine, live at peace with those of their own kind; we only see them unite to make a stand against those of a different species. The fierceness of the lion is not expended in fighting with its own kind; the sting of the serpent is not aimed at the serpent; and the monsters of the sea oven, and the fishes, vent their rage only on those of a different species. But with man,—by Hercules! most of *his* misfortunes are occasioned by man.

(1.) We have already given a general description of the human race in our account of the different nations. Nor, indeed, do I now propose to treat of their manners and customs, which are of infinite variety and almost as numerous as the various groups themselves, into which mankind is divided; but yet there are some things, which, I think, ought not to be omitted; and more particularly, in relation to those peoples which dwell at a considerable distance from the sea; among which, I have no doubt, that some facts will appear of an astounding nature, and, indeed, incredible to many. Who, for instance, could ever believe in the existence of the Æthiopians, who had not first seen them? Indeed what is there that does not appear marvellous, when it comes to our knowledge for the first time? How many things, too, are looked upon as quite impossible, until they have been actually effected? But it is the fact, that every moment of our existence we are distrusting the power and the majesty of Nature, if the mind, instead of grasping her in her entirety, considers her only in detail. Not to speak of peacocks, the spotted skins of tigers and panthers, and the rich colours of so many animals, a trifling thing apparently to speak of, but of inestimable importance, when we give it due consideration, is the existence of so many languages among the various nations, so many modes of speech, so great a variety of expressions; that to another, a man who is of a different country, is almost the same as no man at all. And then, too, the human features and countenance, although composed of but some ten parts or little more, are so fashioned, that among so many thousands of men, there are no two in existence who cannot be distinguished from one another, a result which no art could possibly have produced, when confined to so limited a number of combinations. In most points, however, of this nature, I shall not be content to pledge my own credit only, but shall confirm it in preference by referring to my authorities, which shall be given on all subjects of a nature to inspire doubt. My readers, however, must make no objection to following the Greeks, who have proved themselves the most careful observers, as well as of the longest standing.

4. EGERIA, *DIARY OF A PILGRIMAGE*

The pilgrimage account of Egeria was probably written in the first part of the fifth century A.D. The authorship remains somewhat of a mystery to this day though internal evidence in the document suggests that the author could have been an abbess or another prominent religious woman. Egeria was familiar with Christian liturgical ritual, and her ability to travel for a period of several months through Egypt, Syria, and Palestine also suggests an elevated social stature. There is also some evidence to suggest that the author came from the regions of modern day Spain or France. Egeria's account is enormously important because it is one of the earliest known Christian pilgrimage accounts. It is particularly revealing about Christian life in the East during the fifth century. It shows, for example, that Christians by the fifth century already believed in the spiritual efficacy of touching and experiencing the land walked on by biblical figures such as Christ. This "holy" land was imbued with sacral significance and power, and it could spiritually transform those Christians who visited it. Egeria's account is also important because it is a rarity among classical texts—a book written by a woman which has survived to this day. It is perhaps because she is a woman that Egeria mentions not only several important biblical women but also describes her encounters with religious women as well as men on her travels. In this excerpt, for example, Egeria describes her encounter with a religious woman named Marthana.

Diary of a Pilgrimage

Leaving Tarsus, but still in Cilicia, I reached Pompeiopolis, a city by the sea, and from there I crossed into Isauria, and spent the night in a city called Corycus. On the third day I arrived at a city called Seleucia of Isauria, and, when I got there, I called on the bishop, a very godly man who had been a monk, and saw a very beautiful church in the city. Holy Thecla's is on a small hill about a mile and a half from the city, so, as I had to stay somewhere, it was best to go straight on and spend the night there.

Round the holy church there is a tremendous number of cells for men and women. And that was where I found one of my dearest friends, a holy deaconess called Marthana. I had come to know her in Jerusalem when she was up there on pilgrimage. She was the superior of some cells of apotactites or virgins, and I simply cannot tell you how pleased we were to see each other again. But I must get back to the point. There are a great many cells on that hill, and in the middle a great wall round the martyrium itself, which is very beautiful. The wall was built to protect the church against the Isaurians, who are hostile, and always committing robberies, to prevent them trying to damage the monastery which has been established there. In God's name I arrived at the martyrium, and we had a prayer there, and read the whole Acts of holy Thecla; and I gave heartfelt thanks to God for his mercy in letting me fulfil all my desires so completely, despite all my unworthiness. For two days I stayed there, visiting all the holy monks and apotactities, the men as well as the women; then, after praying and receiving Communion, I went back to Tarsus to rejoin my route.

Arrival in Constantinople (June or July 384)

I stayed there three days before setting off to continue my journey, and then, after a day's travelling, I arrived at a staging-post called Mansucrene below Mount Taurus. We stayed the night there, and the next day we climbed Mount Taurus, and continued along a road we already knew, since our outward journey had brought us along it. Passing through the same provinces of Cappadocia, Galatia, and Bithynia, I reached Chalcedon, and I stayed there because it contains the renowned martyrium of holy Euphemia, long known to me. Next day I crossed the sea and reached Constantinople, giving thanks to Christ our God for seeing fit, through no deserving of mine, to grant me the desire to go on this journey, and the strength to visit everything I wanted and now to return again to Constantinople.

And in all the churches at Constantinople, in the tombs of the apostles, and at many martyria, I never ceased to give thanks to Jesus our God for his grace in showing me such mercy.

So, loving ladies, light of my heart, this is where I am writing to you. My present plan is, in the name of Christ our God, to travel to Asia, since I want to make a pilgrimage to Ephesus, and the martyrium of the holy and blessed Apostle John. 'If after that I am still alive, and able to visit further places, I will either tell you about them face to face (if God so wills), or at any rate write to you about them if my plans change. In any case, ladies, light of my heart, whether I am "in the body" or "out of the body", please do not forget me.

The Weekly Services

On Weekdays

Loving sisters, I am sure it will interest you to know about the daily services they have in the holy places, and I must tell you about them. All the doors of the Anastasis are opened before cock-crow each day, and the "*monazontes* and *parthenae*", as they call them here, come in, and also some lay men and women, at least those who are willing to wake at such an early hour. From then until daybreak they join in singing the refrains to the hymns, psalms, and antiphons.

There is a prayer between each of the hymns, since there are two or three presbyters and deacons each day by rota, who are there with the monazontes, and say the prayers between all the hymns and antiphons.

As soon as dawn comes, they start the Morning Hymns, and the bishop with his clergy comes and joins them. He goes straight into the cave, and into the railed area; he first says the Prayer for All (mentioning any names he wishes) and blesses the catechumens, and then another prayer and blesses the faithful. Then he comes out of the railed area, and everyone comes up to have his hand laid on them. He blesses them one by one, and goes out, and by the time the dismissal takes place it is already day.

Again at midday everyone comes into the Anastasis and says psalms and antiphons until a message is sent to the bishop. Again he enters, and, without taking his seat, goes straight into the railed area in the Anastasis (which is to say into the cave where he went in the early morning), and again, after a prayer, he blesses the faithful and comes out of the railed area, and again they come to have his hand laid on them.

At three o'clock they do once more what they did at midday, but at four o'clock they have *Lychnicon,* as they call it, or in our language, Lucernare. All the people congregate once more in the Anastasis, and the lamps and candles are all lit, which makes it very bright. The fire is brought not from outside, but from the cave—that is from inside the railing—where a lamp is always burning night and day. For some time they have the Lucernare psalms and antiphons; then they send for the bishop, who enters and sits in the chief seat. The presbyters also come and sit in their places, and the hymns and antiphons go on. Then, when they have finished singing everything which is appointed, the bishop rises and goes in front of the railed area (i.e., the cave). One of the deacons make the normal commemoration of individuals, and each time he mentions a name a large group of boys responds *Kyrie eleison* (in our language, "Lord, have mercy"). Their voices are very loud. As soon as the deacon has done his part, the bishop says a prayer and prays the Prayer for All. Up to this point the faithful and the catechumens are praying together, but now the deacon calls every catechumen to stand where he is and bow his head, and the bishop says the blessing over the catechumens from his place. There is another prayer, after which the deacon calls for all the faithful to bow their head, and the bishop says the blessing over the faithful from his place. Thus the dismissal takes place at the Anastasis, and they all come up one by one to have the bishop's hand laid on them.

Then, singing hymns, they take the bishop from the Anastasis to the Cross, and everyone goes with him. On arrival he says one prayer and blesses the catechumens, then another and blesses the faithful. Then again the bishop and all the people go Behind the Cross, and do there what they did Before the Cross; and in both places they come to have the bishop's hand laid on them, as they did in the Anastasis. Great glass lanterns are burning everywhere, and there are many candles in front of the Anastasis, and also Before and Behind the Cross. By the end of all this it is dusk. So these are the services held every weekday at the Cross and at the Anastasis.

On Sunday (Incomplete)

But on the seventh day, the Lord's Day, there gather in the courtyard before cock-crow all the people, as many as can get in, as if it was Easter. The courtyard is the "basilica" beside the Anastasis, that is to say, out of doors, and lamps have been hung there for them. Those who are afraid they may not arrive in time for cock-crow come early, and sit waiting there singing hymns and antiphons, and they have prayers between, since there are always presbyters and deacons there ready for the vigil, because so many people collect there, and it is not usual to open the holy places before cock-crow.

Soon the first cock crows, and at that the bishop enters, and goes into the cave in the Anastasis. The doors are all opened, and all the people come into the Anastasis, which is already ablaze with lamps. When they are inside, a psalm is said by one of the presbyters, with everyone responding, and it is followed by a prayer; then a psalm is said by one of the deacons, and another prayer; then a third psalm is said by one of the clergy, a third prayer, and the Commemoration of All. After these three psalms and prayers they take censers into the cave of the Anastasis, so that the whole Anastasis basilica is filled with the smell. Then the bishop, standing in the sanctuary, takes the Gospel book and goes to the door, where he himself reads the account of the Lord's resurrection. At the beginning of the reading the whole assembly groans and laments at all that the Lord underwent for us, and the way they weep would move even the hardest heart to tears.

When the Gospel is finished, the bishop comes out, and is taken with singing to the Cross; and they all go with him. They have one psalm there and a prayer, then he blesses the people, and that is the dismissal. As the bishop goes out, everyone comes to have his hand laid on them.

Then straight away the bishop retires to his house, and all the monazontes go back into the Anastasis to sing psalms and antiphons until daybreak. There are prayers between all these psalms and antiphons, and presbyters and deacons take their turn every day at the Anastasis to keep vigil with the people. Some lay men and women like to stay on there till daybreak, but others prefer to go home again to bed for some sleep.

At daybreak the people assemble in the Great Church built by Constantine on Golgotha Behind the Cross. It is the Lord's Day, and they do what is everywhere the custom on the Lord's Day. But you should note that here it is usual for any presbyter who has taken his seat to preach, if he so wishes, and when they have finished there is a sermon from the bishop. The object of having this preaching every Sunday is to make sure that the people will continually be learning about the Bible and the love of God.

Because of all the preaching it is a long time till the dismissal, which takes place not before ten or even eleven o'clock. And when the dismissal has taken place in the church—in the way which is usual everywhere—the monazontes lead the bishop with singing to the Anastasis. While they are singing and the bishop approaches, all the doors of the Anastasis basilica are opened, and the people (not the catechumens, only the faithful) all go in. When they are all inside, the bishop enters, and passes straight through the railings of the cave itself, the Witness. They have a thanksgiving to God and the Prayer for All; then the deacon calls every single person to bow his head, and the bishop blesses them from his place inside the middle railing. Then he comes out and, as he does so, everyone comes to kiss his hand. Thus the dismissal is delayed till almost eleven or twelve o'clock.

Lucernare is held in the same way as on other days.

Except on the special days, which we shall be describing below, this order is observed on every day of the year. What I found most impressive about all this was that the psalms and antiphons they use are always appropriate, whether at night, in the early morning, at the day prayers at midday or three o'clock, or at Lucernare. Everything is suitable, appropriate, and relevant to what is being done.

Every Sunday in the year, except one, they assemble in the great Church which Constantine built on Golgotha Behind the Cross; the exception is Pentecost, the Fiftieth Day after Easter, when they assemble on Sion. You will find this mentioned below, but what they do is to go to Sion before nine o'clock after their dismissal in the Great Church. . . .

The Liturgical Year

Epiphany (Incomplete)

. . . "Blessed is he that cometh in the name of the Lord", and so on. They have to go slowly for the sake of the monazontes who are on foot, so they arrive in Jerusalem almost at daybreak, but just before it is light, at the moment when people can first recognize each other.

When they arrive, the bishop goes straight into the Anastasis, and everybody goes with him. Extra lamps have been lighted there. Then they have one psalm and a prayer, and the bishop blesses first the catechumens, and then the faithful. He then retires, and all the people return to the places where they are staying to have a rest, but the monazontes stay there to sing hymns till daybreak.

Just after seven in the morning, when the people have rested, they all assemble in the Great Church on Golgotha. And on this day in this church, and at the Anastasis and the Cross and Bethlehem, the decorations really are too marvellous for words. All you can see is gold and jewels and silk; the hangings are entirely silk with gold stripes, the curtains the same, and everything they use for services at the festival is made of gold and jewels. You simply cannot imagine the number, and the sheer weight of the candles and the tapers and lamps and everything else they use for the services.

They are beyond description, and so is the magnificent building itself. It was built by Constantine, and under the supervision of his mother it was honoured with as much gold, mosaic, and previous marble as his empire could provide, and this not only at the Great Church, but at the Anastasis and the Cross, and the other holy places of Jerusalem as well. But I must get back to the point.

On the first day they have the service in the Great Church on Golgotha, and all the preaching and all that they read or sing is appropriate to the day. Then, after their dismissal in the church, they go with singing to the Anastasis in the usual way, and the dismissal there takes place at about noon. Lucernare that day takes place in the way which is usual every day.

On the second day they assemble in the church on Golgotha, and also on the third, and their rejoicing lasts until noon in Constantine's church on all those three days. On the fourth day they decorate everything and celebrate in the same way on the Eleona (the very beautiful church on the Mount of Olives), on the fifth at the Lazarium, about a mile and a half from Jerusalem, on the sixth on Sion, on the seventh at the Anastasis, and on the eighth at the Cross. The decorations and rejoicing continue for eight days in all these places I have mentioned.

But in Bethlehem they go on for eight days continuously. All the presbyters and clergy of the place, and the monazontes who reside there, take part, but during that season the bishop must celebrate the festival in Jerusalem. So at night everyone goes back with him to Jerusalem; but from that time all the Bethlehem monks keep vigil in the church at Bethlehem, and sing hymns and antiphons till it is day. For the sake of this feast day and the celebrations great crowds come to Jerusalem from all parts, not only monks, but lay men and women as well.

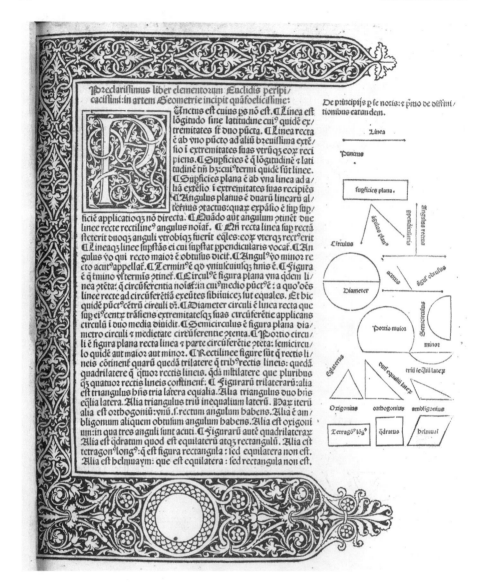

Figure 2.1 Euclid, *Elementa Geometriae*. Venice: Erhard Ratdolt, 1482. Rare Books Division, J. Willard Marriott Library, University of Utah.

Study Questions

1. How does Homer characterize Circe? In what way is she an archetype of femininity in Western society? What masculine values does the figure of Odysseus represent?
2. What features of Egyptian society interest Herodotus? Why does he want to provide such a detailed description of Egypt and other lands?
3. How does Pliny's interpretation of the origins of human nature reflect classical conceptions of human nature?
4. Describe the pilgrimage experience for a Christian living in the Roman Empire during the fifth century A.D.. What does the pilgrimage of Egeria tell us about Christianity during this period? About the role of women?
5. Compare the nature and purpose of travel in the four documents. Was it easy to travel during the periods of ancient Greece and Rome? How did people travel and why? How did travel affect these societies? How did the people of ancient Greece and Rome regard travel?

Suggested Readings

Brown, Peter. *The World of Late Antiquity.* Princeton, NJ: American School of Classical Studies at Athens, 1988.
Cunliffe, Barry. *Greeks, Romans, and Barbarians.* New York: Methuen, 1988.
Finley, M. I. *The World of Odysseus.* New York: St. Martin's Press, 1977.
Lloyd, G. E. R. *Greek Science after Aristotle.* New York: Norton, 1973.
Walbank, F. W. *The Hellenistic World.* Sussex: Harvester Press, 1981.
Whittaker, C. R. *Frontiers of the Roman Empire. A Social and Economic Study.* Baltimore and London: Johns Hopkins University Press, 1994.

Web Sites

1. Bureaucrats and Barbarians: Minoans, Myceneans, and the Greek Dark Ages

   http://www.wsu.edu/~dee/MINOA/CONTENTS.HTM

2. The Karavanis excavation of ancient Rome

   http://www.eawc.evansville.edu/ropage.htm

3. Roman Republic

   http://campus.northpark.edu/history/WebChron/Mediterranean/RomeRep.html

3

Early Medieval Europe
500–1000 A.D.

TEXTS

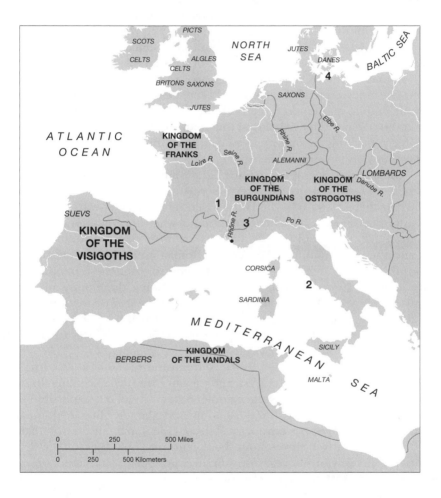

The fall of the Roman Empire after 400 A.D. left a political, economic, and military vacuum in the Western regions of the empire. Far from being a "dark age" as traditionally described, however, the five centuries following the collapse of the Empire saw new cultures emerge that would play an important role in shaping the evolution of Western society. The driving force behind the emergence of these new cultures was the migration of the Germanic peoples into the Western regions of the Roman Empire by the end of the fourth century. It was along the fringes of the Roman Empire in the region then known as Gaul that Julius Caesar first encountered the Germanic and Celtic peoples (ca. 58 B.C.). [1] For a highly educated Roman such as Caesar, those who lived outside Roman culture were not truly civilized. They were "barbarian." Roman attitudes did not change toward these "barbarians" in subsequent centuries even as the Germanic and Celtic peoples began migrating into the empire and entered the ranks of the Roman armies. It is one of the ironies of the later imperial period that many of the Roman generals responsible for protecting the empire from Germanic incursions after 400 A.D. were themselves Germanic in origin.

The initial trickle of Germanic migration became a steady stream by the end of the fourth century as eastern Germanic tribes (Goths, Vandals) were pushed farther westward by the Hun of Central Asia. The Goths were the first to enter the empire as an entire community when they petitioned Emperor Valens in 378. It was not long before tension arose between Roman authorities and these communities. Weakening Roman authority, however, made it impossible for the empire to exert much control over these peoples, especially as other Germanic peoples began penetrating the empire on several fronts. In 429 A.D., the Visigoths had established their own kingdom in modern day Spain, and the Burgundians and the Ostrogoths soon took over the southern part of Gaul and Italy, respectively. By 500, the western part of the Roman Empire was under the control of Germanic peoples.

In the following centuries, Roman administrative and legal structures disintegrated in most parts of the West, and the once vital urban centers shrank as constant warfare made large-scale commercial activity all but impossible. Petty kingdoms, a localized agricultural economy, and a largely illiterate population characterized the Western Europe of 900 A.D. One Roman institution that survived and even thrived throughout these centuries, however, was the Roman Church. Especially in the regions of France and Spain, Germanic monarchs forged alliances with Roman ecclesiastics in their struggle by the end of the seventh century to build more powerful and durable political foundations for their respective authorities. Unlike many of their Germanic conquerors, who were usually more attracted at first to the then popular Arian faith, the majority of the people in the West were followers of Catholic (Western) Christianity. Clovis (482–511 A.D.) was the first Germanic king to convert to Catholicism, and the Visigoth kings converted from Arianism to Catholicism during the seventh century. The Franks in particular encouraged the foundation of monasteries,

[2] a communal and ascetic form of religious life that first emerged in the deserts of Egypt and Syria during the fourth century. The monastery quickly became the center of European intellectual as well as spiritual life and remained so until the emergence of the university in the twelfth century. These monarchs and their successors also promoted the authority of bishops who, in return for royal support of their spiritual activities, recognized the authority of kings as spiritual in nature. To signify the divine origin of royal authority, Visigothic bishops introduced the practice of anointing the royal head with holy oil during the coronation ceremony; this tradition was soon picked up by Frankish and Anglo-Saxon monarchs.

This cooperation between Catholic Church and secular state had important ramifications for the development of both institutions in subsequent centuries, and it was responsible above all for the emergence of a new understanding of the ruler as both a spiritual and temporal leader of society. Germanic influence was also felt in many other ways in the West. Germanic models of kingship based on personal bonds of loyalty between a monarch and a warrior elite replaced the larger, more bureaucratic, imperial state structures. Germanic law codes [3] coexisted alongside Roman law, Germanic marriage and inheritance practices took over from Roman ones, and new languages emerged as a result of cultural interaction between the Germanic peoples and the cultures under their jurisdiction.

The new political, economic, and spiritual institutions which began emerging during this period survived even persistent raiding by the Scandinavian peoples. Hungry for gold, silver, and other treasure, these "Vikings" attacked the coastal regions of the Baltic Sea, France, England, and mainland Russia between the eighth and eleventh centuries. [4] Although the Viking raids did strike terror into the hearts of the Europeans of their day, it is debatable whether they substantially altered European society. Most Viking raids were swift and only moderately destructive. With the exception of England where Scandinavian settlements emerged in greater numbers, furthermore, these peoples usually returned home of were assimilated into the existing population.

1. GREGORY OF TOURS, *THE HISTORY OF THE FRANKS*

Gregory of Tours was the most recent in a long line of bishops in his family when he replaced his cousin as the bishop of Tours in 573 A.D. As a member of the old Gallo-Roman Christian elite, Gregory's ascension to high ecclesiastical office was to be expected. This intellectually and politically influential group controlled virtually all episcopal offices in Gaul long after the region was conquered by the Franks. *The History of the Franks* (ca. 581–591) remains one of the most important sources on Gaul during the sixth century. Gregory of Tours's greatest work reflects a world marked by chronic warfare between petty kingdoms, powerful warrior rulers, treachery, and brutality. Written as it is by a Catholic bishop, the *History* also naturally focuses on the spread of Christianity. The following passage is interesting because here Gregory of Tours pays tribute to the evangelical work of Clovis's wife, Queen Clotilda. Women are rarely given a prominent place in chronicles of the early medieval period. In the *History of the Franks,* however, Queen Clotilda and Queen Radegund play a central role in spreading Christianity throughout the West. The following excerpt concerns Clovis's conversion by his Christian wife Clotilda.

History of the Franks

28. Now the king of the Burgundians was Gundevech, of the family of king Athanaric the persecutor, whom we have mentioned before. He had four sons; Gundobad, Godegisel, Chilperic and Godomar. Gundobad killed his brother Chilperic with the sword, and sank his wife in water with a stone tied to her neck. His two daughters he condemned to exile; the older of these, who became a nun, was called Chrona, and the younger Clotilda. And as Clovis often sent embassies to Burgundy, the maiden Clotilda was found by his envoys. And when they saw that she was of good bearing and wise, and learned that she was of the family of the king, they reported this to King Clovis, and he sent an embassy to Gundobad without delay asking her in marriage. And Gundobad was afraid to refuse, and surrendered her to the men, and they took the girl and brought her swiftly to the king. The king was very glad when he saw her, and married her, having already by a concubine a son named Theodoric.

29. He had a first-born son by queen Clotilda, and as his wife wished to consecrate him in baptism, she tried unceasingly to persuade her husband, saying : "The gods you worship are nothing, and they will be unable to help themselves or any one else. For they are graven out of stone or wood or some metal. And the names you have given them are names of men and not of gods, as Saturn, who is declared to have fled in fear of being banished from his kingdom by his son; as Jove himself, the foul perpetrator of all shameful crimes, committing incest with men, mocking at his kinswomen, not able to refrain from intercourse with his own sister as she herself says: *Jovisque et soror et conjunx.* What could Mars or Mercury do? They are endowed rather with the magic arts than with the power of the divine name. But he ought rather to be worshipped who created by his word heaven and earth, the sea and all that in them is out of a state of nothingness, who made the sun shine, and adorned the heavens with stars, who filled the waters with creeping things, the earth with living things and the air with creatures that fly, at whose nod the earth is decked with growing crops, the trees with fruit, the vines with grapes, by whose hand mankind was created, by whose generosity all that creation serves and helps man whom he created as his own." But though the queen said this the spirit of the king was by no means moved to belief, and he said: "It was at the command of our gods that all things were created and came forth, and it is plain that your God has no power and, what is more, he is proven not to belong to the family of the gods." Meantime the faithful queen made her son ready for baptism; she gave command to adorn the church with hangings and curtains, in order that he who could not be moved by per-

suasion might be urged to belief by this mystery. The boy, whom they name Ingomer, died after being baptized, still wearing the white garments in which he became regenerate. At this the king was violently angry, and reproached the queen harshly, saying: "If the boy had been dedicated in the name of my gods he would certainly have lived; but as it is, since he was baptized in the name of your God, he could not live at all." To this the queen said: "I give thanks to the omnipotent God, creator of all, who has judged me not wholly unworthy, that he should deign to take to his kingdom one born from my womb. My soul is not stricken with grief for his sake, because I know that, summoned from this world as he was in his baptismal garments, he will be fed by the vision of God."

After this she bore another son, whom she named Chlodomer at baptism; and when he fell sick, the king said: "It is impossible that anything else should happen to him than happened to his brother, namely, that being baptized in the name of your Christ, he should die at once." But through the prayers of his mother, and the Lord's command, he became well.

30. The queen did not cease to urge him to recognize the true God and cease worshipping idols. But he could not be influenced in any way to this belief, until at last a war arose with the Alamanni, in which he was driven by necessity to confess what before he had of his free will denied. It came about that as the two armies were fighting fiercely, there was much slaughter, and Clovis's army began to be in danger of destruction. He saw it and raised his eyes to heaven, and with remorse in his heart he burst into tears and cried: "Jesus Christ, whom Clotilda asserts to be the son of the living God, who art said to give aid to those in distress, and to bestow victory on those who hope in thee, I beseech the glory of thy aid, with the vow that if thou wilt grant me victory over these enemies, and I shall know that power which she says that people dedicated in thy name have had from thee, I will believe in thee and be baptized in thy name. For I have invoked my own gods, but, as I find, they have withdrawn from aiding me; and therefore I believe that they possess no power, since they do not help those who obey them. I now call upon thee, I desire to believe thee, only let me be rescued from my adversaries." And when he said this, the Alamanni turned their backs, and began to disperse in flight. And when they saw that their king was killed, they submitted to the dominion of Clovis, saying: "Let not the people perish further, we pray; we are yours now." And he stopped the fighting, and after encouraging his men, retired in peace and told the queen how he had had merit to win the victory by calling on the name of Christ. This happened in the fifteenth year of his reign.

31. Then the queen asked Saint Remi, bishop of Rheims, to summon Clovis secretly, urging him to introduce the king to the word of salvation. And the bishop sent for him secretly and began to urge him to believe in the true God, maker of heaven and earth, and to cease worshipping idols, which could help neither themselves nor any one else. But the king said: "I gladly hear you, most holy father; but there remains one thing: the people who follow me cannot endure to abandon their gods; but I shall go and speak to them according to your words." He met with his followers, but before he could speak the power of God anticipated him, and all the people cried out together: "O pious king, we reject our mortal gods, and we are ready to follow the immortal God whom Remi preaches." This was reported to the bishop, who was greatly rejoiced, and bade them get ready the baptismal font. The squares were shaded with tapestried canopies, the churches adorned with white curtains, the baptistery set in order, the aroma of incense spread, candles of fragrant odor burned brightly, and the whole shrine of the

baptistery was filled with a divine fragrance: and the Lord gave such grace to those who stood by that they thought they were placed amid the odors of paradise. And the king was the first to ask to be baptized by the bishop. Another Constantine advanced to the baptismal font, to terminate the disease of ancient leprosy and wash away with fresh water the foul spots that had long been borne. And when he entered to be baptized, the saint of God began with ready speech: "Gently bend your neck, Sigamber; worship what you burned; burn what you worshipped." The holy bishop Remi was a man of excellent wisdom and especially trained in rhetorical studies, and of such surpassing holiness that he equaled the miracles of Silvester. For there is extant a book of his life which tells that he raised a dead man. And so the king confessed all-powerful God in the Trinity, and was baptized in the name of the Father, Son and holy Spirit, and was anointed with the holy ointment with the sign of the cross of Christ. And of his army more than 3000 were baptized. His sister also, Albofled, was baptized, who not long after passed to the Lord. And when the king was in mourning for her, the holy Remi sent a letter of consolation which began in this way: "The reason of your mourning pains me, and pains me greatly, that Albofled your sister, of good memory, has passed away. But I can give you this comfort, that her departure from the world was such that she ought to be envied rather than mourned." Another sister also was converted, Lanthechild by name, who had fallen into the heresy of the Arians, and she confessed that the Son and the holy Spirit were equal to the Father and was anointed.

2. THE RULE OF SAINT BENEDICT

Christian monasticism began in the deserts of Upper Egypt during the third century when devout individuals sought escape from worldliness by retreating to this harsh landscape. The rigorous asceticism of these hermits, along with their claims of mystical communion with God, quickly attracted imitators. By the fourth century, communities of men and women dedicated to a wholly spiritual life were springing up in the desert. The monastic community of the West, however, was markedly different in character than its Eastern counterpart. Adaptation to the colder climate and violent character of Western European life necessitated a more communal existence. The Benedictine model of monastic community was one of several competing models developed during the early medieval period, and it was ultimately the most successful in the West. In 529, Benedict of Nursia (480–543) developed a set of regulations *(regula)* for his community at Monte Cassino in Italy which became the blueprint for most Western monastic communities from this time forward. The purpose of the *Rule* was to regulate the life of a community of religious men in such a way as to allow them to be economically self-sufficient while pursuing their own salvation and that of others. The religious life outlined in the *Rule* divided the day between work in the fields, prayer, sleeping, and eating. Benedict moderated the rigorous asceticism demanded by Eastern monastic communities so that members could perform mundane, as well as spiritual, tasks. The Benedictine community also revolutionized the monastic movement when it included education as a mandate of the religious life. As one of the few institutions providing education in the West by the sixth century, the monastery quickly became the center of medieval intellectual, as well as spiritual, life.

The Rule of St. Benedict

Chapter I

Of the several kinds of Monks and their lives

It is recognized that there are four kinds of monks. The first are the Cenobites: that is, those who live in a monastery under a Rule or an abbot. The second kind is that of Anchorites, or Hermits, who not in the first fervour of conversion, but after long trial in the monastery, and already taught by the example of many others, have learnt to fight against the devil, are well prepared to go forth from the ranks of the brotherhood to the single combat of the desert. They can now, by God's help, safely fight against the vices of their flesh and against evil thoughts singly, with their own hand and arm and without the encouragement of a companion. The third and worst kind of monks is that of the Sarabites, who have not been tried under any Rule nor schooled by an experienced master, as gold is proved in the furnace, but soft as is lead and still in their works cleaving to the world, are known to lie to God by their tonsure.

These in twos or threes, or more frequently singly, are shut up, without a shepherd; not in our Lord's fold, but in their own. The pleasure of carrying out their particular desires is their law, and whatever they dream of or choose this they call holy; but what they like not, that they account unlawful.

The fourth class of monks is called Gyrovagi (or Wanderers). These move about all their lives through various countries, staying as guests for three or four days at different monasteries. They are always on the move and never settle down, and are slaves to their own wills and to the enticements of gluttony. In every way they are worse than the Sarabites, and of their wretched way of life it is better to be silent than to speak.

Leaving these therefore aside, let us by God's help set down a Rule for Cenobites, who are the best kind of monks.

Chapter VII

On Humility

Brethren, Holy Scripture cries out to us, saying, *Every one who exalteth himself shall be humbled, and he who humbleth himself shall be exalted.* In this it tells us that every form of self-exaltation is a kind of pride, which the prophet declares he carefully avoided, where he says, *Lord, my heart is not exalted, neither are my eyes lifted up; neither have I walked in great things, nor in wonders above myself.* And why? *If I did not think humbly, but exalted my soul: as a child weaned from his mother, so wilt Thou reward my soul.*

Wherefore, brethren, if we would scale the summit of humility, and swiftly gain the heavenly height which is reached by our lowliness in this present life, we must set up a ladder of climbing deeds like that which Jacob saw in his dream, whereon angels were descending and ascending. Without doubt that descending and ascending is to be understood by us as signifying that we descend by exalting ourselves and ascend by humbling ourselves. But the ladder itself thus set up is our life in this world, which by humility of heart is lifted by our Lord to heaven. Our body and soul we may indeed call the sides of the ladder in which our divine vocation has set the divers steps of humility and discipline we have to ascend.

The first step of humility, then, is reached when a man, with the fear of God always before his eyes, does not allow himself to forget, but is ever mindful of all God's commandments. He remembers, moreover, that such as contemn God fall into hell for their sins, and that life eternal awaits such as fear Him. And warding off at each moment all sin and defect in thought and word, of eye, hand or foot, of self-will, let such a one bestir himself to prune away the lusts of the flesh.

Let him think that he is seen at all times by God from heaven; and that wheresoever he may be, all his actions are visible to the eye of God and at all times are reported by the angels. The prophet shows us this when he says that God is ever present to our thoughts: *God searcheth the hearts and minds.* And again, *The Lord knoweth the thoughts of men that they are vain.* He also saith, *Thou hast understood my thoughts afar off;* and again, *The thought of man shall confess Thee.* In order, then, that the humble brother may be careful to avoid wrong thoughts let him always say in his heart, *Then shall I be without spot before Him, if I shall keep me from my iniquity.*

We are forbidden to do our own will, since Scripture tells us, *Leave thy own will and desire.* And again, *We beg of God in prayer that His will may be done in us.*

Rightly are we taught therefore not to do our own will, if we take heed of what the Scripture teaches: *There are ways which to men seem right, the end whereof plungeth even into the deep pit of hell,* And again, when we fear what is said about the negligent, *They are corrupted, and made abominable in their pleasures.* But in regard of the desires of the flesh we ought to believe that God is present with us; as the prophet says, speaking to the Lord, *O Lord, all my desire is before Thee.*

We have therefore to beware of evil desires, since death stands close at the door of pleasure. It is for this reason that Scripture bids us, *Follow not thy concupiscences.* If, therefore, the eyes of the Lord behold both the good and the bad; if He be ever looking down from heaven upon the sons of men to find one who thinks of God or seeks Him; and if day and night what we do is made known to Him—for these reasons, by the angels appointed to watch over us, we should always take heed, brethren, lest God may sometime or other see us, as the prophet says in the Psalm, *inclined to evil and become unprofitable servants.* Even though He spare us for a time, because He is loving and waits for our conversion to better ways, let us fear that He may say to us hereafter, *These things thou hast done and I held my peace.*

The second step of humility is reached when any one not loving self-will takes no heed to satisfy his own desires, but copies in his life what our Lord said, *I came not to do My own will, but the will of Him Who sent Me.* Scripture likewise proclaims that self-will engendereth punishment, and necessity purchaseth a crown.

The third step of humility is reached when a man, for the love of God, submits himself with all obedience to a superior, imitating our Lord, of whom the apostle saith, *He was made obedient even unto death.*

The fourth step of humility is reached when any one in the exercise of his obedience patiently and with a quiet mind bears all that is inflicted on him, things contrary to nature, and even at times unjust, and in suffering all these he neither wearies nor gives over the work, since the Scripture says, *He only that persevereth to the end shall be saved;* also *Let thy heart be comforted, and expect the Lord.* And in order to show that for our Lord's sake the faithful man ought to bear all things, no matter how contrary to nature they may be (the psalmist), in the person of the sufferers, says, *For thee we suffer death all the day long; we are esteemed as sheep for the slaughter.* Secure in the hope of divine reward they rejoice, saying, *But in all things we overcome by the help of Him who hath loved us.*

Elsewhere also Scripture says, *Thou hast proved us, O Lord; Thou hast tried us, as silver is tried, with fire. Thou hast brought us into the snare; Thou hast laid tribulation upon our backs.* And to show that we ought to be subject to a prior (or superior) it goes on, *Thou hast placed men over our heads.* And, moreover, they fulfil the Lord's command by patience in adversity and injury, who, *when on one cheek, offer the other;* when one *taketh away their coat leave go their cloak also,* and who being compelled to carry a burden one mile, go two; who, with Paul the apostle, suffer false brethren, and bless those who speak ill of them.

The fifth step of humility is reached when a monk manifests to his abbot, by humble confession, all the evil thoughts of his heart and his secret faults. The Scripture urges us to do this where it says, *Reveal thy way to the Lord and hope in Him.* It also says, *Confess to the Lord, because He is good, because His mercy endureth for ever.* And the prophet also says, *I have made known unto Thee mine offence, and mine injustices I have not hidden. I have said, I will declare openly against myself mine injustices to the Lord; and Thou hast pardoned the wickedness of my heart.*

The sixth step of humility is reached when a monk is content with all that is mean and vile; and in regard to everything enjoined him accounts himself a poor and worthless workman, saying with the prophet, *I have been brought to nothing, and knew it not. I have become as a beast before Thee, and I am always with Thee.*

The seventh step of humility is reached when a man not only confesses with his tongue that he is most lowly and inferior to others, but in his inmost heart believes so. Such a one, humbling himself, exclaims with the prophet, *I am a worm and no man, the reproach of men and the outcast of the people. I have been exalted and am humbled and confounded.* And again, *It is good for me that Thou hast humbled me, that I may learn Thy commandments.*

The eighth step of humility is reached when a monk does nothing but what the common rule of the monastery, or the example of his seniors, enforces.

The ninth step of humility is reached when a monk restrains his tongue from talking, and, practicing silence, speaks not till a question be asked him, since Scripture says, *In many words thou shalt not avoid sin,* and *a talkative man shall not be directed upon the earth.*

The tenth step of humility is attained to when one is not easily and quickly moved to laughter, for it is written, *The fool lifteth his voice in laughter.*

The eleventh step of humility is reached when a monk, in speaking, do so quietly and without laughter, humbly, gravely and in a few words and not with a loud voice, for it is written, *A wise man is known by a few words.*

The twelfth step of humility is reached when a monk not only has humility in his heart, but even shows it also exteriorly to all who behold him. Thus, whether he be in the oratory at the "Work of God," in the monastery, or in the garden, on a journey, or in the fields, or wheresoever he be, sitting, standing or walking, always let him, with head bent and eyes fixed on the ground, bethink himself of his sins and imagine that he is arraigned before the dread judgment of God. Let him be ever saying to himself, with the publican in the Gospel, *Lord, I a sinner am not worthy to lift mine eyes to heaven;* and with the prophet, *I am bowed down and humbled on every side.*

When all these steps of humility have been mounted the monk will presently attain to that love of God which is perfect and casteth out fear. By means of this love everything which before he had observed not without fear, he shall now begin to do by habit, without any trouble and, as it were, naturally. He acts now not through fear of hell, but for the love of Christ, out of a good habit and a delight in virtue. All this our Lord will vouchsafe to work by the Holy Ghost in His servant, now cleansed from vice and sin.

Chapter XXIII

Of Excommunication for Offences

If any brother be found stubborn, disobedient, proud, murmuring, or in any way acting contrary to the Holy Rule, or contemning the orders of his seniors, let him, according to the precept of our Lord, be secretly admonished by those seniors, once or twice. If he will not amend let him be publicly reproved before all. But if even then he does not correct his faults, let him, if he understand the nature of the punishment, be subject to excommunication. But if he be obstinate he is to undergo corporal punishment.

Chapter XXIV

What the manner of Excommunication should be

The mode of excommunication or punishment should be proportioned to the fault, and the gravity of the fault shall depend on the judgment of the abbot. If any brother be detected in small faults let him be excluded from eating at table with the rest. The punishment of one thus separated from the common table shall be of this kind: in the oratory he shall not intone either psalm or antiphon; neither shall he read any lesson until he has made satisfaction. He shall take his portion of food alone, after the brethren have had their meal, and in such quantity and at such time as the abbot shall think fit. So that if, for example, the brethren take their meal at the sixth hour let him take his at the ninth; if the brethren take theirs at the ninth, let him have his in the evening, till such time as by due satisfaction he obtain pardon.

Chapter XXV

Of Graver Faults

Let the brother who is guilty of some graver fault be excluded both from the common table and from the oratory. None of the brethren shall talk to him or consort with him. Let him be alone at the work which is set him; let him remain in penance and sorrow, and keep before his mind that terrible sentence of the apostle where he says, *Such a one is delivered over to Satan for the destruction of the flesh, that his spirit may be saved in the day of our Lord.* Let him take his food alone, in such quantity and at such time as the abbot shall think fit. Let no one bless him as he passes by, nor ask a blessing on the food that is given him.

Chapter XXVI

Of such as keep company with the Excommunicated without the Abbot's order

If any brother shall presume, without the abbot's order, to have intercourse in any way with an excommunicated brother, to talk with him or send him any message, let him suffer the same penalty of excommunication.

Chapter XXVII

What care the Abbot should have of the Excommunicated

Let the abbot take every possible care of the offending brethren, for *They that are well need not the physician, but they that are sick.* Like a wise physician, therefore, he ought to make use of every remedy; he should send some of the older and wiser brethren as comforters, to console, as it were, in secret their wayward brother, and win him to make humble satisfaction. And let them comfort him that he be not overwhelmed by too great sorrow, but as the apostle saith, *Let charity be confirmed in him and let all pray for him.*

The abbot ought to take the greatest care and to use all prudence and industry to lose none of the sheep entrusted to him. Let him know that he hath undertaken the care of souls that are sick, and not act the tyrant over such as are well. Let him fear the reproach of the prophet in which God speaks thus, *What ye saw to be fat that ye took to yourselves, and what was diseased that ye threw away.* Let him copy the loving example of the Good Shepherd, who, leaving ninety-nine sheep in the mountains, went to seek the one that had gone astray, and on whose infirmity He took such compassion that He deigned to lay it on His shoulders and carry it back to the flock.

Chapter XXVIII

Of those who, being often corrected, do not amend

If any brother does not amend after being often corrected for any fault, and even excommunicated, let a sharper punishment be administered to him, that is, let him be corrected by stripes. And if even after this he shall not correct himself, or being puffed up by pride (which God forbid) shall attempt to defend his doings, then let the abbot act like a wise physician. If after applying the fomentations and ointments of exhortation, the medicine of the Holy Scriptures and the final cautery of excommunication and scourging, he find that his labours have had no effect, then let him try what is more than all this, his own prayer and those of the brethren for him, that the Lord, who can do all things, may work the cure of the sick brother. If he be not healed by this means then let the abbot use the severing knife, according to that saying of the apostle, *Put away the evil one from among you;* and again, *If the faithless one depart, let him depart,* lest one diseased sheep should infect the whole flock....

Chapter XL

Of the measure of Drink

Every one hath his proper gift from God, one thus, another thus. For this reason the amount of other people's food cannot be determined without some misgiving. Still, having regard to the weak state of the sick, we think that a pint of wine a day is sufficient for any one. But let those to whom God gives the gift of abstinence know that they shall receive their proper reward. If either local circumstances, the amount of labour, or the heat of summer require more, it can be allowed at the will of the prior, care being taken in all things that gluttony and drunkenness creep not in.

Although we read that "wine is not the drink of monks at all," yet, since in our days they cannot be persuaded of this, let us at least agree not to drink to satiety, but sparingly, *Because wine maketh even the wise to fall away.*

Chapter XLI

The hours of which the Brethren are to take their Meals

From the holy feast of Easter until Whitsuntide the brethren shall have their first meal at the sixth hour and their supper at night. But from Whitsuntide, throughout the summer, if the monks have not to work in the fields, nor are oppressed by any great heat, let them fast on Wednesdays and Fridays till None; on the other days they may dine at the sixth hour. Dinner at the sixth hour shall be the rule at the discretion of the abbot, if they have work in the fields, or the heat of the summer be great. Let the abbot so temper and arrange everything that souls may be saved, and that what the brethren do may be done without just complaint.

From September the thirteenth till the beginning of Lent the brethren shall always take their meal at the ninth hour. During Lent, however, until Easter their meal shall be at eventide; but this evening meal shall be so arranged that whilst eating they shall not need lamps, and all things be finished in daylight. Indeed, at all times of the year let the hour of meals, whether of dinner or supper, be so arranged that all things be done by daylight.

Chapter XLII

That no one shall speak after Compline

Monks should practise silence at all times, but especially during the night hours. On all days, therefore, whether it be a fast day or otherwise (this shall be the practice). If it be not a fast day, as soon as they shall have risen from supper let all sit together whilst one of them read the *Collations,* or *Lives of the Fathers,* or some other book to edify the hearers. He shall not, however, read the *Heptateuch,* or *Books of Kings,* for at that hour it will not profit weak understandings to listen to this part of Scripture; at other times, however, they may be read. If it be a fast day let the brethren, when Evensong is over, and after a brief interval, come to the reading of the *Collations,* as we have said. Four or five pages are to be read, or as many as time will allow, that during the reading all may come together, even such as have had some work given them to do. When all, therefore, are gathered together let them say Compline, and on coming out from Compline no one shall be permitted to speak at all. If any one shall be found breaking this rule of silence he shall be punished severely, unless the needs of a guest require it, or the abbot shall order something of some one. But even this shall be done with the greatest gravity and moderation.

3. THE SALIC LAW

Salic Law is perhaps most famous to French historians as the law code that justified the exclusion of women from the line of succession to the French throne. In fact, this famous clause was a much later—and fraudulent—addition to the original code. The Salic Law (*Pactus legis Salicae*) was one of several Germanic law codes introduced to the West as early as 400 A.D. Salian Franks once inhabited the northern parts of Gaul. The earliest codification of this law dates to the time of Clovis (481–511 A.D.), and it included only sixty-five sections. The code continued to change and grow over the next three centuries, and it exerted particular influence over French marriage and inheritance practices. As the following excerpt shows, Salic law lacked the complexity and sophistication of Roman law. However, the differences in form and function of Germanic and Roman law codes is itself indicative of the very different character of these cultures. Roman law served the needs of a society that believed that a strong and stable polity was based on reason and justice. A civilized society was a rational society. In contrast, Germanic law codes reflect societies that understood law not as a set of abstract principles but as pragmatic customs which developed over time to regulate relations among members of a society. The following excerpts, for example, point to a society in which vengeance was a familial responsibility and fines were weighted according to one's function in that society. A childbearing woman, for example, exacted a much higher fine than a woman beyond her child-bearing years just as warriors exacted a greater fine than nonwarriors.

Pactus legis Salicae

Here begins the pact of the Salic Laws.

1. With the help of the Lord, it is agreed and resolved among the Franks and their no-bility that they must make every attempt to prevent violence by striving for peace among themselves, and because the assembled [Frankish] people distinguish them-selves from all others by the force of arms, the authority of the laws should also be en-hanced so that disputes might be settled according to the type of complaint.

2. Therefore, among the many selected individuals four men with the following names were chosen: Wisogast, Arogast, Salegast, and Widogast, who were from settlements that lie on the other side of the Rhine—Botheim, Saleheim, and Widoheim; they con-vened in three legal assemblies and carefully discussed all aspects of litigation, and enumerated their judgments individually in the following manner:

28

Concerning secret hirings

1. If a man wishes to hire someone secretly in order that another might be killed and for that reason [the one hired] receives the price, but [the deed] is not done (known in the malberg as *morter*), and it can be proven that [the plotter] did this, let him be held liable for 2500 denarii, which make sixty-two and one-half solidi.

2. If anyone wishes to kill a man hired secretly after receiving the price, but this is not done (known in the malberg as *morter*), and it can be proven that he did this, let him be held liable for 2500 denarii, which make sixty-two and one-half solidi.

3. But if this hiring is conveyed through three men (known in the malberg as *morter*), let these freemen be held liable, if it can be proven that they did this, for 2500 denarii, which make sixty-two and one-half solidi. Indeed, let the donor, recipient and intermediary each be held liable for sixty-two and one-half solidi.

29

Concerning injuries

1. If anyone mutilates another's hand or foot, or knocks out an eye, or cuts off an ear or cuts off a nose (know in the malberg as *sicti*), and it can be proven that he did this, let him be held liable for 4000 denarii, which make 100 solidi.

2. But if he cuts [the other's] hand and it dangles maimed (known in the malberg as *chaminus*), let him be held liable for 2500 denarii, which make sixty-two and one-half solidi.

3. And if this hand is cut through (known in the malberg as *secthe*), let him be held liable for 2500 denarii, which make sixty-two and one-half solidi.

4. If anyone cuts off a thumb or a foot (known in the malberg as *alachtamo*), and it can be proven that he did this, let him be held liable for 2500 denarii.

5. But if this thumb dangles maimed (known in the malberg as *alachtamo chaminis*), let him be held liable for 1200 denarii, which make thirty solidi.

6. But if he cuts off the second finger, with which one shoots an arrow (known in the malberg as *alachtamo briorotero*), let him be held liable for 1400 denarii, which make thirty-five solidi.

7. But if anyone cuts off the other [which is to say] remaining fingers, that is, three [fingers cut off] in one blow at the same time (known in the malberg as *chaminis*), let him be held liable for 1800 denarii, which make forty-five solidi.

8. If he cuts off two [fingers], let him be held liable for thirty-five solidi.

9. But if he cuts off one [finger], let him be held liable for thirty solidi. Indeed, if he cuts off the middle finger (known in the malberg as *taphano*), let him be held liable for 600 denarii, which make fifteen solidi. In fact, for the fourth finger that is cut off (known in the malberg as *melachano*), let him be held liable for nine solidi. For the little finger that is cut off (known in the malberg as *minecleno*), let him be held liable for 600 denarii, which make fifteen solidi.

10. But if the foot is cut and it remains maimed (known in the malberg as *chuldachina chamin*), let him be held liable for 1800 denarii, which make forty-five solidi.

11. But if this foot is cut off (known in the malberg as *chuldachina sichte*), let him be held liable for 2500 denarii, which make sixty-two and one-half solidi.

12. If anyone knocks out another's eye (known in the malberg as *lichauina*), let him be held liable for 2500 denarii, which make sixty-two and one-half solidi.

13. If anyone cuts off another's nose (known in the malberg as *frasito*), let him be held liable for 1800 denarii, which make forty-five solidi.

14. If anyone cuts off another's ear (known in the malberg as *channichleora*), let him be held liable for 600 denarii, which make fifteen solidi.

15. If anyone cuts another's tongue so that he cannot speak (known in the malberg as *alchaltea*), let him be held liable for 4000 denarii, which make 100 solidi.

16. If anyone breaks another's tooth (known in the malberg as *inchlauina*), let him be held liable for 600 denarii, which make fifteen solidi.

17. If anyone castrates a freeman or cuts through his genitals whereby he is made sterile (known in the malberg as *gaferit*), let him be held liable for 100 solidi.

18. But if he cuts off the entire genitalia (known in the malberg as *alacharde*), let him be held liable for 8000 denarii, which make 200 solidi, in addition to nine solidi for the physician.

30

Concerning insults

1. If anyone calls another a louse (known in the malberg as *quintuc*), let him be held liable for 600 denarii, which make fifteen solidi.
2. If anyone calls another a skunk, let him be held liable for 120 denarii, which make three solidi.
3. If anyone, either a man or a woman, calls another freewoman a prostitute (known in the malberg as *strabo*), and it cannot be proven [that she is one], let him be held liable for 1800 denarii, which make forty-five solidi.
4. If anyone calls another a fox, let him be held liable for 120 denarii, which make three solidi.
5. If anyone calls another a hare, let him be held liable for 120 denarii, which make three solidi.
6. If a freeman imputes that another has thrown away his shield and has taken to flight (known in the malberg as *austrapo*), and it cannot be proven that he did this, let him be held liable for 120 denarii, which make three solidi.
7. If anyone calls another an informer or a liar, and he cannot prove it, let him be held liable for 600 denarii, which make fifteen solidi (known in the malberg as *leodardi*).

41

Concerning homicide of freemen

1. But if anyone kills a free Frank or [any] barbarian who is living in accordance with the Salic law, and it can be proven that he did this, let him be held liable for 8000 denarii, which make 200 solidi (known in the malberg as *leodi*).
2. But if he puts him into a well or under water, let him be held liable for 24,000 denarii, which make 600 solidi (known in the malberg as *mathleodi*). And let him be held liable, as we said above, for any kind of concealment.
3. If he is not concealed (known in the malberg as *moantheuthi*), let him be held liable for 8000 denarii, which make 200 solidi.
4. But if he places him under a cover either of branches or skins or conceals him with anything, and it can be proven that he did this, let him be held liable for 24,000 denarii, which make 600 solidi (known in the malberg as *matteleodi*).
5. But if anyone kills [either] him who is in the king's retinue *[trustis]* or a freewoman, and it can be proven that he did this, let him be held liable for 24,000 denarii, which make 600 solidi (known in the malberg as *leodi*).
6. But if he puts him in water or into a well, let him be held liable for 72,000 denarii, which make 1800 solidi.

7. But if he places him under a cover either of branches or skins or conceals him with anything, let him be held liable for 72,000 denarii, which make 1800 solidi (known in the malberg as *matteleodi*).

8. But if he kills a Roman [who has been] a member of the king's court, and it can be proven that he did this, let him be held liable for 12,000 denarii, which make 300 solidi (known in the malberg as *leudi*).

44

Concerning the ring-money

1. If it happens that a man dies, leaving a widow, and [a prospective bridegroom] wishes to take her [in matrimony], let him take her in the presence of the *thunginus* or the *centenarius,* that is, let the *thunginus* or the *centenarius* announce [this fact] in court. And he must have a shield in the same court, and three men [as witnesses] must be asked three questions [by the *thunginus* or the *centenarius*].

2. And then, he who wants to take the widow should have three solidi of equal weight and a denarius. And these three [men] must have weighed the solidi or must prove that the solidi have been weighed, and [when] this deed occurs, if it is agreeable to them, let him to whom she belongs take her.

3. But if he does not do this and he [still] takes her (known in the malberg as *reipus nichalesinus*), he must pay 2500 denarii, which make sixy-two and one-half solidi, to whomever the ring-money belongs.

4. But if, as we said above, he fulfills everything in accordance with the law, let him to whom the ring-money belongs receive the three solidi and one denarius.

5. If this [condition described in laws 44§1 and 2 above] can be discerned [to have occurred, let him] to whom the ring-money belongs [receive it].

6. But if there is a nephew, let him, the eldest sister's son, receive it.

7. But if there is no nephew, let the eldest son of a niece, if there is one, receive this ring-money.

8. But if there is no niece's son, let a son of an aunt receive it. If there are no aunts, let a son of an aunt who is descended from the other's kindred receive it.

9. But if there is no aunt's son, then let the uncle, the mother's brother, receive the ring-money.

45

Concerning migrations [migrantibus]

1. If a man wishes to migrate to another village and one or more of those who live in the village wish to receive him, [but] one or more of those who live there disagree, he shall not have permission to migrate there.

2. But if he attempts to settle in that village contrary to the objection of one or two [of them], then the latter must warn him. And if he refuses to depart, he who warned him must do so with witnesses and must say: "Man, I inform you that you may remain here this next night, as the Salic law specifies, and I [also] inform you that within ten nights you must leave this village." And after ten nights he must come to him and inform him again that he must leave within another ten nights. If [the immigrant] still refuses to

leave after ten nights, let [the resident] again add a third [period of] ten nights to his time period so that in all thirty nights are to be completed. If [the immigrant] still refuses to leave, then let the other summon him and his witnesses to court for each individual [ten-day] period which he had already given to him.

4. VITA ANSKARII

The Danes were already known for their raids along the coasts of England, Scotland, and Normandy when the emperor of the Franks, Louis the Pious, formed an alliance with their king in 822. Eager to spread Christianity to these people, Louis encouraged King Harald I and his wife to visit him at his palace of Ingelheim in 826. Baptized as a Christian, Harald returned to Denmark accompanied by the Benedictine monk Anskar (801–865). Anskar already enjoyed a reputation as a devout religious reformer when he was selected by Louis the Pious and his religious superiors to lead the first Christian mission to Denmark. After three years there, Anskar was sent on a mission to the Swedes. During the next decades, Anskar became in succession the first archbishop of the town of Hamburg and the archbishop of Bremen. As archbishop, Anskar played an influential role in establishing a firm grounding for Christian missions to Scandinavia. The *Life of Anskar* was written by his fellow missionary and successor, Bishop Rimbert (d. 888). The following excerpt recounts Anskar's journey to Sweden in 829. Rimbert's account gives us insight not only into the dangers faced by the missionaries on their travels northward during this period but also into the cultural processes underlying the Christianization of Europe during this period.

Life of Anskar

Chapter X.

In the good providence of God the venerable abbot found for him amongst your fraternity a companion, namely the prior Witmar, who was both worthy and willing to undertake this great task. He further arranged that the good father Gislemar, a man approved by faith and good works, and by his fervent zeal for God, should be with Harald. Anskar then undertook the mission committed to him by the emperor, who desired that he should go to the Swedes and discover whether this people was prepared to accept the faith as their messengers had declared. How great and serious were the calamities which he suffered while engaged in this mission, father Witmar, who himself shared them, can best tell. It may suffice for me to say that while they were in the midst of their journey they fell into the hands of pirates. The merchants with whom they were traveling defended themselves vigorously and for a time successfully, but eventually they were conquered and overcome by the pirates, who took from them their ships and all that they possessed, whilst they themselves barely escaped on foot to land. They lost here the royal gifts which they should have delivered there, together with all their other possessions, save only what they were able to take and carry with them as they left the ship. They were plundered, moreover, of nearly forty books which they had accumulated for the service of God. When this happened some were disposed to turn and go back, but no argument could divert God's servant from the journey which he had undertaken. On the contrary, he submitted everything that might happen to him to God's will, and was by no means disposed to return till, by God's help, he could ascertain whether he would be allowed to preach the gospel in those parts.

Chapter XI.

With great difficulty they accomplished their long journey on foot, traversing also the intervening seas, where it was possible, by ship, and eventually arrived at the Swedish port called Birka.

They were kindly received here by the king, who was called Biörn, whose messengers had informed him of the reason for which they had come. When he understood the object of their mission, and had discussed the matter with his friends, with the approval and consent of all he granted them permission to remain there and to preach the gospel of Christ, and offered liberty to any who desired it to accept their teaching. Accordingly the servants of God, when they saw that matters had turned out propitiously as they had desired, began eagerly to preach the word of salvation to the people of that place. There were many who were well disposed towards their mission and who willingly listened to the teaching of the Lord. There were also many Christians who were held captive amongst them, and who rejoiced that now at last they were able to participate in the divine mysteries. It was thus made clear that everything was as their messengers had declared to the emperor, and some of them desired earnestly to receive the grace of baptism. These included the prefect of this town named Herigar, who was a counselor of the king and much beloved by him. He received the gift of holy baptism and was strengthened in the Catholic faith. A little later he built a church on his own ancestral property and served God with the utmost devotion. Several remarkable deeds were accomplished by this man who afforded many proofs of his invincible faith, as we shall make clear in the following narrative.

Chapter XII.

When the servants of God had spent another half year with them and had attained the object of their mission they returned to the emperor and took with them letters written by the king himself in characters fashioned after the Swedish custom. They were received with great honour and goodwill by the emperor, to whom they narrated all that the Lord had wrought by them, and how in those parts the door of faith was opened by which these nations were bidden to enter. When the most pious emperor heard this, he rejoiced greatly. And as he recalled the beginning which had been made in establishing the worship of God amongst the Danes, he rendered praise and thanks to Almighty God, and, being inflamed with zeal for the faith, he began to enquire by what means he might establish a bishop's see in the north within the limits of his own empire, from which the bishop who should be stationed there might make frequent journeys to the northern regions for the sake of preaching the gospel, and from which all these barbarous nations might easily and profitably receive the sacraments of the divine mystery. As he was pursuing this matter with anxious care he learnt, from information provided by some of his trusty companions, that when his father, the Emperor Charles, of glorious memory, had subdued the whole of Saxony by the sword and had subjected it to the yoke of Christ, he divided it into dioceses, but did not commit to any bishop the furthest part of this province which lay beyond the river Elbe, but decided that it should be reserved in order that he might establish there an archiepiscopal see from which, with the Lord's help, the Christian faith might successively spread to the nations that lay beyond. He, accordingly, caused the first church that was built there to be consecrated by a Gallic bishop named Amalhar. Later on he specially committed the care of this parish to a priest named Heridac, as he did not wish that the neighbouring bishops should have any authority over this place. He had further arranged to have this priest consecrated as a bishop, but his speedy departure from this life prevented this being done. After the death of this much-to-be-remembered emperor his son Ludovic, who was placed on his father's throne, acting on the suggestion of others, divided in two that part of the province which lies beyond the rive Elbe and entrusted it, for the time being, to two neighbouring bishops for he paid no attention to the arrangement which his father had made in regard to this matter, or, possibly, he was altogether ignorant of it. When the time came that the faith of Christ began, by God's grace, to bear fruit in the lands of the Danes and Swedes, and his father's wish became known to him, he was unwilling that this wish should remain unaccomplished and, acting with the approval of the bishops and a largely attended synod, he established an archiepiscopal see in the town of Hamburg, which is situated in the farthest part of Saxony beyond the river Elbe. He desired that the whole Church of the Nordalbingi should be subject to this archbishopric, and that it should possess the power of appointing bishops and priests who for the name of Christ might go out into these districts.

To this see, therefore, the emperor caused the holy Anskar, our lord and father, to be consecrated as archbishop by the hands of Drogo, Bishop of Metz, and at that time principal chaplain at the imperial court. He was assisted by Ebo, Archbishop of Rheims; Hetti, of Trier and Otgar of Mainz, whilst many other bishops who had gathered for the imperial assembly were present. The bishops Helmgaud and Willerick, from whom Anskar took over the above-mentioned parts of this ecclesiastical district, approved and took part in his consecration.

Inasmuch as this diocese was situated in dangerous regions, and it was to be feared that it might come to an end in consequence of the savagery of the barbarians by which it was threatened, and because its area was small, the emperor handed over to his representatives a monastery in Gaul, called Turholt, to be always at its service.

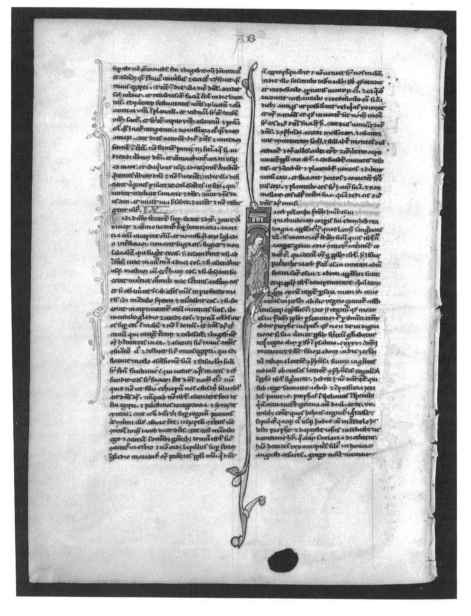

Figure 3.1 Parchment leaf from the Book of Amos 5:23–9:15, Bible (ca. 1240 France). Rare Books Division, J. Williard Marriott Library, University of Utah.

Study Questions

1. What were the defining characteristics of monastic life according to the Benedictine *Rule?* Why was the communal religious life considered an important route to salvation?
2. According to Gregory of Tours, why was Clotilda such an important figure? Does his portrayal shed light on the role of the queen during the early Medieval period?
3. What Germanic social values and customs are expressed in the Salic Law?
4. What were the difficulties faced by Anskar in his mission to Sweden, and what do these difficulties tell us about Northern European society during this period?
5. From the texts, where do we find Germanic traditions influencing the form and development of Christianity in Europe?

Suggested Readings

Geary, Patrick. *Before France and Germany. The Creation and Transformation of the Merovingian World.* New York and Oxford: Oxford University Press, 1988.
McKitterick, Rosamund. *The Frankish Kingdoms under the Carolingians 751–987.* London and New York: Longman, 1983.
Sawyer, P. H. *The Age of the Vikings,* 2d ed. London: Edward Arnold, 1971.
Wells, Peter S. *The Barbarians Speak.* Princeton, NJ: Princeton University Press, 1999.

Web Sites

1. Dark Ages On-line Sources

   http://www.ocf.org/OrthodoxPage/reading/St.Pachomius/bede.html

2. Medieval Europe Documents

   eawc.Evansville.edu/mepage.htm

3. The Salic Law

   www.heraldica.org/topics/france/salic.html

4

Encounters with the East
1100–1400 A.D.

TEXTS

1. Ibn Jubayr, *The Travels of Ibn Jubayr*
2. Friar Jordanus, *The Wonders of the East*
3. Ibn Battuta, *The Travels of Ibn Battuta*
4. Ramón Llull, *The Book of the Lover and the Beloved*
5. Pilgrim's Qu'ran

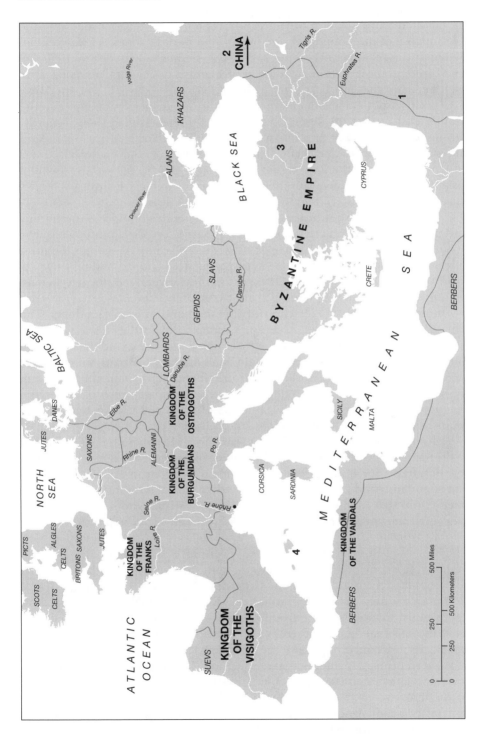

The increasing isolation of Western Europe in the centuries following the collapse of the Roman Empire meant that most Europeans knew very little about the regions lying to the east of the Mediterranean Sea by 1000 A.D. The disintegration of Roman trade routes and a one-system currency, however, were not the only barriers to cultural exchange between East and West. New political powers began emerging among Arabic-speaking peoples in the Middle East during the seventh century and quickly spread their authority throughout the western part of Asia Minor and into North Africa, Spain, and the islands of Corsica and Sicily. Perturbed about these new political powers and the spread of the new monotheistic faith practiced by these peoples (Islam), and preoccupied with their own internal conflicts, Europeans largely stayed away from Eastern regions during these centuries.

By the eleventh century, however, the emergence of more economically and politically stable regimes in the regions of modern day France, Germany, Spain, and Italy stimulated European interest in Islamic kingdoms. Spanish rulers were among the earliest Western powers to begin expanding their authority at the expense of Muslim (Islamic) authority when they turned their attention to the Muslim kingdoms of Spain. Spain of the eleventh century was not one united power but a collection of Christian and Muslim kingdoms. The Christian kingdoms included Léon and Castile in the northwest and the Spanish March in the northeast along the Pyrenees. Eager to expand their political authority, gain military glory, and rid the land of non-Christians, these powers began waging war on the Muslim kingdoms of Southern Spain after 1000 A.D. By 1060 A.D., two Christian kingdoms came to dominate much of Spain: the kingdoms of Alfonso VI (1065–1109), king of Leon and Castile, and Sancho Ramirez (1063–1094), king of Aragon and Navarre.

It was not until 1492 that the last remaining Muslim power, Granada, fell to the Spanish Christian kings. The *reconquista* of the eleventh century, however, was important for initiating a more aggressive European approach to non-Christian lands and peoples from this time forward. Following closely on the heels of the Spanish nobles, furthermore, were Christian monks. Christian nobles gave their support to Christian monks who were eager to transform Spain into a Christian land. The combination of military force and spiritual zeal, which marked the Christian conquest of Muslim Spain, would play a fundamental role in one of the most important political, economic, and spiritual developments of the middle ages: the Crusades. [1] In 1095, Pope Urban II gave the famous address at Clermont which sent European knights and their followers eastward to save Palestine from Muslim rule. Although his speech emphasized the spiritual danger posed by the Islamic faith to Christianity, the pope was clearly also concerned about the Turks as a threat to the political authority of Western princes, including that of the pope. The Byzantine Empire had lost several wealthy regions to the Seljuk Turks following its disastrous loss of the battle of Manzikert in Armenia in 1071. Although Urban was not necessarily concerned about preserving Byzantine wealth, he was worried about the spread of Islam to the frontiers of Western Europe. The Byzantine Empire had long been an effective buffer against the westward spread of Islamic authority. Moreover, presiding as he did over the most powerful European institution at the time, Urban saw in Christian intervention in the Middle East an opportunity for expanding Christian frontiers farther eastward. Regaining control of the Christian holy sites of Palestine, he believed, would stimulate and strengthen Christian piety in the West.

No doubt the Christian nobility who flocked to Palestine following this speech were moved by Urban's appeal to save the Christian holy sites from their Muslim occupiers. Historians have long pointed out, however, that a desire for wealth and military glory were also important factors. Many of the Crusader knights became very wealthy, indeed, in some instances, even carving out their own "kingdoms" in the region. In 1099, the Crusaders conquered the city of Jerusalem, and on Christmas day 1100, a king of Jerusalem was crowned. The Christians managed to hold onto the city for ninety years, but this struggle was never easy. By 1187, Jerusalem was once again in Muslim hands and succeeding Crusades saw Europe lose control of other territories in Palestine. Although the Crusades failed to secure Christian control of the holy sites during these centuries, desire to maintain a foothold in the East remained strong in the West. By the thirteenth century, the papacy was organizing the non-Christian East into administrative territories of the Catholic Church, and members of the new missionary orders of wandering preachers, the Franciscans and Dominicans, were making their way as far as India and China. [2, 4]

Christian desire to convert other cultures, however, was hardly a glorious result of the Crusades because it sprang from spiritual and cultural intolerance. Perhaps the most distasteful legacy of the Crusades to the Christian West was its glorification of the use of violence against people of differing faiths. For many Medieval Christians, Muslims deserved death because they stubbornly resisted following the true faith and worshipped a false god. [1] Christian intolerance also explains Crusader attacks on numerous Jewish communities in the upper Rhineland in Germany which lay along the route of many Crusaders to Palestine. The period of the Crusades may not evoke pride among Europeans today, but it was a significant episode nevertheless because, from this point forward, European attention would always turn to the East, and Christian, Muslim, and Jewish travelers would increasingly cross paths on Eastern roads and at pilgrimage sites as more and more Europeans ventured to the Palestine and other eastern regions. [3]

1. IBN JUBAYR, *THE TRAVELS OF IBN JUBAYR*

The product of an elite Muslim family from the city of Valencia in Spain, Abu 'l-Husayn Muhammad Ahmad ibn Jubayr took a leave from his post as secretary to the governor of Granada in 1183 to go on a pilgrimage to Mecca. Observant Muslims were expected to make at least one pilgrimage to Mecca during their lifetime, and Ibn Jubayr was a devout Muslim. His description of the Muslim pilgrimage is rich in information on the practices of the Islamic faith during this period. A learned as well as pious man, Ibn Jubayr's chronicle of his two-year journey also provides us with a remarkably perceptive and informative account of Egypt, Sicily, and the Middle East during the period just prior to the Third Crusade. Above all, his elegant prose account evokes a world in which cultural exchange as well as political and religious conflict were defining features. Ibn Jubayr describes a land crisscrossed by Christian and Muslim pilgrims, soldiers and merchants, and dotted with Christian, Muslim, and Jewish holy sites and settlements. Despite his dislike of the presence of Christian Europeans in the region, Ibn Jubayr's account shows that he and other Muslims frequently traveled together with Christians and Jews in caravans across the Arabian desert and on Genoese ships bound for European ports. His colorful description of the Norman kingdom of Sicily is particularly revealing about the continuing vibrancy of Islamic culture at the heart of a Christian society. Although Islam was not officially tolerated in Sicily, Islamic art, learning, and religion flourished here among all social groups. The following excerpt provides a distinctly Muslim perspective on Christian presence in the cities of Acre and Tyre. Needless to say, Jubayr's pride in Islamic culture and corresponding conviction that Christians were not true believers provides a useful counterfoil to the decidedly Christian account of the Crusades given by the European William of Tyre, among others.

The Travels of Ibn Jubayr

A Note on the City of Acre

May God exterminate (the Christians in) it and restore it (to the Muslims)

Acre is the capital of the Frankish cities in Syria, the unloading place of 'ships reared aloft in the seas like mountains' [Koran LV, 24], and a port of call for all ships. In its greatness it resembles Constantinople. It is the focus of ships and caravans, and the meeting-place of Muslim and Christian merchants from all regions. Its roads and streets are choked by the press of men, so that it is hard to put foot to ground. Unbelief and unpiousness there burn fiercely, and pigs [Christians] and crosses abound. It stinks and is filthy, being full of refuse and excrement. The Franks ravished it from Muslim hands in the first [last] decade of the sixth [fifth] century, and the eyes of Islam were swollen with weeping for it; it was one of its griefs. Mosques become churches and minarets bell-towers, but God kept undefiled one part of the principle mosque, which remained in the hands of the Muslims as a small mosque where strangers could congregate to offer the obligatory prayers. Near its milhrab is the tomb of the prophet Salih—God bless and preserve him and all the prophets. God protected this part (of the mosque) from desecration by the unbelievers for the benign influence of this holy tomb.

To the east of the town is the spring called 'Ayn al-Baqar [the Spring of the Cattle], from which God brought forth the cattle for Adam—may God bless and preserve him. The descent to this spring is by a deep stairway. Over it is a mosque of which there remains in its former state only the mihrab, to the east of which the Franks have built their own mihrab; and Muslim and infidel assemble there, the one turning to his place of worship, the other to his.

A Note on the City of Sur [Tyre]

May God Most High destroy It

This city has come proverbial for its impregnability, and he who seeks to conquer it will meet with no surrender or humility. The Franks prepared it as a refuge in case of unforeseen emergency, making it a strong point for their safety. Its roads and streets are cleaner than those of Acre. Its people are by disposition less stubborn in their unbelief, and by nature and habit they are kinder to the Muslim stranger. Their manners, in other words, are gentler. Their dwellings are larger and more spacious. The state of the Muslims in this city is easier and more peaceful. Acre is a town at once bigger, more impious, and more unbelieving. But the strength and impregnability of Tyre is more marvellous than is told of. It has only two gates, one landwards, and the other on the sea, which encompasses the city save on one side. The landward gate is reached only after passing through three or four posterns in the strongly-fortified outer walls that enclose it. The seaward gate is flanked by two strong towers and leads into a harbour whose remarkable situation is unique among maritime cities. The walls of the city enclose it on three sides, and the fourth is confined by a mole bound with cement. Ships enter below the walls and there anchor. Between the two towers stretches a great chain which, when raised, prevents any coming in or going forth, and no ships may pass save when it is lowered. At the gate stand guards and trusted watchers, and none can enter or go forth save under their eyes. The beauty of the site of this port is truly wonderful. Acre resembles it in situation and description, but cannot take the large ships, which must anchor outside, small ships only being able to enter. The port of Tyre is more complete, more beautiful, and more animated. Eleven days we tarried in the city, entering it on Thursday, and leaving it on Sunday the 22nd of Jumada, which was the last day of September; this was because the ship in which we had hoped to sail we found to be too small, so that we were unwilling to set forth in it.

An alluring worldly spectacle deserving of record was a nuptial procession which we witnessed one day near the port in Tyre. All the Christians, men and women, had assembled, and were formed in two lines at the bride's door. Trumpets, flutes, and all the musical instruments, were played until she proudly emerged between two men who held her right and left as though they were her kindred. She was most elegantly garbed in a beautiful dress from which trailed, according to their traditional style, a long train of golden silk. On her head she wore a golden diadem covered by a net of woven gold, and on her breast was a like arrangement. Proud she was in her ornaments and dress, walking with little steps of half a span, like a dove, or in the manner of a wisp of cloud. God protect us from the seduction of the sight. Before her went Christian notables in their finest and most splendid clothing, their trains falling behind them. Behind her were her peers and equals of the Christian women, parading in their richest apparel and proud of bearing in their superb ornaments. Leading them all were the musical instruments. The Muslims and other Christian onlookers formed two ranks along the route, and gazed on them without reproof. So they passed along until they brought her to the house of the groom; and all that day they feasted. We thus were given the chance of seeing this alluring sight, from the seducement of which God preserve us. . . .

During our stay in Tyre we rested in one of the mosques that remained in Muslim hands. One of the Muslim elders of Tyre told us that it had been wrested from them in the year 518 [27th of June, 1124], and that Acre had been taken twelve [actually twenty] years earlier [24th of March, 1104], after a long siege and after hunger had overcome them. We were told that it had brought them to such a pass—we take refuge in God from it—that shame had driven them to propose a course from which God had preserved them. They had determined to gather their wives and children into the Great Mosque and there put them to the sword, rather than that the Christians should possess them. They themselves would then sally forth determinedly, and in a violent assault on the enemy, die together. But God made His irreversible decree, and their jurisprudents and some of their godly men prevent them. They thereupon decided to abandon the town, and to make good their escape. So it happened, and they dispersed among the Muslim lands. But there were some whose love of native land impelled them to return and, under the conditions of a safeguard which was written for them, to live amongst the infidels, 'God is the master of His affair' [Koran XII, 21]. Glorious is God, and great is His power. His will overcomes all impediments.

There can be no excuse in the eyes of God for a Muslim to stay in any infidel country, save when passing through it, while the way lies clear in Muslim lands. They will face pains and terrors such as the abasement and destitution of the capitation and more especially, amongst their base and lower orders, the hearing of what will distress the heart in the reviling of him [Muhammad] whose memory God has sanctified, and whose rank He has exalted; there is also the absence of cleanliness, the mixing with the pigs, and all the other prohibited matters too numerous to be related or enumerated. Beware, beware of entering their lands. May God Most High grant His beneficent indulgence for this sin into which (our) feet have slipped, but His forgiveness is not given save after accepting our penitence. Glory to God, the Master. There is no Lord but He.

Among the misfortunes that one who visits their land will see are the Muslim prisoners walking in shackles and put to painful labour like slaves. In like condition are the Muslim women prisoners, their legs in iron rings. Hearts are rent for them, but compassion avails them nothing.

One of the beneficent works of God Most High towards the Maghrib prisoners in these lands of Frankish Syria is that every Muslim of these parts of Syria or elsewhere who makes a will in respect of his property devotes it to the liberation of the Maghribis in particular because of their remoteness from their native land and because, after Great and Glorious God, they have no other to deliver them. They are strangers, cut off from their native land, and the Muslim kings of these parts, the royal ladies, and the persons of ease and wealth, spend their money only in this cause. Nur al-Din—God have mercy on him—during an illness which had struck him, swore to distribute twelve thousand dinars for the ransoming of Maghribi prisoners. When he was cured of his sickness, he sent their ransom, but with them were despatched a group who were not Maghribis, but who were from Hamah, one of his provinces. He ordered their return and the release of Maghribis in their place, saying, 'These men can be ransomed by their kindred and their neighbours; but the Maghribis are strangers and have no kindred (here).'

Consider now the beneficent work of God Most High towards these Maghrib people. He decreed that they should have in Damascus two of the most considerable and wealthy merchants, who were deep in riches. One was named Nasr ibn Qawam and the other Abu 'l-Durr Yaqut, lord of al-'Attafi. Their business is all along this Frankish coast, and there is mention of no one else but them. They have agents who take a share in the profits. Their caravans come and go with their merchandise and stores, bringing great riches; and their influence over the Muslim and Frankish princes is great. Great and Glorious God assigned to them the part of ransoming the Maghribi prisoners with their wealth and that of the bequeathments; for these are made in their name on account of the fame of their probity and integrity and the vast sums of their own wealth that they have spent in this cause. No Maghribi can secure release from captivity save at their hands, and for a long time they have been prodigal of their wealth and efforts in releasing God's servants the Muslims from the hands of His enemies the infidels. May God Most High not fail to reward those who perform these righteous deeds.

By an unhappy chance, from the evils of which we take refuge in God, we were accompanied on our road to Acre from Damascus by a Maghribi from Buna in the district of Bougie who had been a prisoner and had been released by the agency of Abu 'l-Durr and become one of his young men. In one of his patron's caravans he had come to Acre, where he had mixed with the Christians, and taken on much of their character. The devil increasingly seduced and incited him until he renounced the faith of Islam, turned unbeliever, and became a Christian in the time of our stay in Tyre. We left to Acre, but receive news of him. He had been baptised and become unclean, and had put on the girdle of a monk, thereby hastening for himself the flames of hell, verifying the threats of torture, and exposing himself to a grievous account and a long-distant return (from hell). We beg Great and Glorious God to confirm us in the true word in this world and the next, allowing us not to deviate from the pure faith and letting us, in His grace and mercy, die Muslims.

This pig, the lord of Acre whom they call king, lives secluded and is not seen, for God has afflicted him with leprosy. God was not slow to vengeance, for the affliction seized him in his youth, depriving him of the joys of his world. He is wretched here, 'but the chastisement of the hereafter is severer and more lasting' [Koran XX, 127]. His chamberlain and regent is his maternal uncle, the Count, the controller of the Treasury to whom the revenues are paid, and who supervises all with firmness and authority. The most considerable amongst the accursed Franks is the accursed Count, the lord of Tripoli and Tiberias. He has authority and position among them. He is qualified to be king, and indeed is a candidate for the office. He is described as being shrewd and crafty. He was a prisoner of Nur al-Din's for twelve years or more, and then ransomed himself by the payment of a great sum in the time of the first governorship of Saladin, to whom he admits his vassalage and emancipation.

The caravans from Damascus branch away through the territory of Tiberias because its road is smooth, but mule caravans go through Tibnin, which road although rough is direct. The lake of Tiberias is sweet. Its breadth is four or five parasangs, and although statements about its length vary, the nearest to the truth is that it is about six parasangs, albeit we did not see it. There is a dispute as well about the width. In Tiberias there are the tombs of many prophets—God's blessings upon them—such as those of Shu'ayb, Sulayman, Yahuda, Rubil, Shu'ayb's daughter the wife of Moses the Interlocutor, and others—God's blessings upon them all. Nearby is Jabal al-Tur [Tabor]; Between Acre and Bait al-Maqdis [Jerusalem] lies three days journey, and between Damascus and Jerusalem eight. Jerusalem is to the south-west of Acre in the direction of Alexandria. May God restore it to the Muslims, and cleanse it, by His strength and power, from the hands of the polytheists [the believers in the Trinity].

The cities of Acre and Tyre have no gardens around them, and stand in a wide plain that reaches to the shores of the sea. Fruits are brought to them from the orchards that are in the neighbourhood. They possess broad lands and the nearby mountains are furnished with farmsteads from which fruits are brought to them. They are very rich cities. At the eastern extremity of Acre is a torrent course, along the banks of which extending to the sea is a sandy plain, than which I have seen no more beautiful sight. As a course for horses there is none to compare with it. Every morning and evening the Lord of the town rides over it, and there the soldiers parade—destroy them, God. Beside Tyre's landward gate is a fresh spring down to which a stairway leads. The wells and cisterns of the town are many, and there is no house without one. May God Most High, in His grace and favour, restore to it and to its sister (cities) the word of Islam.

On Saturday the 28 of Jumada, being the 6th of October, with the favour of God towards the Muslims, we embarked on a large ship, taking water and provisions. The Muslims secured places apart from the Franks. Some Christians called 'bilghriyin' [from the Italian *pellegrini* = pilgrims] came aboard. They had been on the pilgrimage to Jerusalem, and were too numerous to count, but were more than two thousand. May God in His grace and favour soon relieve us of their company and bring us to safety with His hoped-for assistance and beneficent works; none but He should be worshipped. So, under the will of Great and Glorious God, we awaited a favouring wind and the completion of the ship's stowing.

2. Friar Jordanus, *The Wonders of the East*

Beyond *Wonders of the East,* his travel account of India, little is known about the life and death of the Dominican friar Jordanus. A Frenchman by birth, Jordanus was in India on at least two occasions: 1321–1323 and then again after 1330. Jordanus's journey to India reflects continuing Catholic interest from the time of the Crusades in expanding Western authority farther eastward. Soon after their founding in the early thirteenth century, the Franciscan and Dominican missionary orders were encouraged by the papacy to send friars to proselytize in regions as distant as China and India. By the time of Jordanus's first mission, the Catholic Church had established India as a Catholic province and appointed three bishops to oversee missionary work in the region. The Christian mission in India was, however, never an easy one. After leaving behind four Franciscan companions in the city of Tana in India, for example, Jordanus returned to find these men killed by official authorities. Christianity would never gain much ground in India during the Medieval and Early Modern periods. The following two excerpts from Jordanus's account of this time in India nevertheless reveals why Europeans were fascinated with the exotic East. It was a world full of "marvels and wonder."

Marvels Described

11 In the aforesaid island of Sylen is a very potent king, who hath precious stones of every kind under heaven, in such quantity as to be almost incredible. Among these he hath two rubies, of which he weareth one hung round his neck, and the other on the hand wherewith he wipeth his lips and his beard; and [each] is of greater length than the breadth of four fingers, and when held in the hand it standeth out visibly on either

side to the breadth of a finger. I do not believe that the universal world hath two stones like these, or of so great a price, of the same species.

12 There is also another island where all the men and women go absolutely naked, and have in place of money comminuted gold like fine sand. They make of the cloth which they buy walls like curtains; not do they cover themselves or their shame at any time in the world.

13 There is also another exceeding great island, which is called Jaua, which is in circuit more than seven [thousand?] miles as I have heard, and where are many world's wonders. Among which, besides the finest aromatic spices, this is one, to wit, that there be found pygmy men, of the size of a boy of three or four years old, all shaggy like a he goat. They dwell in the woods, and few are found.

14 In this island are white mice, exceeding beautiful. There also are trees producing cloves, which, when they are in flower, emit an odour so pungent that they kill every man who cometh among them, unless he shut his mouth and nostrils.

15 There too are produced cubebs, and nutmegs, and mace, and all the other finest spices except pepper.

16 In a certain part of that island they delight to eat white and fat men when they can get them.

17 In the Greater Indiana, and in the islands, all the people be black, and go naked from the loins upwards, and from the knee downwards, and without shoes.

18 But the kings have this distinction from others, that they wear upon their arms gold and silver rings, and on the neck a gold collar with a great abundance of gems.

19 In this India never do [even] the legitimate sons of great kings, or princes, or barons, inherit the goods of their parents, but only the sons of their sisters; for they say that they have no surety that those are their own sons, because wives and mistresses may conceive and generate by some one else; but 'tis not so with the sister, for whatever man may be the father they are certain that the offspring is from the womb of their sister, and is consequently thus truly of their blood.

20 In this Greater India many sacrifice themselves to idols in this way. When they are sick, or involved in any grave mischance, they vow themselves to the idol if they should happen to be delivered. Then, when they have recovered, they fatten themselves for one or two years continually, eating and drinking fat things, etc. And when another festival comes round, they cover themselves with flowers and perfumes, and crown themselves with white garlands, and go with singing and playing before the idol when it is carried through the land (like the image of the Virgin Mary here among us at the Rogation tides); and those men who are sacrificing themselves to the idol carry a sword with two handles, like those [knives] which are used in currying leather; and, after they have shown off a great deal, they put the sword to the back of the neck, cutting strongly with a vigorous exertion of both hands, and so cut off their own heads before the idol.

Cathay

7 Cathay is a very great empire, which extendeth over more than C days' journey; and it hath only one lord, whereas the case with the Indies is the very opposite, for there be therein many kings, many princes, not one of whom holdeth himself tributary to another.

8 And the dominion of Æthiopia is great exceedingly; and I believe, and lie not, that the population thereof is, at the least, three times that of our Christendom.

9 But other two empires of the Tartars, as I have heard, to wit, that which was formerly of Cathay, but now is of Osbet, which is called Gatzaria, and the empire of Dua and Cayda, formerly of Capac and now of Elchigaday, extend over more than CC days' journey.

10 The vessels which they navigate in Cathay be very big, and have upon the ship's hull more than C cabins, and with a fair wind they carry X sails, and they are very bulky, being made of three thicknesses of plank, so that the first thickness is as in our great ships, the second cross-wise, the third again long-wise. In sooth, 'tis a very strong affair. It is true that they venture not far out to sea; and that Indian sea is seldom or never boisterous, and when it does rise to such a degree as they deem awfully perilous, it is such weather as our mariners here would deem splendid. For one of the men of our country would there ('tis no lie), be reckoned at sea worth a hundred of theirs and more.

11 Græcia also is of great extent, but of how many days' journey I wot not.

12 One general remark I will make in conclusion; to wit, that there is no better land or fairer, no people so honest, no victuals so good and savoury, dress so handsome, or manners so noble, as here in our own Christendom; and, above all, we have the truth faith, though ill it be kept. For, as God is my witness, ten times better [Christians], and more charitable withal, be those who be converted by the Preaching and Minor friars to our faith, than our own folk here, as experience hath taught me.

13 And of the conversion of those nations of India, I say this: that if there were two hundred or three hundred good friars, who would faithfully and fervently preach the Catholic faith, there is not a year which would not see more than X thousand persons converted to the Christian faith.

14 For, whilst I was among those schismatics and unbelievers, I believe that more than X thousand, or thereabouts, were converted to our faith, and because we, being few in number, could not occupy, or even visit, many parts of the land, many souls (wo is me!) have perished, and exceeding many do yet perish for lack of preachers of the Word of the Lord. And 'tis grief and pain to hear how, through the preachers of the perfidious and accursed Saracens, those sects of the heathen be day by day perverted. For their preachers run about, just as we do, here, there, and everywhere over the whole Orient, in order to turn all to their own miscreance. These be they who accuse us, who smite us, who cause us to be cast into durance, and who stone us; as I indeed have experienced, having been four times cast into prison by them, I mean the Saracens. But how many times I have had my hair plucked out, and been scourged, and been stoned, God himself knoweth and I, who had to bear all this for my sins, and yet have not attained to end my life as a martyr for the faith, as did four of my brethren. For what remaineth God's will be done! Nay, five Preaching Friars and four Minors were there in my time cruelly slain for the Catholic faith.

Wo is me that I was not with them there!

15 I believe moreover that the king of France might subdue the whole world to his own dominion and to the Christian faith, without the aid of any other.

3. Ibn Battuta, *The Travels of Ibn Battuta*

Although the veracity of certain parts of his work is questionable, Ibn Battuta's travel account of Asia Minor and North Africa remains one of the most important sources of information on the political, social, economic, and spiritual life of these regions for the fourteenth century. Born in Tangiers, the Muslim Ibn Battuta (1304–1377) left in 1324 to go on a pilgrimage. Ibn Battuta's travels took him to many places where Western Europeans could not venture because of tensions between Christians and Muslims. Ibn Battuta describes, for example, his visit to many of the sultanates, including Baghdad— the great seat of Islamic power. He discusses the Kurdish people who lived in the city of Sinjar (Balad), the religious sanctuaries found in the city of Shiraz, and the pilgrimage to the Islamic holy site of Mecca. His depiction of Islamic religious life is particularly vivid, suggesting a world marked by pilgrimage routes, religious shrines, theological centers, and communities of holy men and women. Ibn Battuta is clearly fascinated by other cultures. Yet his observations on these societies tell us as much about his own values and beliefs as they do about the societies he encounters. In the following excerpt, Ibn Battuta recounts his visit to the town of Azak in Turkey (Tartary). Ibn Battuta gives the reader a glimpse into the life of this desert people. Among other things he describes the women of Turkey and a "moving city."

Tartary

I proceeded by sea for the city of El Kiram (Crim), but suffered considerable distress in the voyage, and was very near being drowned. We arrived, however, at length, at the port of El Kirash, which belongs to the desert country of Kifjawk. This desert is green and productive: it has, however, neither tree, mountain, hill, nor wood in it. The inhabitants burn dung. They travel over this desert upon a cart, which they call Araba. The journey is one of six months; the extent of three of which belongs to the Sultan Mohammed Uzbek Khān; that of three more to the infidels. I hired one of these carts for my journey from the port of Kirash to the city of El Kafā, which belongs to Mohammed Uzbek. The greater part of the inhabitants are Christians, living under his protection. From this place I travelled in a cart to the city of El Kiram, which is one of the large and beautiful cities of the districts of the Sultan Mohammed Uzbek Khān. From this place I proceeded, upon a cart which I had hired, to the city of El Sarai, the residence of Mohammed Uzbek. The peculiarity of this desert is, that its herbs serve for fodder for their beasts: and on this account their cattle are numerous. They have neither feeders nor keepers, which arises from the severity of their laws against theft, which are these: When any one is convicted of having stolen a beast, he is compelled to return it with nine others of equal value. But, if this is not in his power, his children are taken. If, however, he have no children, he is himself slaughtered just like a sheep.

After several days' journey I arrived at Azāk, which is a small town situated on the sea-shore. In it resides an Emīr on the part of the Sultan Mohammed, who treated us with great respect and hospitality. From this place I proceeded to the city of El Mājar, which is a large and handsome place. The Turkish women of these parts are very highly respected, particularly the wives of the nobles and kings. These women are religious, and prone to almsgiving and other good works. They go unveiled, however, with their faces quite exposed.

I next set out for the camp of the Sultan, which was then in a place called Bish Tāg, or *Five Mountains,* and arrived at a station to which the Sultan with his retinue had just come before us: at this place, which is termed the urdū, or camp, we arrived on the first of the month Ramadān. Here we witnessed a moving city, with its streets, mosques, and cooking-houses, the smoke of which ascended as they moved along. When, however, they halted, all these became stationary. This Sultan Mohammed Uzbek is very powerful, enjoys extensive rule, and is a subduer of the infidels. He is one of the seven great kings of the world; which are, the Sultan of the West, the Sultan of Egypt and Syria, the Sultan of the two Irāks, the Sultan of the Turks Uzbek, the Sultan of Turkistān and Māwarā El Nahar, the Sultan of India, and the Sultan of China.

It is a custom with Mohammed Uzbek to sit after prayer on the Friday, under an alcove called the "golden alcove," which is very much ornamented: he has a throne in the middle of it, overlaid with silver plate, which is gilded and set with jewels. The Sultan sits upon the throne; his four wives, some at his right hand, others at his left, sitting also upon the throne. Beneath the throne stand his two sons, one on his right, the other on his left; before him sits his daughter. Whenever one of these wives enters, he arises, and taking her by the hand, puts her into her place upon the throne. Thus they are exposed to the sight of all, without so much as a veil. After this, come in the great Emīrs, for whom chairs are placed on the right and left, and on these they sit. Before the King stand the princes, who are the sons of his uncle, brothers, and near kinsmen. In front of these, and near the door, stand the sons of the great Emīrs; and behind these, the general officers of the army. People then enter, according to their rank; and saluting the King, return and take their seats at a distance. When, however, the evening prayer is over, the supreme consort, who is Queen, returns; the rest follow, each with their attendant beautiful slaves. The women, who are separated on account of any uncleanness, are seated upon horses; before their carriages are cavalry, behind them beautiful Mamlūks. Upon this day I was presented to the Sultan, who received me very graciously, and afterwards sent me some sheep and a horse, with a leather bag of kimiz, which is the milk of a mare; and very much valued among them as a beverage.

The wives of this King are highly honoured. Each one has a mansion for herself, her followers, and servants. When the Sultan wishes to visit one of them, he sends word, and preparation is made. One of these wives is a daughter of Takfūr, the Emperor of Constantinople. I had already visited each of them, and on this account the Sultan received me: this is a custom among them; and whoever fails in observing it, suffers the imputation of a breach of politeness.

I had formerly heard of the city of Bulgār, and hence I had conceived a desire to see it; and to observe, whether what had been related of it, as to the extremity of the shortness of its nights, and again of its days, in the opposite season of the year, were true or not. There was, however, between that place, and the camp of the Sultan, a distance of ten days. I requested the Sultan, therefore, that he would appoint some one who would bring me thither and back, which he granted.

When, therefore, I was saying the prayer of sun-set, in that place, which happened in the month of Ramadān, I hasted, nevertheless the time for evening prayer came on, which I went hastily through. I then said that of midnight, as well as that termed El Witr; but was overtaken by the dawn. In the same manner also is the day shortened in this place, in the opposite season of the year. I remained here three days, and then returned to the King.

In Bulgār, I was told of the land of darkness, and certainly had a great desire to go to it from that place. The distance, however, was that of forty days. I was diverted, therefore, from the undertaking, both on account of its great danger, and the little good to be derived from it. I was told that there was no travelling thither except upon little sledges, which are drawn by large dogs; and, that during the whole of the journey, the roads are covered with ice, upon which neither the feet of man, nor the hoofs of beast, can take any hold. These dogs, however, have nails by which their feet take firm hold on the ice. No one enters these parts except powerful merchants, each of whom has perhaps a hundred of such sledges as these, which they load with provisions, drinks, and wood: for there we have neither trees, stones, nor houses. The guide in this country is the dog, who has gone the journey several times, the price of which will amount to about a thousand dinars. The sledge is harnessed to his neck, and with him three other dogs are joined, but of which he is the leader. The others then follow him with the sledge, and when he stops they stop. The master never strikes or reprimands this dog; and when he proceeds to a meal, the dogs are fed first: for if this were not done, they would become enraged, and perhaps run away and leave their master to perish. When the travellers have completed their forty days or stages through this desert, they arrive at the land of darkness; and each man, leaving what he has brought with him, goes back to his appointed station. On the morrow they return to look for their goods, and find, instead of them, sable, ermine, and the fir of the sinjāb. If then the merchant likes what he finds, he takes it away; if not, he leaves it, and more is added to it: upon some occasions, however, these people will take back their own goods, and leave those of the merchant's. In this way is their buying and selling carried on; for the merchants know not whether it is with mankind or demons that they have to do; no one being seen during the transaction. It is one of the properties of these firs, that no vermin ever enters them.

I returned to the camp of the Sultan on the 28th of Ramadān; and, after that, travelled with him to the city of Astrachan, which is one of his cities. It is situated on the banks of the river Athal, which is one of the great rivers of the world. At this place the Sultan resides during the very cold weather; and when this river, as well as the adjoining waters, are frozen, the King orders the people of the country to bring thousands of bundles of hay, which they do, and then place it upon the ice, and upon this they travel.

When the King had arrived at Astrachan, one of his wives, who was daughter to the Emperor of Constantinople, and then big with child, requested to be allowed to visit her father, with whom it was her intention to leave her child and then to return: this he granted. I then requested to be permitted to go with her, that I may see Constantinople; and was refused, on account of some fears which he entertained respecting me. I flattered him, however, telling him that I should never appear before her but as his servant and guest, and that he need entertain no fear whatsoever. After this he gave me permission, and I accordingly took my leave. He gave me fifteen hundred dinars, a dress of honour, and several horses. Each of his ladies also gave me some pieces of bullion silver, which they call El Suwam, as did also his sons and daughters.

I set out accordingly on the 10th of the month Shawāl, in company with the royal consort iBailūn, daughter to the Emperor of Constantinople. The Sultan accompanied us through the first stage, in order to encourage her, and then returned. The Queen was attended in her journey by five thousand of the King's army, about five hundred of which were cavalry, as her servants and followers. In this manner we arrived Ukak, which is a moderately sized town but excessively cold. Between this place and El Sarāi which belongs to the Sultan, there is a distance of ten days. At the distance of one day from this place are the mountains of the Russians, who are Christians, with red hair and blue eyes, an ugly and perfidious people. They have silver mines: and from their country is the suwam, *i.e.* the pieces of silver bullion brought. With these they buy and sell, each piece weighing five ounces. After ten days' journey from this place we arrived at the city of

Sūdāk, which is one of the cities of the desert of Kifjāk, and situated on the sea-shore. After this we arrived at a city known by the name of Bābā Saltūk. Saltūk, they say, was a diviner. This is the last district (in this direction) belonging to the Turks; between which, however, and the districts of Room, is a distance of eighteen days, eight of which are over an uninhabited desert without water: but as we entered it during the cold season, we did not want much water.

4. RAMÓN LLULL, *THE BOOK OF THE LOVER AND THE BELOVED*

Ramón Llull (1235–1315) was one of the most influential spiritual and intellectual figures of the late medieval period. A well-known neo-platonic philosopher, mystic, and missionary, Llull was also an early exponent of the Catalan language for use in religious and philosophical works, an author of Arabic texts, and the founder of oriental language schools for Catholic missionaries. Inspired one day by a spiritual vision, the noble-born Llull left his wife and children to convert the Muslims of the North Africa. For nine years he dedicated himself to the study of Arabic and important Islamic religious texts, including the Qu'ran, in order to prepare himself for his mission. Llull's grasp of Arabic was apparently good enough by the end of his studies to permit him to dispute and write in Arabic and to translate Arabic texts. His fascination with Eastern languages, learning, and religion, along with his intense desire to convert Muslim and Jewish peoples, was likely influenced by his experience of growing up in the culturally mixed environment of Mallarca. One-third of Mallarcan society was Muslim by the thirteenth century. The Jewish community was also a strong presence there, and its members frequently acted as ambassadors between Catalonia and Eastern Islamic authorities, as well as bankers for the Catalan government. Llull's profound respect for Muslim and Jewish intellectual and spiritual traditions is reflected in many of his works, including the *The Book of the Gentile and the Three Wise Men*. In this work, Llull describes a remarkably calm and friendly discussion between three wise men who represent the monotheistic faiths of Christianity, Islam, and Judaism. The following passage comes from Lull's celebrated and influential mystical treatise the *Book of the Lover and the Beloved,* a text that many scholars have argued marries eastern and western mystical traditions.

The Book of the Lover and the Beloved

1 The Lover asked his Beloved if there remained in Him anything still to be loved. And the Beloved replied that he had still to love that by which his own love could be increased.

2 Long and perilous are the paths by which the Lover seeks his Beloved. They are people by cares, sighs and tears. They are lit up by love.

3 Many Lovers came together to love One only, their Beloved, who made them all to abound in love. And each declared his Beloved perfection, and his thoughts of Him were very pleasant, making him to suffer pain which brought delight.

4 The Lover wept and said: 'How long shall it be till the darkness of the world is past, that the mad rush of men towards hell may cease? When comes the hour in which water, that flows downwards, shall change its nature and mount upwards? When shall the innocent be more in number than the guilty? Ah! When shall the Lover with joy lay down his life for the Beloved? And when shall the Beloved see the Lover grow faint for love of Him?'

5 Said the Lover to the Beloved: 'Thou that fillest the sun with splendour, fill my heart with love.' And the Beloved answered: 'Wert thou not filled with love, thine eyes had not shed those tears, not hadst thou come to this place to see thy Beloved.'

6 The Beloved made trial of His Lover to see if his love for Him were perfect, and He asked him how the presence of the Beloved differed from His absence. The Lover answered: 'As knowledge and remembrance differ ignorance and oblivion.'

7 The Beloved asked the Lover: 'Hast thou remembrance of anything with which I have rewarded thee, that thou wouldst love Me thus?' 'Yea,' replied the Lover, 'for I distinguish not between the trials that Thou sendest me and the joys.'

8 'Say, O Lover,' asked the Beloved, 'if I double thy trials, wilt thou still be patient?' 'Yea,' answered the Lover, 'so that Thou double also my love.'

9 Said the Beloved to the Lover: 'Knowest thou yet what love meaneth?' The Lover replied: 'If I knew not the meaning of love, I should know the meaning of labour, grief and sorrow.'

10 They asked the Lover: 'Why answerest thou not thy Beloved when He calleth thee?' He replied: 'I brave great perils that He may come, and I speak to Him begging His graces.'

11 'Foolish Lover, why dost thou weary thy body, throw away thy wealth and leave the joys of this world, and go about as an outcast of the people?' 'To honour my Beloved's Name,' he replied, 'for He is hated and dishonoured by more men than honour and love Him.'

12 'Say, Fool of Love, which can be the better seen, the Beloved in the Lover, or the Lover in the Beloved?' The Lover answered, and said: 'By love can the Beloved be seen, and the Lover by sighs and tears, by grief and by labours.'

13 The Lover sought for one who should tell his Beloved how great trials he was enduring for love of Him, and how he was like to die. And he found his Beloved, who was reading in a book wherein were written all the griefs which love made him to suffer for his Beloved, and the graces which He gave him.

14 Our Lady presented her Son to the Lover, that he might kiss His feet, and that he might write in his book concerning Our Lady's virtues.

15 'Sir, thou bird that singest, hast thou placed thyself in the care of my Beloved, that He may guard thee from indifference, and increase in thee thy love?' The bird replied; 'And who makes me to sing but the Lord of love, to whom not to love is to sin.'

16 Between Hope and Fear, Love made her home. She lives on thought, and, when she is forgotten, dies. So unlike the pleasures of this world are her foundations.

17 There was a contention between the eyes and the memory of the Lover, for the eyes said that it was better to see the Beloved than to remember Him. But Memory said that remembrance brings tears to the eyes, and makes the heart to burn with love.

18 The Lover asked the Understanding and the Will which of them was the nearer to his Beloved. And the two ran, and the Understanding came nearer to the Beloved than did the Will.

19 There was strife between the Lover and the Beloved, and another who loved Him saw it and wept, till peace and concord were made between the Beloved and the Lover.

20 Sighs and Tears came to be judged by the Beloved, and asked Him which of them loved Him the more deeply. And the Beloved gave judgment that sighs were nearer to the seat of love, and tears to the eyes.

21 The Lover came to drink of the fountain which gives love to him who has none, and his griefs redoubled. And the Beloved came to drink of the same fountain, that the love of one whose griefs were doubled might be doubled also.

22 The Lover fell sick and thought on the Beloved, who fed him on His merits, quenched his thirst with love, made him to rest in patience, clothed him with humility, and as medicine gave him truth.

23 They asked the Lover where his Beloved was. And he answered: 'See Him for yourselves in a nobler house than all the nobility of creation; but see Him too in my love, my griefs and my tears.'

24 They said to the Lover: 'Whither goest thou?' he answered: 'I come from my Beloved.' 'Whence comest thou?' 'I go to my Beloved.' 'When wilt thou return?' 'I shall be with my Beloved.' 'How long wilt thou be with thy Beloved?' 'As long as my thoughts remain on him.'

25 The birds hymned the dawn, and the Beloved, who is the dawn, awakened. And the birds ended their song, and the Lover died in the dawn for his beloved.

Figure 4.1 Pilgrim's Qu'ran. Rare Books Division, J. Willard Marriott Library, University of Utah.

Note: This pocket-sized Qu'ran contained in a letter pouch would have been carried by Medieval Muslims on their pilgrimages to Mecca and other holy sites.

Study Questions

1. From the accounts of Friar Jordanus and Ibn Battuta, explain why Europeans were fascinated by Eastern regions. How did they perceive these regions? What did they have to offer Europeans?
2. Discuss religious life in the Middle East and India as described in the four texts. How does religious life in these regions compare with Christian religious life?
3. Discuss the portrayal of rulers in the texts of Friar Jordanus, Ibn Battuta, and Ibn Jubayr. What do these portrayals tell us about European and Eastern conceptions of rule?
4. In what ways does Ibn Battuta's account of women reflect the values of his society? Why does he find Turkish treatment of women so unusual? How did Medieval European society understand the place of women in society?
5. Where do we see the influence of Eastern philosophy upon Llull in *the Book of the Lover and the Beloved*?

Suggested Reading

Elsner, Jas, and Joan-Pau Rubiés, eds. *Voyages and Visions: Towards a Cultural History of Travel*. London: Reaktion Books, 1999.

Kadar, Benjamin *Crusade and Mission. European approaches to Islam*. Princeton: Princeton University, 1985.

Maier, Christopher, *The Preaching of the Friars*. Cambridge: Cambridge University Press, 1994.

Riley-Smith, Jonathon *The Crusaders: A Short History*. New Haven: Yale University Press, 1987

Web Sites

1. The Crusades

   http://history.idbsu.edu/westciv/crusades/00.htm

2. The Holy Sepulchre in Jerusalem

   www.christusrex.org/www1/jhs/TSspmain.html

3. Marco Polo and His Travels

   www.silk-road.com/artl/marcopolo.shtml

5

Eastern Influence on Europe
1100–1400 A.D.

TEXTS

1. Giovanni Villani, *Croniche Fiorentine*

2. *Justinian Code*

3. Averroes, *On the Harmony of Religion and Philosophy*

4. Thomas Aquinas, *Summa Theologica*

5. Islamic astronomy text. Ibn Ezra, Abraham ben Meir. *De nativitatibus*

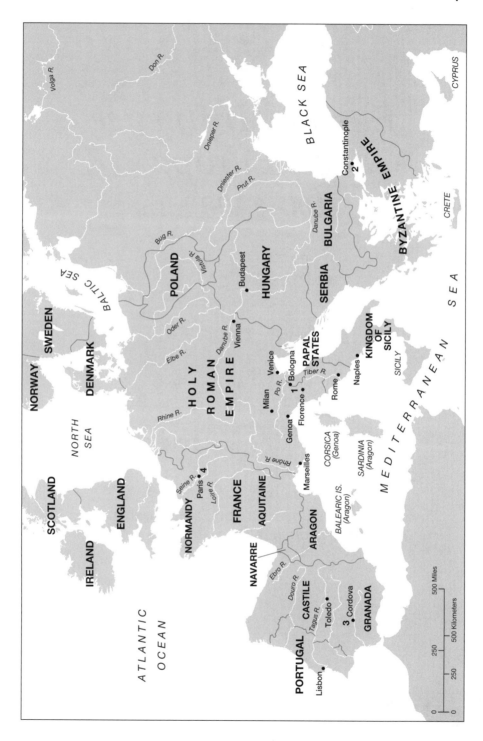

The Crusades may have been one of the least glorious episodes in the history of European toleration, but they did mark a dramatic shift in European interest in kingdoms east of the Mediterranean. As much as Christian Europeans detested Islam, those who went to Palestine and its neighboring regions developed a profound appreciation for the sophistication and cosmopolitan character of eastern cultures. In particular, the city of Constantinople evoked awe, but European crusaders and missionaries alike were also struck by the cultural and economic vibrancy of other cities such as Antioch, Tripoli, and Jaffa on the west coast of Asia Minor. They were also impressed by tales of the grandeur and wealth of the great Muslim cities of Baghdad and Damascus which were largely inaccessible to Christians. These Christian travelers returned to Europe with a taste for eastern luxury goods such as silk, perfume, and spices, thereby adding greater impetus to European trade with the East.

Before the first Crusades set out for Palestine, however, European trade in eastern luxury goods was already on the rise as was European trade in general. During the eleventh century, increasing European commercial activity in the Baltic Sea and along the western shores of Northern Europe was matched by a revival of European trade with the East as Italian merchants from the port cities of Venice and Genoa in particular capitalized on Western demand for eastern goods. Genoese and Venetian merchants established mercantile settlements in Alexandria in Egypt, as well as in many of the principal ports of Asia Minor. In these commercial centers, they received goods brought by Arab merchants from the famous markets of Baghdad and Damascus. By the end of the twelfth century, Genoa and Venice had established themselves as wealthy, cosmopolitan urban centers in their own right. Growing trade with the East also played a role in the emergence of the city of Florence at the end of the next century as the great center of banking in Europe. [1]

European interest in Eastern goods was matched by a growing fascination with Eastern learning. What impressed them was not only Islamic knowledge in the fields of mathematics, astronomy, and medicine, but also the much wider availability of ancient Greek and Roman texts in the Islamic and Byzantine worlds. The majority of these texts were new to Europeans of the twelfth century because of the shift of learning from secular society to the monastery which took place in the West in the centuries following the collapse of the Roman Empire. European education was in the hands of clerics throughout the Middle Ages, and few clerics saw any use in preserving and studying works written by non-Christians. By the tenth century, classical texts which did survive in the West lay molding largely forgotten in monastic libraries when not expurgated of their non-Christian content to serve the needs of a Christian society.

For European of the twelfth century, these ancient Greek and Roman texts suddenly found new relevance. Classical treatises on politics, jurisprudence, philosophy, and science immediately found an audience among European scholars and political leaders alike because they spoke to the needs of an increasingly urbanized and commercial society. The discovery of the sixth-century codification of Roman civil law known as the Justinian Code [2] sparked a revolution in jurisprudence in Europe because it provided a legal system and theory of law which was at once more rational and comprehensive than the Germanic codes used throughout the Medieval period.

The rediscovery of the Justinian Code did more, however, than change European legal systems. It also contributed to the emergence of an altogether new and unique intellectual institution in Europe: the university. The scholarship of such men as Gratian (ca. 1090–1150) transformed the city of Bologna into a prominent center of Roman law by the early twelfth century as students began flocking here in large numbers to receive legal training. Frequently in conflict with townsmen, the students of Bologna organized themselves into a union to protect themselves. It was not long before they also used their combined authority to regulate the teaching of law. Similar institutions for the fields of medicine and theology were also emerging at the same time. By the thirteenth century, universities dotted the map of Western Europe. Padua became a famous center of medicine, and the University of Paris developed into the most prestigious theological center in Europe.

Providing the foundation for these new institutions was the study of the ancient Greek and Roman, Arabic, and Byzantine texts discovered by Western Europeans on their journeys eastward, as well as Medieval Christian texts. From the middle of the twelfth to the middle of the thirteenth centuries, Muslim, Jewish, and Christian scholars in the cities of Toledo and Palermo collaborated on translations of Islamic mathematical, astronomical, and medical texts, and to a lesser extent, on philosophical texts. Averroes's commentaries on Aristotle, for example, were translated into Castilian and Latin, along with other Islamic texts.

The first journeys to Constantinople in search of Greek texts began in the thirteenth century. European scholars relied on these different authorities to create a new, more critical approach to the examination of ancient texts in each field of study. The new approach that emerged is better known as scholasticism. Of all the classical authorities used by Medieval scholars, none was more important than the Greek philosopher Aristotle. Simply referred to by many Medieval scholars as "the philosopher," Aristotle first received wide exposure in the West through Islamic translations and surviving Greek editions of his work. Most of the Aristotlean corpus was translated into Arabic between 750 and 1000 A.D. Between 900 and 1200 A.D., a number of enterprising and ambitious Islamic thinkers such as Avicenna (d. 1051) and Averroes (d. 1198) [3] tried to harmonize Aristotle with Islam. These individuals were only partially known to the West during this period. However, their interpretations of Aristotle's work came to exert enormous influence in the

West in subsequent centuries, particularly the fields of philosophy and theology. There is no better example of their influence upon Western thought than the work of the most famous medieval scholastic theologian of all, Thomas Aquinas (1225–1274).**[4]**

1. GIOVANNI VILLANI, *CRONICHE FIORENTINE*

Giovanni Villani (ca. 1276–1348) was a Florentine by birth and a close friend of the famous author Dante Aligheri. Like Dante, Villaini was a member of a prominent Florentine banking family, but he is best known as the author of an early history of Florence, *The Croniche Fiorentine.* Villani's work is an especially important historical source on the political and military events surrounding the rise of Florence as a republican regime by the end of the thirteenth century. The *Croniche* also highlights the changing character of Florence during this period. It was during the thirteenth century that Florence began emerging as one of the most powerful city-states in Italy. Ruled by a merchant elite, Florence profited from growing trade between Italian merchants and their Muslim and Byzantine counterparts. Florence developed into a vital center of banking and textile manufacturing during this period. Its coin, the *florin,* was considered the most stable currency throughout Europe and the Mediterranean. Florentine pride in its wealth and self-rule also laid the foundation for the emergence of a new intellectual and artistic movement known as the Renaissance. The following brief excerpts highlight the economic and political vitality of fourteenth-century Florence.

Croniche Fiorentine

§ 50. —*How the bridge Santa Trinita was built.*
In this time, the city of Florence being in happy state under the rule of the Popolo, a bridge was built over the Arno from Santa Trinita to the house of the Frescobaldi in Oltrarno, and in this the zeal of Lamberto Frescobaldi helped much, which was a noted Ancient in the Popol, and he and his had come to great state and riches.
§ 53. —*How the golden florins were first made in Florence.*
The host of the Florentines having returned, and being at rest after the victories aforesaid, the city increased greatly in state and in riches and lordship and in great quietness; for the which thing the merchants of Florence, for the honour of the commonwealth, ordained with the people and commonwealth that golden coins should be struck at Florence; and they promised to furnish the gold, for before the custom was to strike silver coins of 12 pence the piece. And then began the good coins of gold, 24 carats fine, the which are called golden florins, and each was worth 20 soldi. And this was in the time of the said M. Filippo degli Ugoni of Brescia, in the month of November, the year of Christ 1252. The which florins weighed eight to the ounce, and on one side

was the stamp of the lily and on the other of S. John. By reason of the said new money of the golden florin there fell out a pretty story, and worth narrating. The said new florins having begun to circulate through the world, they were carried to Tunis in Barbary; and being brought before the king of Tunis, which was a worthy and wise lord, they pleased him much, and he caused them to be tried; and finding them to be of fine gold, he much commended them, and having caused his interpreters to interpret the imprint and legend on the florin, he found that it said: S. John the Baptist, and on the side of the lily, Florence. Perceiving it to be Christian money, he sent to the Pisan merchants who were then free of the city and were much with the king (and even the Florentines traded in Tunis through the Pisans), and asked them what manner of city among Christians was this Florence which made the said florins. The Pisans answered spitefully through envy, saying: "They are our inland Arabs: which is to say, our mountain rustics." Then answered the king wisely: "It does not seem to me the money of Arabs. O you Pisans, what manner of golden money is yours?" Then were they confused, and knew not how to answer. He asked if there were among them any one from Florence, and there was found there a merchant from Oltrarno, by name Pera Balducci, discreet and wise. The king asked him of the state and condition of Florence, whom the Pisans called their Arabs; the which answered wisely, showing the power and magnificence of Florence, and how Pisa in comparison was neither in power nor in inhabitants the half of Florence, and that they had no golden money, and that the florin was the fruit of many victories gained by the Florentines over them. For the which cause the Pisans were shamed, and the king, by reason of the florin and by the words of our wise fellow-citizen, made the Florentines free of the city, and allowed them a place of habitation and a church in Tunis, and he gave them the same privileges as the Pisans. And this we knew to be true from the said Pera, a man worthy of faith, for we were among his colleagues in the office of prior.

Political Life

§ 1. —In the year of Christ 1292, on the 1st day of February, the city of Florence being in great and powerful state, and prosperous in all things, and the citizens thereof waxing fat and rich, and by reason of excessive tranquility, which naturally engenders pride and novelties, being envious and arrogant among themselves, many murders, and wounds, and outrages were done by one citizen upon another; and above all the nobles known as magnates and potentates, alike in the country and in the city, wrought upon the people who might not resist them, force and violence both against person and goods, taking possession thereof. For the which thing certain good men, artificers and merchants of Florence, which desired good life, considered how to set a remedy and defence against the said plague, and one of the leaders therein, among others, was a man of worth, an ancient and noble citizen from among the popolani, rich and powerful, whose name was Giano della Bella, of the people of S. Martin, with he following and counsel of other wise and powerful propolani. And instituting in Florence an order of judges to correct the statutes and our laws, as by our ordinances the custom was of old to do, they ordained certain laws and statutes, very strong and weighty, against such magnates and men of power as should do wrong or violence against the people; increasing the common penalties in divers ways, and enacting that one member of a family of magnates should be held answerable for the others; and two bearing witness to public fame and report should be held to prove such crimes; and the public accounts should be revised. And these laws they called the Ordinances of Justice. And to the intent they might be maintained and put into execution, it was decreed that beyond the number of six Priors which governed the city, there should be a gonfalonier of justice appointed by the several sesti in succession, changing every two months, as do the Priors. And when the hammer-bells were sounded, the people were to rally to the church of San Piero Scheraggio and give out the banner of justice, which before was not the custom. And they decreed that not one of the Priors should be of the noble houses called magnates; for before this good and true merchants had often been made Priors, albeit they chanced to be of some great and noble house. And the ensign and standard of the said Popolo was decreed to be a white field with a red cross; and there were chosen 1000 citizens, divided according to the sesti, with certain standard-bearers for each region, with fifty footmen to each standard, which were to be armed, each one with hauberk and shield marked with the cross; and they were to assemble at every tumult or summons of the gonfalonier, at his house or at the palace of the Priors, to do execution against the magnates; and afterwards the number of the chosen footmen increased to 2,000, and then to 4,000. And a like order of men-at-arms for the people, with the said ensign, was enrolled in each country and district of Florence, and they were called the Leagues of the People. And the first of the said gonfaloniers was one Baldo de' Ruffoli of the Porte del Duomo; and in his time the standard sallied forth with armed men to destroy the goods of a family named Galli of Porta S. Marie, by reason of a murder which one of them had committed in the kingdom of France on the person of a popolano. This new decree of the people, and change in the State was of much importance to the city of Florence, and had afterwards many and divers consequences both ill and good to our commonwealth, as hereafter in due time we shall make mention. And in this new thing and beginning of the Popolo, the popolani would have been hindered by the power of the magnates had it not been that in those times the said magnates of Florence were in broils and discords among themselves, since that the Guelfs were returned to Florence; and there was great war between the Adimari and the Tosinghi, and between the Rossi and the Tornaquinci, and between the Bardi and the Mozzi, and between the Gherardini and the Manieri, and between the Calvalcanti and the Bondelmonti, and between certain of the Bondelmonti and the Giandonati, and between the Visdomini and the Falconieri, and between the Bostichi and the Foraboschi, and between the Foraboschi and the Malispini, and among the Frescobaldi themselves, and among the family of the Donati themselves, and many other noble houses. [And therefore let not the reader marvel because we have put this event at the head of our book, forasmuch as the most strange events arose from this beginning, and not only to our city of Florence, but to all the region of Italy.]

2. Justinian Code

One of the most important administrative reforms introduced by Emperor Justinian I (483–565 A.D.) during his rule of the Byzantine Empire was the codification of Roman law. The Byzantine Empire was formed out of the eastern part of the Roman Empire, and it maintained the Roman civil law (*corpus iuris civilis*) as the basis of its legal structure long after the Roman empire disappeared in the West. By the sixth century, however, centuries of legislation had transformed Roman civil law into a large and unruly body of law. The Justinian Code (529–565) was one early and largely successful attempt to impose a more orderly and rational structure to the *corpus iuris civilis*. The Code organizes Roman law into three parts: the *Digest, Pandects,* and the *Institutes*. A fourth section, the *Novellae,* comprises legal decrees that were introduced subsequent to the formulation of the Code. The Justinian Code became enormously important in the West when it was brought from Constantinople to Italy during the eleventh century. European legal scholars and authorities immediately recognized the use of Roman law for their own society. Roman law was at once a more comprehensive and rational system of law than the *Salic Law* and other customary codes that were then in use in medieval Europe. This legal system was designed for a complex, urban society, and Europe of the eleventh and twelfth centuries, Italy above all, was increasingly that. By the end of the twelfth century, legal scholars such as Gratian (ca. 1090–1150) had transformed the city of Bologna into a great center of legal studies because of their work on the *corpus iuris civilis*. The University of Bologna, one of the first universities in Europe, remained the most highly regarded of the many schools of legal studies to emerge during the Medieval and Early Modern periods.

Justinian Code

On Corrupting a Slave

ULPIANUS (*on the Edict* 23) The Prætor says:—"Where a man is alleged to have harboured a slave of either sex belonging to another or induced him or her maliciously to act in any way with intent to deteriorate his or her character, I will allow an action against him for twice what the matter comes to." 1. A man who is a *bona fide* purchaser of the slave will not be liable under this Edict, nor can he himself bring an action for corrupting the slave, as he has no interest in the slave not being corrupted; in fact, it is clear that, if his right to sue were admitted, two persons would have a good right of action for corruption of the slave, which is absurd. It may be added that, according to the received opinion, the action cannot be brought by one who has *bona fide* the services of a free man. 2. With regard to the word "harboured" (*recepisse*), as used by the Prætor, what this is taken to refer to is the case of a man taking in another man's slave at his own place of abode; "harbouring" is, strictly speaking, affording a slave a refuge with a view to concealing him, whether it be on the party's own ground or in a place or building belonging to another. 3. To induce (*persuadere*) is *to compel and constrain a person to obey you;* but "induce" is a kind of neutral term, as the incitement may be applied by giving good advice as well as bad; accordingly the Prætor adds the words "maliciously" and "with intent to deteriorate the slave's character." So that one who solicits a slave to do or to plan something objectionable must be the kind of person who is held up to observation in this Edict. 4. Is a man, however, liable only where he has driven a well-conducted slave to commit an offence, or is he equally so where he instigates a bad slave, or shows a bad slave the way to commit it? The truer view is that even where he shows a bad slave how to commit an offence he is liable. Indeed, if the slave had made up his mind independently to run away or to commit a theft, and the party in question is shown to have applauded his design, he is liable; the slave's bad disposition ought not to be made worse still by approbation. Accordingly, whether a man makes a good slave bad or makes a bad slave worse, he will be held to corrupt him. 5. A person too makes a slave worse who induces him to commit wrongful damage or theft or to run away or to instigate a slave belonging to some other person to commit such offences, or to make his *peculium* undistinguishable, or to go after girls, or to loiter about, or to give himself up to magical arts, or to spend too much time at public shows, or to engage in riots, or again who induces [a slave who is] a bailiff, either by words or bribes, to mutilate [or[falsify his master's accounts or even to confuse an account put in his hands,

PAULUS (*on the Edict* 19) or who encourages a slave to live expensively, or to be insubordinate, or induces him to submit to *stuprum*.

ULPIANUS (*on the Edict* 23) By adding the expression "maliciously" the Prætor stigmatizes craft on the part of the person who induces; whereas if a man deteriorates a slave's character without wrongful intention he incurs no stigma; and he is not liable where he does it for a practical joke. 1. Hence arises this question: suppose a man incites the slave of another to climb on a roof or to go down a well, and the slave accordingly climbs up or goes down, and so falls and breaks his leg or breaks any limb or is killed, will the party be liable? The answer is that, if he did it without malice, he is not liable, but, if it was done maliciously, he is;

PAULUS (*on the Edict* 19) but the more convenient plan is to hold him liable to an *utilis* [*actio* framed on the] *lex Aquilia.*

ULPIANUS (*on the Edict* 23) The word "maliciously" must be applied equally in the case of one who harbours a slave, so that a man is not liable unless he harbours maliciously; if he harboured the slave with a view to keeping him safely on his owner's behoof or from motives of humanity or out of pity or on some other approved and lawful ground, he is not liable. 1. If anyone maliciously induces a slave whom he took for a free man to do anything, I should say that he ought to be held liable, as one who corrupts a slave whom he believes to be free commits a still greater offence [than if he knew him to be a slave], consequently, if the man really is a slave, the party will be liable. 2. The action is for twofold damages, even where the defendant admits his guilt, though the Aquilian action only inflicts that penalty on one who denies. 3. Where the offender is a slave of either sex, the action is allowed with the option of surrender for *noxa.* 4. The action relates to the date at which the slave was corrupted or harboured, and not the date of the application, so that if the slave should be dead or have been disposed of or manumitted, the action may none the less be brought, and, the right to bring it having once accrued, it is not lost by manumission, …

PAULUS (*on the Edict* 27) Where the person whose funeral has been held was subject to *potestas,* the right to bring an *actio funeraria* exists against the *paterfamilias,* according to his position and means.

ULPIANUS (*on the Edict* 25) We read in Celsus:—on the death of a married woman, the funeral expenses should always be a charge on the *dos* remaining in the hands of the husband and on the general property of the deceased, in proportion to their respective values.

PAULUS (*on the Edict* 27) For example, if the *dos* is worth a hundred and the estate of the deceased two hundred, the heir must contribute two thirds of the expense and the husband one third;

ULPIANUS (*on the Edict* 25) and this, according to Julianus, without deducting legacies,

PAULUS (*on the Edict* 27) or the value of slaves who are manumitted,

POMPONIUS (*on Sabinus* 15) or deducting debts.

ULPIANUS (*on the Edict* 25) In this way the husband and the heir have to contribute to the funeral in proportion [to the amounts they receive]. 1. There can be no *actio funeraria* against the husband, if he handed over the *dos* to his wife during the coverture, so Marcellus tells us, and this is a sound opinion,—that is to say, in those cases in which the statutes allow the husband to act in the way described. 2. I may add that in my opinion a husband can be compelled to pay by means of the *actio funeraria* only to the extent of his means; the fact is that he is the richer by the amount which he would have had to hand over to his wife if she had sued him.

POMPONIUS (*on Sabinus* 15) Should there be no *dos,* then, according to Atilicinus, the whole expense ought to be paid by the father; or else by the heirs of the woman, supposing, that is, she should be emancipated. Should the woman have left no heirs, and the father be insolvent, the husband, he says, can be sued to the extent of his means, with the object of preventing its being set down to his misconduct that his late wife was left unburied.

GAIUS (*on the Provincial Edict* 19) If a woman who is divorced marries another man and then dies, Fulcinius holds that the first husband is not chargeable with funeral expenses, although he is the richer by the amount of the *dos.* 1. A man who holds the funeral of a married woman who was under *potestas* has a good right to sue the husband, so long as the *dos* is not restored to the woman's father; if it has been restored, his claim will be against the father; but, in any case, where the husband has been sued, he need hand over the less to the woman's father by the amount [which he has paid the plaintiff in the action].

POMPONIUS (*on Sabinus* 15) Conversely, whatever the father disbursed for the funeral of his [married] daughter or hands over in consequence of an *actio funeraria* brought against him by another, he can recover from her husband in an action *de dote.* 1. But if a married woman who has been emancipated dies during coverture, her heirs or *bonorum possessores* will have to contribute, and so will the father in proportion to the amount of the *dos* which he has received, and the husband in proportion to the amount of it by which he is the richer.

On Carrying in a Dead Body and Building a Sepulchral Monument

ULPIANUS (*on the Edict* 68) The Prætor says:—"Whither and wheresoever such a one has a right to carry in a dead body without your leave, I forbid the use of force to prevent him from being free to take the body thereto and there to bury it." 1. Where a man has a right to bury, he is not [to be] hindered from doing so, and it is held that he is so hindered when either he is prevented from taking the body on to the ground in question or his approach to it is obstructed. 2. The bare proprietor of the piece of ground can have recourse to the interdict as to carrying in a body; in fact it is equally available in respect of ordinary land. 3. Again, if I have a right of way to a plot of ground, and I wish to carry in a body to that plot, but my approach is hindered, the law is that I can take proceedings by way of this interdict, inasmuch as, being hindered from using the right of way, I am hindered from carrying in the body, and a similar rule must be held to apply where I have any other servitude. 4. That this is a prohibitory interdict is plain on the face of it. 5. The Prætor says:—"Wheresoever such a one has a right to carry in a body without your leave, I forbid force being used to prevent him from being free to erect on the spot a sepulchral monument, he doing the same without malicious intent." 6. The reason why this interdict is offered is that the construction and ornamentation of monuments is desirable in the interests of religion. 7. No one is to be hindered from making a tomb or a monument on a spot where he has right to do so. 8. A man is held to hinder the making of a structure even where he prevents the materials being brought to the spot which are required for purposes of construction. On the same principle, if a man prevents the necessary workmen from coming to the spot, the interdict will apply, also if he hinders the fixing of apparatus, assuming that he does so on a spot which is subject to the servitude; but, of course, if you attempt to set up your appliances on my ground, I shall not be liable to the interdict, if, in exercise of my rights, I decline to allow you to proceed. 9. A man must be understood to construct not only when he undertakes some fresh work of his own, but equally so when his object is to execute repairs. 10. A man who takes measures to make a sepulchral structure fall over is exposed to this interdict.

MARCELLUS (*Digest* 28) One of the "Royal Statutes" lays down that, on the death of a woman with child, she will not be buried until the unborn infant is extracted; anyone who transgresses this rule may be said to have taken away the prospect of the living child in disposing of the body of the pregnant woman.

POMPONIUS (*on Sabinus* 9) If a man is erecting a sepulchral monument close to your house, you can serve on him a "notification of novel structure," but, when the work is finished, the only right of action you will have is that for an interdict *quod vi aut clam*. 1. If a body is once carried in close to the house of a stranger, that is over the statutable limits, the owner of the house cannot after that prevent the person [who does it] from carrying in another body to the same place, or from constructing a monument, if the act was originally done with he knowledge of such owner.

ULPIANUS (*Responsa* 2) The right to a burial-place is not acquired by long possession by one to whom it does not legally belong.

THE SAME (*Opinions* 1) If human remains are laid within some structure which is averred to be incomplete, there is no reason, so far, why it should not be completed. 1. But, if the place is already made religious, the *pontifices* ought to decide how far it is possible to meet the need of putting the structure in proper condition with due regard to religion.

3. AVERROES, *ON THE HARMONY OF RELIGION AND PHILOSOPHY*

The preservation of ancient Greek and Roman texts in the East owes a great deal to the revival of Eastern interest in these works after the ninth century, particularly in certain Islamic intellectual centers such as Baghdad in the Middle East and Cordoba in Spain. Islamic rulers encountered Greek learning when they conquered Syria during the seventh century. Greek studies were still vital in these regions, and in the ninth century, the Muslim caliphs of Baghdad encouraged the translation of works by Euclid, Archimedes, Ptolemy, Galen, Hippocrates, and Aristotle into Arabic. These translations laid the basis for the golden age of Islamic scholarship of the tenth and eleventh centuries when men such as al-Khwarizimi (d. 846), al-Razid (d. 925), Alfarabi (d. 950) and Avicenna (d. 1037) combined classical and Islamic learning to advance knowledge on medicine and mathematics far beyond that of Western Europe. Al-Khwarizmi was particularly important for developing algebra. Geometry was familiar to Islamic scholars but algebra and other fields of mathematics developed from the numerical system devised by Al-Kwarizmi. He combined his knowledge of Indian mathematics with that of the Greeks, developing in the process the numbers 0 through 9. The spread of Muslim knowledge about mathematics to the West by the sixteenth century laid the foundations for the groundbreaking work of Early Modern individuals such as Galileo Galilei in astronomy, mechanics, physics, and other scientific fields.

Islamic absorption of Greek philosophy, along with mathematics, also brought previously unknown Greek philosophical texts by Aristotle, Plato, and others to the attention of Western philosophers. Along with Avicenna, one of the most important of the Muslim transmitters of Aristotle to the west was Averroes (1226–1198). Averroes (Ibn Rushd) was born in Cordoba in Spain. So influential was he during the Middle Ages that his Eastern-influenced interpretation of Aristotlean thought stimulated the emergence of a philosophical school at the University of Paris, the most important theological center in Western Europe, by the end of fifteenth century. The following text by Averroes was not known until much later in the West, but it nevertheless reflects the influence of classical learning, particularly that of Aristotle and Plato, on Islamic religious thought by the end of the eleventh century. Averroes revered ancient Greek philosophy, and he considered Aristotle the greatest of all the Greek philosophers. His profound admiration for the pagan Aristotle convinced him that the philosopher was singled out for greatness by the God of Islam as an agent of divine authority on earth. In the following excerpt, Averroes explains why rational philosophy is not antithetical to Muslim scripture (the Qu'ran).

The Decisive Treatise, Determining the Nature of the Connection Between Religion and Philosophy

[What Is the Attitude of the Law to Philosophy?]

Thus spoke the lawyer, *imām*, judge, and unique scholar, Abul Walīd Muhammad Ibn Abmad Ibn Rushd:

Praise be to God with all due praise, and a prayer for Muhammad His chosen servant and apostle. The purpose of this treatise is to examine, from the standpoint of the study of the Law, whether the study of philosophy and logic is allowed by the Law, or prohibited, or commanded—either by way of recommendation or as obligatory.

[Chapter One]

[The Law Makes Philosophic Studies Obligatory]

[If Teleological Study of the World is Philosophy, and If the Law Commands Such a Study, Then the Law Commands Philosophy.]

We say: If the activity of 'philosophy' is nothing more than study of existing beings and reflection on them as indications of the Artisan, i.e inasmuch as they are products of art (for beings only indicate the Artisan through our knowledge of the art in them, and the more perfect this knowledge is, the more perfect the knowledge of the Artisan becomes), and if the Law has encouraged and urged reflection on beings, then it is clear that what this name signifies is either obligatory or recommended by the Law.

[The Law Commands Such a Study.]

That the Law summons to reflection on beings, and the pursuit of knowledge about them, by the intellect is clear from several verses of the Book of God, Blessed and Exalted, such as the saying of the Exalted, 'Reflect, you have vision:' this is textual authority for the obligation to use intellectual reasoning, or a combination of intellectual and legal reasoning. Another example is His saying, 'Have they not studied the kingdom of the heavens and the earth, and whatever things God has created?: this is a text urging the study of the totality of beings. Again, God the Exalted has taught that one of those whom He singularly honoured by this knowledge was Abraham, peace on him, for the Exalted said, 'So we made Abraham see the kingdom of the heavens and the earth, that he might be' [and so on to the end of the verse]. The Exalted also said, 'Do they not observe the camels, how they have been created, and the sky, how it has been raised up?', and He said, 'and they give thought to the creation of the heavens and the earth', and so on in countless other verses.

[This Study Must be Conducted in the Best Manner, by Demonstrative Reasoning.]

Since it has now been established that the Law has rendered obligatory the study of beings by the intellect, and reflection on them, and since reflection is nothing more than inference and drawing out of the unknown from the known, and since this is reasoning or at any rate done by reasoning, therefore we are under an obligation to carry on our study of beings by intellectual reasoning. It is further evident that this manner of study, to which the Law summons and urges, is the most perfect kind of study using the most perfect line of reasoning; and this is the kind called 'demonstration'.

[To master this instrument the religious thinker must make a preliminary study of logic, just as the lawyer must study legal reasoning. This is no more heretical in the one case than in the other. And logic must be learned from the ancient masters, regardless of the fact that they were not Muslims.]

The Law, then, has urged us to have demonstrative knowledge of God the Exalted and all the beings of His creation. But it is preferable and even necessary for anyone, who wants to understand God the Exalted and the other beings demonstratively, to have first understood the kinds of demonstration and their conditions [of validity], and in what respects demonstrative reasoning differs from dialectical, rhetorical and fallacious reasoning. But this is not possible unless he has previously learned what reasoning as such is, and how many kinds it has, and which of them are valid and which invalid. This in turn is not possible unless he has previously learned the parts of reasoning, of which it is composed, i.e. the premisses and their kinds. Therefore he who believes in the Law, and obeys its command to study beings, ought prior to his study to gain a knowledge of these things, which have the same place in theoretical studies as instruments have in practical activities.

For just as the lawyer infers from the Divine command to him to acquire knowledge of the legal categories that he is under obligation to know the various kinds of legal syllogisms, and which are valid and which invalid, in the same way he who would know [God] ought to infer from the command to study beings that he is under obligation to acquire a knowledge of intellectual reasoning and its kinds. Indeed it is more fitting for him to do so, for if the lawyer infers from the saying of the Exalted, 'Reflect, you who have vision', the obligation to acquire a knowledge of legal reasoning, how much more fitting and proper that he who would know God should infer from it the obligation to acquire a knowledge of intellectual reasoning!

It cannot be objected: 'This kind of study of intellectual reasoning is a heretical innovation since it did not exist among the first believers.' For the study of legal reasoning and its kinds is also something which has been discovered since the first believers, yet it is not considered to be a heretical innovation. So the objector should believe the same about the study of intellectual reasoning. (For this there is a reason, which it is not the place to mention here.) But most <masters> of this religion support intellectual reasoning, except a small group of gross literalists, who can be refuted by [sacred] texts.

Since it has now been established that there is an obligation of the Law to study intellectual reasoning and its kinds, just as there is an obligation to study legal reasoning, it is clear that, if none of our predecessors had formerly examined intellectual reasoning and its kinds, we should be obliged to undertake such an examination from the beginning, and that each succeeding scholar would have to seek help in that task from his predecessor in order that knowledge of the subject might be completed. For it is difficult or impossible for one man to find out by himself and from the beginning all that he needs of that subject, as it is difficult for one man to discover all the knowledge that he needs of the kinds of legal reasoning; indeed this is even truer of knowledge of intellectual reasoning.

But if someone other than ourselves has already examined that subject, it is clear that we ought to seek help towards our goal from what has been said by such a predecessor on the subject, regardless of whether this other one shares our religion or not. For when a valid sacrifice is performed with a certain instrument, no account is taken, in judging the validity of the sacrifice, of whether the instrument belongs to one who shares our religion or to one who does not, so long as it fulfils the conditions for validity. By 'those who do not share our religion' I refer to those ancients who studied these matters before Islam. So if such is the case, and everything that is required in the study of the subject of intellectual syllogisms has already been examined in the most perfect manner by the ancients, presumably we ought to lay hands on their books in order to study what they said about the subject; and if it is all correct we should accept it from them, while if there is anything incorrect in it, we should draw attention to that.

[After logic we must proceed to philosophy proper. Here too we have to learn from our predecessors, just as in mathematics and law. Thus it is wrong to forbid the study of ancient philosophy. Harm from it is accidental, like harm from taking medicine, drinking water, or studying law.]

When we have finished with this sort of study and acquired the instruments by whose aid we are able to reflect on beings and the indications of art in them (for he who does not understand the art does not understand the product of art, and he who does not understand the product of art does not understand the Artisan), then we ought to begin the examination of beings in the order and manner we have learned from the art of demonstrative syllogisms.

And again it is clear that in the study of beings this aim can be fulfilled by us perfectly only through successive examinations of them by one man after another, the later ones seeking the help of the earlier in that task, on the model of what has happened in the mathematical sciences. For if we suppose that the art of geometry did not exist in this age of ours, and likewise the art of astronomy, and a single person wanted to ascertain by himself the sizes of the heavenly bodies, their shapes, and their distances from each other, that would not be possible for him—e.g. to know the proportion of the sun to the earth or other facts about the sizes of the stars—even though he were the most intelligent of men by nature, unless by a revelation or something resembling revelation. Indeed if he were told that the sun is about 150 or 160 times as great as the earth, he would think this statement madness on the part of the speaker, although this is a fact which has been demonstrated in astronomy so surely that no one who has mastered that science doubts it.

But what calls even more strongly for comparison with the art of mathematics in this respect is the art of the principles of law; and the study of law itself was completed only over a long period of time. And if someone today wanted to find out by himself all the arguments which have been discovered by the theorists of the legal schools on controversial questions, about which debate has taken place between them in most countries of Islam (except the West), he would deserve to be ridiculed, because such a task is impossible for him, apart from the fact that the work has been done already. Moreover, this is a situation that is self-evident not in the scientific arts alone but also in the practical arts; for there is not one of them which a single man can construct by himself. Then how can he do it with the art of arts, philosophy? If this is so, then whenever we find in the works of our predecessors of former nations a theory about beings and a reflection on them conforming to what the conditions of demonstration require, we ought to study what they said about the matter and what they affirmed in their books. And we should accept from them gladly and gratefully whatever in these books accords with the truth, and draw attention to and warn against what does not accord with the truth, at the same time excusing them.

From this it is evident that the study of the books of the ancients is obligatory by law, since their aim and purpose in their books is just the purpose to which the Law has urged us, and that whoever forbids the study of them to anyone who is fit to study them, i.e. anyone who unites two qualities, (1) natural intelligence and (2) religious integrity and moral virtue, is blocking people from the door by which the Law summons them to knowledge of God, the door of theoretical study which leads to the truest knowledge of him; and such an act is the extreme of ignorance and estrangement from God the Exalted.

And if someone errs or stumbles in the study of these books owing to a deficiency in his natural capacity, or bad organization of his study of them, or being dominated by his passions, or not finding a teacher to guide them to an understanding of their contents, or a combination of all or more than one of these causes, it does not follow that one should forbid them to anyone who is qualified to study them. For this manner of harm which arises owing to them is something that is attached to them by accident, not by essence; and when a thing is beneficial by its nature and essence, it ought not to be shunned because of something harmful contained in it by accident. This was the thought of the Prophet, peace on him, on the occasion when he ordered a man to give his brother honey to drink for his diarrhoea, and the diarrhoea increased after he had given him the honey: when the man complained to him about it, he said, 'God spoke the truth; it was your brother's stomach that lied.' We can even say that a man who prevents a qualified person from studying books of philosophy, because some of the most vicious people may be thought to have gone astray through their study of them, is like a man who prevents a thirsty person from drinking cool, fresh water until he dies of thirst, because some people have choked to death on it. For death from water by choking is an accidental matter, but death by thirst is essential and necessary.

Moreover, this accidental effect of this art is a thing which may also occur accidentally from the other arts. To how many lawyers has law been a cause of lack of piety and immersion in this world! Indeed we find most lawyers in this state, although their art by its essence calls for nothing but practical virtue. Thus it is not strange if the same thing that occurs accidentally in the art which calls for practical virtue should occur accidentally in the art which calls for intellectual virtue.

4. THOMAS AQUINAS, *SUMMA THEOLOGICA*

The recovery of Aristotle's entire corpus of work during the twelfth century radically transformed European intellectual and spiritual life. The appeal of this fourth-century B.C. pagan Greek philosopher for medieval Christian thinkers lay not only in his sophisticated, comprehensive, and systematic study of such diverse fields as biology, politics, philosophy, rhetoric, and poetics, but also in Aristotle's pronounced preoccupation with morality and ethics. Like his teacher Plato, Aristotle believed that a real understanding of the cosmos and the individual's place within it was possible, and that the exercise of human reason would lead toward this understanding. For these ancient thinkers, the correct exercise of reason would lead to enlightenment, and enlightenment guided the individual to virtue. Aristotle's preoccupation with ethics had a profound influence upon many scholastic theologians, including Thomas Aquinas (1225–1274), one of the greatest Christian theologians. The son of a southern Italian baron, the Count of Aquino, Thomas Aquinas joined the Dominican order in 1244. After spending years studying under the great Dominican scholar Albertus Magnus (1206/7–1280) in Cologne, Aquinas was sent to teach at the Dominican school at the University of Paris in 1252. It was here at Paris that Aquinas undertook and completed his massive synthesis of Christian learning known as the *Summa Theologica*. In this work, Aquinas uses rational inquiry to examine and resolve inconsistencies in Christian spiritual texts. He was convinced that classical philosophy was essential to salvation, and his challenge with the *Summa* was to reconcile classical emphasis upon reason with Christian insistence upon faith. However, his admiration for classical philosophy never outweighed his belief in divine revelation. Aquinas asserts in his *Summa Theologica* that divine revelation was necessary for humans because certain truths essential to salvation could not be attained by human reason. Reason was ultimately subordinated to faith as a source of truth in the work of Aquinas, and he did not hesitate to criticize Aristotle when his conclusions contradicted divine revelation. The following excerpt discussing the unity of the body and soul reflects the influence of Aristotlean logic and natural philosophy upon Aquinas.

Summa Theologica

Question LXXVI

Of the Union of Body and Soul. (In Eight Articles.)

We now consider the union of the soul with the body; and concerning this there are eight points for inquiry: (1) Whether the intellectual principle is united to the body as its form? (2) Whether the intellectual principle is multiplied numerically according to the number of bodies; or is there one intelligence for all men? (3) Whether in the body the form of which is an intellectual principle, there is some other soul? (4) Whether in the body there is any other substantial form? (5) Of the qualities required in the body of which the intellectual principle is the form? (6) Whether it be united to such a body by means of another body? (7) Whether by means of an accident? (8) Whether the soul is wholly in each part of the body?

First Article. Whether the Intellectual Principle Is United to the Body as Its Form?

We proceed thus to the First Article:—

Objection 1. It seems that the intellectual principle is not united to the body as its form. For the Philosopher says (*De Anima* iii. 4) that the intellect is *separate,* and that it is not the act of any body. Therefore it is not united to the body as its form.

Obj. 2. Further, every form is determined according to the nature of the matter of which it is the form; otherwise no proportion would be required between matter and form. Therefore if the intellect were united to the body as its form, since every body has a determinate nature, it would follow that the intellect has a determinate nature; and thus, it would not be capable of knowing all things, as is clear from what has been said (Q. LXXV., A. 2); which is contrary to the nature of the intellect. Therefore the intellect is not united to the body as its form.

Obj. 3. Further, whatever receptive power is an act of a body, receives a form materially and individually; for what is received must be received according to the condition of the receiver. But the form of the thing understood is not received into the intellect materially and individually, but rather immaterially and universally: otherwise the intellect would not be capable of the knowledge of immaterial and universal objects, but only of individuals, like the senses. Therefore the intellect is not united to the body as its form.

Obj. 4. Further, power and action have the same subject; for the same subject is what can, and does, act. But the intellectual action is not the action of a body, as appears from above (Q. LXXV., A. 2). Therefore neither is the intellectual faculty a power of the body. But virtue or power cannot be more abstract or more simple than the essence from which the faculty or power is derived. Therefore neither is the substance of the intellect the form of a body.

Obj. 5. Further, whatever has *per se* existence is not united to the body as its form; because a form is that by which a thing exists: so that the very existence of a form does not belong to the form by itself. But the intellectual principle has *per se* existence and is subsistent, as was said above (Q. LXXV., A. 2). Therefore it is not united to the body as its form.

Obj. 6. Further, whatever exists in a thing by reason of its nature exists in it always. But to be united to matter belongs to the form by reason of its nature; because form is the act of matter, not by any accidental quality, but by its own essence; otherwise matter and form would not make a thing substantially one, but only accidentally one. Therefore a form cannot be without its own proper matter. But the intellectual principle, since it is incorruptible, as was shown above (Q. LXXV., A. 6), remains separate from the body, after the dissolution of the body. Therefore the intellectual principle is not united to the body as its form.

On the contrary, According to the Philosopher, *Metaph.* viii. (Did. vii. 2), difference is derived from the form. But the difference which constitutes man is *rational,* which is applied to man on account of his intellectual principle. Therefore the intellectual principle is the form of man.

I answer that, We must assert that the intellect which is the principle of intellectual operation is the form of the human body. For that whereby primarily anything acts is a form of the thing to which the act is to be attributed: for instance, that whereby a body is primarily healed is health, and that whereby the soul knows primarily is knowledge; hence health is a form of the body, and knowledge is a form of the soul. The reason is because nothing acts except so far as it is in act; wherefore a thing acts by that whereby it is in act. Now it is clear that the first thing by which the body lives is the soul. And as life appears through various operations in different degrees of living things, that whereby we primarily perform each of all these vital actions is the soul. For the soul is the primary principle of our nourishment, sensation, and local movement; and likewise of our understanding. Therefore this principle by which we primarily understand, whether it be called the intellect or the intellectual soul, is the form of the body. This is the demonstration used by Aristotle (*De Anima* ii. 2).

But if anyone say that the intellectual soul is not the form of the body he must first explain how it is that this action of understanding is the action of this particular man; for each one is conscious that it is himself who understands. Now an action may be attributed to anyone in three ways, as is clear from the Philosopher (*Phys.* v. 1); for a thing is said to move or act, either by virtue of its whole self, for instance, as a physician heals; or by virtue of a part, as a man sees by his eye; or through an accidental quality, as when we say that something this is white builds, because it is accidental to the builder to be white. So when we say that Socrates or Plato understands, it is clear that this is not attributed to him accidentally; since it is ascribed to him as man, which is predicated of him essentially. We must therefore say either that Socrates understands by virtue of his whole self, as Plato maintained, holding that man is an intellectual soul; or that intelligence is a part of Socrates. The first cannot stand, as was shown above (Q. LXXV., A. 4), for this reason, that it is one and the same man who is conscious both that he understands, and that he senses. But one cannot sense without a body: therefore the body must be some part of man. It follows therefore that the intellect by which Socrates understands is a part of Socrates, so that in some way it is united to the body of Socrates.

The Commentator held that this union is through the intelligible species, as having a double subject, in the possible intellect, and in the phantasms which are in the corporeal organs. Thus through the intelligible species the possible intellect is linked to the body of this or that particular man. But this link or union does not sufficiently explain the fact, that the act of the intellect is the act of Socrates. This can be clearly seen from comparison with the sensitive faculty, from which Aristotle proceeds to consider things relating to the intellect. For the relation of phantasms to the intellect is like the relation of colours to the sense of sight, as he says in *De Anima* iii. 5, 7. Therefore, as the species of colours are in the sight, so are the species of phantasms in the possible intellect. Now it is clear that because the colours, the images of which are in the sight, are on a wall, the action of seeing is not attributed to the wall: for we do not say that the wall sees, but rather that it is seen. Therefore, from the fact that the species of phantasms are in the possible intellect, it does not follow that Socrates, in whom are the phantasms, understands, but that he or his phantasms are understood.

Some, however, tried to maintain that the intellect is united to the body as its motor; and hence that the intellect and body form one thing so that the act of the intellect could be attributed to the whole. This is, however, absurd for many reasons. First, because the intellect does not move the body except through the appetite, the movement of which presupposes the operation of the intellect. The reason therefore why Socrates understands is not because he is moved by his intellect, but rather, contrariwise, he is moved by his intellect because he understands. Secondly, because, since Socrates is an individual in a nature of one essence composed of matter and form, if the intellect be not the form, it follows that it must be outside the essence, and then the intellect is to the whole Socrates as a motor to the thing moved. Whereas the act of intellect remains in the agent, and does not pass into something else, as does the action of heating. Therefore the action of understanding cannot be attributed to Socrates for the reason that he is moved by his intellect. Thirdly, because the action of a motor is never attributed to the thing moved, except as to an instrument; as the action of a carpenter to a saw. Therefore if understanding is attributed to Socrates, as the action of what moves him, it follows that it is attributed to him as to an instrument. This is contrary to the teaching of the Philosopher, who holds that understanding is not possible through a corporeal instrument (*De Anima* iii. 4). Fourthly, because, although the action of a part be attributed to the whole, as the action of the eye is attributed to a man; yet it is never attributed to another part, except perhaps indirectly; for we do not say that the hand sees because the eye sees. Therefore if the intellect and Socrates are united in the above manner, the action of the intellect cannot be attributed to Socrates. If, however, Socrates be a whole composed of a union of the intellect with whatever else belongs to Socrates, and still the intellect be united to those other things only as a motor, it follows that Socrates is not one absolutely, and consequently neither a being absolutely, for a thing is a being according as it is one.

There remains, therefore, no other explanation than that given by Aristotle—namely, that this particular man understands, because the intellectual principle is his form. Thus from the very operation of the intellect it is made clear that the intellectual principle is united to the body as its form.

The same can be clearly shown from the nature of the human species. For the nature of each thing is shown by its operation. Now the proper operation of man as man is to understand; because he thereby surpasses all other animals. Whence Aristotle concludes (*Ethic.* x. 7) that the ultimate happiness of man must consist in this operation as properly belonging to him. Man must therefore derive his species from that which is the principle of this operation. But the species of anything is derived from its form. It follows therefore that the intellectual principle is the proper form of man.

But we must observe that the nobler a form is, the more it rises above corporeal matter, the less it is merged in matter, and the more it excels matter by its power and its operation; hence we find that the form of a mixed body has another operation not caused by its elemental qualities. And the higher we advance in the nobility of forms, the more we find that the power of the form excels the elementary matter; as the vegetative soul excels the form of the metal, and the sensitive soul excels the vegetative soul. Now the human soul is the highest and noblest of forms. Wherefore it excels corporeal matter in its power by the fact that it has an operation and a power in which corporeal matter has no share whatever. This power is called the intellect.

It is well to remark that if anyone holds that the soul is composed of matter and form, it would follow that in no way could the soul be the form of the body. For since the form is an act, and matter is only in potentiality, that which is composed of matter and form cannot be the form of another by virtue of itself as a whole. But if it is a form by virtue of some part of itself, then that part which is the form we call the soul, and that of which it is the form we call the *primary animate,* as was said above (Q. LXXV., A. 5).

Reply Obj. 1. As the Philosopher says (*Phys.* ii. 2), the ultimate natural form to which the consideration of the natural philosopher is directed is indeed separate; yet it exists in matter. He proves this form the fact that *man and the sun generate man from matter.* It is separate indeed according to its intellectual power, because the intellectual power does not belong to a corporeal organ, as the power of seeing is the act of the eye; for understanding is an act which cannot be performed by a corporeal organ, like the act of seeing. But it exists in matter so far as the soul itself, to which this power belongs, is the form of the body, and the term of human generation. And so the Philosopher says (*De Anima* iii.) that the intellect is separate, because it is not the faculty of a corporeal organ.

From this it is clear how to answer the Second and Third objections: since, in order that man may be able to understand all things by means of his intellect, and that his intellect may understand immaterial things and universals, it is sufficient that the intellectual power be not the act of the body.

Reply Obj. 4. The human soul, by reason of its perfection, is not a form merged in matter, or entirely embraced by matter. Therefore there is nothing to prevent some power thereof not being the act of the body, although the soul is essentially the form of the body.

Reply Obj. 5. The soul communicates that existence in which it subsists to the corporeal matter, out of which and the intellectual soul there results unity of existence; so that the existence of the whole composite is also the existence of the soul. This is not the case with other non-subsistent forms. For this reason the human soul retains its own existence after the dissolution of the body; whereas it is not so with other forms.

Reply Obj. 6. To be united to the body belongs to the soul by reason of itself, as it belongs to a light body by reason of itself to be raised up. And as a light body remains light, when removed from its proper place, retaining meanwhile an aptitude and an inclination for its proper place; so the human soul retains its proper existence when separated from the body, having an aptitude and a natural inclination to be united to the body.

Figure 5.1 Ibn Ezra, Abraham ben Meir. *De nativitatibus*. Venice: Erhard Ratdolt, 1485. Rare Books Division. J. Willard Marriott Library, University of Utah.

Note: Ibn Ezra (1092–1167) was a well-known Arabic twelfth-century astronomer. The *De Nativitatibus* is one of eight astrological treatises written by him in 1148, and this particular treatise describes the planetary influences upon man's fate at the time of his birth. The publishing of this text in Venice during the fifteenth century reflects the continuing influence of Arabic learning upon Western thought. In fact, it is probable that this work was translated by Peter D'Abano, a famous fifteenth-century scholar of astronomy at the University of Padua.

Study Questions

1. Why was the Justinian Code so useful for twelfth-century Europe?
2. Why do Averroes and Thomas Aquinas try to reconcile Aristotle with their own spiritual traditions?
3. Why do you think that Avereroes's work became so influential in Western Europe?
4. From the account of Villani, how did contact with the East shape fourteenth-century Florence?

Suggested Readings

Abulafia, David. *The Two Italies: Economic Relations between the Norman Kingdom of Sicily and the Northern Communes.* Cambridge: Cambridge University Press, 1977.

Brundage, James A. *Medieval Canon Law.* New York: Longman, 1995.

Cipolla, Carlo M. *Before the Industrial Revolution: European Society and Economy, 1000–1700.* New York: Norton, 1980.

Colish, Marsha L. *Medieval Foundations of the Western Intellectual Tradition, 400–1400.* New Haven: Yale University Press, 1997.

Web Sites

1. Thomas Aquinas

   http://plato.stanford.edu/entries/aquinas

2. Gratian's *Decretum*

   http://www.dia.org/collections/euroart/introduction/61.248.html

3. Giovanni Villani, *Chronicle*

   http://www.fordham.edu/halsall/source/villani.html

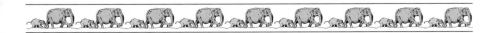

6

General Worldview on the Eve of Exploration
1480–1600 A.D.

TEXTS

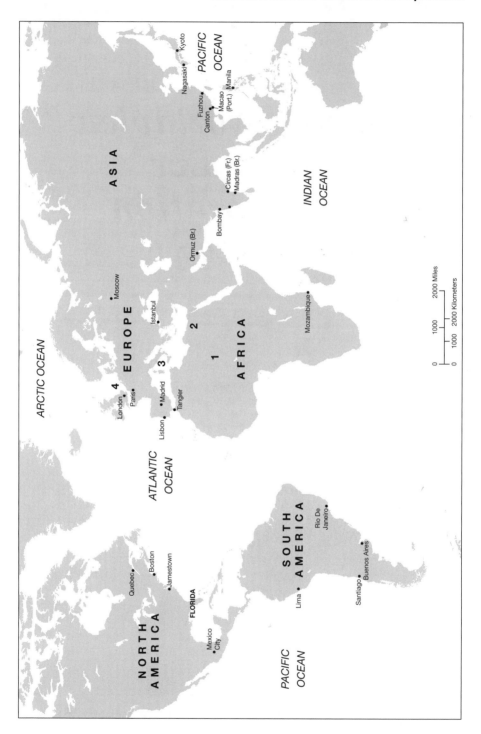

The explorers who set out across the Atlantic at the end of the fifteenth century were products of a very different European society than were their crusader predecessors. European cities were larger, and once small kingdoms were growing in size and power under the rule of expansionist monarchs such as Charles VIII (1483–1498) and Louis XII (1498–1515) of France, Henry VII (1485–1509) of England, and the Spanish rulers Isabella of Castile (1474–1504) and Ferdinand II of Aragon (1479–1516). Literacy was increasing, and the new invention, the printing press, was making popular as well as scholarly texts more affordable and accessible. European society was also in the throes of a new literary and artistic culture known as the Renaissance. The Renaissance owed its initial impetus to Francesco Petrarch (1304–1374) who found in classical Latin literature a rhetorical style and moral content more appealing to him than that of most medieval literature. For Petrarch, the entire period from the fall of the Roman Empire to his own day was an intellectual "dark age," an age in which scholastic thinkers debated unimportant philosophical and theological points rather than wrestling with the more pertinent concerns of humankind. Petrarch and later Renaissance (humanist) scholars were particularly drawn to classical celebration of the "rational" nature of humanity, urban life, and the pursuit of virtue in human society rather than in withdrawal from it. Thirsty for ancient moral and ethical wisdom, Renaissance scholars searched in monastic and private libraries across Europe, North Africa, and the Middle East in pursuit of previously undiscovered texts. They copied, translated, and edited these works for broader public consumption and used the printing press to transmit these works throughout Europe. The men and women who engaged in the "new learning" became famous for their mastery of ancient and modern languages, classical prose style, and, above all, their critical analysis of ancient texts.

By the fifteenth century, humanist linguistic and textual skills were applied to nonliterary fields such as law, science, and medicine. Humanism had a particularly profound impact, however, on religion. Concern about the state of religion in Europe was growing in Europe by the middle of the fifteenth century, especially with regard to the leadership of the Catholic Church. The return of the papacy to Rome following the end of the Babylonian Captivity and the papal Schism (1378–1415) did not lead to the general spiritual reformation hoped for by many lay and clerical Catholics. Renaissance popes such as Alexander IV (1492–1503) showed more interest in expanding their own political power and wealth than in reforming a church that was already notorious for the selling of clerical offices, moral laxity, and the poor training of priests. Convinced that the church had strayed from its true spiritual role, scholars such as Desiderius Erasmus (1466–1536) applied humanist critical methodology to the texts of the early Christian Church fathers in pursuit of a purer model of Christian community and source of Christian doctrine. In using these texts to attack the existing church structure and practices, however, these Christian humanists unleashed enormous religious debate in Europe and arguably paved the way for Martin Luther's public rejection of the Catholic Church in 1521. Christian humanism was not responsible, however, for the increasing violence with which Catholic Europeans began to treat those of differing faiths over the course of the sixteenth century. The Spanish monarchs Ferdinand and Isabella in particular earned a reputation by the end of the fifteenth century as rulers determined to transform their kingdoms of Aragon and Castile into wholly Christian lands. Between 1478 and 1492, these two monarchs defeated the last Muslim kingdom in Spain, Granada, and introduced an Inquisition to investigate Muslim *(moriscos)* and Jewish *(conversos)* converts suspected of returning to their old faith. In 1492, Isabella and Ferdinand expelled all professed Jews from their kingdoms. As many as 150,000 of 200,000 estimated Jews fled Spain as a result of this decree. The same year, therefore, that saw Columbus reach the Americas and sparked European interest in lands across the Atlantic also initiated a new period of increasing spiritual intolerance on the part of Europeans.

The four texts selected here reflect some of the more important ideological conceptions that informed the minds of the first generation of Early Modern European explorers. The medieval travelogue *The Travels of Sir John Mandeville* [1] and Strabo's *Geography* [2] were two texts relied upon by Columbus and his contemporaries as authorities on distant lands, showing the continuing power during this period of classical and Medieval assumptions about the world. The treatises of Pico della Mirandola and Desiderius Erasmus [3, 4] reflect the influence of Renaissance conceptions of humanity and spirituality during the late fifteenth and sixteenth centuries.

1. THE TRAVELS OF SIR JOHN MANDEVILLE

Although its authorship was contested from early on, the popular Medieval travel text *Travels of Sir John Mandeville* (ca. 1356) continued to circulate widely in Europe throughout the Early Modern period. This text recounts the fictional pilgrimage of Sir John Mandeville to Palestine. His travels, however, also take him much farther east to India and to Cathay (China). In its determination to provoke in the reader a desire for spiritual reformation, the *Travels* is typical of medieval pilgrimage accounts. However, its colorful, sensual descriptions of eastern lands captured the imaginations of Europeans such as Christopher Columbus. Columbus took his copy of the *Travels* with him when he left Spain in 1492 in search for a new route to the eastern spice trade. For Columbus, as for many of his contemporaries, the *Travels* was considered a reliable source of geographic and cultural information on regions in the East until the exploratory journeys of the late fifteenth and sixteenth centuries provided more accurate information. The following excerpt is a description of the kingdom of Prester John. During a time when Muslim cultures predominated in North Africa and Asia Minor, tales of the distant, beautiful, wealthy Christian kingdom ruled by Prester John appealed enormously to Christian Europeans. The *Travels* provide one of many competing descriptions of this land. According to the *Travels,* the land of Prester John lay somewhere in Cathay.

The Travels of Sir John Mandeville

Chapter XXXI

Of the Devil's Head in the Valley Perilous. And of the Customs of Folk in diverse Isles that be about in the Lordship of Prester John.

Beside that Isle of Mistorak upon the left side nigh to the river of Pison is a marvelous thing. There is a vale between the mountains, that dureth nigh a four mile. And some men clepe it the Vale Enchanted, some clepe it the Vale of Devils, and some clepe it the Vale Perilous. In that vale hear men often-time great tempests and thunders, and great murmurs and noises, all days and nights, and great noise, as it were sound of tabors and of nakers and of trumps, as though it were of a great feast. This vale is all full of devils, and hath been always. And men say there, that it is one of the entries of hell. In that vale is great plenty of gold and silver. Wherefore many misbelieving men, and many Christian men also, go in oftentime for to have of the treasure that there is; but few come again, and namely of the misbelieving men, ne of the Christian men neither, for anon they be strangled of devils.

And in mid place of that vale, under a rock, is an head and the visage of a devil bodily, full horrible and dreadful to see, and it sheweth not but the head, to the shoulders. But there is no man in the world so hardy, Christian man ne other, but that he would be adread to behold it, and that it would seem him to die for dread, so is it hideous for to behold. For he beholdeth every man so sharply with dreadful eyen, that be evermore moving and sparkling as fire, and changeth and stirreth so often in diverse manner, with so horrible countenance, that no man dare not neighen towards him. And from him cometh out smoke and stinking fire and so much abomination, that unnethe no man may there endure.

But the good Christian men, that be stable in the faith, enter well without peril. For they will first shrive them and mark them with the token of the holy cross, so that the fiends ne have no power over them. But albeit that they be without peril, yet, natheles, ne be they not without dread, when that they see the devils visibly and bodily all about them, that make full many diverse assaults and menaces, in air and in earth, and aghast them with strokes of thunder-blasts and of tempests. And the most dread is, that God will take vengeance then of that that men have misdone against his will.

And ye shall understand, that when my fellows and I were in that vale, we were in great thought, whether that we durst put our bodies in adventure, to go in or not, in the protection of God. And some of our fellows accorded to enter, and some not. So there were with us two worthy men, friars minors, that were of Lombardy, that said, that if any man would enter they would go in with us. And when they had said so, upon the gracious trust of God and of them, we let sing mass, and made every man to be shriven and houseled. And then we entered fourteen persons; but at our going out we were but nine. And so we wist never, whether that our fellows were lost, or else turned again for dread. But we saw them never after; and those were two men of Greece, and three of Spain. And our other fellows that would not go in with us, they went by another coast to be before us; and so they were.

And thus we passed that perilous vale, and found therein gold and silver, and precious stones and rich jewels, great plenty, both here and there, as us seemed. But whether that it was, as us seemed, I wot never. For I touched none, because that the devils be so subtle to make a thing to seem otherwise than it is, for to deceive mankind. And therefore I touched none, and also because that I would not be put out of my devotion; for I was more devout then, than ever I was before or after, and all for the dread of fiends that I saw in diverse figures, and also for the great multitude of dead bodies, that I saw there lying by the way, by all the vale, as though there had been a battle between two kings, and the mightiest of the country, and that the greater part had been discomfited and slain. And I trow, that unnethe should any country have so much people within him, as lay slain in that vale as us thought, the which was an hideous sight to see. And I marveled much, that there were so many, and the bodies all whole without rotting. But I trow, that fiends made them seem to be so whole without rotting. But that might not be to mine advice that so many should have entered so newly, ne so many newly slain, without stinking and rotting. And many of them were in habit of Christian men, but I trow well, that it were of such that went in for covetise of the treasure that was there, and had overmuch feebleness in the faith; so that their hearts ne might not endure in the belief for dread. And therefore were we the more devout a great deal. And yet we were cast down, and beaten down many times to the hard earth by winds and thunders and tempests. But evermore God of his grace holp us. And so we passed that perilous vale without peril and without encumbrance, thanked be Almighty God.

After this, beyond the vale, is a great isle, where the folk be great giants of twenty-eight foot long, or of thirty foot long. And they have no clothing but of skins of beasts that they hang upon them. And they eat no bread, but all raw flesh; and they drink milk of beasts, for they have plenty of all bestial. And they have no houses to lie in. And they eat more gladly Man's flesh than any other flesh. Into that isle dare no man gladly enter. And if they see a ship and men therein, anon they enter into the sea for to take them.

And men said us, that in an isle beyond that were giants of greater stature, some of forty-five foot, or of fifty foot long, and, as some men say, some of fifty cubits long. But I saw none of those, for I had no lust to go to those parts, because that no man cometh neither into that isle ne into the other, but if he be devoured anon. And among those giants be sheep as great as oxen here, and they bear great wool and rough. Of the sheep I have seen many times. And men have seen, many times, those giants take men in the sea out of their ships, and brought them to land, two in one hand and two in another, eating them going, all raw and all quick.

Another isle is there toward the north, in the sea Ocean, where that be full cruel and full evil women of nature. And they have precious stones in their eyen. And they be of that kind, that if they behold any man with wrath, they slay him anon with the beholding, as doth the basilisk.

Another isle is there, full fair and good and great, and full of people, where the custom is such, that the first night that they be married, they make another man to lie by their wives for to have their maidenhead: and therefore they take great hire and great thank. And there be certain men in every town that serve of none other thing; and they clepe them cadeberiz, that is to say, the fools of wanhope. For they of the country hold it so great a thing and so perilous for to have the maidenhead of a woman, that them seemeth that they that have first the maidenhead putteth him in adventure of his life. And if the husband find his wife maiden that other next night after that she should have been lain by of the man that is assigned therefore, peradventure for drunkenness or for some other cause, the husband shall plain upon him that he hath not done his devoir, in such cruel wise as though the officers would have slain him. But after the first night that they be lain by, they keep them so straitly that they be not so hardy to speak with no man. And I asked them the cause why that they held such custom: and they said me, that of old time men had been dead for deflowering of maidens, that had serpents in their bodies that stung men upon their yards, that they died anon: and therefore they held that custom, to make other men ordained therefore to lie by their wives, for dread of death, and to assay the passage by another [rather] than for to put them in that adventure.

After that is another isle where that women make great sorrow when their children be y-born. And when they die, they make great feast and great joy and revel, and then they cast them into a great fire burning. And those that love well their husbands, if their husbands be dead, they cast them also in the fire with their children, and burn them. And they say that the fire shall cleanse them of all filths and of all vices, and they shall go pured and clean into another world to their husbands, and they shall lead their children with them. And the cause why that they weep, when their children be born is this; for when they come into this world, they come to labour, sorrow and heaviness. And why they make joy and gladness at their dying is because that, as they say, then they go to Paradise where the rivers run milk and honey, where that men see them in joy and in abundance of goods, without sorrow and labour.

In that isle men make their king evermore by election, and they ne choose him not for no noblesse nor for no riches, but such one as is of good manners and of good conditions, and therewithal rightfull, and also that he be of great age, and that he have no children. In that isle men be full rightfull and they do rightfull judgments in every cause both of rich and poor, small and great, after the quantity of the trespass that is mis-done. And the king may not doom no man to death without assent of his barons and other men wise of counsel, and that all the court accord thereto. And if the king do any homicide or any crime, as to slay a man, or any such case, he shall die there for. But he shall not be slain as another man; but men shall defend, in pain of death, that no man be so hardy to make him company ne to speak with him, ne that no man give him, ne sell him, ne serve him, neither of meat ne of drink; and so shall he die in mischief. They spare no man that hath trespassed, neither for love, ne for favour, ne for riches, ne for noblesse; but that he shall have after that he hath done.

Beyond that isle is another isle, where is great multitude of folk. And they will not, for no thing, eat flesh of hares, ne of hens, ne of geese; and yet they bring forth enough, for to see them and to behold them only; but they eat flesh of all other beasts, and drink milk. In that country they take their daughter and their sisters to their wives, and their other kinswomen. And if there be ten men or twelve men or more dwelling in an house, the wife of everych of them shall be common to them all that dwell in that house; so that every man may lie with whom he will of them on one night, and with another, another night. And if she have any child, she may give it to what man that she list, that hath companied with her, so that no man knoweth there whether the child be his or another's. And if any man say to them, that they nourish other men's children, they answer that so do other men theirs.

In that country and by all Ind be great plenty of cockodrills, that is a manner of a long serpent, as I have said before. And in the night they dwell in the water, and on the day upon the land, in rocks and in caves. And they eat no meat in all the winter, but they lie as in a dream, as do the serpents. These serpents slay men, and they eat them weeping; and when they eat they move the over jaw, and not the nether jaw, and they have no tongue.

In that country and in many other beyond that, and also in many on this half, men put in work the seed of cotton, and they sow it every year. And then groweth it in small trees, that bear cotton. And so do men every year, so that there is plenty of cotton at all times. Item; in this isle and in many other, there is a manner of wood, hard and strong. Whoso covereth the coals of that wood under the ashes thereof, the coals will dwell and abide all quick, a year or more. And that tree hath many leaves, as the juniper hath. And there be also many trees, that of nature they will never burn, ne rot in no manner. And there be nut trees, that bear nuts as great as a man's head.

There also be many beasts, that be clept orafles. In Arabia, they be clept gerfaunts. That is a beast, pomely or spotted, that is but a little more high than is a steed, but he hath the neck a twenty cubits long; and his croup and his tail is as of an hart; and he may look over a great high house. And there be also in that country many camles; that is a little beast as a goat, that is wild, and he liveth by the air and eateth nought, ne drinketh nought, at no time. And he changeth his colour often-time, for men see him often sithes, now in one colour and now in another colour; and he may change him into all manner colours that him list, save only into red and white. There be also in that country passing great serpents, some of six score foot long, and they be of diverse colours, as rayed, red, green, and yellow, blue and black, and all speckled. And there be others that have crests upon their heads, and they go upon their feet, upright, and they be well a four fathom great, or more, and they dwell always in rocks or in mountains, and they have always the throat open, of whence they drop venom always. And there be also wild swine of many colours, as great as be oxen in our country, and they be all spotted, as be young fawns. And there be also urchins, as great as wild swine here; we clepe them Porcz de Spine. And there be lions all white, great and mighty. And there be also of other beasts, as great and more greater than is a destrier, and men clepe them Loerancs; and some men clepe them odenthos; and they have a black head and three long horns trenchant in the front, sharp as a sword, and the body is slender; and he is a full felonious beast, and he chaseth and slayeth the elephant. There be also many other beasts, full wicked and cruel, that be not mickle more than a bear, and they have the head like a boar, and they have six feet, and on every foot two large claws, trenchant; and the body is like a bear, and the tail as a lion. And there be also mice as great as hounds, and yellow mice as great as ravens. And there be geese, all red, three sithes more great than ours here, and they have the head, the neck and the breast all black.

And many other diverse beasts be in those countries, and elsewhere there-about, and many diverse birds also, of the which it were too long for to tell you. And therefore, I pass over at this time.

2. STRABO, GEOGRAPHY

Strabo (64/3 B.C.–ca. 21 A.D.) was a highly respected historian and geographer at a time when the Roman Empire was growing in power throughout the Mediterranean. His peripatetic life brought him to Rome and Egypt for lengthy stays, and it was while in Egypt in particular that he gathered much of his geographical material. The *Geography* is one of his few works to survive, but in itself it is a massive intellectual achievement. Comprising twelve books, the *Geography* is as much a work of historical geography as it is of the philosophy of geography. It gathers together such classical authorities as Herodotus and Polybius and critically evaluates their interpretations. Rich in detailed information, Strabo's most famous work came to exert enormous influence in Europe by the end of the thirteenth century, and it remained a vital source of information for Europeans into the sixteenth century, even though by this time many knew that his text was more accurate on Asia Minor and the Mediterranean lands than it was on Northern Europe and other regions. The continuing reliance of Europeans on Strabo in the face of changing knowledge about the world testifies to the powerful hold classical learning continued to exercise upon the intellectual life of Europeans in the Early Modern period. The following excerpt is taken from the first book of the *Geography*. Here Strabo explains his understanding of the nature and importance of geography as a field of investigation.

The Geography of Strabo

Book I

1. The science of Geography, which I now propose to investigate, is, I think, quite as much as any other science, a concern of the philosopher; and the correctness of my view is clear for many reasons. In the first place, those who in earliest times ventured to treat the subject were, in their way, philosophers—Homer, Anaximander of Miletus, and Anaximander's fellow-citizen Hecataeus—just as Eratostheries had already said; philosophers, too, were Democritus, Eudoxus, Dicaearchus, Ephorus, with several others of their times; and further, their successors—Eratosthenes, Polybius, and Poseidonius—were philosophers. In the second place, wide learning, which alone makes it possible to undertake a work on geography, is possessed solely by the man who has investigated things both human and divine—knowledge of which, they say, constitutes philosophy. And so, too, the utility of geography—and its utility is manifold, not only as regards the activities of statesmen and commanders but also as regards knowledge both of the heavens and of things on land and sea, animals, plants, fruits, and everything else to be seen in various regions—the utility of geography, I say, presupposes in the geographer the same philosopher, the man who busies himself with the investigation of the art of life, that is, of happiness.

2. But I must go back and consider each one of these points in greater detail; and, first, I say that both I and my predecessors, one of whom was Hipparchus himself, are right in regarding Homer as the founder of the science of geography; for Homer has surpassed all men, both of ancient and modern times, not only in the excellence of his poetry, but also, I might say, in his acquaintance with all that pertains to public life. And this acquaintance made him busy himself not only about public activities, to the end that he might learn of as many of them as possible and give an account of them to posterity, but

also about the geography both of the individual countries and of the inhabited world at large, both land and sea; for otherwise he would not have gone to the uttermost bounds of the inhabited world, encompassing the whole of it in his description.

3. In the first place, Homer declares that the inhabited world is washed on all sides by Oceanus, and this is true; and then he mentions some of the countries by name, while he leaves us to infer the other countries from hints; for instance, he expressly mentions Libya, Ethiopia, Sidonians, and Erembians—and by Erembians he probably means Arabian Troglodytes—whereas he only indicates in general terms the people who live in the far east and the far west by saying that their countries are washed by Oceanus. For he makes the sun to rise out of Oceanus and to set in Oceanus; and he refers in the same way to the constellations: "Now the sun was just beating on the fields as he climbed heaven from the deep stream of gently-flowing Oceanus." "And the sun's bright light dropped into Oceanus, drawing black night across the earth." And he declares that the stars also rise from Oceanus "after having bathed in Oceanus."

4. As for the people of the west, Homer makes plain that they were prosperous and that they lived in a temperate climate—doubtless having heard of the wealth of Iberia, and how, in quest of that wealth, Heracles invaded the country, and after him the Phoenicians also, the people who in earliest times became masters of most of the country (it was at a later date that the Romans occupied it). For in the west the breezes of Zephyrus blow; and there it is that Homer places the Elysian Plain itself, to which he declares Menelaus will be sent by the gods: "But the deathless gods will convey thee to the Elysian Plain and the ends of the earth, where is Rhadamanthys of the fair hair, where life is easiest. No snow is there, nor yet great storm; but always Oceanus sendeth forth the breezes of the clear-blowing Zephyrus."

11. For the moment what I have already said is sufficient, I hope, to show that Homer was the first geographer. And, as every one knows, the successors of Homer in geography were also notable men and familiar with philosophy. Erathosthenes declares that the first two successors of Homer were Anaximander, a pupil and fellow-citizen of Thales, and Hecataeus of Miletus; that Anaximander was the first to publish a geographical map, and that Hecataeus left behind him a work on geography, a work believed to be his by reason of its similarity to his other writings.

12. Assuredly, however, there is need of encyclopaedic learning for the study of geography, as many men have already stated; and Hipparchus, too, in his treatise *Against Eratosthenes,* correctly shows that it is impossible for any man, whether layman or scholar, to attain to the requisite knowledge of geography without the determination of the heavenly bodies and of the eclipses which have been observed; for instance, it is impossible to determine whether Alexandria in Egypt is north or south of Babylon, or how much north or south of Babylon it is, without investigation through the means of the "climata." In like manner, we cannot accurately fix points that lie at varying distances from us, whether to the east or the west, except by a comparison of the eclipses of the sun and the moon. That, then, is what Hipparchus says on the subject.

13. All those who undertake to describe the distinguishing features of countries devote special attention to astronomy and geometry, in explaining matters of shape, of size, of distances between points, and of "climata," as well as matters of heat and cold, and, in general, the peculiarities of the atmosphere. Indeed, an architect in constructing a house, or an engineer in founding a city, would make provision for all these conditions; and all the more would they be considered by the man whose purview embraced the

whole inhabited world; for they concern him more than anyone else. Within the area of small countries it involves no very great discrepancy if a given place be situated more towards the north, or more towards the south; but when the area is that of the whole round of the inhabited world, the north extends to the remote confines of Scythia and Celtica, and the south to the remote confines of Ethiopia, and the difference between these two extremes is very great. The same thing holds true also as regards a man's living in India or Iberia; the one country is in the far east, and the other is in the far west; indeed, they are, in a sense, the antipodes of each other, as we know.

3. GIOVANNI PICO DELLA MIRANDOLA, *ORATION ON THE DIGNITY OF MAN*

Giovanni Pico della Mirandola (1463–1494) was arguably the most brilliant of the Renaissance philosophers. Pico was the son of Francesco, the count of Mirandola and Concordia in Italy. He left his studies at the University of Bologna at the age of sixteen to wander around Europe. His fascination with theology and philosophy took him to the University of Paris where he studied scholastic theology, Latin, Greek, Hebrew, and even developed an interest in Arabic. Pico made his reputation when he attempted to publish his work *Conclusiones* in Rome during his visit there in 1486. Comprising 900 articles, the *Conclusiones* was supposed to be a summary of all learning, and Pico challenged any and all scholars to public debate. His text was never published, however, because its orthodoxy was soon questioned by papal authorities. Nevertheless, the audaciousness of the young Pico and his evident brilliance had already brought him to the attention of such scholars as Marsilio Ficino with whom he shared an interest in classical philosophy. Both men were particularly drawn to neo-Platonism, the philosophical system developed by the Greek thinker Plotinus during the second century A.D. Ficino was the founder of the Florentine school of neo-Platonism, and Pico was one of his students. During his short life, Pico wrote a number of theological texts. The *Oration on the Dignity of Man,* however, remains his most famous work. The appeal of this text lies not only in its beautiful mastery of a classical Latin prose style which was so cherished by Renaissance writers but also in its optimistic view of human nature. For Pico, Ficino, and other Christian neo-Platonists, humans were glorious creations of God and mediators between the heavenly and earthly realms. Made in the image of God, humans ruled on earth much as God ruled in heaven. Like God they were creators in their own realm. In contrast to medieval Catholic theology, which tended to view human pursuits and the human world as transient and corrupt, Pico's celebration of humanity as glorious reflects a profound change in European attitudes by the end of the fifteenth century. The men and women of the Renaissance believed that the natural focus of their attention should be on their own humanity. Because earth and its other creatures were all creations of

God, furthermore, exploring the world as well as exploring humanity were important routes to divine understanding.

Oration on the Dignity of Man

I have read in the records of the Arabians, reverend Fathers, that Abdala the Saracen, when questioned as to what on this stage of the world, as it were, could be seen most worthy of wonder, replied: "There is nothing to be seen more wonderful than man." In agreement with this opinion is the saying of Hermes Trismegistus: "A great miracle, Asclepius, is man." But when I weighed the reason for these maxims, the many grounds for the excellence of human nature reported by many men failed to satisfy me—that man is the intermediary between creatures, the intimate of the gods, the king of the lower beings, by the acuteness of his senses, by the discernment of his reason, and by the light of his intelligence the interpreter of nature, the interval between fixed eternity and fleeting time, and (as the Persians say) the bond, nay, rather, the marriage song of the world, on David's testimony but little lower than the angels. Admittedly great though these reasons be, they are not the principal grounds, that is, those which may rightfully claim for themselves the privilege of the highest admiration. For why should we not admire more the angels themselves and the blessed choirs of heaven? At last it seems to me I have come to understand why man is the most fortunate of creatures and consequently worthy of all admiration and what precisely is that rank which is his lot in the universal chain of Being—a rank to be envied not only by brutes but even by the stars and by minds beyond this world. It is a matter past faith and a wondrous one. Why should it not be? For it is on this very account that man is rightly called and judged a great miracle and a wonderful creature indeed.

2. But hear, Fathers, exactly what this rank is and, as friendly auditors, conformably to your kindness, do me this favor. God the Father, the supreme Architect, had already built this cosmic home we behold, the most sacred temple of His godhead, by the laws of His mysterious wisdom. The region above the heavens He had adorned with Intelligences, the heavenly spheres He had quickened with eternal souls, and the excrementary and filthy parts of the lower world He had filled with a multitude of animals of every kind. But, when the work was finished, the Craftsman kept wishing that there were someone to ponder the plan of so great a work, to love its beauty, and to wonder at its vastness. Therefore, when everything was done (as Moses and Timaeus bear witness), He finally took thought concerning the creation of man. But there was not among His archetypes that from which He could fashion a new offspring, nor was there in His treasurehouses anything which He might bestow on His new son as an inheritance, nor was there in the seats of all the world a place where the latter might sit to contemplate the universe. All was now complete; all things had been assigned to the highest, the middle, and the lowest orders. But in its final creation it was not the part of the Father's power to fail as though exhausted. It was not the part of His wisdom to waver in a needful matter through poverty of counsel. It was not the part of His kindly love that he who was to praise God's divine generosity in regard to others should be compelled to condemn it in regard to himself.

3. At last the best of artisans ordained that that creature to whom He had been able to give nothing proper to himself should have joint possession of whatever had

been peculiar to each of the different kinds of being. He therefore took man as a creature of indeterminate nature and, assigning him a place in the middle of the world, addressed him thus: "Neither a fixed abode nor a form that is thine alone nor any function peculiar to thyself have we given thee, Adam, to the end that according to thy longing and according to thy judgment thou mayest have and possess what abode, what form, and what functions thou thyself shalt desire. The nature of all other beings is limited and constrained within the bounds of laws prescribed by Us. Thou, constrained by no limits, in accordance with thine own free will, in whose hand We have placed thee, shalt ordain for thyself the limits of thy nature. We have set thee at the world's center that thou mayest from thence more easily observe whatever is in the world. We have made thee neither of heaven nor of earth, neither mortal nor immortal, so that with freedom of choice and with honor, as though the maker and molder of thyself, thou mayest fashion thyself in whatever shape thou shalt prefer. Thou shalt have the power to degenerate into the lower forms of life, which are brutish. Thou shalt have the power, out of thy soul's judgment, to be reborn into the higher forms, which are divine."

4. O supreme generosity of God the Father, O highest and most marvelous felicity of man! To him it is granted to have whatever he chooses, to be whatever he wills. Beasts as soon as they are born (so says Lucilius) bring with them from their mother's womb all they will ever possess. Spiritual beings, either from the beginning or soon thereafter, become what they are to be for ever and ever. On man when he came into life the Father conferred the seeds of all kinds and the germs of every way of life. Whatever seeds each man cultivates will grow to maturity and bear in him their own fruit. If they be vegetative, he will be like a plant. If sensitive, he will become brutish. If rational, he will grow into a heavenly being. If intellectual, he will be an angel and the son of God. And if, happy in the lot of no created thing, he withdraws into the center of his own unity, his spirit, made one with God, in the solitary darkness of God, who is set above all things, shall surpass them all. Who would not admire this our chameleon? Or who could more greatly admire aught else whatever? It is man who Asclepius of Athens, arguing from his mutability of character and from his self-transforming nature, on just grounds says was symbolized by Proteus in the mysteries. Hence those metamorphoses renowned among the Hebrews and the Pythagoreans.

5. For the occult theology of the Hebrews sometimes transforms the holy Enoch into an angel of divinity whom they call "Mal'akh Adonay Shebaoth," and sometimes transforms others into other divinities. The Pythagoreans degrade impious men into brutes and, if one is to believe Empedocles, even into plants. Mohammed, in imitation, often had this saying on his tongue: "They who have deviated from divine law become beasts," and surely he spoke justly. For it is not the bark that makes the plant but its senseless and insentient nature; neither is it the hide that makes the beast of burden but its irrational, sensitive soul; neither is it the orbed form that makes the heavens but their undeviating order; nor is it the sundering from body but his spiritual intelligence that makes the angel. For if you see one abandoned to his appetites crawling on the ground, it is a plant and not a man you see; if you see one blinded by the vain illusions of imagery, as it were of Calypso, and, softened by their gnawing allurement, delivered over to his senses, it is a beast and not a man you see. If you see a philosopher determining all things by means of right reason, him you shall reverence: he is a heavenly being and not of this earth. If you see a pure contemplator, one unaware of the body and confined to the inner reaches of the mind, he is neither an earthly nor a heavenly being; he is a more reverend divinity vested with human flesh.

6. Are there any who would not admire man, who is, in the sacred writings of Moses and the Christians, not without reason described sometimes by the name of "all flesh," sometimes by that of "every creature," inasmuch as he himself molds, fashions, and changes himself into the form of all flesh and into the character of every creature? For this reason the Persian Euanthes, in describing the Chaldaean theology, writes that man has no semblance that is inborn and his very own but many that are external and foreign to him; whence this saying of the Chaldaeans: "Hanorish tharah sharinas," that is, "Man is a being of varied, manifold, and inconstant nature." But why do we emphasize this? To the end that after we have been born to this condition—that we can become what we will—we should understand that we ought to have especial care to this, that it should never be said against us that, although born to a privileged position, we failed to recognize it and became like unto wild animals and senseless beasts of burden, but that rather the saying of Asaph the prophet should apply: "Ye are all angels and sons of the Most High," and that we may not, by abusing the most indulgent generosity of the Father, make for ourselves that freedom of choice He has given into something harmful instead of salutary. Let a certain holy ambition invade our souls, so that, not content with the mediocre, we shall pant after the highest and (since we may if we wish) toil with all our strength to obtain it.

7. Let us disdain earthly things, despise heavenly things, and, finally, esteeming less whatever is of the world, hasten to that court which is beyond the world and nearest to the Godhead. There, as the sacred mysteries relate, Seraphim, Cherubim, and Thrones hold the first places; let us, incapable of yielding to them, and intolerant of a lower place, emulate their dignity and their glory. If we have willed it, we shall be second to them in nothing.

4. DESIDERIUS ERASMUS, *IN PRAISE OF FOLLY*

Desiderius Erasmus (ca. 1466–1536) is the most famous of the sixteenth-century Christian humanist scholars. Born the illegitimate son of a Dutch cleric and a physician's daughter, Erasmus was destined from an early age for a career in the Catholic Church. During his long and celebrated life as a scholar, Erasmus traveled widely across Europe and was a close friend and colleague of Thomas More, John Colet, and many other celebrated humanist scholars. A superb Latin and Greek linguist and an admirer of classical rhetorical style, Erasmus was best known in his day as a humanist who placed his linguistic and textual skills at the service of spiritual and moral reform. Erasmus's calling as a religious reformer grew out of his disillusionment with the corrupt and lax state of the Catholic Church and his desire for a more personal, emotional, and simpler form of piety. Heavily influenced by the *Devotio Moderna,* the spiritual reform movement that began sweeping through Northern Europe during the late fifteenth century, Erasmus wrote books designed to incite Europeans to reform themselves. Many of his works were commentaries and corrected translations of early Christian (patristic) texts because he believed that these sources were more authentic reflections of the original Christian ideal. Erasmus also found satire a useful literary genre for inspiring moral reform. His best known satire, *In Praise of Folly,* uses the voice of the goddess Folly to poke at the pretensions and hypocrisies of his contemporaries. No one is spared, especially not worldly monks and popes.

In Praise of Folly

The next to be placed among the regiment of fools are such as make a trade of telling or enquiring after incredible stories of miracles and prodigies: never doubting that a lie will choke them, they will muster up a thousand several strange relations of spirits, ghosts, apparitions, raising of the devil, and such like bugbears of superstition, which the farther they are from being probably true, the more greedily they are swallowed, and the more devoutly believed. And these absurdities do not only bring an empty pleasure, and cheap divertisement, but they procure a comfortable income to such priests and friars as by this craft get their gain. To these again are nearly related such others as attribute strange virtues to the shrines and images of saints and martyrs, and so would make their credulous proselytes believe, that if they pay their devotion to St. Christopher in the morning, they shall be guarded and secured the day following from all dangers and misfortunes: if soldiers, when they first take arms, shall come and mumble over such a set prayer before the picture of St. Barbara, they shall return safe from all engagements: or if any pray to Erasmus on such particular holidays, with the ceremony of wax candles, and other fopperies, he shall in a short time be rewarded with a plentiful increase of wealth and riches. The Christians have now their gigantic St. George, as well as the Pagans had their Hercules; they paint the saint on horseback, and picture the horse in splendid trappings, very gloriously accoutred, they scarce refrain in a literal sense from worshiping the very beast.

What shall I say of such as cry up and maintain the cheat of pardons and indulgences? that by these compute the time of each soul's residence in purgatory, and assign them a longer or shorter continuance, according as they purchase more or fewer of these paltry pardons, and saleable exemptions? Or what can be said bad enough of others, who pretend that by the force of such magical charms, or by the fumbling over their beads in the rehearsal of such and such petitions (which some religious imposters invented, either for diversion, or what is more likely, for advantage), they shall procure riches, honor, pleasure, health, long life, a lusty old age, nay, after death a sitting at the right hand of our Saviour in His kingdom; though as to this last part of their happiness, they care not how long it be deferred, having scarce any appetite toward a tasting the joys of heaven, till they are surfeited, glutted with, and can no longer relish their enjoyments on earth.

By this easy way of purchasing pardons, any notorious highwayman, any plundering soldier, or any bribe-taking judge, shall disburse some part of their unjust gains, and so think all their grossest impieties sufficiently atoned for; so many perjuries, lusts, drunkenness, quarrels, bloodsheds, cheats, treacheries, and all sorts of debaucheries, shall all be, as it were, struck a bargain for, and such a contract made, as if they had paid off all arrears, and might now begin upon a new score. . . .

The custom of each country challenging their particular guardian-saint, proceeds from the same principles of folly; nay, each saint has his distinct office allotted to him, and is accordingly addressed to upon the respective occasions: as one for the tooth-ache, a second to grant an easy delivery in child-birth, a third to recover lost goods, another to protect seamen in a long voyage, a fifth to guard the farmer's cows and sheep, and so on; for to rehearse all instances would be extremely tedious.

There are some more catholic saints petitioned to upon all occasions, as more especially the Virgin Mary, whose blind devotees think it manners now to place the mother before the son.

And of all the prayers and intercessions that are made to these respective saints, the substance of them is no more than downright Folly. . . .

The next to these are another sort of brainless fools, who style themselves monks, or members of religious orders, though they assume both titles very unjustly: for as to the last, they have very little religion in them; and as to the former, the etymology of the word monk implies a solitariness, or being alone; whereas they are so thick abroad that we cannot pass any street or alley without meeting them: and I cannot imagine which degree of men would be more hopelessly wretched if I did not stand their friend, and buoy them up in that lake of misery, which by the engagements of a religious vow they have voluntarily immerged themselves into.

But when these sort of men are so unwelcome to others, as that the very sight of them is thought ominous, I yet make them highly in love with themselves, and fond admirers of their own happiness. The first step whereunto they esteem a profound ignorance, thinking carnal knowledge a great enemy to their spiritual welfare, and seem confident of becoming greater proficients in divine mysteries, the less they are influenced with any human learning.

They imagine that they bear a sweet consort with the heavenly choir, when they tone out their daily tally of psalms, which they rehearse only by rote, without permitting their understanding or affections to go along with their voice.

Among these, some make a good and profitable trade by beggary, going about from house to house, not like the apostles, to break, but to beg, their bread; nay, they thrust themselves into all public-houses, come aboard the passage-boats, get into the traveling wagons, and omit no opportunity of time or place for craving people's charity, and doing a great deal of injury to common highway beggars by interfering with their traffic of alms.

And when they are thus voluntarily poor, destitute, not provided with two coats, nor with any money in their purse, they have the impudence to pretend that they imitate the first disciples, whom their master expressly sent out in such an equipage.

It is amusing to observe how they regulate all their actions, as it were by weight and measure, to so exact a proportion, as if the whole loss of their religion depended upon the omission of the least punctilio.

Thus, they must be very critical in the precise number of knots requisite for tying on their sandals; what distinct colors their respective habits should be, and of what material made; how broad and long their girdles; how big, and in what fashion, their hoods; whether their bald crowns be to a hair's-breadth of the right cut; how many hours they must sleep, at what minute rise to prayers, etc.

And these several customs are altered according to the humors of different persons and places.

While they are sworn to the superstitious observance of these trifles, they not only despise all others, but are even inclined to fall out among themselves; for though they make profession of an apostolical charity, yet they will pick a quarrel, and be implacably passionate for such slight provocations as for putting on a coat the wrong way, for wearing clothes a little too dark in color, or any such nicety not worth speaking of.

Some are so obstinately superstitious that they will wear their upper garment of some coarse dog's hair stuff, and that next their skin as soft as silk: but others on the contrary, will have linen frocks outermost, and their shirts of wool, or hair. Some again will not touch a piece of money, though they make no scruple of the sin of drunkenness, and the lust of the flesh.

All their several orders are mindful of nothing more than of their being distinguished from each other by their different costumes and habits. They seem indeed not so careful of becoming like Christ, and of being known to be his disciples, as the being unlike to one another, and distinguishable for followers of their several founders.

A great part of their religion consists in their title. Some will be called Cordeliers, and these subdivided into Capuchines, Minors, Minims, and Mendicants; some again are styled Benedictines, others of the order of St. Bernard, others of that of St. Bridget; some are Augustin Monks, some Willielmites, and others Jacobists, as if the common name of Christian were too mean and vulgar. . . .

And now for some reflections upon popes, cardinals, and bishops, who in pomp and splendor have almost equaled if not outdone secular princes.

Now, if any one considers that their upper crochet of white linen is to signify their unspotted purity and innocence; that their forked mitres, with both divisions tied together by the same knot, are to denote the joint knowledge of the Old and New Testament; that their always wearing gloves, represents their keeping their hands clean and undefiled from lucre and covetousness; that the pastoral staff implies the care of a flock committed to their charge; that the cross carried before them expresses their victory over all carnal affections; he (I say) that considers this, and much more of the like nature, must needs conclude that they are entrusted with a very weighty and difficult office. But, alas, they think it sufficient if they can but feed themselves; and as to their flock, either commend them to the care of Christ himself, or commit them to the guidance of some inferior vicars and curates; not so much as remembering what their name of bishop imports, to wit, labor, pains, and diligence, but by base simoniacal contracts, they are in a profane sense, *Episcopi, i.e.,* overseers of their own gain and income.

So cardinals, in like manner, if they did but consider that the church supposes them to succeed in the room of the apostles; that therefore they must behave themselves as their predecessors, and so not be lords, but dispensers of spiritual gifts, of the disposal whereof they must one day render a strict account. Or if they would but reflect a little on their habit, and thus reason with themselves, What means this white upper garment but only an unspotted innocence? What signifies my inner purple but only an ardent love and zeal to God? What imports my outermost pall, so wide and long that it covers the whole mule when I ride, nay, should be big enough to cover a camel, but only a diffusive charity, that should spread itself for a succor and protection to all, by teaching, exhorting, comforting, reproving, admonishing, composing of differences, courageously withstanding wicked princes, and sacrificing for the safety of our flock our life and blood, as well as our wealth and riches; though indeed riches ought not to be at all possessed by such as boast themselves successors to the apostles, who were poor, needy, and destitute. I say, if they did but lay these considerations to heart they would never be so ambitious of being promoted to this honor, they would willingly resign it when conferred upon them, or at least would be as industrious, watchful and laborious as the primitive apostles were.

Now as to the popes of Rome, who pretend themselves Christ's vicars, if they would but imitate his exemplary life, in the being employed in an unintermitted course of preaching; in the being attended with poverty, nakedness, hunger, and a contempt of this world; if they did but consider the import of the word Pope, which signifies a father; or if they did but practice their surname of most holy, what order or degrees of men would be in a worse condition?

There would be then no such vigorous making of parties and buying of votes in the Conclave, upon a vacancy of that See: and those who by bribery, or other indirect courses, should get themselves elected, would never secure their sitting firm in the chair by pistol, poison, force, and violence.

How much of their pleasure would be abated if they were but endowed with one dram of wisdom? Wisdom, did I say? Nay, with one grain of that salt which our Savior bade them not to lose the savor of.

All their riches, all their honors, their jurisdictions, their Peter's patrimony, their offices, their dispensations, their licenses, their indulgences, their long train of attendants (see in how short a compass I have abbreviated all their marketing of religion); in a word, all their perquisites would be forfeited and lost; and in their room would succeed watchings, fastings, tears, prayers, sermons, hard studies, repenting sighs, and a thousand such like severe penalties: nay, what's yet more deplorable, it would then follow, that all their clerks, amanuenses, notaries, advocates, proctors, secretaries, the offices of grooms, ostlers, serving-men, pimps, (and somewhat else, which for modesty's sake I shall not mention); in short, all these troops of attendants, which depend on his holiness, would all lose their several employments. This indeed would be hard, but what yet remains would be more dreadful: the very Head of the Church, the spiritual prince, would then be brought from all his splendor to the poor equipage of a scrip and staff.

But all this is upon the supposition only that they understood the circumstances they are placed in; whereas now, by a wholesome neglect of thinking, they live as well as heart can wish.

Whatever of toil and drudgery belongs to their office, that they assign over to St. Peter or St. Paul, who have time enough to mind it; but if there be any thing of pleasure and grandeur, that they assume to themselves, as being "herunto called:" so that by my influence no sort of people live more to their own ease and content.

They think to satisfy that Master they pretend to serve, our Lord and Savior, with their great state and magnificence, with the ceremonies of installments, with the titles of reverence and holiness, and with exercising their episcopal function only in blessing and cursing.

The working of miracles is old and out-dated; to teach the people is too laborious; to interpret scripture is to invade the prerogative of the schoolmen; to pray is too idle; to shed tears is cowardly and unmanly; to fast is too mean and sordid; to be easy and familiar is beneath the grandeur of him, who, without being sued to and intreated, will scarce give princes the honor of kissing his toe; finally, to die for religion is too self-denying; and to be crucified as their Lord of Life, is base and ignominious.

Their only weapons ought to be those of the Spirit; and of these indeed they are mighty liberal, as of their interdicts, their suspensions, their denunciations, their aggravations, their greater and lesser excommunications, and their roaring bulls, that fright whomsoever they are thundered against; and these most holy fathers never issue them out more frequently than against those, who, at the instigation of the devil, and not having the fear of God before their eyes, do feloniously and maliciously attempt to lessen and impair St. Peter's patrimony: and though that apostle tells our Savior in the gospel, in the name of all the other disciples, we have left all and followed you, yet they challenge as his inheritance, fields, towns, treasures, and large dominions; for the defending whereof, inflamed with a holy zeal, they fight with fire and sword, to the great loss and effusion of Christian blood, thinking they are apostolical maintainers of Christ's spouse, the church, when they have murdered all such as they call her enemies; though indeed the church has no enemies more bloody and tyrannical than such impious popes, who give dispensations for the not preaching of Christ; evacuate the main effect and design of our redemption by their pecuniary bribes and sales; adulterate and gospel by their forced interpretations, and undermining traditions; and lastly, by their lusts and wickedness grieve the Holy Spirit, and make their Savior's wounds to bleed anew.

Farther, when the Christian church has been all along first planted, then confirmed, and since established by the blood of her martyrs, as if Christ, her head, would be wanting in the same methods still of protecting her, they invert the order, and propagate their religion now by arms and violence, which was wont formerly to be done only with patience and suffering.

And though war be so brutish, as that it becomes beasts rather than men; so extravagant, that the poets feigned it an effect of the furies; so licentious, that it stops the course of all justice and honesty, so desperate, that it is best waged by ruffians and banditti, and so unchristian, that it is contrary to the express commands of the gospel; yet magure all this, peace is too quiet, too inactive, and they must be engaged in the boisterousness of war.

Among which latter undertaking you shall have some popes so old that they can scarce creep, and yet they will put on a young, brisk resolution,—will resolve to stick at no pains, to spare no cost, nor to waive any inconvenience, so they may involve laws, religion, peace, and all other concerns, whether sacred or civil, in unappeasable tumults and distractions.

And yet some of their learned fawning courtiers will interpret this notorious madness for zeal, and piety, and fortitude, having found out the way how a man may draw his sword, and sheathe it in his brother's bowels, and yet not offend against the commandment whereby we are taught to love our neighbors as ourselves.

It is yet uncertain whether these Romish fathers have taken example from, or given precedent to, such other German bishops who, omitting their ecclesiastical habit, and other ceremonies, appear openly armed cap-a-pie, like so many champions and warriors, thinking no doubt that they come short of the duty of their function, if they die in any other place than the open field, fighting the battles of the Lord.

The inferior clergy, deeming it unmannerly not to conform to their patrons and diocesans, devoutly tug and fight for their tithes with syllogisms, and arguments, as fiercely as with swords, sticks, stones, or anything that came next to hand. When they read the rabbis, fathers, or other ancient writings, how quick-sighted are they in spying out any sentences that they may frighten the people with, and make them believe that more than the tenth is due, passing by whatever they meet with in the same authors that reminds them of the duty and difficulty of their own office.

They never consider that their shaven crown is a token that they should pare off and cut away all the superfluous lusts of this world, and give themselves wholly to divine meditation; but instead of this, our bald-pated priests think they have done enough, if they do but mumble over such a fardel of prayers; which it is a wonder if God should hear or understand, when they whisper them so softly, and in so unknown a language, which they can scarce hear or understand themselves. This they have in common with other mechanics, that they are most subtle in the craft of getting money, and wonderfully skilled in their respective dues of tithes, offerings, perquisites, &c.

Thus they are all content to reap the profit, but as to the burden, that they toss as a ball from one hand to another, and assign it over to any they can get or hire. For as secular princes have their judges and subordinate ministers to act in their name, and supply their stead; so ecclesiastical governors have their deputies, vicars, and curates, nay, many times turn over the whole care of religion to the laity. The laity, supposing they have nothing to do with the church (as if their baptismal vow did not initiate them members of it), make it over to the priests; of the priests again, those that are secular, thinking their title implies them to be a little too profane, assign this task over to the regulars, the regulars to the monks, the monks bandy it from one order to another, till it light upon the mendicants; they lay it upon the carthusians, which order alone keeps honesty and piety among them, but really keep them so close that nobody could ever yet see them.

Thus the Popes, thrusting out their sickle into the harvest of profit, leave all the other toil of spiritual husbandry to the bishops, the bishops bestow it upon the pastors, the pastors on their curates, and the curates commit it to the mendicants, who return it again to such as well know how to make good advantage of the flock, by securing the benefit of their fleece.

Figure 6.3 Frontispiece of the *Novum Organum* in Francis Bacon, *Francisci de Verulamio, summi Angliae cancellarii. Instauratio magna. Multi pertransibunt et augebitur scientia.* 1st ed., London: Joannem Billium, Typographum Regium, 1620. Rare Books Division, J. Willard Marriott Library, University of Utah.

Note: The title-page to Francis Bacon's (1561–1626) *Novum Organum,* a treatise on logical reasoning, shows Bacon piloting his ship through the Pillars of Hercules. For centuries, the mythical Pillars of Hercules were regarded as the boundaries of the known world. The image of Bacon as explorer symbolizes Bacon's own conscious efforts to expand human knowledge by developing a new method of reasoning, and it shows that he is equating his intellectual voyaging with the geographic wanderings of many of his contemporaries.

Study Questions

1. Discuss Mandeville's description of Prester John. Why would Christian Europeans have been fascinated by Prester John?
2. Why were classical works like Strabo's *Geography* still so influential at the end of the fifteenth century?
3. How does Pico della Mirandola describe the nature of man?
4. Where do we see the influence of humanism upon both Pico della Mirandola and Desiderius Erasmus? What is humanism?
5. What is Erasmus criticizing in *Folly* and why? How does this text reflect the spiritual concerns of sixteenth-century Europe?

Suggested Readings

Hankings, John. *Plato in the Italian Renaissance.* Leiden: E. J. Brill, 1990.

Kamen, Henry. *The Spanish Inquisition. An Historical Revision.* New Haven: Yale University Press, 1998.

Rummel, Erika. *The Humanist-Scholastic Debate in the Renaissance and Reformation.* Cambridge: Harvard University Press, 1995.

Tracy, James. *Erasmus of the Low Countries.* Berkeley: University of California Press, 1996.

Trinkaus, Charles. *In Our Image and Likeness: Humanity and Divinity in the Italian Renaissance.* Chicago: University of Chicago Press, 1970.

Web Sites

1. Desiderius Erasmus, *In Praise of Folly*

   http://smith2.sewanee.edu/Erasmus/pof.html

2. Giovanni Pico della Mirandola, *Oration on the Dignity of Man*

   http://www.wsu.edu:8000/~dee/ren/pico.htm

7

Early Modern Contact
1500–1700 A.D.

TEXTS

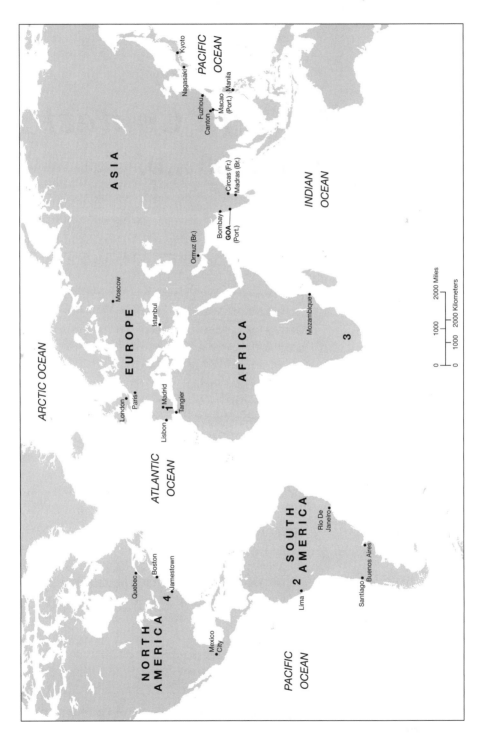

The voyage of Christopher Columbus across the Atlantic in 1492 was a pivotal moment in the history of Europe, as well as the Americas. From this time forward, Europeans looked westward as well as eastward to fuel their growing economies and satiate the European taste for exotic goods and adventure. Silver and gold from Mexico and South America transformed Spain into one of the most powerful European nations during the sixteenth century while the exploitation of New World timber, fur, fish, and plants played an important role in the emergence of England, France, and the Netherlands as powerful maritime empires by the end of the seventeenth century. Equally importantly, exposure to new cultures gradually but irrevocably altered European self-perceptions, as well as their perceptions of other peoples.

The Europeans who first ventured across the Atlantic, however, did not immediately foresee the dramatic consequences of their voyages. Their intention was simply to find a more direct route to the lucrative spice trade of the Indies. The term "Indies" did not refer to a specific region but rather was a general European designation for all lands east of the Arabian Peninsula and south of the Sahara Desert. The rise of Islam in the Mediterranean during the seventh century effectively ended direct contact between Western Europe and these Eastern regions. However, eastern spices and luxury goods continued to flow into Europe through Arab merchants who brought these goods to the major markets of Constantinople, Baghdad, and Alexandria. Genoese and Venetian merchants acted as brokers for these goods, bringing them to western markets. By the fifteenth century, the rising maritime powers of Portugal and Spain decided to break into the Arab-Italian monopoly of the spice trade. The growing power of the Ottoman Turks in the East, however, convinced both kingdoms that it was best not to try and challenge this monopoly on the Mediterranean. The Ottomans were much less tolerant of Christian presence than their predecessors the Mamluk Turks, and their vessels frequently harassed Christian ones when they encountered them.

The Portuguese and Spanish decision to find a new route to the Indies by crossing the Atlantic was more than a novel idea; it was an impressive act of will. From the time of the ancient Greeks, the Atlantic was considered a vast and dangerous body of water that swallowed all who tested her. Ptolemy's *Geographica* filled the ocean with monsters, and other accounts transformed the Atlantic into a burning zone. Convinced that the Indies could be reached by circumnavigating Africa, the Portuguese were the first to rave the waters of the Atlantic. Successive exploratory ventures along the African coast after the middle of the fifteenth century contributed slowly to the amassing of Portuguese knowledge about the land, waters, and cultures of the great continent. By the time Bartolomeo Dias rounded the Cape of Good Hope in 1487, the Portuguese were experienced Atlantic travelers, and Lisbon attracted would-be adventurers such as Christopher Columbus from across Europe to study navigation and seek their fortune. It must be said that the success of Portugal at Atlantic exploration during this period owed no small debt to the financial and political encouragement of its rulers. From the time of Prince Henry "the Navigator" (1438–1460) to the reign of Kings John II (1481–1495) and Manuel I (1495–1521), Portuguese rulers patronized the collection and translation of Greek and Arabic texts on navigation, astronomy, and geography; commissioned new maps; and funded exploratory voyages. Manuel I personally oversaw the provisioning of the fleet that Vasco da Gama took around Africa and into the Indian Ocean in 1497/98. In many ways, these monarchs were emblematic of the new breed of ruler that emerged during the Renaissance. They were humanist-educated individuals who were eager to transform their kingdoms into powerful, wealthy, and unified polities and who believed that exploration offered one means to do so.

The documents in this chapter represent a cross-section of early exploration accounts. Da Gama [1] and Leo Africanus [5] ventured into India and Africa, respectively. Columbus, [2] Cartier, [4] and Cortes [3] crossed the Atlantic to the Americas. The account of Leo Africanus is somewhat unique because Africanus, though born in Granada, spent most of his life in the city of Fez in Morocco. Moreover, except for the years he spent in Italy as a Christian, Africanus was a practicing Muslim. For this reason he was able to travel freely through Muslim African kingdoms which were then inaccessible to early modern Europeans. European cosmographers such as André Thevet relied enormously on his descriptions and analysis of these forbidden zones. Largely respectful of the African cultures, Africanus's account provides an alternative voice to the decidedly Western European voices of the other authors included here.

The tracts of the other four authors are more representative of early modern values. They show, for example, that though profit and power were important motivations for explorers and their monarchs, religion was undeniably a motivation as well. Cartier was not the first explorer to plant crosses wherever his ships landed, and Columbus himself was convinced that his own voyage was a matter of divine providence. For many of the early explorers, proselytizing was an accepted component of their ventures abroad. Da Gama's famous comment to King Manuel I in 1497 that he was traveling in pursuit of "Christians and spices" reminds us forcibly that these Europeans were confident in the veracity and universality of Catholic Christian spiritual beliefs, and they were eager to spread their faith abroad—by force if necessary.

The documents used here also suggest that curiosity was another important factor in European exploration. Whether Europeans were truly more "curious" than other peoples as some recent historians have suggested is perhaps debatable. However, the popularity of travel literature throughout the Medieval and Early Modern periods shows that Europeans were always intrigued by tales of exotic lands. During the Renaissance, scholars and merchants alike studied foreign languages such as Arabic and Greek in order to read eastern texts and communicate with eastern cultures. The following exploration accounts show that early modern explorers were similarly fascinated by the sights and sounds of the worlds they were encountering. However, this fascination did not necessarily translate into toleration for other cultures. Moreover, their excitement about these new experiences was always matched by uneasiness. As Columbus quickly discovered, his experiences were not easily reconciled with traditional European assumptions about the nature of the world. The profoundly transformative effect of cultural encounter upon the European psyche was therefore yet another significant legacy of early modern exploration.

1. Gaspar Correa, *Lendas da India*

The Portuguese were worried about news of Columbus's voyage but not because they believed he had found Cathay. Their own recent explorations around the African coast convinced them that the Indies lay closer to the east than to the west of Portugal. What the Portuguese worried about, however, was Spanish competition for dominance in the Atlantic. To secure Portuguese control of the waters off of the African coast, King John II "the perfect" (1481–1495) encouraged Spain to sign the Treaty of Tordesillas with Portugal in September 1494. This treaty had enormous consequences for the future of European exploration because it divided the Atlantic on a north-south axis into two zones. Spain was guaranteed control of the waters to the west, and Portugal claimed waters to the east. John II had secured Portuguese control of the West African coast, but it was left to his successor, Manuel I (1495–1521), to oversee the successful completion of the so-called "plan of the Indies." Manuel was only twenty-six years old but eager to continue the royal legacy of exploration. It was during his reign that Portuguese ships under the direction of Vasco da Gama (d. 1524) finally reached India. Born into a noble family just outside of Lisbon, da Gama spent many years at sea before receiving the royal commission in 1497 to round the African Cape. Da Gama's fleet survived strong winds, mutiny, and conflict with Turkish vessels before reaching the Indian coast on May 20, 1498, 207 days after leaving Lisbon. The delighted monarch rewarded da Gama and his men well, giving da Gama in particular a coat of royal arms, the admiralship of the Indian seas, and a generous pension among other rewards. Manuel's generosity was more than understandable. He knew that a century of Portuguese exploration had come to fruition. Within a few years of da Gama's voyage, the Portuguese succeeded in ending the Arab-Italian monopoly of the spice trade and Lisbon and became the great European market for eastern goods.

The following account is taken from Gaspar Correa's *Lendas da India* (ca. 1515), a sixteenth-century history of Portuguese exploration. Correa arrived in India in 1514. His remarkably even-handed account is not only one of the earliest but also one of the most detailed of the early chronicles. Correa considered da Gama a good leader, but in the following passage he reveals the ruthless side of da Gama's character. Particularly during his second voyage in 1502, da Gama was more than willing to use violence once diplomacy failed to secure Portuguese control of the Indies trade.

Lendas da India, Chapter VIII

How the Captain-major with all the fleet arrived before the city of Calecut, and of the damage and destruction which was done to it, and of the case of a miracle which happened.

The captain-major, on arriving at Calecut, was in a passion because he found the port cleared, and in it there was nothing to which he could do harm, because the Moors, knowing of his coming, had all fled, and hid their vessels and sumbuks in the rivers; for they knew what the captain major had done at Onor and Batticala, and what he had done to the ship Mount Dely, which belonged to a brother of Coja Casem, the factor of the sea of the King of Calecut. The King of Calecut thought that he might gain time, so that the captain-major should not do him harm; and when his fleet arrived he sent him a Brahman of his in a boat with a white cloth fastened to a pole, as a sign of peace. This Brahman came dressed in the habit of a friar, one of those who had been killed in the country; and on reaching the ship, he asked for a safe conduct to enter. When it was known that he was not a friar,—for the captain-major and everyone had been joyful, thinking that he was one of our friars,—seeing that he was not, the captain-major gave him a safe conduct, and bade him enter the ship. He said to the captain-major: "Sir, I clothed myself with this habit that they might not drive me away from the ships, and that I might come and give you a good message; for the King sends to tell you that he will send you here, where you are, twelve Moors, whom he has arrested for some time since, who were the chief men who induced him to make the great mistakes which he made, by which he is so dishonoured; and with the Moors he sends you twenty thousand cruzados, which he took from them, for payment of the goods which were plundered in the factory: and this he does only for his honour's sake; and with you he wishes for neither peace nor war; and, if you please, he will immediately send these, as soon as your answer arrives." The captain-major was greatly enraged, for he understood the evil; but he dissembled, and ordered the Brahman to write the reply, as he had brought palm-leaves for that purpose; and the captain-major drew up a document for the King, and sent to tell him that he greatly rejoiced that he recognised the fault which he had committed; and that since he did justice on those who had made him do it, he thus acted like a good King, and that he would take what he, sent him; that with respect to the Moors, he grieved that they were few out of the many who had done the evil, and that he would be better pleased with them than with the money, for at Mount Dely he had burned a few of them, who had offered him so much money as ransom, as he (the King of Calecut) already knew; and this was his answer, and that the King might do as he pleased: for his friar whom he had sent would remain waiting until his answer returned. Upon this he sent away the Indian boat, and ordered the friar to be well secured.

Next day the King sent to say, by the same boat, that the Moors whom he had got to send offered for themselves twenty thousand pardaos more, if he pleased that he should send them. The captain-major did not choose to answer, because he was losing time. He then ordered all the fleet to draw in close to the shore, and all day, till night, he bombarded the city, by which he made a great destruction; and he did not choose to fire more, on account of the damage received thereby by the ships which had to return to the kingdom. Then he stood out to sea, and ordered Vicente Sodré to remain before Calecut in a small ship of Diego Fernandes Correa; and Bras Sodré, his brother, in the small ship of Ruy da Cuuha; and in another small ship of Joan Fernandes de Mello he put Pero d'Ataide, his relation, and Joan Rodrigues Badarças, Antao Vaz, and Antonio Fernandes Roxo, with three caravels. In these six sail he put as many as two hundred men, amongst whom were many cross-bow men,—for at that time there were not yet any fire-locks,—and he gave them more artillery and munitions. Whilst they were doing this business, there came in from the ofling two large ships, and twenty-two sambuks and Malabar vessels, which came from Coromandel laden with rice, which the Moors of Calecut had ordered to be laden there, as its price there was very cheap, and they gained much by it; and they came to fetch the port, thinking that our ships, if they had come, would already be at Cochym, and not at Calecut; but our fleet having sighted them, the caravels went to them, and the Moors could not fly, as they were laden, and the caravels brought them to the captain-major, and all struck their sails. Six nakhodas of the sambuks then came to the captain-major, saying they were from Cananor, and mentioned the names of the factor and of Fuy de Mendanha, and other Portuguese, at which the captain-major was pleased. He then ordered the boats to go and plunder the small vessels, which were sixteen, and the two ships, in which they found rice, and many jars of butter, and many bales of stuffs. They then gathered all this together into the ships, with the crews of the two large ships, and he ordered the boats to get as much rice as they wanted, and they took that of four of the small vessels, which they emptied, for they did not want more. Then the captain-major commanded them to cut off the hands and ears and noses of all the crews, and put all that into one of the small vessels, into which he ordered them to put the friar, also without ears, or nose, or hands, which he ordered to be strung round his neck, with a palm-leaf for the King, on which he told him to have a curry made to eat of what his friar brought him. When all the Indians had been thus executed, he ordered their feet to be tied together, as they had no hands with which to untie them: and in order that they should not untie them with their teeth, he ordered them to strike upon their teeth with staves, and they knocked them down their throats; and they were thus put on board, heaped up upon the top of each other, mixed up with the blood which streamed from them; and he ordered mats and dry leaves to be spread over them, and the sails to be set for the shore, and the vessel set on fire: and there were more than eight hundred Moors; and the small vessel with their friar, with all the hands and ears, was also sent on shore under sail, without being fired. These vessels went at once on shore, where many people flocked together to put out the fire, and draw out those whom they found alive, upon which they made great lamentations.

The friar went to the King's presence, with the wives and relations of the dead, to make clamour for the so great evil of which he was the cause. The King soothed them, taking great oaths that he would expend the whole of his kingdom in avenging them. But as he was a tyrant, in order not to expend his own property, he summoned before him the principal Moors of the city, and said to them, that they well saw the great dishonour which had been done him, which was through his taking their counsel, and that, besides his dishonour, his heart grieved at the crises and lamentations of the women and people, who were relations of the slain; and he made oaths that he would avenge them, and would therefore spend all his treasure for vengeance; that they should therefore take the trouble to make and bring together a fleet throughout all his kingdom, as large as they could, and for all of it he would give pay, at his cost, to the men-at-arms. The Moors, when they heard this, gave him great praises, and offered to spend their lives and properties for vengeance: especially Coja Kasim, who was present, with grief for the death of his brother, who was killed in the ship at Marabia, and they at once elected him to be captain-major. So all set to work with great diligence throughout the kingdom of Calecut, which has many rivers, to construct many armed paraos and large rowing vessels and sambuks, and large ships, decided on fighting with our fleet when it should come laden, and to board it, and set fire to it with a quantity of dry leaves, which they would carry for that purpose; and having lighted the fire which was to burn our ships and theirs, they would throw themselves into the sea, and escape by swimming in the boats which they would take equipped for that purpose. So they made a very great fleet, with which they went out to fight ours, as I will relate further on.

The captain-major ordered Vicente Sodré to return to Cananor with his fleet, and to take there the two ships and the six small vessels; and if they belonged to Cananor, as they said, and if the King said so too, he was to let them go; and from the ships and twelve small vessels of Calcecut the factor was to collect as much rice as he could, and the butter, and what had remained over in the ships and small vessels, and give it all to the King; and that the Indians might relate what they saw done to those of Calecut, which being related by them caused great dread amongst the people, who praised the King for the good peace which he had established with the Portuguese, by which they were free from such great evils. The captain-major also ordered Vicente Sodré that after leaving the small vessels at Cananor, he was to return at once and go to Cochym, doing all the damage which he could. Vicente Sodré then went to Cananor, and the captain-major sailed for Cochym.

In this occurrence with these Malabar vessels, there happened a case which it seemed to me, in reason, ought not to be forgotten. There came in these vessels of Moors of Choromandel, natives of the country, who, seeing the executions which were being carried out,—for they hung up some men by the feet in the vessels which were sent ashore, and when thus hung up the captain-major ordered the cross-bow men to shoot arrows into them, that the people on shore might see it; and when it was intended to do the same to these men of Choromandel, they called out that they should make them Christians, naming Thomas, who had been in their country; and they shouted this out, and raised their hands to heaven. This, from pity, was repeated to the captain-major, who ordered them to be told, that even though they became Christians, that still he would kill them. They answered, that they did not beg for life, but only to be made Christians. Then, by order of the captain-major, a priest gave them holy baptism. They were three, who entreated the priest, saying that they wished for once only to say our prayer; and the priest said the *Pater noster* and *Ave Maria,* which they also repeated. When this was finished, then they hung them up strangled, that they might not feel the arrows. The cross-bow men shot arrows and transfixed the others; but the arrows which struck these did not go into them nor make any mark upon them, but fell down. This having been seen, in the case of many arrows which they shot at them to confirm themselves,—for it was always so,—and no arrow wounded them, it was told to the captain-major, and grieved him much; and he ordered them to be shrouded and put into baskets; and the priest commended them with his psalms for the dead, and they cast them into the sea, all saying prayers for their souls, as for faithful Christians, which the Lord was pleased of His great mercy to show in those who were Gentiles, who went in the company of the Moors gaining their livelihood.

2. BARTOLOMÉ DE LAS CASAS, THE JOURNAL OF HIS FIRST VOYAGE

The historical legacy of Christopher Columbus (1451–1506) has been shrouded in debate in recent years for understandable reasons. Columbus's eurocentric designation as "discoverer" of the Americas ignores the fact that aboriginal peoples had inhabited these lands long before his arrival, and that African as well as Scandinavian voyagers had also crossed the Atlantic centuries earlier. Columbus's "discovery" of America, furthermore, has become synonymous for many with ruthless European exploitation of its lands and peoples. Death through war and disease, slavery, and the mass transportation of African peoples throughout the world were some of the more inglorious consequences of his voyage in 1492.

That being said, no one can deny that by bringing Europe into regular contact with the Americas Columbus forever altered the course of European and American history. This son of a Genoese merchant set out from Spain in 1492 to find a new and faster route to the Indies. With three ships under this command and a commission from the Spanish monarchs Isabella and Ferdinand, Columbus was as surprised as everyone else to discover a previously unknown land mass, and he remained convinced until his death that he had reached Cathay in Asia. The following two excerpts come from an account written by the Dominican friar Bartolomé de las Casas who accompanied Columbus on his early voyages. Las Casas says that he based his account on the no longer extant journal of Columbus. The first excerpt reveals a man determined to find the known world in the unknown even when it meant denying the evidence of his own senses. Armed with his well-thumbed copies of Pierre d'Ailly's *Imago Mundi* and the *Travels of John Mandeville*, Columbus concludes here that Cuba must be the fabled island of Cipango mentioned by Mandeville. Cipango was supposedly off the coast of Asia. The second excerpt shows Columbus interpreting his initial encounters with the men and women of other cultures within a decidedly European frame of reference.

First Voyage of Columbus

Tuesday, Oct. 23d. It is now my determination to depart for the island of *Cuba*, which I believe to be *Cipango*, from the accounts I have received here, of the multitude and riches of the people. I have abandoned the intention of staying here and sailing round the island in search of the king, as it would be a waste of time, and I perceive there are no gold mines to be found. Moreover it would be necessary to steer many courses in making the circuit, and we cannot expect the wind to be always favourable. And as we are going to places where there is great commerce, I judge it expedient not to linger on the way, but to proceed and survey the lands we meet with, till we arrive at that most favourable for our enterprise. It is my opinion that we shall find much profit there in spices; but my want of knowledge in these articles occasions me the most excessive regrets, inasmuch as I see a thousand sorts of trees, each with its own species of fruit, and as flourishing at the present time, as the fields in Spain, during the months of May and June; likewise a thousand kinds of herbs and flowers, of all which I remain in ignorance as to their properties, with the exception of the aloe, which I have directed to-day to be taken on board in large quantities for the use of your Highnesses. I did not set sail to-day for want of wind, a dead calm and heavy rain prevailing. Yesterday it rained much without cold; the days here are hot, and the nights mild like May in Andalusia. . . .

Tuesday, Nov. 6th. Last night, says the Admiral, the two men whom I had sent into the country returned, and related as follows. After having travelled a dozen leagues they came to a town containing about fifty houses, where there were probably a thousand inhabitants, every house containing a great number; they were built in the manner of large tents. The inhabitants received them after their fashion with great ceremony; the men and women flocked to behold them, and they were lodged in their best houses. They signified their admiration and reverence of the strangers by touching them, kissing their hands and feet, and making signs of wonder. They imagined them come from heaven, and signified as much to them. They were feasted with such food as the natives had to offer. Upon their arrival at the town they were led by the arms of the principal men of the place, to the chief dwelling, here they gave them seats, and the Indians sat upon the ground in a circle round them. The Indians who accompanied the Spaniards explained to the natives the manner in which their new guests lived, and gave a favourable account of their character. The men then left the place, and the women entered, and seated themselves around them in the same manner, kissing their hands and feet, and examining whether they were flesh and bone like themselves. They entreated them to remain there as long as five days. The Spaniards showed them the cinnamon, pepper and other spices which they had received from the Admiral, and they informed them by signs that there was much of these in the neighbourhood at the southeast, but they knew not of any in this place. The Spaniards not discovering any great number of towns here, resolved to return to the ships, and had they chosen to admit the natives to accompany them, might have been attended back by more than five hundred men and women, who were eager to bear them company, thinking they were returning to heaven. They took none along with them but one of the principal inhabitants with his son; with these the Admiral held some conversation, and showed them great civilities; the Indian described to him by signs many countries and islands in these parts, and the Admiral thought to carry him home to Spain, but says he was unable to find whether the Indian was willing. At night he seemed to grow fearful, and wished to go on shore; the Admiral says that having the ship aground he thought it not advisable to oppose him, and so let him return, requesting him to come back the next morning, but they saw him no more. The Spaniards upon their journey met with great multitudes of people, men and women with firebrands in their hands and herbs to smoke after their custom. No village was seen upon the road of a larger size than five houses, but all the inhabitants showed them the same respect. Many sorts of trees were observed, and herbs and odoriferous flowers. Great numbers of birds they remarked, all different from those of Spain except the nightingales, who entertained them with their songs, and the partridges and geese, which were found in abundance. Of quadrupeds they descried none except dumb dogs. The soil appeared fertile and under good cultivation, producing the *mames* aforementioned and beans very dissimilar to ours, as well as the grain called panic-grass. They saw vast quantities of cotton, spun and manufactured, a single house contained above five hundred *arrobas;* four thousand quintals might be collected here per annum. The Admiral says it appears to him that they do not sow it, but that it is productive the whole year round; it is very fine with an exceeding long staple. Everything which the Indians possessed they were ready to barter at a very low price; a large basket of cotton they would give for a leather thong, or other trifling thing which was offered them. They are an inoffensive, unwarlike people, naked, except that the women wear a very slight covering at the loins; their manners are very decent, and their complexion not very dark, but lighter than that of the inhabitants of the Canary Islands. "I have no doubt, most serene Princes," says the Admiral, "that were proper devout and religious persons to come among them and learn their language, it would be an easy matter to convert them all to Christianity, and I hope in our Lord that your Highnesses will devote yourselves with much diligence to this object, and bring into the church so many multitudes, inasmuch as you have exterminated those who refused to confess the Father, Son and Holy Ghost, so that having ended your days (as we are all mortal) you may leave your dominions in a tranquil condition, free from heresy and wickedness, and meet with a favourable reception before the eternal Creator, whom may it please to grant you a long life and great increase of kingdoms and dominions, with the will and disposition to promote, as you always have done, the holy Christian religion, Amen.

"This day I launched the ship, and made ready to depart in the name of God, next Thursday, for the S.E. in quest of gold and spices, as well as to discover the country." These are the words of the Admiral, who expected to sail on Thursday, but the wind being contrary, detained him till the twelfth day of November.

Monday, Nov. 12th. They sailed from the port and river, *de Mares* at daybreak: they directed their course in search of an island which the Indians on board affirmed repeatedly was called *Babeque,* where as they related by signs, the inhabitants collected gold at night by torchlight upon the shore, and afterwards hammered it into bars. In order to reach this island they directed to steer East by South. Having sailed eight leagues along the coast, they discovered a river, and four leagues further onward, another, very large, exceeding in size all which they had seen. The Admiral was unwilling to remain, and put into either of them, for two reasons, the first and principal one, because the wind and weather were favourable to proceed to the above-mentioned island of *Babeque;* the other was, that were there any large towns near the sea, they might easily be discovered, but in case they were far up the rivers, they could only be reached by ascending the stream in small vessels, which those of his fleet were not. A desire, therefore, not to waste time determined him not to explore these rivers, the last of which was surrounded with a well-peopled country; he named it *Rio del Sol.* He states that the Sunday previous he had thought it would be well to take a few of the natives from the place where the ships lay for the purpose of carrying them to Spain, that they might acquire our language, and inform us what their country contained, besides becoming Christians and serving us at their return as interpreters, "for I have observed," says he, "that these people have no religion, neither are they idolaters, but are a very gentle race, without the knowledge of any iniquity; they neither kill, nor steal, nor carry weapons, and are so timid that one of our men might put a hundred of them to flight, although they will readily sport and play tricks with them. They have a knowledge that there is a God above, and are firmly persuaded that we have come from heaven. They very quickly learn such prayers as we repeat to them, and also to make the sign of the cross. Your Highnesses should therefore adopt the resolution of converting them to Christianity, in which enterprise I am of opinion that a very short space of time would suffice to gain to our holy faith multitudes of people, and to Spain great riches and immense dominions, with all their inhabitants; there being, without doubt, in these countries vast quantities of gold, for the Indians would not without cause give us such descriptions of places where the inhabitants dug it from the earth, and wore it in massy bracelets at their necks, ears, legs, and arms. Here are also pearls and precious stones, and an infinite amount of spices. In the river *de Mares,* which I left last evening, there is undoubtedly a great deal of mastick, and the quantity might be increased, for the trees transplanted easily take root; they are of a lofty size, bearing leaves and fruit like the lentisk; the tree, however, is taller and has a larger leaf than the lentisk, as is mentioned by Pliny, and as I have myself observed in the island of Scio in the Archipelago. I ordered many of these trees to be tapped in order to extract the resin, but as the weather was rainy all the time I was in the river, I was unable to procure more than a very small portion, which I have preserved for your Highnesses. It is possible also that this is not the proper season for collecting it, which, it is likely, may be in the spring, when they begin to put forth their blossoms; at present the fruit upon them is nearly ripe. Great quantities of cotton might be raised here, and sold, as I think, profitably, without being carried to Spain, but to the cities of the *Great Can,* which we shall doubtless discover, as well as many others belonging to other sovereigns; these may become a source of profit to your Highnesses by trading thither with the productions of Spain and the other European countries."

3. HERNAN CORTES, *THE LETTERS OF CORTES*

Product of a respectable but poor noble Spanish family, Fernando Cortes (1485–1547) went to seek his fortune in the newly established colony of Cuba in 1514. The colony was then under the direction of Diego Velasquez, a nobleman well connected at the Spanish court and a man determined to enhance his own wealth and power through exploration of the newly discovered lands. Velasquez authorized numerous ventures led by Spanish colonists of Cuba to the nearby islands, among them the well-known adventurer Francisco Hernandes de Cordoba. Hernan Cortes was one of the captains of the four vessels that sailed to the coast of Mexico in 1519, two years after Cordoba's voyage to Cozumel. Cortes's reputation as conqueror of Mexico has tarnished in recent years because of his brutal treatment of indigenous peoples and destruction of the once thriving Aztec civilization. Taken from his second letter to the King of Spain (1521), the following excerpt describes Cortes's first impression of the great city of Tenochitlan, the seat of the Aztec empire. Cortes is clearly impressed by the sophistication and wealth of Aztec society but nevertheless views these people as inferior to Europeans because of their different cultural traditions.

The Letters of Cortes

To give an account, Very Powerful Lord, of the greatness, and the strange and marvellous things of this great city of Temixtitan to Your Royal Excellency, and of all the dominions and splendour of Montezuma its sovereign; of all the rites and customs which these people practise, and of the order prevailing in the government, not only of this city, but also of others belonging to this lord, much time and many very expert narrators would be required. I shall never be able to say one-hundredth part of what might be told respecting them, but, nevertheless, as far as I am able, I shall speak of some of the things I have seen, which although badly described, I know very well will cause so much wonder, that they will hardly be believed, because even we, who see them here with our own eyes, are unable to comprehend their reality. Your Majesty may be assured, that, if there be anything wanting in my relation, it will be rather in falling short, than by overdrawing, not only in this, but in all other matters of which I shall give an account to Your Highness; but it seems to me only just towards my Prince and Sovereign to tell him very clearly the truth, without interpolating matters which diminish or exaggerate it.

Before beginning to describe this great city, and the others which I mentioned in the other chapter, it appears to me that to understand them better I should describe Mexico, which is where this great city, some others of which I have spoken, and the principal seat of Montezuma's dominion are. This province is ciroular, and completely surrounded by high and rugged mountains. Its plain is perhaps seventy leagues in circumference, in which there are two lakes, occupying almost all of it, for a canoe travels fifty leagues within their borders, and one of these lakes is of fresh water, and the other larger one is salt. The lakes are divided from one another on one side by a small chain of very high hills, in the middle of one end of this plain, except for a strait between these hills and the high mountains; the strait is about a bow shot across. Communication between one lake and the other, and between the cities, and the other towns round about, is by means of canoes, with no need of going by land. The large salt lake rises and falls in its tides like the sea; its waters, whenever it rises, falling into the fresh-water lake as rapidly as though it were a great river; and when it ebbs, the fresh water then runs into the salt lake.

This great city of Temixitan is built on the salt lake, and from the mainland to the city is a distance of two leagues, from any side from which you enter. It has four approaches by means of artificial causeways, two cavalry lances in width. The city is as large as Seville or Cordoba. Its streets (I speak of the principal ones) are very broad and straight, some of these, and all the others, are one half land, and the other half water on which they go about in canoes. All the streets haev openings at regular intervals, to let the water flow from one to the other, and at all of these openings, some of which are very broad, there are bridges, very large, strong, and well constructed, so that, over many, ten horsemen can ride abreast. Perceiving that, if the inhabitants wished to practise any treachery against us, they had plenty of opportunity, because the said city being built as I have described, they might, by raising the bridges at the exits and entrances, starve us without our being able to reach land, as soon as I entered the city, I made great haste to build four brigantines, which I had completed in a short time, capable whenever we might wish, of taking three hundred men and the horses to land.

The city has many squares where markets are held, and trading is carried on. There is one square, twice as large as that of Salamanca, all surrounded by arcades, where there are daily more than sixty thousand souls, buying and selling, and where are

found all the kinds of merchandise produced in these countries, including food products, jewels of gold and silver, lead, brass, copper, zinc, stone, bones, shells, and feathers.
Stones are sold, hewn and unhewn, adobe bricks, wood, both in the rough and manufactured in various ways. There is a street for game, where they sell every sort of bird, such as
chickens, partridges, quails, wild ducks, fly-catchers, widgeons, turtle-doves, pigeons, reed-
birds, parrots, owls, eaglets, owlets, faclons, sparrow-hawks and kestrels, and they sell the
skins of some of these birds of prey with their feathers, heads, beaks, and claws. They sell
rabbits, hares, and small dogs which they castrate, and raise for the purpose of eating.

There is a street set apart for the sale of herbs, where can be found every sort of
root and medical herb which grows in the country. There are houses like apothecary
shops, where prepared medicines are sold, as well as liquids, ointments, and plasters.
There are places like our barber's shops, where they wash and shave their heads. There
are houses where they supply food and drink for payment. There are men, such as in
Castile are called porters, who carry burdens. There is much wood, charcoal, braziers
made of earthenware, and mats of divers kinds for beds, and others, very thin, used as
cushions, and for carpeting halls, and bed-rooms. There are all sorts of vegetables, and especially onions, leeks, garlic, borage, nasturtium, water-cresses, sorrel, thistles, and artichokes. There are many kinds of fruits, amongst others cherries, and prunes, like the
Spanish ones. They sell bees-honey and wax, and honey made of corn stalks, which is as
sweet and syrup-like as that of sugar, also honey of a plant called maguey, which is better
than most; from these same plants they make sugar and wine, which they also sell.

They also sell skeins of different kinds of spun cotton, in all colours, so that it seems
quite like one of the silk markets of Granada, although it is on a greater scale; also as many
different colours for painters as can be found in Spain and of as excellent hues. They sell
deer skins with all the hair tanned on them, and of different colours; much earthenware,
exceedingly good, many sorts of pots, large and small, pitchers, large tiles, an infinite variety of vases, all of very singular clay, and most of them glazed and painted. They sell maize,
both in the grain and made into bread, which is very superior in its quality to that of the
other islands and mainland; pies of birds, and fish, also much fish, fresh, salted, cooked, and
raw; eggs of hens, and geese, and other birds in great quantity, and cakes made of eggs.

Finally, besides those things I have mentioned, they sell in the city markets everything else which is found in the whole country and which, on account of the profusion
and number, do not occur to my memory, and which also I do not tell of, because I do
not know their names.

Each kind of merchandise is sold in its respective street, and they do not mix their
kinds of merchandise of any species; thus they preserve perfect order. Everything is sold
by a kind of measure, and, until now, we have not seen anything sold by weight.

There is in this square a very large building, like a Court of Justice, where there are
always ten or twelve persons, sitting as judges, and delivering their decisions upon all
cases which arise in the markets. There are other persons in the same square who go
about continually among the people, observing what is sold, and the measures used in
selling, and they have been seen to break some which were false.

This great city contains many mosques, or houses for idols, very beautiful edifices
situated in the different precincts of it; in the principal ones of which are the religious orders of their sect, for whom, besides the houses in which they keep their idols, there are
very good habitations provided. All these priests dress in black, and never cut or comb
their hair from the time they enter the religious order until they leave it; and the sons of

all the principal families, both of chiefs as well as noble citizens, are in these religious orders and habits from the age of seven or eight years till they are taken away for the purpose of marriage. This happens more frequently with the first-born, who inherit the property, than with the others. They have no access to women, nor are any allowed to enter the religious houses; they abstain from eating certain dishes, and more so at certain times of the year than at others.

Amongst these mosques, there is one principal one, and no human tongue is able to describe its greatness and details, because it is so large that within its circuit, which is surrounded by a high wall, a village of five hundred houses could easily be built. Within, and all around it, are very handsome buildings, in which there are large rooms and galleries, where the religious who live there are lodged. There are as many as forty very high and well-built towers, the largest having fifty steps to reach the top; the principal one is higher than the tower of the chief church in Seville. They are so well built, both in their masonry, and their wood work, that they could not be better made nor constructed anywhere; for all the masonry inside the chapels, where they keep their idols, is carved with figures, and the wood work is all wrought with designs of monsters, and other shapes. All these towers are places of burial for the chiefs, and each one of their chapels is dedicated to the idol to which they have a particular devotion. Within this great mosque, there are three halls wherein stand the principal idols of marvellous grandeur in size, and much decorated with carved figures, both of stone and wood; and within these halls there are other chapels, entered by very small doors, and which have no light, and nobody but the religious are admitted to them. Within these are the images and figures of the idols, although, as I have said, there are many outside.

The principal idols in which they have the most faith and belief I overturned from their seats, and rolled down the stairs, and I had those chapels, where they kept them, cleansed, for they were full of blood from the sacrifices; and I set up images of Our Lady, and other Saints in them, which grieved Montezuma, and the natives not a little. At first they told me not to do it, for, if it became known throughout the town, the people would rise against me, as they believed that these idols gave them all their temporal goods, and, in allowing them to be ill-treated, they would be angered, and give nothing, and would take away all the fruits of the soil, and cause the people to die of want. I made them understand by the interpreters how deceived they were in putting their hope in idols, made of unclean things by their own hands, and I told them that they should know there was but one God, the Universal Lord of all, who had created the heavens, and earth, and all things else, and them, and us, who was without beginning, and immortal; that they should adore, and believe in Him, and not in any creature, or thing. I told them all I knew of these matters, so as to win them from their idolatries, and bring them to a knowledge of God, Our Lord; and all of them, especially Montezuma, answered that they had already told me they were not natives of this country, and that it was a long time since their forefathers had come to it, therefore they might err in some points of their belief, as it was so long since they left their native land, whilst I, who had recently arrived, should know better than they what they should believe, and hold; and if I would tell them, and explain to them, they would do what I told them, as being for the best. Montezuma and many chiefs of the city remained with me until the idols were taken away and the chapels cleansed, and the images put up, and they all wore happy faces. I forbade them to sacrifice human beings to the idols, as they were accustomed to do, for besides its being very hateful to God, Your Majesty had also prohibited it by your laws, and commanded that those who killed should be put to death. Henceforth they abolished it, and, in all the time I remained in the city, never again were they seen to sacrifice any human creature.

The figures of the idols, in which those people believe, exceed in size the body of a large man. They are made of a mass of all the seeds and vegetables which they eat, ground up and mixed with one another, and kneaded with the hearts' blood of human beings, whose breasts are opened when alive, the hearts being removed, and, with the blood which comes out, is kneaded the flour, making the quantity necessary to construct a great statue. When these are finished the priests offer them more hearts, which have likewise been sacrificed, and besmear the faces with the blood. The idols are dedicated to different things, as was the custom of the heathen who anciently honoured their gods. Thus, to obtain favours in war these people have one idol, for harvests another, and for everything in which they desire any good, they have idols whom they honour and serve.

There are many large and handsome houses in this city, and the reason for this is that all the lords of the country, vassals of Montezuma, inhabit their houses in the city a certain part of the year; moreover there are many rich citizens, who likewise have very good houses. Besides having very good and large dwelling places, all these people have very beautiful flower gardens of divers kinds, as well in the upper, as in the lower dwellings.

Along one of the causeways which lead to the city, three are two conduits of masonry each two paces broad, and five feet deep, through one of which a volume of very good fresh water, the bulk of a man's body, flows into the heart of the city, from which all supply themselves, and drink. The other which is empty brings the water, when they wish to clean the first conduit, for, while one is being cleaned, the water flows through the other. Conduits as large round as an ox's body bring the fresh water across the bridges, thus avoiding the channels by which the salt-water flows, and in this manner the whole city is supplied, and everybody has water to drink. Canoes peddle the water through all the streets, and the way they take it from the conduits is this: the canoes stop under the bridges where the conduits cross, where men are stationed on the top who are paid to fill them. At the different entrances to the city, and wherever the canoes are unloaded, which is where the greatest quantity of provisions enter the city, there are guards, in huts to collect a *certum quid* of everything that comes in. I do not know whether this goes to the sovereign, or to the city, because up till now I have not been able to ascertain, but I believe it is for the sovereign, for, in other market places of other provinces, that contribution has been seen to be paid to the ruler. There are to be found daily in the markets and public places of the city many workmen, and masters of all trades, waiting to be hired.

The people of this city had better manners, and more luxury in their dressing and service, than those of other provinces and cities, for the reason that the sovereign, Montezuma, always resided there, and all the nobles, his vassals, frequented the city, so better manners, and more ceremony prevailed. But to avoid being prolix in describing the things of the city (though I would fain continue), I will not say more than that, in the service and manners of its people, their fashion of living was almost the same as in Spain, with just as much harmony and order; and considering that these people were barbarous, so cut off from the knowledge of God, and other civilised peoples, it is admirable to see to what they attained in every respect. As far as the service surrounding Montezuma is concerned, and the admirable attributes of his greatness and state, there is so much to write that I assure Your Highness I do not know where to begin, so as to finish what I would say of any part respecting it. For, as I have already said, what greater grandeur can there be, than that a barbarian monarch, like him, should have imitations in gold, silver, stones, and feather-work, of all the things existing under heaven in his dominion?—gold, and silver, things, so like to nature, that there is not a silversmith in the world who could do it better; and, respecting the stones, there is no imagination which can divine the instruments with which they were so perfectly executed; and respecting the feather-work, neither in wax, nor in embroidery, could nature be so marvellously imitated.

4. JACQUES CARTIER, *THE SECOND VOYAGE OF JACQUES CARTIER*

It did not take long for other European countries to see the economic possibilities offered by crossing the Atlantic. France, England, and the Netherlands began sending out regular exploratory ventures during the sixteenth century under the leadership of such men as Ferdinand Magellan (ca. 1480–1521), Jean Cabot (ca. 1450–ca. 1499), and Martin Frobisher (ca. 1535–1594). Jacques Cartier (1491–1557) was one such explorer. Born in 1491 in the great French seaport of St Malo, Brittany, Jacques Cartier traveled to Brazil and Newfoundland before receiving a commission in 1534 from the king of France to lead his own fleet across the Atlantic in pursuit of a new route to the Indies. Of course, what he found was not the Indies but the northern lands of the Americas. The following excerpt is the preface to Cartier's account of his second voyage to New France (1535–1536) which he dedicates to the King of France. This preface is interesting for the insight it sheds not only into the political and spiritual motivations underlying French sponsorship of transatlantic ventures but also the intellectual and psychological consequences of exploration. In contrast to Columbus, however, Cartier seems to welcome exploration as a source of knowledge that could challenge accepted European assumptions about the world.

The Second Voyage of Jacques Cartier

To the Most Christian King

Considering, O my most redoubted Prince, the great benefits and favours it has pleased God, the Creator, to grant to His creatures, and amongst others to place and fix the sun, upon which the lives and existence of all depend, and without which none can bring fourth fruit nor generate, at that place where it is, where it moves and sets in a motion contrary and different from that of the other planets, by which rising and setting all the creatures on earth, no matter where they live, are able in the sun's year, which is 365 days and six hours, to have as much visual sight of it, the one as the other. Not that its beams and rays are as warm and hot in some places as in others, nor the division, of days and nights of like equality everywhere, but it suffices that its heat is of such a nature and so temperate that the whole earth is or may be inhabited, in any zone, climate or parallel whatsoever, and that these zones, with their waters, trees, plants and all other creatures of whatever kind or sort they be, may through the sun's influence, give forth fruit and off-spring according to their natures for the life and sustinence of humanity. And should any persons wish to uphold the contrary of the above, by quoting the statements of the wise philosophers of ancient times, who have written that the earth was divided into five zones, three of which they affirmed to be uninhabitable, namely the torrid zone which lies between the two tropics or solstices, on account of the great heat and the reflection of the sun's rays, which passes over the heads of the inhabitants of that zone, and the arc-tic and antarctic zones, on account of the great cold which exists there, owing to their small elevation above the said sun's horizon, I confess that they have so written and firmly believe they were of that opinion, which they formed from some natural reason-ings whence they drew the basis of their argument, and with these contented them-selves without adventuring or risking their lives in the dangers they would have incurred, had they tried to test their statements by actual experience. But I shall simply reply that the prince of those philosophers left among his writings a brief maxim of great import, to the effect that "Experience is the master of all things," by which teaching I have dared to set before the eyes of Your Majesty this preface as an introduction to this little work; for the simple mariners of to-day, not being so afraid at your royal command to run the risk of those perils and dangers, as were the ancients; and being desirous of doing you some humble service to the increase of the most holy Christian faith, have con-vinced themselves by actual experience of the unsoundness of that opinion of the an-cient philosophers.

I have set forth the above for the reason that just as the sun which rises every day in the east and sets in the west, goes round and makes the circuit of the earth, giving light and heat to everyone in twenty-four hours, which is a natural day, without any interrup-tion of its movement and natural course, so I, in my simple understanding, and without being able to give any other reason, am of opinion that it pleases God in His divine good-ness, that all human beings inhabiting the surface of the globe, just as they have sight and knowledge of the sun, have had and are to have in time to come knowledge of and belief in our holy faith. For first our most holy faith was sown and planted in the Holy Land, which is in Asia to the east of our Europe, and afterwards by succession of time, it has been carried and proclaimed to us, and at length to the west of our Europe, just like the sun, carrying its light and its heat from east to west, as already set forth. And likewise also, we have seen this most holy faith of ours in the struggle against wicked herectics and false law-makers here and there sometimes go out and then suddenly shine forth again and exhibit its brightness more clearly than before. And even now at present, we see how the wicked Lutherans, apostates and imitators of Mahomet, from day to day strive to cloud it over and finally to put it out altogether, if God and the true members of the same did not guard against this with capital punishment, as one sees daily by the good regulations and orders you have instituted throughout your territories and king-dom. Likewise also one sees the princes of Christendom and the true pillars of the Catholic church, unlike the above infants of Satan, striving day by day to extend and en-large the same, as the Catholic king of Spain has done in the countries discovered to the west of his lands and kingdoms, which before were unknown to us, unexplored and without the pale of our faith, as New Spain, Isabella, the Spanish Main and other islands, where innumerable peoples have been found, who have been baptized and brought over to our most holy faith.

And now through the present expedition undertaken at your royal command for the discovery of the lands in the west formerly unknown to you and to us, lying in the same climates and parallels as your territories and kingdom, you will learn and hear of their fertility and richness, of the immense number of peoples living there, of their kindness and peacefulness, and likewise of the richness of the great river, which flows through and waters the midst of these lands of yours, which is without comparison the largest river that is known to have ever been seen. These things fill those who have seen them with the sure hope of the future increase of our most holy faith and of your possessions and most Christian name, as you may be pleased to see in this present booklet wherein is fully set forth everything worthy of note that we saw or that happened to us both in the course of the above voyage and also during our stay in those lands and territories of yours, as well as the routes, dangers and situation of those lands.

5. LEO AFRICANUS, WASF IFRIQIYA: THE HISTORY AND DESCRIPTION OF AFRICA

One of the most influential accounts of Africa during the sixteenth century was Leo Africanus's *The History and Description of Africa*. Born into a Muslim family in Granada in 1491, Hassan el-Ouzzan emigrated to the city of Fez in Morocco with his family while still a child. The *Description* is based on his travels in North and West Africa between 1513 and 1519 while in the service of the king of Morocco. Ouzzan received the designation "Leo Africanus" after being kidnaped in Mauritania and taken to Italy. Here he was handed to Pope Leo X. Ouzzan soon converted to Christianity, taking the name "John Leo" in honor of his powerful patron. Africanus's obvious stature as a learned individual quickly earned him a warm reception from humanist circles in Rome and later Bologna. During his many years in Italy, Africanus taught Arabic at the University of Bologna and produced numerous scholarly works, including an Arabic grammar, several Latin translations of Arabic texts, and the humanist-influenced biographical study the *Book of Illustrious Arabic Men*. In 1528, Africanus left Italy for Tunis where he spent his final years reconciled to Islam, the religion of his birth. Africanus wrote the *Description of Africa* while still in Italy. The work quickly became an important authority on Africa among sixteenth-century European cosmographers such as the Frenchman André Thevet because Christians could not travel easily through the mostly Muslim kingdoms of North and West Africa. In the following excerpt, Africanus describes his own city of Fez. This passage reveals not only his profound respect for Islamic culture but also shows Africanus's gift of observation and meticulous description, two qualities that appealed to Early Modern scholars and explorers alike.

Regarding the Diversity of Artisans, Shops and Places

The artisans in this city are separated from one another. The most noble are around the great temple, such as the notaries, who have around eighty shops. One side of each shop is joined to the walls of the temple, the other faces outward, and there are two notaries in each shop. Towards the west there are approximately thirty bookstores and on the south side of the temple are the shoe merchants who have approximately fifty shops. These merchants buy shoes and boots in large quantity from the cobblers who sell them individually. A little further are the cobblers who make shoes for children, and they comprise roughly fifty shops. On the east side of the temple are those who sell leather goods. On the other side towards the great western door are the fruit sellers who have around fifty shops.

Further on we find those who sell wax which they use to mold the most beautiful works that I have ever seen, and from there one comes across the grocers who are few in number. Soon thereafter are around twenty-five flower shops . . . but these flowers are such a beautiful sight because of their mottled appearance and unparalleled perfume that one could believe one was in a green field filled with beautiful smelling flowers, or perhaps regarding a gorgeous, colorful portrait. Further on we find the milk sellers whose houses are decorated with majolica vases and who buy the milk from certain farmers. The farmers feed the cows for their merchandise then send it every morning in wooden vases, linked with iron circles, which are narrow at the mouth and large at the base, to the milk shops. That which remains at the evening or morning is bought by resellers who make butter and who leave part of it to go sour and congeal in order to sell it to the populace. It is believed that they sell more than twenty-five tons of milk, bitter as well as fresh, in the city each day.

Later on is the place of the porters who number three hundred. They have a consul or chief who has the authority to elect and chose those who must work and manage matters during the entire week. The money which they receive for their salary is placed in a box with several locks and the keys are guarded by different chiefs. At the end of the week, the money is divided between those who worked during the week. These individuals bear such friendship for one another that they seem almost like natural brothers. When one of them dies and leaves behind a small child, the company takes care of the widow until she remarries. Regarding children, they take marvelous care of them until they are of an age to work, and when any of them marries or his wife is in childbirth, he holds a banquet for all those who give a gift. The lords of the company have the privilege of not paying any salt tax or other tax, and they can cook their bread at the bakers if they wish too. And if by chance one of them commits a capitol crime, he has the right not to be punished publicly. When members are working, they wear a short habit bearing the same livery but when they finish working, they all wear different clothes. So many of them are honest men of good life.

Beyond this place and towards the mountain is the herbery. There one sells cabbages and other herbs which one eats with meat, and it contains around forty shops. Thereafter is the place where one finds smoke shops. This is where one sells bread fried in oil, similar to the bread coated in honey which we call spiced bread, and those who make it employ in their shops many boys and use many cooking instruments in order to make the bread in an orderly fashion. They sell a great quantity of bread each day because it is the custom here even on feast days to eat the bread for lunch with the roti, honey, or even with a salted soup made with meat which is cut after it is cooked. It is not their custom to cook their roti quickly but rather to place two ovens one upon the other and light the flame in the lower one so that the higher one is very hot. Then they place an entire mutton in the higher one which has a hole in the side so that they do not burn their hands. This ensures that the meat is perfectly-cooked, so that it takes color while retaining a very delicate flavor. To accomplish this one must ensure that the smoke does not overwhelm the meat and that the fire is not too fierce, because the meat must cook slowly throughout the entire night.

Figure 7.1 Frontispiece to Hernan Cortes, *Historia de Nueva-España*. Mexico: Impr. del superior goblerno, J. A. de Hogal, 1770. Rare Books Division, J. Willard Marriott Library, University of Utah.

Note: The title-page of the *Historia* provides a decidedly Eurocentric view of the conquest. Here Cortes presents Mexico to the king of Spain. Nearby, indigenous representatives prostrate themselves before the king to signify their recognition of his authority over the land. In the far right, Franciscan missionaries look onto the scene.

Study Questions

1. What specific references in the text suggest that Columbus was convinced that he had arrive in the Indies?
2. Why were da Gama and his men so upset that a Muslim envoy arrive on their ship dressed in the clothing of a friar? Discuss the relationship between identity and clothing for early modern Europeans.
3. Da Gama was not the only early explorer to use violence against other peoples. Columbus, Cartier, and Cortes all kidnaped indigenous peoples to learn their languages, and Cortes brutally crushed Aztec society. What role did violence play in Early Modern society in general?
4. What does Cartier mean when he quotes "experience is the master of all things"? To what extent does this quotation reflect a change in early modern attitudes regarding the pursuit of knowledge? The knowledge of ancient Greek and Roman thinkers? The relationship between exploration and knowledge?
5. Africanus and Cortes both provide a detailed description of a city. Compare Fez with Tenochitlan. How do Africanus and Cortes view the two societies? Do their attitudes reflect fundamentally different cultural perspectives?
6. According to these documents, what factor was the most important in stimulating European thirst for exploration: economic expansion, political expansion, religion, intellectual curiosity? Why?
7. What European attitudes are expressed in the title-page of Cortes's *Historia de Nueva-España* with regard to the New World?

Suggested Readings

Clendinnen, Inga. *Ambivalent Conquests. The Maya and Spaniard in Yucatan, 1517–1570.* Cambridge: Cambridge University Press, 1987.

Schwartz, Stuart, ed. *Implicit Understandings: Observing, Reporting, and Reflecting on the Encounters between Europeans and Other Peoples in the Early Modern Era.* Cambridge: Cambridge University Press, 1994.

Seed, Patricia. *Ceremonies of Possession in Europe's Conquest of the New World, 1492–1640.* New York: Cambridge University Press, 1995.

Thorton, John. *Africa and Africans in the Making of the Atlantic World, 1400–1800,* 2d ed. Cambridge: Cambridge University Press, 1998.

Web Sites

1. Jacques Cartier—The Virtual Museum of New France

   http://www.vmnf.civilization.ca/explor/carti_el.html

2. The European Voyages of Exploration

   http://www.ucalgary.ca/HIST/tutor/eurvoya/Imperial.html

3. Expulsion of the Jews, 1492

   http://www.fordham.edu/halsall/jewish/1492-jews-spain1.html

8

The New World: Barbarian, Slave, or Subject?
1500–1700 A.D.

TEXTS

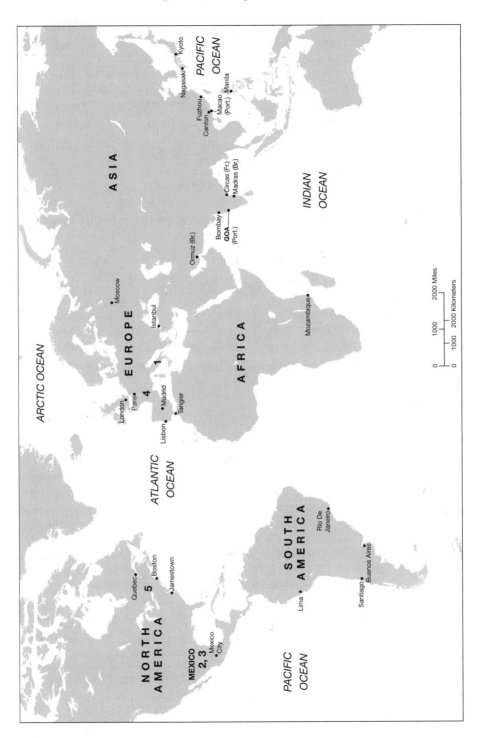

It was not long after the first exploratory voyagers to the New World that concern arose in Spain and elsewhere in Europe over the nature of the Spanish Conquest. In 1493, a series of papal bulls recognized Spanish dominion over all newly discovered lands in the Atlantic which were not occupied by other Christian princes. The two most significant of these bulls, *Inter Caetera* and *Eximie devotionis,* extended to Spain the same rights and privileges that it had granted Portugal over its possessions in Africa. These rights included one that would soon arouse a storm of protest throughout Europe: the Spanish right to enslave the New World peoples. The papacy's justification for conceding these rights was grounded in its role as the most important spiritual authority in Europe. Alexander VI believed that enslavement by a Christian nation such as Spain would facilitate the process of Christianization in the Atlantic regions. Not surprisingly, the Spanish monarchy made these papal concessions the foundation of its claim to jurisdiction in the New World.

The first outright attack on Spanish dominion came in 1511 from the Dominican Antonio de Montesinos. Montesinos bitterly harangued Spanish colonists of Hispania during a Sunday sermon in 1511 for their cruel treatment of the indigenous population. The furious colonists turned to King Ferdinand for redress against the outspoken cleric, but Montesino's attacks were soon joined by the public criticisms of other members of the Dominican order. As tales of Spanish cruelty toward New World peoples reached Europe, the Dominicans soon found influential supporters in the prominent group of Spanish scholars known as the School of Salamanca. Francesco de Vitoria (ca. 1492–1546), Domingo de Soto (1494–1560), Melchor Cano (1509–1560), Francisco Suarez (1548–1617), and Luis de Molina (1535–1600) were among the scholars who applied their broad training in law, physics, and theology as well as jurisprudence and moral philosophy to defend the New World indigenous peoples form abusive Spanish rule. These scholars attacked the legitimacy of the Spanish conquest on a number of fronts, but at the heart of their defense of the indigenous populations of the New World was profound disagreement with the Spanish monarchy over its conceptualization of the nature of humanity. Supporters of Spanish royalist policy initially justified the subjugation of these peoples on the basis of Aristotle's conception of natural slavery and Christian conceptions of a spiritually elect community. Aristotle's conception of natural slavery rested on the classical association of reason with the establishment of urban polities (*polis*). For Aristotle, the city was a product of human reason. It was an orderly world regulated by a code of laws, and it was the natural site of human intellectual, spiritual, and creative activity. It was in the city that humans could pursue virtue. Those who lived outside of the city were barbarians because they could not share in Greek culture. Even though barbarians were human in form, they could not be considered wholly human in nature because they lacked the cultural formation that made them truly rational and therefore truly human. Such people, he believed, were naturally subject to the authority of those whose rational character was fully developed.

This classical interpretation of cultural superiority was infused over the course of the Medieval period with a Christian understanding of salvation. By the fifteen century, many Europeans, including the Spanish apologists, viewed barbarians as those who were ignorant of Christianity. The fact that many of the peoples first encountered by Columbus and other early Spanish explorers in the Americas did not live in recognizably urban societies also bolstered Spanish conviction that these peoples were not "civilized." Juan Ginés de Sepúlveda was among the royal apologists who argued that the peoples of the New World were inferior cultures. Slavery for such people, he believed, could only be spiritually as well as culturally beneficial. The scholars associated with the School of Salamanca, however, disagreed. In his influential treatise *relectio de indis* (1537), Francesco Vitoria relied on theories of natural law to argue that the indigenous people of the New World were rational beings and therefore could not be deprived of the right to consent to their own rule. As rational beings, the indigenous peoples could only be Spanish subjects and not Spanish slaves. Making war on these people, he says, was like making war on the inhabitants of Seville.

Vitoria was not disputing Spanish dominion over the people of the New World, nor was he questioning European assumptions of cultural superiority. He and the other Salamancan scholars were inclined to view the New World cultures as ones that had yet to reach their full potential and that would benefit from European guidance—forced or otherwise. With European guidance, these indigenous peoples could one day become free and independent citizens of the Spanish state. The insistence of the Salamancan scholars on the inherent rationality and humanity of the New World peoples, however, was enormously important for stimulating all later European debates on the legal and political implications of European conquest, notions of empire, and, above all, European perceptions of human nature. The following documents reflect differing European and non-European perspectives on human nature in the wake of the Spanish Conquest. The papal bull *Inter Caetera* [1] states the position of the papacy during the first days of European discovery of the New World. The Dominican Bartolomé de las Casas attacks Spanish treatment of Amerindian peoples in the polemic *Tears of the Indians,* [2] whereas Michel de Montaigne's *On Cannibals* [4] provides a decidedly humanist cast to the sixteenth-century debate. Morton's *New English Canaan* similarly emphasizes the shared humanity of indigenous peoples, [5] and Book 12 of the *Florentine Codex* [3] provides a necessary corrective to traditionally Eurocentric discussions on the sixteenth-century debate on human nature, showing that New World peoples were inclined to view their European conquerors as "barbarians" themselves.

1. POPE ALEXANDER VI, *INTER CAETERA*

Within four years of his return to Europe, Columbus's official account of his first voyage to the Americas had been published in several different languages. One of the first European institutions to see the potential implications of Columbus's encounter with new cultures was, not surprisingly, the papacy. Papal power was still recovering from its ignominious fall from grace during the fourteenth century, when as many as three officially recognized popes competed for control of the church. Reunified in one person after the Council of Constance in 1415, a succession of popes sought to restore the spiritual and political authority of the office. Alexander IV (1492–1503) was one of these popes. Famous for his immorality, political corruption, and ruthless pursuit of personal power, Alexander IV was also eager to strengthen the spiritual authority of the papacy. In 1493, he granted Spain political jurisdiction over the new lands discovered in the Atlantic in order to harness Spanish might to the service of the church. Spain became an agent of Catholic authority in the New World from this point on, and the interactions of church and state during this period played a formative role in the evolution of Spanish colonial institutions. The bull *Inter Caetera* (May 4, 1493) is an important document for many reasons, not the least for the insight it sheds into Catholic—and in particular papal—perception of non-Christian peoples. As the document suggests, papal perception of the Jewish and Muslim cultures as being inherently different from the societies of the New World was important for shaping the Catholic Church's political as well as evangelical treatment of these societies.

Inter Caetera

Alexander, bishop, servant of the servants of God, to the illustrious sovereigns, our very dear son in Christ, Ferdinand, king, and our very dear daughter in Christ. Isabella, queen of Castile, Leon, Aragon, Sicily, and Granada, health and apostolic benediction. Among other works well pleasing to the Divine Majesty and cherished of our heart, this assuredly ranks highest, that in our times especially the Catholic faith and the Christian religion be exalted and be everywhere increased and spread, that the health of souls be cared for and that barbarous nations by overthrown and brought to the faith itself. Wherefore inasmuch as by the favor of divine clemency, we, though of insufficient merits, have been called to this Holy See of Peter, recognizing that as true Catholic kings and princes, such as we have known you always to be, and as your illustrious deeds already known to almost the whole world declare, you not only eagerly desire but with every effort, zeal, and diligence, without regard to hardships, expenses, dangers, with the shedding even of your blood, are laboring to that end; recognizing also that you have long since dedicated to this purpose your whole soul and all your endeavors—as witnessed in these times with so much glory to the Divine Name in your recovery of the kingdom of Granada from the yoke of the Saracens—we therefore are rightly led, and hold it as our duty, to grant you even of our own accord and in your favor those things whereby with effort each day more hearty you may be enabled for the honor of God himself and the spread of the Christian rule to carry forward your holy and praiseworthy purpose so pleasing to immortal God. We have indeed learned that you, who for a long time had intended to seek out and discover certain islands and mainlands remote and unknown and not hitherto discovered by others, to the end that you might bring to the worship of our Redeemer and the profession of the Catholic faith their residents and inhabitants, having been up to the present time greatly engaged in the siege and recovery of the kingdom itself of Granada were unable to accomplish this holy and praiseworthy purpose; but the said kingdom having at length been regained, as was pleasing to the Lord, you, with the wish to fulfill your desire, chose our beloved son, Christopher Columbus, a man assuredly worthy and of the highest recommendations and fitted for so great an undertaking, whom you furnished with ships and men equipped for like designs, not without the greatest hardships, dangers, and expenses, to make diligent quest for these remote and unknown mainlands and islands through the sea, where hitherto no one had sailed; and they at length, with divine aid and with the utmost diligence sailing in the ocean sea, discovered certain very remote islands and even mainlands that hitherto had not been discovered by others; wherein dwell very many peoples living in peace, and, as reported, going unclothed, and not eating flesh. Moreover, as your aforesaid envoys are of opinion, these very peoples living in the said islands and countries believe in one God, the Creator in heaven, and seem sufficiently disposed to embrace the Catholic faith and be trained in good morals. And it is hoped that, were they instructed, the name of the Savior, our Lord Jesus Christ, would easily be introduced into the said countries and islands. Also, on one of the chief of these aforesaid islands the said Christopher has already caused to be put together and built a fortress fairly equipped, wherein he has stationed as garrison certain Christians, companions of his, who are to make search for other remote and unknown islands and mainlands. In the islands and countries already discovered are found gold, spices, and very many other precious things of divers kinds and qualities. Wherefore, as becomes Catholic kings and princes, after earnest consideration of all matters, especially of the rise and spread of the Catholic faith, as was the fashion of your ancestors, kings of renowned memory, you have purposed with the favor of divine clemency to bring under your sway the said mainlands and islands with their residents and inhabitants and to bring them to the Catholic faith. Hence, heartily commending in the Lord this your holy and praiseworthy purpose, and desirous that it be duly accomplished, and that the name of our Savior be carried into those regions, we exhort you very earnestly in the Lord and by your reception of holy baptism, whereby you are bound to our apostolic commands, and by the bowels of the mercy of our Lord Jesus Christ, enjoin strictly, that inasmuch as with eager zeal for the truth faith you design to equip and despatch this expedition, you purpose also, as is your duty, to lead the peoples dwelling in those islands and countries to embrace the Christian religion; nor at any time let dangers or hardships deter you therefrom, with the stout hope and trust in your hearts that Almighty God will further your undertakings. And, in order that you may enter upon so great an undertaking with greater readiness and heartiness endowed with the benefit of our apostolic favor, we, of our own accord, not at your instance nor the request of anyone else in your regard, but of our own sole largess and certain knowledge and out of the fullness of our apostolic power, by the authority of Almighty God conferred upon us in blessed Peter and of the vicarship of Jesus Christ, which we hold on earth, do by tenor of these presents, should any of said islands have been found by your envoys and captains, give, grant, and assign to you and your heirs and successors, kings of Castile and Leon, forever, together with all their dominions, cities, camps, places, and villages, and all rights, jurisdictions, and appurtenances, all islands and main-lands found and to be found, discovered and to be discovered towards the west and south, by drawing and establishing a line from the Arctic pole, namely the north, to the Antarctic pole, namely the south, no matter whether the said mainlands and islands are found and to be found in the direction of India or towards any other quarter, the said line to be distant one hundred leagues towards the west and south from any of the islands commonly known as the Azores and Cape Verde. With this proviso however that none of the islands and mainlands, found and to be found, discovered and to be discovered, beyond that said line towards the west and south, be in the actual possession of any Christian king or prince up to the birthday of our Lord Jesus Christ just past from which the present year one thousand four hundred and ninety-three begins. And we make, appoint, and depute you and your said heirs and successors lords of them with full and free power, authority, and juris-diction of every kind; with this proviso however that by this our gift, grant, and assignment no right acquired by any Christian prince, who may be in actual possession of said islands and mainlands prior to the said birthday of our Lord Jesus Christ, is hereby to be under-stood to be withdrawn or taken away. Moreover we command you in virtue of holy obedi-ence that, employing all due diligence in the premises, as you also promise—nor do we doubt your compliance therein in accordance with your loyalty and royal greatness of spirit—you should appoint to the aforesaid mainlands and islands worthy, God-fearing, learned, skilled, and experienced men, in order to instruct the aforesaid inhabitants and residents in the Catholic faith and train them in good morals. Furthermore, under penalty of excommunication *late sententie* to be incurred *ipso facto,* should anyone thus contra-vene, we strictly forbid all persons of whatsoever rank, even imperial and royal, or of what-soever estate, degree, order, or condition, to dare, without your special permit or that of your aforesaid heirs and successors, to go for the purpose of trade or any other reason to the is-lands or mainlands, found and to be found, discovered and to be discovered, towards the west and south, by drawing and establishing a line from the Arctic pole to the Antarctic pole, no matter whether the mainlands and islands, found and to be found, lie in the di-rection of India or toward any other quarter whatsoever, the said line to be distant one hun-dred leagues towards the west and south, as is aforesaid, from any of the islands commonly known as the Azores and Cape Verde; apostolic constitutions and ordinances and other de-crees whatsoever to the contrary notwithstanding. We trust in Him from whom empires and governments and all good things proceed, that, should you, with the Lord's guidance, pursue this holy and praiseworthy undertaking, in a short while your hardships and en-deavors will attain the most felicitous result, to the happiness and glory of all Christendom. But inasmuch as it would be difficult to have these present letters sent to all places where desirable, we wish, and with similar accord and knowledge do decree, that to copies of them, signed by the hand of a public notary commissioned therefor, and sealed with the seal of any ecclesiastical officer or ecclesiastical court, the same respect is to be shown in court and outside as well as anywhere else as would be given to these presents should they thus be exhibited or shown. Let no one, therefore, infringe, or with rash boldness contra-vene, this our recommendation, exhortation, requisition, gift, grant, assignment, constitu-tion, deputation, decree, mandate, prohibition, and will. Should anyone presume to attempt this, be it known to him that he will incur the wrath of Almighty God and of the blessed apostles Peter and Paul. Given at Rome, at St. Peter's, in the year of incarnation of our Lord one thousand four hundred and ninety-three, the fourth of May, and the first year of our pontificate.

Gratis by order of our most holy lord, the pope.

June. For the referendary, , For J. Bufolinus, A. de Mucciarellis. A. Santoseverino. L. Podocatharus.

2. Bartolomé de Las Casas, *Tears of the Indians*

An experienced explorer who traveled with Columbus to the New World and wrote the only known firsthand account of his voyages, Bartolomé de las Casas (1474–1566) is equally famous as one of the early European defenders of indigenous peoples against Spanish cruelty. Like many Spanish men of his generation, Las Casas traveled to the New World in pursuit of land and fortune. The brutal massacre of indigenous peoples by Spaniards in Cuba, however, galvanized him into political action. In 1515, he made the first of several visits to the Spanish court to protest Spanish treatment of indigenous peoples. Las Casas later joined the Dominican order in 1522, an order that already had a reputation as an outspoken critic of the Spanish in the Americas. In 1544, he was named the bishop of Chiapa, Mexico. Six years later he was invited to debate with Juan Ginés de Sepúlveda before a Spanish royal commission on the just nature of the Spanish conquest. A royal historian and respected theologian, Sepúlveda argued that the American peoples were ignorant, unreasoning, vice-ridden, and incapable of learning more than the mechanical arts. Natural law dictated that inferior cultures should be ruled by superior cultures, and Spain, according to Sepúlveda, was superior in reason and virtue, as well as might. Las Casas's published response to Sepúlveda, *In Defense of the Indians,* relied on his broad learning in law, theology, and history to present a more optimistic view of the nature of the New World peoples. During his lifetime, Las Casas also wrote several histories and polemical treatises decrying Spanish brutality. His pamphlet the *very brief account of the Destruction of the Indies* played no small role in spreading the "black Spanish" reputation, and it helped ensure the passage of the New Laws (1542), legislation that fundamentally transformed Spanish policy regarding colonization by restricting colonial enslavement of New World peoples. The excerpt is taken from another polemic work which circulate during Las Casas's lifetime, *Tears of the Indians.*

Tears of the Indians, or Inquisition for Bloud: Being the Relation of the Spanish Massacre There.

In the year 1492, the West-Indies were discovered, in the following year they were inhabited by the Spaniards: a great company of the Spaniards going about 49 years ago. The first place they came to, was Hispaniola, being a most fertile Island, and for the bigness of it very famous, it being no less than six hundred miles in compass. Round about it lie an innumerable company of Islands, so thronged with Inhabitants, that there is not to be found a greater multitude of people in any part of the world. The Continent is distant from this about Two hundred miles, stretching it self out in length upon the sea side for above Ten thousand miles in length. This is already found out, and more is daily discovered. These Countries are inhabited by such a number of people, as if God had assembled and called together to this place, the greatest part of Mankind.

This infinite multitude of people was so created by God, as that they were without fraud, without subtility or malice, to their natural Governours most faithful and obedient. Towards the Spaniards whom they serve, patient, meek and peaceful, who laying all contentious and tumultuous thoughts aside, live without any hatred or desire of revenge; the people are most delicate and tender, enjoying such a feeble constitution of body as does not permit them to endure labour, so that the Children of Princes and great persons here, are not more nice and delicate than the Children of the meanest Country-man in that place. The Nation is very poor and indigent, possessing very little, and by reason that they gape not after temporal goods, neither proud nor ambitious. Their diet is such that the most holy Hermite cannot feed more sparingly in the wilderness. They go naked, only hiding the undecencies of nature, and a poor shag mantle about an ell or two long is their greatest and their warmest covering. They lie upon mats, only those who have larger fortunes, lie upon a kind of net which is tied at the four corners, and so fasten'd to the roof, which the Indians in their natural language call Hamecks. They are of a very apprehensive and docible wit, and capable of all good learning, and very apt to receive our Religion, which when they have but once tasted, they are carried on with a very ardent and zealous desire to make a further progress in it; so that I have heard divers Spaniards confess that they had nothing else to hinder them from enjoying Heaven, but their ignorance of the true God.

To these quiet Lambs, endued with such blessed qualities, came the Spaniards like most cruel Tigers, Wolves, and Lions, enrag'd with a sharp and tedious hunger; for these forty years past, minding nothing else but the slaughter of these unfortunate wretches, whom with divers kinds of torments neither seen nor heard before, they have so cruelly and inhumanely butchered, that of three millions of people which Hispaniola itself did contain, there are left remaining alive scarce three hundred persons. And for the Island of Cuba, which contains as much ground in length, as from Valladolid to Rome; it lies wholly desert, untill'd and ruin'd. The Islands of St. John and Jamaica lie waste and desolate. The Lucayan Islands neighbouring toward the North upon Cuba and Hispaniola, being above Sixty or thereabouts with those Islands that are vulgarly called the Islands of the Gyants, of which that which is least fertile is more fruitful then the King of Spains Garden at Sevil, being situated in a pure and temperature air, are now totally unpeopled and destroyed; the inhabitants thereof amounting to above 500000 souls, partly killed, and partly forced away to work in other places: so that there going a ship to visit those parts and to glean the remainder of those distressed wretches, there could be found no more than eleven men. Other Islands there were near the Island of St. John more then thirty in number, which were totally made desert. All which Islands, though they amount to such a number containing in length of ground the space of above Two thousand miles, lie now altogether solitary without any people or Inhabitant.

Now to come to the Continent, we are confident, and dare affirm upon our own knowledge, that there were ten Kingdomes of as large an extent as the Kingdoms of Spain, joining to it both Arragon, and Portugal, containing above a thousand miles every one of them in compass, which the unhumane and abominable villanies of the Spaniards have made a wilderness of, being now as it were stript of all their people, and made bare of all their inhabitants, though it were a place formerly possessed by vast and infinite numbers of men; And we dare confidently aver, that for those Forty years, wherin the Spaniards exercised their abominable cruelties, and detestable tyrannies in those parts, that there have innocently perish'd above Twelve millions of souls, women and children being numbred in this sad and fatal list; moreover I do verily believe that I should speak within compass, should I say that above Fifty millions were consumed in this Massacre.

As for those that came out of Spain, boasting themselves to be Christians, they took two several ways to extirpate this Nation from the face of the Earth, the first whereof was a bloody, unjust, and cruel war which they made upon them: a second by cutting off all that so much as sought to recover their liberty, as some of the stouter sort did intend. And as for the Women and Children that were left alive, they laid so heavy and grievous a yoke of servitude upon them that the condition of beasts was much more tolerable.

Upon these two heads all the other several torments and inhumanities which they used to the ruin of these poor Nations may be reduced.

That which led the Spaniards to these unsanctified impieties was the desire of Gold, to make themselves suddenly rich, for the obtaining of dignities & honours which were no way fit for them. In a word, their covetousness, their ambition, which could not be more in any people under heaven, the riches of the Country, and the patience of the people gave occasion to this their devilish barbarism. For the Spaniards so contemned them (I now speak what I have seen without the least untruth) that they used them not like beasts, for that would have been tolerable, but looked upon them as if they had been but the dung and filth of the earth, and so little they regarded the health of their soul, that they suffered this great multitude to die without the least light of Religion; neither is this less true then what I have said before, and that which those tyrants and hangmen themselves dare not deny, without speaking a notorious falsehood, that the Indians never gave them the least cause to offer them violence, but received them as Angels sent from heaven, till their excessive cruelties, the torments and slaughters of their Countrymen mov't them to take arms against the Spaniards.

Of *Hispaniola*

In the Island of Hispaniola, to which the Spaniards came first, these slaughters and ruins of mankind took their beginning. They took away their women and children to serve them, though the reward which they gave them was a sad and fatal one. Their food got with great pain and dropping sweat, the Spaniards still consumed, not content with what the poor Indians gave them gratis out of their own want; One Spaniard consuming in one day as much as would suffice three families, every one containing ten persons. Being thus broken with so many evils, afflicted with so many torments, and handled so ignominiously, they began at length to believe that the Spaniards were not sent from Heaven. And therefore some of them hid their Children, others their Wives, others their Victuals in obscure and secret places; Others not being able to endure a Nation that conversed among them with such a boisterous impiety sought for shelter in the most abrupt and inaccessible mountains. For the Spaniards while they were among them did not only entertain them with cruel beating them with their fists, and with their staves, but presumed also to lay violent hands upon the Rulers and Magistrates of their Cities: and they arriv'd at that height of impudence and unheard of boldness, that a certain private Captain scrupled not to force the Wife of the most potent King among them. From which time forward they began to think what way they might take to exel the Spaniards out of their Country. But good God! what sort of armies had they? such as were as available to offend or defend as bullrushes might be. Which when the Spaniards saw, they came with their Horsemen well armed with Sword and Launce, making most cruel havocks and slaughters among them. Overrunning Cities and Villages, where they spared no sex nor age; neither would their Cruelty pity Women with child, whose bellies they would rip up, taking out the Infant to hew it in pieces. They would often lay wagers who should with most dexterity either cleave or cut a man in the middle, or who could at one blow soonest cut off his head. The children they would take by the feet and dash their innocent heads against the rocks, and when they were fallen into the water, with a strange and cruel derision they would call upon them to swim. Sometimes they would run both Mother and Infant, being in her belly quite through at one thrust.

They erected certain Gallowses, that were broad but so low, that the tormented creature might touch the ground with their feet, upon every one of which they would hang thirteen persons, blasphemously affirming that they did it in honour of our Redeemer and his Apostles, and then putting fire under them, they burnt the poor wretches alive. Those whom their pity did think fit to spare, they would send away with their hands half cut off, and so hanging by the skin. Thus upbraiding their flight, *Go carry letters to those who lie hidden in the mountains that are fled from us.*

This death they found out also for the Lords and Nobles of the Land; they stuck up forked sticks in the ground, and then laid certain perches upon them, and so laying them upon those perches, they put a gentle fire under, causing the fire to melt them away by degrees, to their unspeakable torment.

One time above the rest I saw four of the Nobles laid upon these perches, and two or three other of these kind of hurdles furnished after the same manner; the clamours and cries of which persons being troublesome to the Captain, he gave order that they should be hang'd, but the Executioner whose name I know, and whose parents are not obscure, hindred their Calamity from so quick a conclusion, stopping their mouths, that they should not disturb the Captain, and still laying on more wood, till being roasted according to his pleasure, they yielded up the ghost. Of these and other things innumerable I have been eye-witness; Now because there were some that shun'd like so many rocks the cruelty of a Nation so inhumane, so void of piety and love to mankind, and therefore fled from them to the mountains; therefore they hunted them with their Hounds, whom they bred up and taught to pull down and tear the Indians like beasts: by these Dogs much human blood was shed; and because the Indians did now and then kill a Spaniard, taking him at an advantage, as justly they might; therefore the Spaniards made a Law among themselves, that for one Spaniard so slain, they should kill a hundred Indians.

Of the *Kingdoms* which the *Island* of *Hispaniola* Did Contain

The Island of Hispaniola had in it five very great Kingdoms, and five very potent Kings, to whom the other Lords, of which there was a very great number were for the most part subject; for there were some few Lords of peculiar Countries that did not acknowledge the jurisdiction of these Kings; one of the Kingdomes is called Maqua, which signifies a plain. This Plain if ther be any thing in the world worth taking notice, claims a very nice observation. For from the South to the North it is stretcht forward fourscore miles in length; in breadth it takes up sometimes eight, sometimes five, and sometimes ten miles, on all sides it is shut up with very high mountains; it is watered by thirty thousand Rivers and Rivolets, whereof twelve are not less then either *Duerus, Ebrus,* or *Guadalgevir:* and all the Rivers which run from the Mountains on the West side, whose number is twenty thousand, do all of them abound with gold. With which Mountain the Province of *Cibao* is bounded, where are the mines of *Cibao,* that afford the most exquisite and pure God which is so much valued among us. This Kingdom was govern'd by *Guarionex,* who had under his jurisdiction as his vassals, Lords and Governors so potent, that every one of them was able to bring into the field for the service of *Guarionex* above Sixteen thousand men apiece. Some of which Lords I very well knew; this King was not meanly vertuous, by nature peaceful, and much devoted to the King of Castile. This King commanded his subjects that they should present to the Spaniards a bell full of Gold, which when they were not able to do by reason that the people had but little skill how to dig out the Gold, he there upon commanded them to present the Spaniards with as much as they could fill.

Here a Cacius or Governour offer'd himself to the service of the King of Castile, upon condition, that he would take care that all the Country from Isabella to St. Domingo, being five hundred miles in length, might be till'd; which promises I am very confident he would cheerfully performed; and then might the King of Castile have had a revenue of above Three millions of Castilian Crowns, and there have been still remaining in the Island above Fifty Cities as large all of them as Sevill.

But what was the recompense which they afforded to this mild and bountiful Prince? they suffered one of the Spanish Captains unworthy of the name of a Christian to vitiate his Wife. He might have raised an army and endeavoured a revenge, but he rather chose to leave his Kingdom and his dignity, and to live a banished person in Province of Coquaios, where a potent vassal and subject of his inhabited. But the Spaniards hearing of this flight, resolved not to let him lurk any where; but immediately making war upon him that had received them so liberally, they never rested till they had wasted all the Kingdom to find him out, at length he fell into their hands; and no sooner had they taken him, but they fettered him immediately, putting him into a ship that was bound for Spain; but the ship was wrackt by the way, many Spaniards perishing, and great treasure of Gold being lost; God so taking revenge upon their enormities.

Another Kingdom was called Marien, where there is a port at one end of the plain that looks toward the North, being larger and more fertile then the Kingdom of Portugal, and which very well deserves to be better peopled; for it abounds with Mountains wherein are great store of Gold Mines. The name of the King that there ruled was Guacanagari, under whom there were many other potent Lords, some of whom I knew: To this place came the old sea Captain that first discovered America, who was received with so much courtesy and friendship by Guacanagari, who gave him and his associates all the help and assistance that might be (for his ship was there sunk) that upon his return into Spain he would often affirm, that his own parents in his own Country were never so friendly to him. This King flying from the cruelty and enormous murders of the Spaniards, being depriv'd of his Kingdom, died poorly in the mountains. The rest of his Nobles ended their lives in that servitude and slavery which shall be hereafter related.

The third Kingdom was Maquana, a Country very temperate and fertile, where the best Sugar in that Island is made. In this Country at that time Canabao did reign, who for power, dignity, gravity, and the ceremonies which were used towards him, far exceeded the rest. This King suspecting nothing less, was by the craft and subtlety of the Spaniards taken in his own house; whom when they had taken they put a shipboard to send him to Castile; but there being six ships in the Port ready to set sail, the sea began to swell so high, and to be so unruly, that all the six ships with the Spaniards in them, together with King Canabao, all perished in the waves. The great God showing the Judgements of his wrath upon these unjust and wicked wretches as he had done upon the others. This King had three or four brothers stout and valiant men, who being offended at the captivity of their Lord and King, hearing of the deprivations and rapines daily committed by the Spaniards in these Countries, and understanding that their brother was dead, resolved to take arms for the relief of their Country; but the Spaniards meeting them with a certain number of horse, which are a very great terror to the Indians made such a slaughter among them, that they depopulated the greatest part of this Country.

3. *FLORENTINE CODEX*

Early indigenous accounts of contact between Europeans and New World peoples are rare until the middle of the sixteenth century. One of the earliest is the *Florentine Codex* (1578–1579) an encyclopic account of the history of the Nahua peoples of Central Mexico compiled under the direction of the Spanish friar Bernardino de Sahagùn (d. 1590). Sahagùn applied his humanist training in language and textual criticism to prepare a history that he believed was an accurate representation of preconquest Nahua society and culture. In the prologue to Book I, Sahagùn asserts that the Codex would be "as authoritative and reliable as what was written by Vergil, Cicero, and other Latin authors." Written decades after the arrival of the Europeans and under the supervision of a European, the Codex cannot be considered an entirely accurate reflection of Mexican attitudes at the moment of conquest. Historians have disputed in particular its portrayal of Montezuma as a weak ruler who believed that Cortes was the returned God Quetzalcoatl. Although likely not accurate, this interpretation has shaped European perceptions of the success of Cortes and his small band of warriors at conquering the mighty Aztec empire. The excerpt is taken from Book Twelve of the Codex. Book Twelve is considered to be the most authentic and therefore the most important of the texts included in the Codex. The account demonstrates that the Nahua saw little to admire in the behavior of the Europeans. According to these Nahua writers, European greed, lack of respect for native customs, and violent nature made them a decidedly inferior culture.

Florentine Codex

Fortieth Chapter. Here is told how the men of Tlatilulco and Tenochtitlan and their leaders yielded to the Spaniards, and what befell when they were among them.

And when they had betaken themselves to bring him and disembark him, thereupon all the Spaniards came to see. They drew him along; the Spaniards took him by the hand. After that they took him up to the roof-top, where they went to stand him before the Captain, the war leader. And when they had proceeded to stand him before [Cortés], they looked at Quauhtemoc, made much of him, and stroked his hair. Then they seated him with [Cortés] and fired the guns. They hit no one with them, but only made them go off above, [so that] they passed over the heads of the common folk. Then [some Mexicans] took and got into a boat and guided it there to the house of Coyoueutetzin. And when they arrived, then they climbed up to the roof-top, whereupon once again they slew men and many died there. But [the Mexicans] only fled. With this the war reached its end.

Then there was shouting; they said: "Enough! Let it end! Eat greens!" When they heard this, the common folk thereupon issued forth. On this, they went, even into the lagoon.

And as they departed, leaving by the great road, once more they there slew some, wherefore the Spaniards were wroth that still some again had taken up their obsidian-bladed swords and their shields. Those who dwelt in house clusters went straightway to Amaxac; they went direct to where the ways divide. There the common folk separated. So many went toward Tepeyacac, so many toward Xoxouiltitlan, so many toward Nonoalco. But toward Xolloco and toward Maçatzintamalco no one went.

And all who lived in boats and [in houses] on poles, and those at Tolmayecan, went into the water. On some, the water reached to the stomach; some, to the chest; and on some it reached to the neck. And some were all submerged, there in the deeps. Little children were carried on the backs [of their elders]; cries of weeping arose. Some went on happy and rejoicing as they traveled crowding on the road. And those who owned boats, all the boatmen, left by night, and even [continued to] leave all day. It was as if they pushed and crowded one another as they set out.

And everywhere the Spaniards were seizing and robbing the people. They sought gold; as nothing did they value the green stone, quetzal feathers, and turquoise. [The gold] was everywhere in the bosoms or in the skirts of the wretched women. And as for the men, it was everywhere in their breech clouts and in their mouths.

And [the Spaniards] seized and set apart the pretty women—those of light bodies, the fair [-skinned] ones. And some women, when they were [to be] assaulted, covered their faces with mud and put on old, mended skirts and rags for their shifts. They put all rags on themselves.

And also some men were singled out—those who were strong, grown to manhood, and next the young boys, of whom they would make messengers, who would be their servants, and who were known as their runners. And on some they burned [brand marks] on their cheeks; on some they put paint on their cheeks; on some they put paint on their lips.

And when the shield was laid down, when we gave way, it was the year count Three House and the day count was One Serpent.

And when Quauhtemoc went to deliver himself, up, they then took him, after nightfall, to Acachinanco. And on the morrow, when already a little sun shone, once more the Spaniards, a good many of them, came forth likewise to put an end [to the fray]—girt for war, [in] iron corselets and iron helmets, but not with their iron swords nor their shields. They all only pressed white linen cloths against their noses as they passed by; [for] the dead sickened them; they already smelled foul and stank.

All went forth afoot holding, by their capes, Quauhtemoc, Coanacotzin, and Tetlepanquetzatzin—grasping only these three. [And also appeared] the ruler's vicar

Tlacotzin, the lords' judge Petlauhtzin, the captain of the armies Motelchiuhtzin, the constable of Mexico, the lord priest Coatzin, the keeper Tlaçolyaotl—the men who guarded all the gold.

Then they went straightway to Atactzinco, to the house of the chieftain and commanding general Coyoueuetzin. The Spaniards came in files; they stretched out in two rows, which went to their ends at a distance and extended far. And when they had reached the house of Coyoueuetzin, then they climbed up to the roof-top, on to a platform. Then they sat down. With a many-colored cloth they made a canopy for the Captain. Then the Marquis sat there, and with him stood Marina.

And Quauhtemoc was by the Captain. He had bound on the cape of quetzal feathers, each half of different color, with humming bird feathers, after the manner of those of Ocuillan. It looked soiled. He had only this. Then, after him, came Coanacotzin, ruler of Texcoco, who had bound on only a maguey fiber cape bordered with flowers and with a design of radiating flowers. It also seemed dirty. Then after him came Tetlepanquetzatzin, ruler of Tlacopan. He likewise was covered by a cape of maguey fiber, also very dirty—much soiled. Then, next, came the chief justice Auelitoctzin, and last walked Yopicatl Popocatzin, a prince. On the other side were the men of Tenochtitlan—Tlacotzin, Petlauhtzin, Motelchiuhtzin, the constable of Mexico, the lord priest Coatzin, and the keeper Tlaçolyaotl.

4. MICHEL DE MONTAIGNE, *ON CANNIBALS*

A member of the French magistracy and a known political and religious moderate, Michel de Montaigne (1533–1592) survived the factionalism of the French Wars of Religion (1562–1594) to become one of the most celebrated humanists of his day. The *Essays* remain his best known literary contribution, in part because it introduced an altogether new genre of literature: the autobiography. Written in the form of a series of seemingly unrelated prose texts or "essays," Montaigne's *Essays* explore his own thoughts on a wide range of moral and philosophical issues. In his classically influenced rhetorical style, reliance on ancient authors, and his praise of indigenous self-sufficiency and moderation, Montaigne betrays his humanist leanings. What is reflected in the text above all, however, is Montaigne's profound distaste for human cruelty. For Montaigne, war was destructive not glorious, and he was as harshly critical of the brutality of fellow Frenchmen during the Wars of Religion as he was of Spanish treatment of the Amerindian populations. Several of his essays concern human brutality. His essay entitled "Coaches," for example, describes indigenous communities destroyed and people massacred through European pursuit of "pearls and pepper." His essay "On Cannibals," which is reproduced here, is particularly interesting because it challenges European conceptions of cultural superiority by debating the very categories used to define cultural superiority.

On Cannibals

When King Pyrrhus invaded Italy, after he had surveyed the army that the Romans had went out against him, drawn up in battle array, "I know not," he said, "what barbarians these are" (for the Greeks so called all foreign nations), "but the disposition of this army that I see is in no wise barbarian." The Greeks said the same of the army that Flaminius led into their country; (c) and Philip, when he saw from a little hill the order and arrangement of the Roman camp in his kingdom under Publius Sulpicius Galba. (a) Thus we see how we should beware of adhering to common opinions, and that we must weigh them by the test of reason, not by common report.

I had with me for a long time a man who had lived ten or twelve years in that other world which has been discovered in our time in the region where Villegaignon made lande, and which he christened Antarctic France. This discovery of a boundless country seems to be worth consideration. I do not know whether I can be assured that some other may not hereafter be found, so many greater personages having been deceived about this one. I fear that our eyes may be greater than our stomachs, and that we have more curiosity than capacity. We grasp at every thing, but clutch nothing but wind. Plato speaks of Solon narrating that he learned from the priests of the city of Sais in Egypt that in times past, and before the Deluge, there was a large island called Atlantidis, just at the mouth of the Strait of Gibraltar, which was of greater extent than Africa and Asia together, and that the kings of that country—who not only possessed that island, but had extended their dominion so far on the continent that they held the breadth of Africa as far as Egypt, and the length of Europe as far as Tuscany—undertook to stride into Asia and to subdue all the nations on the shores of the Mediterranean as far as the Euxine; and to this end they traversed all Spain, Gaul, and Italy, even to Greece, where the Athenians resisted them; but, some time later, the Athenians and they and their island were swallowed up by the Deluge. It is very probable that that immense inundation made strange changes in the inhabited places of the earth, as it is thought that the sea cut off Sicily from Italy,—

> (b) Hæc loca, vi quondam et vasta convulsa ruina, Dissiluisse ferunt, cum protinus utraque tellus Una foret,—

(a) Cyprus from Syria, and the island of Negropont from the mainland of Bœotia; and elsewhere joined lands that were formerly separate, filling with mud and sand the channels between them,—

> sterilisque diu palus aptaque remis
> Vicinas urbes alit, et grave sentit aratrum.

But there is no great likelihood that this new world that we have just discovered is that island; for it almost touched Spain, and it would be an incredible effect of the inundation to have moved it away, as it is, more than twelve hundred leagues; besides which, the explorations of modern navigators have almost made sure that this is not an island, but mainland, connected with the East Indies on one side, and elsewhere with the countries that lie under the two poles; or, if divided from them, it is by so narrow a passage that it is not thereby entitled to be called an island. *(b)* It seems as if there may be motions in those great bodies as in our own, *(c)* some natural, others irregular. *(b)* When I see the encroach-ment that my river Dordogne is making on its right bank, in my own day, and how much it has gained in twenty years, and has undermined the foundations of several buildings, I see clearly that it is an unusual disturbance; for if the river had always so done, or if it were al-ways so to do, the face of the world would be subverted. But they are subject to changes: sometimes they overflow on one side, sometimes on the other; sometimes they keep within their banks. I am not speaking of sudden inundations, of which we can lay our hand on the causes. In Medoc, along the seacoast, my brother, Sieur D'Arsac, saw an estate of his buried under the sand which the sea threw upon it; the roofs of some buildings are still visible; his revenues and domain are transformed into very poor pastures. The people of the place say that for some time past the sea pushes on so effectually toward them, that they have lost four leagues of land. These sands are her harbingers; *(c)* and we see great moving sand dunes that march half a league before her and steadily advance.

(a) The other assertion of ancient times with which it is attempted to connect this discovery, is in Aristotle—that is, if that little treatise of *Unheard-of Wonders* be his. He there relates that certain Carthaginians, having started across the Atlantic Sea from the Strait of Gibraltar, and having sailed a long while, finally discovered a large, fertile island, well covered with forests, and watered by broad and deep rivers, far distant from any mainland; and that they, and others after them, attracted by the bounty and fertility of the soil, went thither with their wives and children, and set up their habitation there. The lords of Carthage, seeing that their country was being gradually depopulated, expressly forbade, upon pain of death, that any more of their people should go thither, and ex-pelled these new settlers, fearing, so it is said, that, as time passed, they might so multiply that they would supplant themselves, and ruin their state. This narrative of Aristotle's agrees no better with our newly-discovered territories.

This man that I had was a simple, plain fellow, which is a nature likely to give true testimony; for intelligent persons notice more things and scrutinise them more carefully; but they comment on them; and to make their interpretation of value and win belief for it, they can not refrain from altering the facts a little. They never represent things to you just as they are: they shape them and disguise them according to the aspect which they have seen them bear; and to win faith in their judgment and incline you to trust it, they readily help out the matter on one side, lengthen it, and amplify it. It needs a man either very truthful or so ignorant that he has no material wherewith to construct and give verisimilitude to false conceptions, and one who is wedded to nothing. My man was such a one; and, besides, he on divers occasions brought to me several sailors and traders whom he had known on his travels. So I am content with this information, with-out enquiring what the cosmographers say about it. We need topographers who would give us a detailed description of the places where they have been. But when they have the advantage over us of having seen Palestine, they desire to enjoy the privilege of telling us news about all the rest of the world. I could wish that every one would write what he knows and as much as he knows, not about one subject alone, but about all oth-ers; for one may have some special knowledge or experience as to the nature of a river or a fountain, who about other things knows only what everyone knows. He will under-take, however, in order to give currency to that little scrap of knowledge, to write on the whole science of physics. From this fault spring many grave disadvantages.

Now, to return to what I was talking of, I think that there is nothing barbaric or un-civilised in that nation, according to what I have been told, except that every one calls "barbarism" whatever he is not accustomed to. As, indeed, it seems that we have no other criterion of truth and of what is reasonable than the example and type of the opinions and customs of the country to which we belong: therein [to us] always is the perfect religion, the perfect political system, the perfect and achieved usage in all things. They are wild men, just as we call those fruits wild which Nature has produced unaided and in her usual course; whereas, in truth, it is those that we have altered by our skill and removed from the common kind which we ought rather to call wild. In the former the real and most useful and natural virtues are alive and vigorous—we have vitiated them in the latter, adapting them to the gratification of our corrupt taste; *(c)* and yet nevertheless the special savour and delicacy of divers uncultivated fruits of those regions seems excellent even to our taste in comparison with our own. *(a)* It is not reasonable that art should gain the preëminence over our great and puissant mother Nature. We have so overloaded the beauty and richness of her works by our contrivances that we have altogether smothered her. Still, truly, whenever she shines forth unveiled, she wonderfully shames our vain and trivial undertakings.

> *(b)* Et veniunt ederæ sponte sua melius,
> Surgit et in solis fromosior arbutus antris,
> Et volucres nulla dulcius arte canunt.

(a) All our efforts can not so much as reproduce the nest of the tiniest birdling, its contexture, its beauty, and its usefulness; nay, nor the web of the little spider. *(c)* All things, said Plato, are produced either by nature, or by chance, or by art; the greatest and most beautiful by one or other of the first two, the least and most imperfect by the last.

(a) These nations seem to me, then, wild in this sense, that they have received in very slight degree the external forms of human intelligence, and are still very near to their primitive simplicity. The laws of nature still govern them, very little corrupted by ours; even in such pureness that it sometimes grieves me that the knowledge of this did not come earlier, in the days when there were men who would have known better than we how to judge it. I am sorry that Lycurgus and Plato had not this knowledge; for it seems to me that what we see in intercourse with those nations surpasses not only all the paintings wherewith poetry has embellished the golden age, and all its conceptions in representing a happy condition of mankind, but also the idea and aspiration, even, of philosophy. They could not conceive so pure and simply an artlessness as we by experience know it to be; nor could they believe that human society could be carried on with so little artificiality and human unitedness. It is a nation, I will say to Plato, in which there is no sort of traffic, no acquaintance with letters, no knowledge of numbers, no title of magistrate or of political eminence, no custom of service, of wealth, or of poverty, no contracts, no successions, no dividings of property, no occupations except leisurely ones, no respect for any kinship save in common, no clothing, no agriculture, no metals, no use of wine or grain. The very words that signify falsehood, treachery, dissimulation, avarice, envy, slander, forgiveness, are unheard of. How far from such perfection would he find the Republic he imagined: *(c) viri a diis recentes.*

> *(b)* Hos natura modos primum dedit.

(a) For the rest, they live in a country with a most agreeable and pleasant climate; consequently, according to what my witnesses have told me, it is a rare thing to see a sick man there; and they have assured me that any one palsied, or blear-eyed, or toothless, or bent

with old age is never to be seen. These people are settled on the sea-shore, and are shut in, landward, by a chain of high mountains, leaving a strip a hundred leagues or thereabouts in width. They have a great abundance of fish and meats, which bear no resemblance to ours, and they eat them without other elaboration than cooking. The first man who rode a horse there, although he had been with them on several other voyages, so terrified them in that guise that they shot him to death with arrows before they could recognise him.

Their buildings are very long and can hold two or three hundred souls; they are built of the bark of large trees, fastened to the earth at one end and resting against and supporting one another at the ridge-pole, after the fashion of some of our barns, the roofing whereof falls to the ground and serves for side and end walls. They have wood so hard that they cut with it and make swords of it, and gridirons for cooking their meat. Their beds are a cotton web, hung from the roof like those in our ships, each person having his own, for the women lie apart from their husbands. They rise with the sun and eat immediately after rising, for the whole day's need; for they have no other meal than this. They do not drink then, *(b)* as Suidas says of certain Oriental nations who drank when not eating; *(a)* they drink many times during the day, and a great deal. Their beverage is made of some root, and is of the colour of our light wines; they drink it only luke-warm. This beverage will keep only two or three days; it is rather sharp in taste, not at all intoxicating, good for the stomach, and laxative for those who are not accustomed to it; it is a very pleasant drink for those wonted to it. Instead of bread they use a certain substance like preserved coriander. I have tasted it; its flavour is sweetish and rather insipid. The whole day is passed in dancing. The young men go hunting wild animals with bows. A part of the women employ themselves meanwhile in warming their drink, which is their chief duty. Some one of the old men, in the morning, before they begin to eat, counsels the whole collected household, walking from end to end of the building and repeating the same phrase many times, until he has completed the turn (for the buildings are fully a hundred paces in length). He enjoins upon them only two things—valour against the enemy and friendship for their wives. And they never fail, by way of response, to note the obligation that it is their wives who keep their drink warm and well-seasoned for them. There can be seen in many places, and, among others, in my house, the fashion of their beds, of their twisted ropes, of their wooden swords and the wooden armlets with which they protect their wrists in battle, and of the long staves, open at one end, by the sound of which they mark time in their dancing. They are clean-shaven, and they shave much more closely than we do, with no other razor than one of wood or stone.

They believe their souls to be immortal, and that they who have deserved well of the gods have their abode in that quarter of the heavens where the sun rises; the accursed, in the Occident. They have I know not what kinds of priests and prophets, who very rarely come among the people, having their abode in the mountains. On their arrival a great festival and solemn asemblage of several villages takes place. (Each building such as I have described is a village, and they are about a French league distant one from another.) The prophet speaks to them in public, inciting them to virtue and to their duty; but their whole moral teaching contains only these two articles: resoluteness in war and affection for their wives. He prophesies things to come and the results they may hope for from their undertakings; shows them the way toward war, or dissuades them from it; but all this is under the condition that, when he fails to prophesy truly, and if it chances them otherwise than he predicted to them, he is chopped into a thousand pieces if they catch him, and condemned as a false prophet. For this reason, he who has once erred is never seen gain. *(c)* Divination is a gift of God; that is why the misuse of it should be a punishable imposture. Among the Scythians, when the soothsayers failed in their venture, they were laid, loaded with chains, in carts filled with brushwood and drawn by oxen, in which they were burned alive. Those who manage things subject to the guidance of human knowledge are excusable if they do with them what they can; but these others, who come cheating us with assurances of an extraordinary power which is beyond our ken—must not they be punished, both because they do not carry out the fact of their promise, and for the foolhardiness of their imposture?

(a) They wage wars against the tribes that live on the other side of their mountains, farther inland, to which they go entirely naked, with no other weapons than bows, or wooden swords pointed at the end like the heads of our boar spears. The obstinacy of their combats is wonderful, and they never end save with slaughter and bloodshed; for as to routs and panic, they do not know what those are. Every man brings back as his trophy the head of the foe he has killed, and fastens it at the entrance of his abode. After they have for a long while treated their prisoners well and supplied them with all the comforts they can think of, the head man summons a great assemblage of his acquaintances. He ties a rope to one of the prisoner's arms, *(c)* by the end of which he holds him at a distance of some paces, for fear of being injured by him; *(a)* the other arm he gives to his dearest friend to hold in the same way; and they two, before the assembly, kill him with their swords. That done, they roast him, and all eat him in common and send portions to those of their friends who are absent. This is not, as some think, for sustenance, as the Scythians of old did, but to indicate an uttermost vengeance. And therefore, having observed that the Portuguese, who had allied themselves with their adversaries, made use, when they captured them, of another sort of death for them, which was to bury them to the waist and cast many darts at the rest of their bodies, and hang them afterward, they thought that these people from the other part of the world, who had spread the knowledge of many villanies among their neighbours, and who were much more expert than they in all sorts of evil-doing, would not choose that sort of vengeance without good reason, and that it must be more painful than theirs; and they began to lay aside their old fashion and to follow this one.

I am not sorry that we note the savage horribleness there is in such an action; but indeed I am sorry that, while rightly judging their misdeeds, we are very blind to our own. I think there is more barbarism in eating a living man than a dead one, in rending by torture and racking a body still quick to feel, in slowly roasting it, in giving it to dogs and swine to be torn and eaten (as we have not only read but seen in recent days, not among long-time foes, but among neighbours and fellow citizens, and, what is worse, in the guise of piety and religion), than in roasting it and eating it after it is dead. Chrysippus and Zeno, heads of the Stoic school, did indeed think that there was no harm in using a dead body for any thing demanded by our need, and in deriving sustenance from it; like our ancestors, who, being besieged by Cæsar in the town of Alexia, determined to relieve hunger during the siege by the bodies of old men, women, and other persons useless for fighting.

(b) Vascones, fama est, alimentis talibus usi Produxere animas.

(a) And physicians do not fear to make use of it in every sort of way for our health, whether to be applied internally or externally; but there was never found an opinion so

unreasonable as to excuse treachery, disloyalty, tyranny, and cruelty, which are our common faults.

We can, then, rightly call them barbarians with respect to the rules of reason, but not with respect to ourselves, who surpass them in every sort of barbarism. Their warfare is wholly noble and honourable, and has as much excuse and beauty as that malady of mankind can have. With them it has no other motive than simply eagerness of prowess. They are not at strife for the conquest of new territories, for they still enjoy that natural fertility which supplies them, without labour and without trouble, with all things necessary, in such abundance that they have no reason to enlarge their boundaries. They are still at that fortunate point of desiring only so much as is ordained by their natural needs: every thing beyond that is superfluous for them. They generally call those of the same age brothers, those younger, children; and the old men are fathers to all the others. They leave to their heirs in common the undivided full possession of property, without other title than that flawless one which Nature gives to her creatures on bringing them into the world. If their neighbours come over the mountains to attack them and win the victory over them, the victor's gain is glory, and the advantage of having proved the superior in valour and prowess; for no otherwise do they give heed to the property of the vanquished; and they turn back to their own country, where they lack nothing that is necessary, nor do they lack that great gift of knowing how to enjoy their condition happily and to be content with it. When the turn of the others comes, they do the same; they ask no other ransom of their prisoners than the admission and acknowledgement that they are conquered; but there is not one found in a whole age who does not prefer death rather than to abate, either by manner or by word, a single jot of the grandeur of an invincible courage; not one is seen who does not prefer to be killed rather than merely to ask not to be. They give them every liberty, so that life may be all the dearer to them; and they entertain them usually with threats of their future death, of the torments they will have to suffer, of the preparations that are being made to that end, of the lopping off of their limbs, and of the feast there will be at their expense. All this is done for the sole purpose of extorting from their lips some faltering or downcast word, or of making them long for flight, in order to obtain this advantage of having frightened them and of having shaken their firmness. For, it rightly understood, true victory consists in this single point:—

(c) Victoria nulla est Quam quæ confessos animo quoque subjugat hostes.

The Hungarians, very valorous fighters, did not formerly carry their point beyond reducing their enemy to their mercy; for, having extorted this admission from him, they let him go without injury and without ransom, save, at the most, forcing him to promise not henceforth to take arms against them.

(a) We obtain many advantages over our enemies, which are borrowed advantages, not our own. It is the quality of a porter, not of merit, to have stouter arms and legs; it is a lifeless and corporeal faculty to be always ready; it is a stroke of fortune to make our enemy stumble, and to dazzle his eyes by the glare of the sun; it is a trick of art and knowledge—which may fall to a dastardly and worthless person—to be skilled in fencing. A man's estimation and value depend upon his heart and his will; that is where his true honour lies; valour is strength, not of arms and legs, but of the mind and the soul; it does not depend upon the worth of our horse or of our armour, but upon our own. He who falls persistent in his will, *(c) si succederit de genu pugnat.* (a) He who abates no

whit of his firmness and confidence for any danger from death not far away; he who, while yielding up his soul, still gazes at his foe with an unshrinking and disdainful eye— he is beaten, not by us, but by fortune; he is killed, not conquered. *(b)* The most valiant are sometimes the most unfortunate. *(c)* So too there are defeats no less triumphant than victories. Nor did those four sister victories, the most splendid that the eyes of the sun can ever have seen,—of Salamis, Platæa, Mycale, and Sicily,—ever venture to compare all their combined glory to the glory of the defeat of King Leonidas and his men at the pass of Thermopylæ.

Who ever rushed with a more praiseworthy and more ambitious longing to the winning of a battle than did Captain Ischolas to the loss of one? Who ever more skilfully and carefully assured himself of safety than he of his destruction? He was appointed to defend a certain pass in the Peloponnesus against the Arcadians; finding himself wholly unable to do this because of the nature of the place and the inequality of the forces, and making up his mind that all who should meet the enemy would by necessity remain on the field; on the other hand, deeming it unworthy, both of his own valour and nobleness of spirit and of the Lacedæmonian name, to fail in his commission, he took a middle course between those two extremes, in this way: the youngest and most active of his force he preserved for the protection and service of their country, and sent them back to it; and with those who would be less missed, he decided to hold the pass, and by their deaths to make the enemy purchase the entrance thereto as dearly as possible. And so it fell out: for, being presently surrounded on all sides by the Arcadians, after he and his had made a great slaughter of them, they were all killed. Is there any trophy assigned to victors, which would not be more justly due to these vanquished? The real surmounting had for its part strife, not safety; and the honour of courage consists in fighting, not in winning.

(a) To return to our narrative, these prisoners, despite all that is done to them, are so far from yielding that, on the contrary, during the two or three months that they are kept in captivity, they bear themselves cheerfully; they urge their masters to make haste to put them to that test; they defy them, insult them, upbraid them with their cowardice and with the number of battles they have lost in mutual combat. I have a ballad written by a prisoner wherein is this taunt: Let them come boldly every one, and gather together to dine upon him; for they will at the same time eat their own fathers and grandfathers, who have served as food and nourishment for his body; "these muscles," he says, "this flesh, and these veins are your own, poor fools that you are; you do not recognise that the substance of your ancestors' limbs still clings to them. Taste them carefully, and you will find in them the flavour of your own flesh"—a conceit which has no smack of barbarism. Those who depict them when dying, and who describe the act of putting them to death, depict the prisoner as spitting in the faces of those who kill him and making mouths at them. In truth, they do not, to their last gasp, cease to brave and defy them by word and look. Verily, in comparison with ourselves these men are savages indeed; for it must be that they are so, or else that we are so; there is a wonderful distance between their behaviour and ours.

The men have several wives, and they have the larger number in proportion to their reputation for valour. A notably beautiful thing in their marriages is that the same eagerness that our wives have to keep us from the friendship and good-will of other women, theirs have to an equal degree to obtain this for their husbands. Being more solicitous for their husband's honour than for any other thing, they seek, and make it their care to have, as many companions as they can, forasmuch as it is a testimony to the husband's valour. *(c)* Our wives will cry out on this as a miracle: it is not so; it is a properly matrimonial virtue, but of the highest type. And in the Bible, Leah, Rachel, Sarah, and the wives of Jacob gave their beautiful maidservants to their husbands; and Livia seconded the appetites of Augustus, to her own detriment; and the wife of King Dejotarus, Straton-ica, not only lent to her husband for his use a very beautiful young maid in her service, but carefully brought up their children and gave them a helping hand toward the suc-cession to their father's estates. *(a)* And, to the end that it may not be thought that all this is done from simple and slavish compliance with usage, and by the influence of the au-thority of their ancient customs, without reflection and without judgement, and because their wits are so dull that they can not take any other course, some examples of their ability should be brought forward. Besides what I have just quoted from one of their war-like songs, I have another, an amorous one, which begins in this way: "Adder, stay thee; stay thee, adder, to the end that my sister may make, after the pattern of thy markings, the fashion and workmanship of a rich girdle, which I may give to my love; so shall thy beauty and thy grace be for all time more highly esteemed than all other serpents." This is the first couplet, and it is the refrain of the ballad. Now I have enough knowledge of poetry to form this judgement, that not only is there nothing barbaric in this conception, but that it is quite Anacreontic. Their language, moreover, is a soft language and has a pleasant sound, and much resembles the Greek in its terminations.

Three of this people—not knowing how dear the knowledge of the corruption of this country will some day cost their peace of mind and their happiness, and that from this intercourse will be born their ruin, which conjecture may be already in process of confirmation; most miserable in having allowed themselves to be tricked by the desire for things unknown, and in having left the sweetness of their own skies, to come to gaze at ours—were at Rouen at the time that the late King Charles the Ninth was there. The king talked with them a long while; they were shown our modes of life, our magnifi-cence, and the outward appearance of a beautiful city. Thereafter some one asked them what they thought of all this, and wished to learn from them what had seemed to them most worthy of admiration. They mentioned in reply three things, of which I have forgot-ten the third, and am very sorry for it; but I remember two. They said that, in the first place, they thought it very strange that so many tall, bearded men, strong and well armed, who were about the king (they probably referred to the Swiss of the Guard), should humble themselves to obey a child, and that they did not rather choose some one of themselves to command them. Secondly (they have a fashion of speech of call-ing men halves of one another), they had perceived that there were among us some men gorged to the full with all sorts of possessions, and that their other halves were beg-gars at their doors, gaunt with hunger and destitution; and they thought it strange that these poverty-stricken halves could suffer such injustice, and that they did not take the others by the throat or set fire to their houses. I talked with one of them a very long while; but I had an interpreter who followed me so badly, and who was so hindered by his stupidity from grasping my ideas, that I could not have any pleasure in it. When I asked what advantage he derived from his superior position among his people (for he was a captain and our seamen called him king), he said that it was the privilege of marching at their head in war. By how many men he was followed. He indicated a cer-tain extent of ground, as if to signify that it was by as many men as that space would hold—perhaps four or five thousand. Whether, when there was no war, all his authority was at an end. He said that he still retained the right, when he visited the villages that were in his dependence, to have paths made for him through the thickets of their forests, by which he could travel easily.

All this does not seem too much amiss; but then, they do not wear breeches!

5. Thomas Morton, *New English Canaan*

A lawyer by training, Thomas Morton arrived in New England in 1622 to begin a new life as a landowner and cultivator. Unlike many of his neighbors, however, Morton left England in pursuit of economic gain rather than spiritual freedom, and within a very short period of time, he ran afoul of the Puritan-dominated governments of Massachusetts Bay. He was imprisoned at least three times. The Puritan governments may have harshly treated Morton because he was competing with them in the fur trade, but they were also clearly uneasy over his reputation for licentious living. Disapproving neighbors referred to Morton's plantation of Maremount as "merrymount" because of the lively mixed English and indigenous society that gathered there. Morton's scathing depiction of Puritan settlements in his treatise the *New English Canaan* (1637) also did little to quell local unease about his presence. Religious bias aside, Morton's detailed treatise remains one of the most important sources on early colonial life in New England. As the following excerpt shows, one of the striking features of his account is its optimistic and respectful view of indigenous culture. Here Morton discusses the possible origins of the native cultures in the New World. For this unconventional Englishman, the issue is not whether the native peoples are human but rather which human society produced them.

New English Canaan

In the yeare since the incarnation of Christ, 1622, it was my chance to be landed in the parts of New England, where I found two sortes of people, the one Christians, the other Infidels; these I found most full of humanity, and more friendly then the other: as shall hereafter be made apparant in Dew-Course by their severall actions from time to time, whilest I lived among them. After my arrivall in those partes, I endeavoured by all the wayes and meanes that I could to find out from what people, or nation, the Natives of New England might be conjectured originilly to proceede; and by continuance and conversation amongst them, I attaned to so much of their language, as by all probable conjecture may make the same manifest: for it hath been found by divers, and those of good judgement, that the Natives of this Country doe use very many wordes, both of Greeke and Latine, to the same signification that the Latins and Greekes have done; as *en animia,* when an Indian expresseth that hee doth anything with a good will; and *Pascopan* signifieth greedy gut, this being the name of an Indian that was so called of a Child, through the greedinesse of his minde and much eating, for *Pasco* in Latine signifieth to feede, and *Pan* in Greeke signifieth all; and *Pasco nantum, quasi pasco nondum,* halfe starved, or not eating, as yet; *Equa coge,* set it upright; *Mona* is an Island in their language, *quasi Monon,* that is alone, for an Island is a peece or plott of ground standing alone, and devided from the mane Land by force of water.

Cos is a Whetstone with them. *Hame* an instrument to take fish. Many places doe retaine the name of *Pan,* as Pantneket an *Matta pan,* so that it may be thought that these people heretofore have had the name of *Pan* in great reverence and estimation, and it may bee have worshipped *Pan* the great God of the Heathens: Howsoever they doe use no manner of worship at all now: and it is most likely that the Natives of this Country are descended from people bred upon that part of the world which is towardes the Tropicke of Cancer, for they doe still retaine the memory of some of the Starres one that part of the Cælestiall Globe, as the North-Starre, which with them is called Maske, for Maske in their Languace signifieth a Beare: and they doe divide the windes into eight partes, and it seemes originally have had some litterature amongst them, which time hath Cancelled and worne out of use.

And whereas it hath beene the opinion of some men, which shall be nameless, that the Natives of New-England may proceede from the race of the Tartars, and come from Tartaria into those partes, over the frozen Sea, I see no probability for any such Conjecture; for as much as a people once setled must be remooved by compulsion, or else tempted thereunto in hope of better fortunes, upon commendations of the place unto which they should be drawne to remoove: and if it may be thought that these people came over the frozen Sea, then would it be by compulsion? if so, then by whome, or when? or what part of this mane continent may be thought to border upon the Country of the Tartars, it is yet unknown: and it is not like, that a people well enough at ease will of their one accord undertake to travayle over a Sea of Ice, considering how many difficulties they shall encounter with; as first, whether there be any Land at the end of their unknown way, no Land being in view; then want of Food to sustane life in the meane time upon that Sea of Ice; or how should they doe for Fuell, to keepe them at night from freezing to death, which will not bee had in such a place. But it may perhaps be granted that the Natives of this Country might originally come of the scattered Trojans: For after that Brutus, who was the forth from Aneas, left Latium upon the conflict had with the Latines, (where although hee gave them a great overthrow, to the Slaughter of their grand Captaine and many other of the Heroes of Latium, yet hee held it more safety to depart unto some other place and people, then by staying to runne the hazard of an unquiet life or doubtfull Conquest, which as history maketh mention hee performed,) this people were dispersed: there is no question but the people that lived with him, by reason of their conversation with the Græcians and Latines, had a mixed language that participated of both, whatsoever was that which was proper to their owne nation at first I know not; for this is commonly seene where 2. nations traffique together, the one indevouring to understand the others meaning makes them both many times speak a mixed language, as is approved by the Natives of New England, through the covetous desire they have to commerce with our nation and wee with them.

And when Brutus did depart from Latium, we doe not finde that his whole number went with him at once, or arrived at one place; and being put to Sea might encounter with a storme that would carry them out of sight of Land, and then they might sayle God knoweth whether, and so might be put upon this Coast, as well as any other. Compasse I beleeve they had none in those dayes; Sayles they might have, (which Dædalus the first inventor thereof left to after ages, having taught his Sonne Icarus the use of it, who to this Cost found how dangerous it is for a Sonne not to observe the precepts of a wise Father, so that the Icarian Sea now retaines the memory of it to this day,) and Victuals they might have good store, and many other things fittinge; oares without all question they would store themselves with, in such a case; but for the use of Compasse, there is no mention made of it at that time (which was much about Sauls time, the first that was made King of Israell.) Yet it is thought (and that not without good reason for it) that the use of the Loadstone and Compasse was knowne in Salomons time, for as much as hee sent Shippes to fetch of the gould of Ophir, to adorne and bewtify that magnificent Temple of Hierusalem by him built for the glory of Almighty God, and by his speciall appointment: and it is held by Cosmographers to be 3. yeares voyage from Hierusalem to Ophir, and it is conceaved that such a voyage could not have beene performed, without the helpe of the Loadstone and Compasse.

And why should any man thinke the Natives of New England to be the gleanings of all Nations, onely because by the pronounciation and termination their words seeme to trench upon severall languages, when time hath not furnished him with the interpretation thereof. The thinge that must induce a man of reasonable capacity to any maner of conjecture of their originall, must be the sence and signification of the words, principally to frame this argument by, when hee shall drawe to any conclusion thereupon: otherwise hee shall but runne rounde about a maze (as some of the fantasticall tribe use to do about the tythe of mint and comin.) Therefore, since I have had the approbation of Sir Christopher Gardiner, Knight, an able gentl. that lived amongst them, and of David Tompson, a Scottish gentl. that likewise was conversant with those people, both Scollers and Travellers that were diligent in taking notice of these things, as men of good judgement, and that have bin in those parts any time, besides others of lesse, now I am bold to conclude that the originall of the Natives of New England may be well conjectured to be from the scattered Trojans, after such time as Brutus departed from Latium.

Figure 8.1 Theodore deBry, "The Town of Secota," 1585-88. Service Historique dela Marine, Vincennes, France. Giraudon/Art Resource, NY.

Note: John White, the artist, was sent by Sir Walter Raleigh to his colony of Roanoake in 1577 to record native life as well as natural resources. He returned there as governor in 1587. White's watercolor paintings were later transformed into engravings by Theodore de Bry for his work *America*. White's depictions of the indigenous population are considered among the most sensitive images at the moment of contact. This portrayal of a Secota village suggests an orderly and well-governed community.

Study Questions

1. In what significant ways were the Jews and Muslims different from the peoples of the New World according to the papal bull *Inter Caetera?*
2. How does Las Casas define the nature of the New World peoples?
3. Where do we see humanist influence in *On Cannibals?*
4. Compare Morton's understanding of the character of the indigenous peoples with that of Montaigne. Do you think that their versions differ because Montaigne never visited the Americas whereas Morton did? What cultural values does the painting of the Secota village by John White suggest?
5. In what ways were the Spanish an "inferior" culture according to the Nahua authors of the *Florentine Codex?* Does this reflect a different perception of human nature in comparison with the European interpretations?

Suggested Readings

Kupperman, Karen Ordahl. *Settling with the Indians.* Totowa, NJ: Rowman and Littlefield, 1980.

Lockheart, James. *The Nahuas after the Conquest. A Social and Cultural History of the Indians of Central Mexico, Sixteenth through Eighteenth Centuries.* Stanford, CA: Stanford University Press, 1992.

Pagden, Anthony. *The Fall of Natural Man. The American Indian and the Origins of Comparative Ethnology.* Cambridge: Cambridge University Press, 1982.

Web Sites

1. Bartolomé de Las Casas

    http://www.lamp.ac.uk/tairona/a4casas.html

2. Michel de Montaigne, *On Cannibals*

    http://www.humanities.ccny.cuny.edu/history/reader/cannibal.htm

9

Early Colonization
1500–1700 A.D.

TEXTS

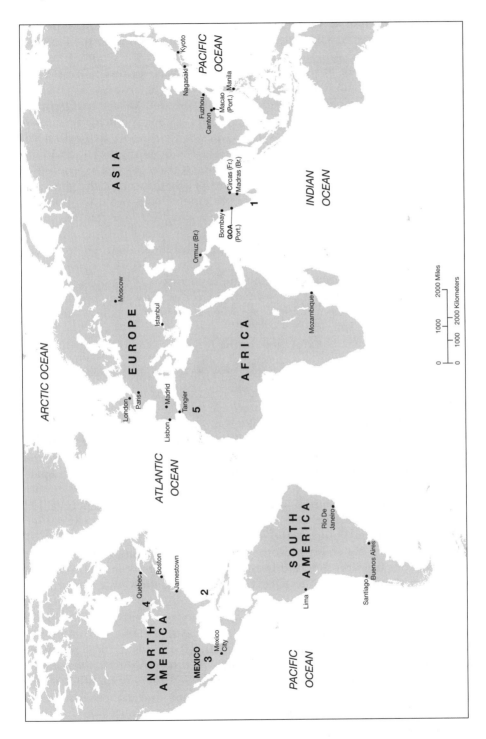

PACIFIC OCEAN

Kyoto

Nagasaki

Fuzhou

Canton

Macao (Port.)

Manila

A S I A

Circas (Fr.)

Madras (Br.)

1

Bombay

GOA (Port.)

INDIAN OCEAN

Ormuz (Br.)

Moscow

E U R O P E

Istanbul

A F R I C A

Mozambique

London

Paris

Madrid

Tangier

5

Lisbon

ATLANTIC OCEAN

0   1000   2000 Miles

0   1000   2000 Kilometers

ARCTIC OCEAN

Quebec

Boston

Jamestown

4

2

N O R T H   A M E R I C A

MEXICO

3

Mexico City

S O U T H   A M E R I C A

Rio De Janeiro

Lima

Santiago

Buenos Aires

PACIFIC OCEAN

Within a decade of Columbus's voyage across the Atlantic, prospective settlers began making their way in increasing numbers to the coasts of West Africa and the Americas. The impetus behind early colonization was largely economic. For Portuguese settlers, the coastal regions of West Africa offered lucrative trade first in the form of slaves and later in the form of exotic foodstuffs. The gold and silver mines discovered in Mexico and Peru encouraged many Europeans to settle in these Spanish-held territories. Although the British and French settlers who went farther to the north never discovered the same rich mineral deposits as the Spanish, they soon found that northern resources such as timber, fur, and tobacco, as well as a variety of different foods, had a ready market in Europe. By the end of the sixteenth century, two somewhat distinct colonial settlement zones begin to appear in the Western Atlantic along an east-west axis: a southern zone that was dominated by the Spanish, Portuguese, and to a lesser extent the French, and a northern zone occupied largely by the English and the French. The southern zone included modern day Latin America, Mexico, and the Caribbean whereas the northern zone comprised the eastern coastal regions of modern day North America. During the subsequent century, the Dutch would also begin to play an increasingly important role as a colonizing culture in Africa, East India, and the Americas.

The settlements that emerged during the early years of European colonization varied enormously in character from region to region. The earliest Portuguese communities in Africa, Asia, and the Americas were typically merchant communities located along important trading routes rather than agricultural settlements. By the 1500s, however, the plantation system began to emerge in the Portuguese Atlantic islands off the coast of Africa for the production of sugar. This system was soon widely imitated by the other colonial empires, appearing in the French and English Caribbean territories and some of the British colonies in North America. Laying the basis of the Spanish colonial system was the *encomienda,* a royal grant that entitled certain Spanish settlers to the labor of a specified number of indigenous people. [1] This labor usually took the form of agricultural or domestic work on the settler's *hacienda* (farm), but it could also include work in the mines. The economic structures that emerged in the northernmost regions of the Americas were different from those found in the Spanish colonies. Smaller landholdings characterized the northern colonies, and agriculture was the primary source of wealth. [4]

These differences in settlement patterns are only partly explainable in terms of cultural differences among the European settlers. Also important factors were the native cultures themselves and the kinds of local resources available for European exploitation. Europeans discovered that it was easier to exploit human labor in more highly urbanized regions such as central Mexico, for example, than in regions where hunter and gathering societies predominated. Nomadic communities such as these could easily leave the area in which European settlers were organizing a native labor force. European settlers in New England and New France consequently relied on African slaves, indentured European servants, and their own labor to develop the land.

There is no question that the European colonies were founded on the exploitation of indigenous populations. The mass displacement of African peoples to the plantations of Brazil, the Caribbean islands, and North America remains one of the most disturbing and destructive moments in European history [3] though by no means the only one. Indigenous and European accounts make it clear that European settlers were frequently intolerant of native cultural and religious practices and were willing to use excessive violence to exert control. Growing European presence in the New World after 1600 only served to heighten the tension between Europeans and indigenous peoples, especially as European control of land and labor increasingly threatened indigenous self-sufficiency and autonomy. As devastating as the colonial experience was for the Africans, Amerindians, and other indigenous populations subjected to European rule, recent studies on the early years of colonization emphasize the persistence of indigenous culture in the face of European authority. Far from being able to impose European structures on a passive, receptive population, succeeding generations of European rulers, administrators, and settlers were forced to work with and adapt colonial structures to existing indigenous social, political, economic, and spiritual patterns of organization. In Mexico and Peru, for example, Spanish local administrative structures followed indigenous ones. Cultural interaction ultimately laid the groundwork for the emergence of altogether new and distinct societies in the colonies as the mingling of European and native peoples created new racial mixtures [2] and new linguistic groups among other unique cultural formations.

1. THE *REQUERMIENTO*

Increasing competition with the Portuguese over jurisdiction in the Atlantic led the Spanish to devise one of the most famous documents of the early colonial period: the Requirement (*Requermiento*). One of the cornerstones of early Spanish colonial policy, the *Requermiento* became law in 1526. The *Requermiento* articulated Spanish claims to jurisdiction in the New World based on Roman law and the Bible. Spanish explorers and settlers were ordered to read aloud this document as they entered and claimed each new region. Clearly the indigenous peoples were not expected to understand the document because it was written in Spanish, a fact that reflects early Spanish attitudes of governance. Like other European colonial powers, the Spanish were eager to build a juridical foundation for their control of New World territories. Spanish claims of just rule, however, revolved around the assumption that the peoples of the New World were incapable of ruling themselves.

The Requermiento

"On the part of the king, Don Fernando, and of Doña Juana, his daughter, queen of Castile and Leon, subduers of the barbarous nations, we their servants notify and make known to you, as best we can, that the Lord our God, living and eternal, created the heaven and the earth, and one man and one woman, of whom you and we, and all the men of the world, were and are descendants, and all those who come after us. But, on account of the multitude which has sprung from this man and woman in the five thousand years since the world was created, it was necessary that some men should go one way and some another, and that they should be divided into many kingdoms and provinces, for in one alone they could not be sustained.

"Of all these nations God our Lord gave charge to one man, called St. Peter, that he should be lord and superior of all the men in the world, that all should obey him, and that he should be the head of the whole human race, wherever men should live, and under whatever law, sect, or belief they should be; and he gave him the world for his kingdom and jurisdiction.

"And he commanded him to place his seat in Rome, as the spot most fitting to rule the world from; but also he permitted him to have his seat in any other part of the world, and to judge and govern all Christians, Moors, Jews, Gentiles, and all other sects. This man was called Pope, as if to say Admirable Great Father and Governor of men. The men who lived in that time obeyed that St. Peter, and took him for lord, king, and superior of the universe" (imagine what Tiberius or Nero would have said to this assertion!); "so also they have regarded the others who after him have been elected to the pontificate, and so has it been continued even till now, and will continue till the end of the world.

"One of these pontiffs, who succeeded that St. Peter as lord of the world in the dignity and seat which I have before mentioned, made donation of these isles and Terra-firma to the aforesaid king and queen and to their successors, our lords, with all that there are in these territories, as is contained in certain writings which passed upon the subject as aforesaid, which you can see if you wish.

"So their highnesses are kings and lords of these islands and land of Terra-firma by virtue of this donation; and some islands, and indeed almost all those to whom this has been notified, have received and served their highnesses, as lords and kings, in the way that subjects ought to do, with good will, without any resistance, immediately, without delay, when they were informed of the aforesaid facts. And also they received and obeyed the priests whom their highnesses sent to preach to them and to teach them our Holy faith; and all these, of their own free will, without any reward or condition, have become Christians, and are so, and their highnesses have joyfully and benignantly received them, and also have commanded them to be treated as their subjects and vassals; and you too are held and obliged to do the same. Wherefore, as best we can, we ask and require you that you consider what we have said to you, and that you take the time that shall be necessary to understand and deliberate upon it, and that you acknowledge the Church as the ruler and superior of the whole world (*por Señora y Superiora del universo mundo*), and the high priest called Pope, and in his name the king and queen Doña Juana our lords, in his place, as superiors, and lords, and kings of these islands and this Terra-firma by virtue of the said donation, and that you consent and give place that these religious fathers should declare and preach to you the aforesaid.

"If you do so you will do well, and that which you are obliged to do to their highnesses, and we in their name shall receive you in all love and charity, and shall leave you your wives, and your children, and your lands free without servitude, that you may do with them and with yourselves freely that which you like and think best, and they shall not compel you to turn Christians, unless you yourselves, when informed of the truth, should wish to be converted to our holy Catholic faith, as almost all the inhabitants of the rest of the islands have done; and, besides this, their highnesses award you many privileges and exemptions" (hard words in a new world!), "and will grant you many benefits.

"But, if you do not do this, and maliciously make delay in it, I certify to you that, with the help of God, we shall powerfully enter into your country, and shall make war against you in all ways and manners that we can, and shall subject you to the yoke and obedience of the Church and of their highnesses; we shall take you, and your wives, and your children, and shall make slaves of them, and as such shall sell and dispose of them as their highnesses may command; and we shall take away your goods, and shall do you all the mischief and damage that we can, as to vassals who do not obey, and refuse to receive their lord, and resist and contradict him; and we protest that the deaths and losses which shall accrue from this are your fault, and not that of their highnesses, or ours, nor of these cavaliers who come with us. And that we have said this to you, and made this Requisition, we request the notary here present to give us his testimony in writing, and we ask the rest who are present that they should be witnesses of this Requisition."

2. YNCA GARCILAZO DE LA VEGA, *THE ROYAL COMMENTARIES OF THE INCAS*

The *Royal Commentaries* is one of the most famous indigenous accounts of European colonization in Peru. Ynca Garcilaso de la Vega (1537–1616) was the son of a Spanish nobleman, Garcilaso de la Vega, and an Inca Princess. His penetrating account of Spanish colonization of Peru reflects the dramatic changes taking place in Peruvian society as a result of the Spanish Conquest during the first generation of settlement. The following excerpt discusses the introduction of Spanish plants and foodstuffs to Peru and, even more importantly, the new racial groups emerging from the mixtures of European, African, and indigenous peoples. Garcilaso himself was a product of a mixed marriage, and throughout his life he was constantly aware of both of his cultural heritages.

The Royal Commentaries

Chapter XXIX

Of the Garden Stuffs and Herbs, and Concerning Their Growth
None of the vegetables that are eaten in Spain were found in Peru; neither lettuces, endives, radishes, spinach, beetroot, mint, coriander, artichokes, asparagus, carrots, parsley, penny-royal, nor any of the useful herbs of Spain. Of the seeds they had neither beans,

peas, mustard, caraway, anise, rice, lavender, cumin, marjoram, fennel, poppy, clover, nor camomile; nor had they roses, pinks, jessamine, lilies, nor white musk roses.

But now they have all these herbs and flowers in such abundance that some of them are becoming mischievous, such as the mustard, mint, and camomile, which have spread to such an extent in some of the valleys that they have overcome the power and diligence of the inhabitants in pulling them up, and have even changed the ancient names of the valleys. Thus the Valley of Mint, on the sea coast, used to be called Rucma, and there are other instances. In the City of the Kings the first endives and spinach multiplied in such a way that a horse could not force its way through them. The monstrous size and great abundance of the legumes and cereals that were first sown is almost incredible. Wheat, in many parts, at first yielded three hundred *fanegas* and more for one *fanega* that was planted.

In the Valley of Huarcu, in a village that the Viceroy Don Andres Hurtado de Mendoza, Marquis of Cañete, has recently ordered to be established, when I was passing through on my way to Spain, in the year 1560, a citizen, named Garci Vasquez, who had been a servant of my father, took me to his house and gave me some supper. He said: "Eat of this bread, which is part of a yield of three hundred *fanegas,* and take the news with you to Spain." I was astonished at the great yield, for I had not been accustomed to hear of anything like it. Garci Vasquez then said to me: "Do not be hard of belief, for what I tell you is true, on the word of a Christian. I sowed two and a half *fanegas* of wheat, and I have reaped six hundred and eighty, besides losing as much again for want of reapers."

I told the same story to Gonzalo Silvestre, of whom we have said much in our history of Florida, and of whom we shall make further mention, if we reach so far, in this work. He answered that it was not very wonderful; for that, in the province of Chuquisaca, near the river Pillcumayu, on some land of his, he raised four hundred and five hundred *fanegas* from one. In 1556, when Don Garcia de Mendoza, son of the Viceroy, was on his way to the government of Chile, and touched at Arica, they told him that, in a neighbouring valley called Cusapa, there was a radish of such a marvellous size, that five horses were tethered under its shade; and they wanted him to come and see it. Don Garcia said that he must see it with his own eyes, that he might be able to vouch for the story. He went with several others, and saw that what had been told him was true. The radish was so thick that a man could scarcely make his arms meet round it, and so tender that it was afterwards brought to the lodging of Don Garcia, and eaten by many of the company. In the valley called the Valley of Mint they have measured many shoots which were two and a half yards long. The person who measured them is now with me in my house, and I write this on his authority.

In May 1595, I was talking with a gentleman named Don Martin de Contreras, nephew of the famous Francisco de Contreras, Governor of Nicaragua, in the holy cathedral church of Cordova; and I observed that I feared to mention the size of the cereals and vegetables of Peru, in this part of my history, because it would appear incredible to persons who had only seen those of Spain. He told me not to omit anything, that people might believe or not as they pleased, and that it was sufficient for me to state the truth. He added, "I am myself an eye-witness of the size of the radish at Cusapa; for I am one of those who accompanied Don Garcia de Mendoza, and I give my word of honour as a gentleman, that I saw the five horses tied to its branches, and afterwards I ate part of it, with the others. You may add that, during the same journey, I saw a melon at Yca that weighed four arrobas and three pounds; and this was registered before a notary, that such a wonderful thing might have credible witnesses. And in the valley of Yucay I ate a lettuce that weighed seven and a half pounds." This gentleman told me many other things touching the cereals, vegetables, and fruits, which I omit in order not to tire those that may read my work.

The Father Acosta, in the nineteenth chapter of his fourth book, where he treats of the vegetables and fruits of Peru, writes as follows, copied word for word:—

"I have not found that the Indians had gardens for vegetables, but they broke the ground up for legumes such as they have, called *frijoles*, which they use instead of beans and peas. They had none of the garden-stuffs of Spain, but the Spaniards have introduced them, and in some places they thrive better in Peru, especially the melons in the valley of Yca, where they form a trunk, and last for years. They prune them as if they were trees, a thing which I do not believe to be practised in any part of Spain."

Thus far is from Father Acosta, whose authority encourages me to speak, without fear, of the great fertility of that land, as shown when the Spanish fruits were first planted, and throve in so wonderful and incredible a manner. That which the Father writes is not the least wonderful, and it may be added that the melons displayed another excellence. None of them became bad when they were left to ripen, and this was another sign of the fertility of the soil. As the first melons in the valley of Rimac gave rise to a good story, it will be well to insert it here, and thus show the simplicity of the Indians in ancient times. A citizen of the City of the Kings, and one of the first conquerors, named Antonio Solar, had an estate in Pachacamac, four leagues from the City of the Kings, which was managed by a Spaniard. This manager sent ten melons to his master, on the backs of two Indians, with a letter. On setting out, the manager told them not to eat any of the melons, because if they did, the letter would tell of them. The Indians set out, and when they got half way, they unloaded themselves to rest. One of them, moved by the spirit of gluttony, said to the other, "Shall we not taste this fruit from the estate of our master?" The other answered, "No; for if we eat it, this letter will tell of us, as the manager says." The first replied, "It will be a good plan to put the letter out of sight, and if it does not see us eating, it will not be able to say anything." His companion was satisfied with this proposal, and, hiding the letter, they ate one of the melons. In those early days the Indians did not know what letters were, and thought that the letters the Spaniards wrote were like messengers, and that they spoke what the Spaniards told them. They fancied also that they were like spies, and that they reported what they saw on the road. This was the reason that one Indian proposed to the other to put the letter out of sight, that it might not see them when they were eating. When they were getting ready to proceed on their journey, the Indian who had five melons in his load said to the other, "Do not let us go unequally laden, it will be well for us to make the loads equal; for, if you carry four and I five, they will suspect that we have eaten the odd one." His companion rejoined, "You say well." Then, in order to conceal one fault they committed another, and ate a second melon. They presented the eight that were left to their master, who, after reading the letter, asked them where the two missing melons were? They both answered at once, saying that they only received eight. Antonio Solar said, "Why do you lie to me, when this letter says that you were given ten. You must have eaten two of them." The Indians were astonished that the letter should openly tell their master what they had done in secret. They were confused, and knew not how to deny the truth. They went out, saying that the Spaniards might well be called gods, and have the name Uira-ccocha, when they could find out such great secrets.

Gomara tells a similar story touching what took place when Cuba was first occupied. It is not wonderful that the same sort of ignorance should be displayed in different places, by various nations, for the simplicity of the Indians of the New World, regarding things beyond their experience, was the same everywhere. They attributed to a supernatural cause every advantage that the Spaniards had over them, such as riding horses, ploughing with oxen, making mills, spanning great rivers with arches, firing guns so as to kill at two hundred paces, and other similar things. Hence also the two Indians called their master a god, because of the letter.

Chapter XXX

Of Flax, Asparagus, Carrots, and Anise

They had no flax in Peru. Doña Catalina de Retes, a native of the town of San Lucar de Barrameda, and mother-in-law of Francisco de Villafuerte, one of the first conquerors, a native of Cuzco, and a very noble and religious woman, and one of the first inhabitants of the convent of Santa Clara of Cuzco, sent to Spain for linseed to sow, and for a loom to weave linen in her home, in 1560. I left Peru in that year, and did not hear whether she received them or not. I have since heard that they gather plenty of flax, but I do not know whether my relations, Spanish and Indians, have become great weavers; for I never saw them at work. But I have seen them work and sew; for they had no flax when I was in the country, only very fine cotton, and beautiful wool which the Indian girls worked up with exquisite skill. They spun and carded the cotton and wool with their fingers; for they had no teazels, nor wheels for spinning. If they were not great workers of linen, they had an excuse, for they had not the means.

Returning to the subject of the great value that the Spaniards in Peru at first set upon the commonest things that came from Spain, as soon as they arrived; I remember that, in 1555 or 1556, Garcia de Melo, a native of Truxillo, and then treasurer of his Majesty's finances in Cuzco, sent three stalks of asparagus to my Lord Garcilasso de la Vega. He sent a message to say that they were the first that had been seen in Cuzco, and for that reason he sent them. They were very fine, two being as large round as the fingers of a man's hand, and a *tercia* in length. The third was thicker and shorter. They all were so tender that they broke of themselves. My father, to do more honour to the vegetables of Spain, ordered that they should be cooked in his own apartment, at the *brasero* that stood there, in presence of seven or eight gentlemen who were having supper with him. When the asparagus was cooked, he sent for salt and vinegar, and Garcilasso my Lord divided the two largest with his own hand, giving each of his guests a mouthful. He took the third for himself, saying that they must pardon him, for that, as it was a thing of Spain, he wished to have the advantage for that time. In this manner they ate the asparagus with great pleasure and enjoyment; and, though I waited upon them, and brought all the trimmings, I did not get any.

At the same time the Captain Bartolomè de Terrazas brought my father, as a great present, three carrots from Spain. They were served up at dinner when he had the next party, and, for greater magnificence, he gave a *pajuela* for them.

Anise was brought to Cuzco at about the same time, and was baked in the bread as a thing of great value, as if it had been the nectar or the ambrosia of the gods. All the things of Spain were valued in the same way, when they first began to arrive from Spain. I write an account of these things, though they may seem to be of little importance, because in time to come, which is the period when histories are of most use, men may rejoice to hear them. The other plants, cereals and legumes, have multiplied in the way that has been mentioned. They have also planted mulberries, and imported silk-worms, which were also unknown in Peru, but they have not been able to work the silk, owing to a very great difficulty that has arisen.

Chapter XXXI

New Names to Distinguish Different Generations

One of the chief things that have happened in the Indies, which must not be forgotten, is the introduction of Negroes, whom the Spaniards have brought there as slaves to work for them; for there were none in my country before the conquest. From these two races others have arisen, mixed in various ways, and they have given them different names for distinction. In our history of Florida we said something on this subject, but it will be well to repeat it here, as this is the proper place. They call a Spanish man or woman who comes from Spain a Spaniard or a Castillian; for they have both names there for the same thing, and I have used them in my history of Florida. The sons of a Spanish man and woman, born in the country, are called *Creoles,* which means that they are born in the country. It is a name that was invented by the Negroes. Among them it means a Negro born in the Indies, as distinguished from one born in Guinea. They hold those who are born in their native country in more honour than the children who are born in a strange land, and the parents are offended if they are called *Creoles.* The Spaniards, to express the same thing, have adopted the word into their language, to designate those born in the country. Thus both Spaniards and Negroes born in the Indies are called *Creoles.* The Negro who comes from Africa is called *Negro* or *Guineo.* The son of a Negro by an Indian woman, or of an Indian by a Negress, is called a *Mulatto.* Their children are called *Cholos,* a word brought from the Windward Islands, and meaning dog. The Spaniards use the word as a term of contempt and reproach. The sons of a Spaniard by an Indian woman, or of an Indian by a Spanish woman are called *Mestizos,* which means that we are a mixture of both nations. It was adopted by the first Spaniards who had children by Indian women; and, being a name given by our parents, I call myself by it with open mouth, and pride myself upon it. But the Indians look upon it as an insult, if anyone calls them *Mestizos.* Hence they adopted, with great joy, the name *Montañes,* which, with other vituperative epithets, the Spaniards gave them in place of that of *Mestizos.* The Spaniards do not consider that even in Spain the term *Montañes* is an honourable appellation, by reason of the privileges that were granted to the mountaineers of Asturias and Biscay. But to call any one by that name who is not a native of those provinces is an insult, for, in its usual signification, it means a thing of the mountains; as the great master, Antonio de Lebrija, who has the credit of all the sound Latinity of which Spain can now boast, says in his vocabulary. The equivalent word in the general language of Peru is *Sacha-runa,* which properly means a savage. That excellent master, Lebrija, called men *Montañeses* when he wished to insinuate covertly that they were savages. But my relations, not understanding the malicious design in applying that name, set store by their affront; instead of hating and detesting it, and calling themselves by the names of their fathers, while refusing to receive new and insulting appellations. The son of a Spaniard and a *Mestiza,* or of a *Mestizo* and a Spanish woman, is called *Quatralvo,* meaning that he is three parts Spanish and one Indian. The son of a *Mestizo* and an Indian woman, or of an Indian and *Mestiza* is called *Tresalvo,* having three parts Indian and one Spanish. All these names, and others which I do not mention to avoid being tedious, have been invented in my country to designate the generations that have risen up since the arrival of the Spaniards; and we may say that the Spaniards brought them with the other things, as they were not there before. We will now return to the Kings Yncas, sons of the great Huayna Ccapac, who are calling us that they may occupy us with grand events.

3. JOURNAL OF JAN VAN RIEBEECK

Born into an old and respected Dutch merchant family, Jan Van Riebeeck began working for the Dutch East Indies Company in 1639. In 1640, he was sent on his first trip to South Africa. Three years later, Riebeeck's administrative abilities brought him to Japan. After a brief return to the Netherlands, Riebeeck left for the Cape of Good Hope in 1651 as merchant and commander of the company. The *Journal* records the period in which Riebeeck governed the Dutch community; it is an interesting document for what it reveals about the internal workings of the Dutch East Indies Company. Founded in 1602 as a joint stock company, the Dutch East Indies Company was an enormous institution by the middle of the seventeenth century. It included several branch offices and a complex administrative hierarchy that exercised economic and political jurisdiction over colonies in Africa, the East Indies, and the New World. The detailed nature of the *Journal* reflects an administration trying to maintain close watch over its wide-flung offices in order to ensure that its directives were followed. By 1650, every office was asked to produce a journal recording company affairs. Valuable as an administrative document, the *Journal* is also a rich source of information on early colonial relations between European settlers and native peoples. The following two excerpts show that the survival of the colonial settlements was a constant struggle. The first excerpt highlights the important role played by native interpreters Eva and Doman in securing the survival of European settlements. Of the two, we know the most about Eva. Christianized by the Dutch and given the name Eva, her native name was Krotoa. Eva worked in the household of Riebeeck from an early age, and it was during these years that she learned Dutch. Valued for their linguistic skills, interpreters such as Eva and Doman occupied an ambiguous place in the early settlements. Europeans depended on them to establish harmonious working relations with the native peoples, but they did not always trust them to serve European interests. There is also some question as to what role these individuals played in native society as well as a result of their access to the colonial power structure. The second excerpt shows that Dutch concern about threats posed by indigenous peoples was matched by fear of potential rebellion within the African slave population.

Journal of Jan Van Riebeeck

JULY 1658

Sunday 7th Fine, lovely, sunny weather in the morning. The cattle were counted and found to number 227 in all, both young and old. From this we deducted the number the Hon. Company had originally possessed, viz. 117, leaving 110, which represented the number from Harry. Valued at 5 guilders per head, practically the purchase price, they were worth *f* 550, plus 260 sheep at 25 stivers each, *f* 325, making a total value of *f* 875. The value of what he had stolen from the Hon. Company was calculated in order to set it off against the above amount, viz. 43 head of cattle at 5 guilders each, *f* 215. The following articles entrusted to him for buying cattle in the interior, for which he delivered only 10 head of cattle, the rest being misappropriated to himself: 404 lbs. of copper at *f* 50 per 100 lbs., 202 guilders; 44 lbs. of tobacco at *f* 6 per 100 lbs., *f* 26.8; 1½ gross pipes at *f* 1.10; 24 brass chains at 27 stivers, *f* 32.8; and some beads and bric-a-brac valued at *f* 22.14, making a total of *f* 500. This value, when deducted from the above-mentioned figure of *f* 875, leaves *f* 375 as compensation for the loss suffered by the Hon. Company through interference with the increase.

Harry was accordingly told that there was no intention to return anything to him, as it was estimated that what had been recovered was less than what would have accrued to us from the increase of the livestock, while the question of the murder of the boy had yet to be settled and was not forgotten.

After the sermon to-day the articles of peace negotiated with the Kaapmans were read out and affixed everywhere. During the morning service 60 or 70 Hottentots had been loitering nearby, intending to steal the cattle from the Hon. Company once more, but seeing 25 or 26 stalwart soldiers guarding them, they retired as if they had merely come to have a look. The interpreter Eva was asked who they were and what this meant, and replied that they were Kaapmans who had come to spy how our cattle were guarded and were seeking an opportunity to steal them from us. She also said that the Fat Captain, Gogosoa, had made peace merely to free his son Osinghkhimma or Schacher, and Osaoa, and that they intended, when the Commander and the sergeant went out to the grain-fields or elsewhere, to seize the opportunity to kill them because the Commander had imprisoned Schacher and the sergeant had killed their comrade in the encounter yesterday, whereafter, so they believed, they would be able to overpower the rest as well. On being asked about the honourable peace they had made, she said that it had been made with the mouth, but they had not meant what they said. When the interpreter Doman was told this, he flatly contradicted it and maintained that these were the intentions of Harry's people. He stated that the men seen nearby had been to collect mussels on the rocks at the beach behind the Lion Mountain when the tide was out. These two interpreters are therefore contradicting each other with the greatest vigour, with the result that we are discovering many things. Eva stated that the Kaapmans intended entering into a general alliance with the others in the interior for the purpose of attacking us together. We replied to Eva that we hoped that they would come with many cattle so that our booty might be larger, and that we were a match for all the Hottentots should they dare to attempt it, but that it would be better for them to observe the conditions of the treaty, so that we might live as brethren as we had mutually agreed to do. To this Doman replied: "Yes, *Mijnheer*, the Kaapmans wish to do so, and this will be evident, when ships arrive, from their supply of cattle and their invitation to other natives to come here to trade with the Commander." Eva thereupon said: "Take care, *Mijnheer* Van Riebeeck, Doman lies and cajoles (meaning to say deceives) you, but I shall tell you the truth, for I overheard Schacher myself. If *Mijnheer* releases Harry and allows him to live at the fort with 4 or 5 milch cows, his people will always assist you against the Kaapmans." She talks thus from devotion to her uncle Harry, so that no credence can be given to it. Doman's statements must likewise be treated with reserve. When the latter was asked who among the Kaapmans would accompany him when proceeding to board ships on arrival here for the purpose of obtaining bread, etc., he replied: Osinghkhimma, alias Schacher, or perhaps Chaihantima, who is an important headman or chief of the Chainouquas, often mentioned before and from whom the most cattle were obtained approximately two years ago. We therefore concluded that if Schacher dared to go aboard, we need not fear what Eva had communicated to us. Orders were nevertheless given for a good watch to be kept and proper care to be exercised everywhere.

8th Fine, calm, clear, sunny morning, as yesterday. The Commander summoned the Council and, to augment it, also skipper Claes Franssen Bordingh, of the yacht *Maria* lying here in the roadstead. With his assistance the following resolution was passed....

AUGUST 1658

26th Overcast sky and westerly wind and mist. The Commander Riebeecq had 1,200 rooted branches as well as unrooted cuttings from the cut vines planted on the Bosheuvel, about three hours distant from the fort, by his private agriculturists and slaves, and also gave to the freemen as many as they wanted. The original stocks were left standing in the Company's gardens. Some of them already bore fruit last year, while most of them will evidently bear this year. By next season a fair quantity of cuttings will be obtainable from them and from those now planted for himself by the Commander at suitable places as aforesaid.

The Commander went out to-day for this purpose and also to make his customary visit to the freemen everywhere, inspecting their agricultural work and that of the Company and exhorting everyone to do his duty. To reach his own lands, he has to pass those of the freemen and the Company. He learned that 14 male and female slaves of the free sawyers had deserted the night before, and also one of his own, who, with two of the female slaves mentioned, had been recaptured. The sawyers were given some soldiers to assist them to recapture the others, as there were no Hottentots at hand who could be told of this in good time. Besides, Doman, the interpreter, who is a rascal, tries to thwart the Hon. Company in everything and is thrice as bad and harmful as Harry ever was throughout his life, as we discover daily and as Eva testifies. She states openly that he is the chief opponent of the Hon. Company; he calls her a lickspittle or flatterer, and makes her odious among her own people by saying that she speaks more in favour of the Dutch than the Hottentots. When she comes to interpret, he calls out: "See, there comes the advocate of the Dutch; she will tell her people some stories and lies and will finally betray them all", and anything which will serve to make her odious to them. We wish that this scamp had never left the Cape and that he could be seized without causing unrest and removed to the Robben Island.

In the afternoon the freemen's vessels *Peguijn* and the *Zeeleeuw* returned to the jetty from the Dassen Island, which they had left this morning, with 3 half-aums train-oil and 3,500 lbs. salted seal meat, as well as some eggs and fish, etc.

27th Dark, cloudy sky in the morning.

28th Somewhat clearer weather. Two female slaves were recovered, who made known by signs that their menfolk had intended to cut the throats of the free sawyers during the night while they were asleep if they could only have got hold of knives.

The freeman Harman Remajenne also came with 2 slaves who had run away from him, and asked for a chain with which to fetter them; this was given to him. The aforesaid recaptured female slaves had been seen by the Commander's agriculturists from the top of the Bosheuvel, where they were busy ploughing and from where they had a view over the whole of the flats. They had pursued the slaves and brought them out of the brushwood; the tracks of the others were being followed according to the directions of the women. Two of the Hon. Company's slaves also had absconded from the chief gardener during the night, after breaking out of the building outside the fort in which they had been locked up. Eva and Doman were therefore told to inform the two Kaapmans at present at the fort of the desertion of the slaves and to tell them to make it known to their people and to urge them to try and recapture the fugitives, now about 30 in number, at once, so that we might chain them, otherwise they might very likely attack the Kaapmans and rob them of their cattle, arms and other possessions, for once the slaves were armed, the Hottentots would be unable to master them and would be increasingly plagued by them and robbed and murdered. The slaves would also multiply in the course of time, having about a third of their women with them, and might become masters of all the Hottentots, who have only small mat huts and who are not as well protected as the Dutch, and therefore might easily be overcome by them; they were further told anything else which might encourage them to help in the search.

4. Thomas Hariot, *Narrative of the First English Plantation of Virginia*

Printed accounts of early settlements in the New World were eagerly absorbed by a fascinated European readership throughout the early modern period. Typical is the following account written by Thomas Hariot in 1588. Thomas Hariot was one of the earliest settlers to write about the native peoples in North America. His *Narrative* was first published in 1588 and was later included in Theodore de Bry's *America*. The intent of Hariot's work is clearly polemic as well as informative for he mentions recent slandering in Europe of Roanoke, the settlement established by Walter Raleigh on the island of Roanoke off the coast of Virginia. Like many other English travel writers of the period, Hariot was intent on encouraging English interest in the colonization of the new lands. Not surprisingly, his text paints a portrait of a land rich in natural resources and peopled by friendly and cooperative indigenous peoples. His intimate knowledge of native clothing, institutions, and cultural practices points to the coexistence and constant interaction of European and indigenous societies in this region. Although Hariot's view of the native peoples as culturally inferior was typical of his age, he nevertheless admires many facets of native culture. Hariot even went so far as to study the Algonquian language because he believed that only through communication with the native peoples could he truly come to understand their societies and give an accurate description of their cultural life.

Narrative of the First English Plantation of Virginia

Of the Nature and Manners of the People

It resteth I speake a word or two of the naturall inhabitants, their natures and maners, leauing large discourse thereof vntill time more conuenient hereafter: nowe onely so farre foorth, as that you may know, how that they in respect of troubling our inhabiting and planting, are not to be feared; but that they shall haue cause both to feare and loue vs that shall inhabite with them.

They are a people clothed with loose mantles made of Deere skins, & aprons of the same rounde about their middles; all els naked; of such a difference of statures only as wee in England; hauing no edge tooles or weapons of yron or steele to offend vs with-all, neither know they how to make any: those weapons that they haue, are onlie bowes made of Witch hazle, & arrowes of reeds; flat edged truncheons also of wood about a yard long, neither haue they any thing to defend themselues but targets made of barcks; and some armours made of stickes wickered together with thread.

Their townes are but small, & neere the sea coast but few, some containing but 10 or 12 houses; some 20. the greatest that we haue seene haue bene but of 30 houses: if they be walled it is only done with barks of trees made fast to stakes, or els with poles onely fixed vpright and close one by another.

Their houses are made of small poles made fast at the tops in rounde forme after the maner as is vsed in many arbories in our gardens of England, in most townes couered with barkes, and in some with artificiall mattes made of long rushes; from the tops of the houses downe to the ground. The length of them is commonly double to the breadth, in some places they are but 12 and 16 yardes long, and in other some wee haue seene of foure and twentie.

In some places of the countrey one onely towne belongeth to the gouernment of a *Wiróans* or chiefe Lorde; in other some two or three, in some sixe, eight, & more; the greatest *Wiróans* that yet we had dealing with had but eighteene townes in his gouernmẽt, and able to make not aboue seuen or eight hundred fighting men at the most: The language of euery gouernment is different from any other, and the farther they are distant the greater is the difference.

Their maner of warres amongst themselues is either by sudden surprising one an other most commonly about the dawning of the day, or moone light; or els by ambushes, or some suttle deuises: Set battels are very rare, except it fall out where there are many trees, where eyther part may haue some hope of defence, after the deliuerie of euery arrow, in leaping behind some or other.

If there fall out any warres between vs & them, what their fight is likely to bee, we hauing aduantages against them so many maner of waies, as by our discipline, our strange weapons and deuises els; especially by ordinance great and small, it may be eas-ily imagined; by the experience we haue had in some places, the turning vp of their heeles against vs in running away was their best defence.

In respect of vs they are a people poore, and for want of skill and iudgement in the knowledge and vse of our things, doe esteeme our trifles before thinges of greater value: Notwithstanding in their proper manner considering the want of such meanes as we haue, they seeme very ingenious; For although they haue no such tooles, nor any such craftes, sciences and artes as wee; yet in those thinges they doe, they shewe excel-lencie of wit. And by howe much they vpon due consideration shall finde our manner of knowledges and craftes to exceede theirs in perfection, and speed for doing or execu-tion, by so much the more is it probable that they shoulde desire our friendships & loue, and haue the greater respect for pleasing and obeying vs. Whereby may bee hoped if meanes of good gouernment bee vsed, that they may in short time be brought to ciuili-tie, and the imbracing of true religion.

Some religion they haue alreadie, which although it be farre from the truth, yet beyng as it is, there is hope it may bee the easier and sooner reformed.

They beleeue that there are many Gods which they call *Montóac*, but of different sortes and degrees; one onely chiefe and great God, which hath bene from all eternitie. Who as they affirme when hee purposed to make the worlde, made first other goddes of a principall order to bee as meanes and instruments to bee vsed in the creation and gouernment to follow; and after the Sunne, Moone, and Starres, as pettie goddes and the instruments of the other order more principall. First they say were made waters, out of which by the gods was made all diuersitie of creatures that are visible or inuisible.

For mankind they say a woman was made first, which by the woorking of one of the goddes, conceiued and brought foorth children: And in such sort they say they had their beginning.

But how manie yeeres or ages haue passed since, they say they can make no relation, hauing no letters nor other such meanes as we to keepe recordes of the particularities of times past, but onelie tradition from father to sonne.

They thinke that all the gods are of human shape, & therfore they represent them by images in the formes of men, which they call *Kewasowok,* one alone is called *Kewás;* Them they place in houses appropriate or temples which they call *Mathicómuck;* Where they woorship, praie, sing, and make manie times offerings vnto them. In some *Machicómuck* we haue seene but one *Kewas,* in some two, and in other some three; The common sort thinke them to be also gods.

They beleeue also the immortalitie of the soule, that after this life as soone as the soule is departed from the bodie according to the workes it hath done, it is eyther carried to heauen the habitacle of gods, there to enjoy perpetuall blisse and happinesse, or els to a great pitte or hole, which they thinke to bee in the furthest partes of their part of the worlde towarde the sunne set, there to burne continually: the place they call *Popogusso.*

For the confirmation of this opinion, they tolde mee two stories of two men that had been lately dead and reuiued againe, the one happened but few yeres before our coming in the countrey of a wicked man which hauing beene dead and buried, the next day the earth of the graue beeing seene to moue, was taken vp againe; Who made declaration where his soule had beene, that is to saie very neere entring into *Popogusso,* had not one of the gods saued him & gaue him leaue to returne againe, and teach his friends what they should doe to auoid that terrible place of torment.

The other happened in the same yeere wee were there, but in a towne that was threescore miles from vs, and it was told mee for straunge newes that one beeing dead, buried and taken vp againe as the first, shewed that although his bodie had lien dead in the graue, yet his soule was aliue, and had trauailed farre in a long broade waie, on both sides whereof grewe most delicate and pleasaunt trees, bearing more rare and excellent fruites then euer hee had seene before or was able to expresse, and at length came to most braue and faire houses, neere which hee met his father, that had beene dead before, who gaue him great charge to goe backe againe and shew his friendes what good they were to doe to enjoy the pleasures of that place, which when he had done he should after come againe.

What subtilty soeuer be in the *Wiroances* and Priestes, this opinion worketh so much in manie of the common and simple sort of people that it maketh them haue great respect to their Gouernours, and also great care what they do, to auoid torment after death, and to enjoy blisse; although notwithstanding there is punishment ordained for malefactours, as stealers, whoremoongers, and other sortes of wicked doers; some punished with death, some with forfeitures, some with beating, according to the greatnes of the factes.

And this is the summe of their religion, which I learned by hauing special familiarity with some of their priestes. Wherein they were not so sure grounded, nor gaue such credite to their traditions and stories but through conuersing with vs they were brought into great doubts of their owne, and no small admiration of ours, with earnest desire in many, to learne more than we had meanes for want of perfect vtterance in their language to expresse.

Figure 9.1 Clay stamp with jaguar design. Rare Books Division, J. Willard Marriott Library, University of Utah.

Note: Long before contact with the Europeans, many of the indigenous cultures of modern day Mexico and South America already had their own writing systems. These writing systems were composed largely of pictograms and ideograms. The jaguar, for example, was often a symbol for a warrior in Mayan texts. The indigenous communities of these regions created a wide variety of texts, ranging from genealogical and historical works to ones containing calendars and descriptions of rituals. Virtually no texts dating from the preconquest period survived the conquest.

Study Questions

1. On what basis does the *Requermiento* justify Spanish right of jurisdiction in the New World?
2. What new racial mixtures are appearing in Peru according to de la Vega?
3. In what ways does Riebeeck's journal highlight the importance of the Dutch East Indies Company in the life of the colony?
4. Compare the accounts of Riebeeck and Hariot. In what ways do their accounts portray very different relations with native peoples? In what ways are they similar?
5. From the accounts of Riebeeck and de la Vega, what influential role is African slavery playing in the colonial societies during this period?

Suggested Readings

Blackburn, Robin. *The Making of New World Slavery: From the Baroque to the Modern, 1492–1800.* New York: Verso, 1998.

Curtin, Philip. *The Rise and Fall of the Plantation Complex: Essays in Atlantic History.* Cambridge: Cambridge University Press, 1990.

Kupperman, Karen Ordahl. *Settling with the Indians.* Totowa, NJ: Rowman and Littlefield, 1980.

Spalding, Karen. *Huarochiri. An Andean Society under Inca and Spanish Rule.* Stanford, CA: Stanford University Press, 1984.

Web Sites

1. Encounters in America

   http://lcweb.loc.gov/rr/hispanic/guide/encameri.html

2. Indians of North America

   http://www.csulb.edu/~gcampus/libarts/am-indian/index.html#north

3. Las Cronicas de America—People

   http://web.reed.edu/academic/departments/spanish/spanish%20380/people.html

4. Maps of Colonial America

   http://scarlett.libs.uga.edu/darchive/hargrett/maps/colamer.html

10

Evangelization
1500–1700 A.D.

TEXTS

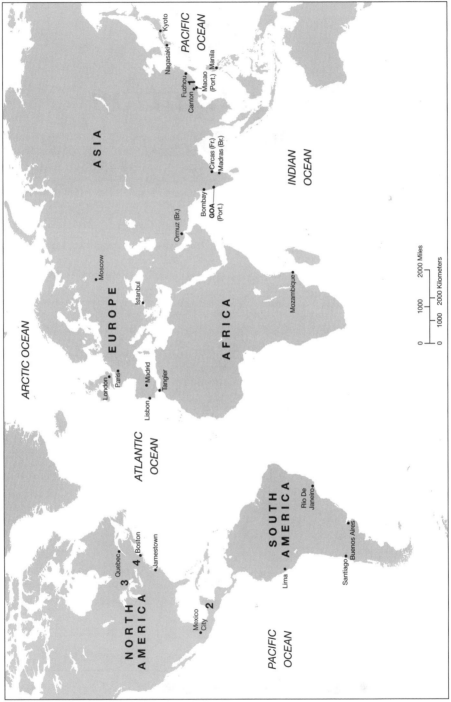

The desire to convert nonbelievers to the one "true" faith was characteristic of the Christian tradition throughout its history, and it became a particularly powerful force in Europe by the end of the fifteenth century. Growing Ottoman power in the East, the Spanish Christian conquest of the Muslim kingdom of Granada, the spread of the lay devotional movement the *Devotio Moderna,* and European encounters with non-Christian peoples across the Atlantic were among the forces that sparked this new crusading zeal. Among the first missionaries to make their way across the Atlantic in the service of the "true" faith were the Franciscans and Dominicans. Formed during the thirteenth century, these orders of wandering preachers were accustomed to working in distant lands. During the Middle Ages, Franciscan and Dominican missionaries made it as far as China and East India. Twelve Franciscans accompanied Cortes to Mexico in 1521, and the Dominicans soon followed. The formation of the Jesuit order in 1534 introduced yet another active, competing missionary organization to the New World by the end of the sixteenth century. By 1630, numerous monastic communities dotted the landscapes of Mexico, Brazil, and Peru, as well as the region of New France in the northern part of the Americas. [3] Female religious communities like the Ursulines also began appearing in the New World to provide native children with a Christian education.

The numerous writings that flowed from the pens of these missionaries and circulated in Europe throughout the Early Modern period belie the small scale of the majority of these missions. The Franciscan presence in Mexico, for example, grew from twelve in 1521 to no more than 380 at the end of the seventeenth century, even though the friars were working in a native population comprised of several millions of people. The number of Jesuits working in North America during the seventeenth century was smaller still. Although small, these missions were remarkably influential. Because the purpose of many of the Catholic missions was not simply conversion but cultural assimilation, however, their influence was often more destructive than constructive. Europeans generally viewed the New World cultures as spiritually and culturally inferior to both their own societies and those of China, India, and the Middle East. [1] European missions to the New World frequently encouraged the implantation of European cultural traditions at the expense of native ones. The Franciscans working in Mexico, for example, forced baptism and weekly religious instruction on many Amerindian communities, as well as introduced European language and writing systems, economic practices, and moral values. Although it was true that many of the missionaries were active defenders of the native peoples from European physical and political abuse, many were not above using force to ensure conversion. The brutal treatment of forty-five hundred Indians in the Yucatan peninsula in 1562 for practicing their own religious traditions is vivid testimony to European intolerance of cultural difference. [2]

Protestant migrations to the New World from England by the end of the sixteenth century introduced a new religion into the Americas, and these settlers were as determined to save the native peoples from the Catholic influence as they were from indigenous spiritual traditions. The Puritans were among the first Protestant settlers to arrive, eager to establish their own independent spiritual communities far from the arm of English authority. [4] Ironically, Puritan experience with religious intolerance in England did not make these Protestant settlers any more tolerant than their Catholic neighbors. Gruding respect constantly battled with assumptions of cultural superiority in their treatment of native peoples. Protestant and Catholic efforts at evangelization, however, were fraught with difficulty throughout the Early Modern period in part because of competition between the different missionary efforts and in part because of the natives themselves. Early modern missionary accounts reflect a noticeable shift in tone from optimism during the early mission years about the "docile" and "receptive" nature of native peoples to a sense of disillusionment and betrayal as European missionaries came to realize that the native peoples were not so willing to abandon their own religious traditions after all. It is perhaps this sense of betrayal that explains the remarkable ferocity of the Franciscan De Landa's response to the Mayan peoples in 1562 after discovering that many of the people had not abandoned their traditional faith.

1. MATTEO RICCI, *JOURNALS*

The mission of the Italian Jesuit Matteo Ricci (1552–1610) to China during the sixteenth century provides a nice contrast to Catholic missions to the New World. From its inception in 1534 onward, the Jesuit order always emphasized flexibility in the field to best ensure the success of its evangelization. The following text is taken from a letter sent by Ricci to the general of the order. Here Ricci candidly discusses his efforts to adapt his mission to a society that was more intellectually and culturally sophisticated than those found in Europe. A learned man himself, Ricci studied Chinese, and by 1595, he was sufficiently fluent to translate Christian texts into Chinese. As the following letter suggests, however, linguistic fluency did not guarantee European missionaries a Chinese audience for the Christian message.

China in the 16th Century

In order that the appearance of a new religion might not arouse suspicion among the Chinese people, the Fathers did not speak openly about religious matters when they began to appear in public. What time was left to them, after paying their respects and civil compliments and courteously receiving their visitors, was spent in studying the language of the country, the methods of writing and the customs of the people. They did, however, endeavor to teach this pagan people in a more direct way, namely, by virtue of their example and by the sanctity of their lives. In this way they attempted to win the good will of the people and little by little, without affectation, to dispose their minds to receive what they could not be persuaded to accept by word of mouth, without endangering what had been thus far accomplished. The great difficulty in attempting to preach openly at that time lay in a lack of knowledge of the language and in the natural indisposition of the people. From the time of their entrance they wore the ordinary Chinese outer garment, which was somewhat similar to their own religious habits; a long robe reaching down to the heels and with very ample sleeves, which are much in favor with the Chinese.

The Mission House, as it was called, had two rooms on either side, with an open hall space between, which served as a chapel, with an altar in the center and above it a picture of the Madonna. In order to couple the idea of authority with the name of God, instead of saying God, the missionaries always used the title Thien-ciu, meaning, Lord of Heaven. They could hardly have chosen a more appropriate expression, because there is no consonant sound of D in the Chinese language, and to them there was something magnificent and a touch of the divine in this particular name. In fact, this title, first used at the beginning of our missionary work, is still in vogue today when God is mentioned in discourse and in writing, though several others have been introduced by way of amplification and for clearer understanding. Among the titles most commonly employed are, Sovereign Director of All Things, and First Cause of All Things. The Blessed Virgin is known as The Glorious Mother of God. When people came to visit the Fathers, Magistrates and other holders of literacy degrees, the common people, and even those who offered sacrifice to idols, everyone in short, paid reverence to the Madonna in her picture above the altar, with the customary bows and kneeling and touching of the forehead to the floor. All of this was done with an air of real religious sentiment. They never ceased to admire the beauty and the elegance of this painting; the coloring, the very natural lines and the lifelike posture of the figure. Before long it became evident, and for several reasons, that it would be better to remove the picture of the Virgin Mother from above the altar and replace it with one of Christ the Saviour. First, so that they would not believe, as rumor had already announced, that we adored a woman as our God; and secondly, that they might more easily be taught the doctrine of the Word made Flesh.

Once the Mission was established, frequent visitors came uninvited to hear something of the principal articles of our faith. The Chinese are a thinking people who frequently entertain doubts, and not without reason, about the many absurdities contained in their own religious beliefs. Copies of the Commandments were printed in Chinese and given out to all who asked for them. Many who received them said they would live in the future according to these commandments, because as they claimed, they were in such perfect accord with the voice of conscience and with the natural law. Their reverence for the Christian law increased with their admiration for it. Some of them, without being asked or told of it, began to bring incense for the benedictions, others brought oil for the sanctuary lamp and a few made voluntary offerings for the support of the house.

If they had wished to accept the generosity of the Governor, the Fathers might have obtained a grant of land that was originally intended for a temple of idols, but they deemed it wiser not to compromise the newborn liberty of Christianity by subjecting it to the power of the governing Magistrates. Their refusal to accept the offer served to exempt Christianity from any suspicion of cupidity or avarice, and it became known among the people from the very beginning that the preachers of the divine law were not looking for material gain from their religion. This gave them an easy entrée to the palaces of the officials who knew that when the European priests came they were not looking for favors, as was generally the case with those who cultivated the friendship of all civil rulers. Thus the method of mute publication, substituting deeds for words, was more than a little effective in spreading the reputation of the newly arrived Christianity. No doubt, many who came to see a Christian service were prompted by curiosity, but many returned touched with admiration of the evidence of the divine. At times some of the more learned Chinese, who were interested in the religious customs of the Christian world, requested that we discuss the whole question more openly and freely and also the question of Chinese Idols. These discussions were carried on through interpreters and at times without them, but the latter method was rather awkward because of a lack of knowledge of the language, which forced the foreigners to say what they could, rather than what they wanted to say. What the Fathers continually endeavored to emphasize in these talks was the fact that the Christian law was in perfect accord with the innate light of conscience. It was, as they maintained, by this same light of conscience that the most ancient of the Chinese scholars had approached to this same doctrine of Christianity in their writings, centuries before the appearance of the idols. They explained, also, that they themselves were not abolishing the natural law, rather they were adding to it what was lacking, namely, the supernatural as taught by God who Himself had become a man. All this seemed to have met with more applause than approval, because the pride of the Chinese was not as yet reduced to such a state that they could accept a new religion of foreigners, which none of their race had ever embraced.

The first one in the Chinese Kingdom to make open profession of the Christian faith was from the very lowest rank of the people. God had evidently chosen the lesser things of earth to confound the greater. This man was afflicted with an incurable disease, and when the doctors held out no hope of betterment, his people, who could no longer support him, cruelly put him out of the house, and he was left lying abandoned on a public road. When the Fathers heard of the case they went out and found the man, told him there was no hope of curing his bodily ailments, but that there was a means of taking care of his soul and of leading him to salvation and eternal happiness. His reaction was as joyful as it was courageous, and he answered that any law offering such sympathy and pity to its observers was quite acceptable to him.

2. Diego de Landa, *Relación de las Cosas de Yucatan*

Diego de Landa (1524–1579) remains one of the most controversial figures of the early colonial period in Spanish America. A member of the Franciscan order, Landa arrived in the Yucatan in 1549 as a missionary. During his many years in Mexico he would rise first to the position of custodian of the Franciscan province of Yucatan and later the office of bishop. The office of custodian gave de Landa substantial political and spiritual authority in the Yucatan because the papacy had extended all powers normally exercised by bishops to the leaders of the Franciscan order in the New World. Famous for his choleric temper, de Landa was also a fervent religious reformer who used his jurisdiction in the

Yucatan to further Franciscan Christianization of the Mayan peoples. The *Relación* (1566) is de Landa's account of the Spanish mission in the Yucatan. The following excerpt gives some indication as to why this Franciscan was constantly in conflict with colonial officials and settlers. It also describes in simple but explicit fashion the torture and imprisonment of several thousand Mayan peoples in 1562 for practicing their own religious traditions. Several Mayans were even executed. This repression was sparked by the discovery of a cave full of Mayan idols and human skulls. After over thirty years of missionary work in the Yucatan, de Landa and other Franciscans were shocked to discover that many natives had in fact not renounced their ancient religious traditions but rather continued to practice them alongside the newer Christian tradition.

Relación de las Cosas de Yucatan

The Spaniards were displeased to see the friars were building monasteries, and drove away the sons of the Indians from their *repartimientos,* in order to keep them from going to learn Christianity, and twice they burned the monastery of Valladolid, with its church which was of wood and straw. Things reached such a pass that the friars were obliged to go and live among the Indians, and when the Indians of this province rose in rebellion, they (the Spaniards) wrote to the Viceroy, Don Antonio, that they had revolted from love of the friars. And the Viceroy investigated and found that at the time when the rebellion took place, the friars had not yet arrived in that province. And they kept watch of the friars during the night, to the great scandal of the Indians, and made inquiries into their lives and took away the alms from them.

The friars, seeing this danger, sent a friar to the very excellent judge, Cerrato, the President (of the *Audiencia*) of Guatemala, (so as) to give him an account of what was going on; and he, seeing the disorder and the unchristian conduct of the Spaniards, since they were collecting just as much tribute as they could without an order from the King, and were enforcing personal service in all sorts of work and even hiring them to carry burdens, established a rate of taxation, which, though high, was yet endurable. In this he made it known what things belonged to the Indian, after paying his tribute to his *encomendero,* and that everything should not absolutely belong to the Spaniard. But they appealed from this, and from fear of the tax they (the Spaniards) took from the Indians more than before; and the friars went back to the *Audencia,* and sent to Spain; and they did so much that the *Audiencia* of Guatemala sent an *oidor,* who decided the taxes to be paid in this country and abolished personal service, and he obliged some of them to marry and took away from them the houses which were filled with women. This (*oidor*) was the Licentiate Tomas Lopez, a native of Tendilla, and this made them (the Spaniards) hate the friars even more, and they published defamatory libels against them, and stopped going to hear their masses.

This hate was precisely the cause why the Indians became attached to the friars, as they saw all the toil which they endured, without any private interest, and the freedom which resulted from their efforts, so that they did nothing without informing the friars and taking their advice, and this gave cause for the Spaniards to be envious and to say that the friars had acted in this way, so that they could have the government of the Indies and could thus enjoy the things of which they had deprived them.

The vices of the Indians were idolatries and repudiation of their wives, and orgies of public drunkenness, and buying and selling slaves; and they came to hate the friars because they tried to make them give up these things. Among the Spaniards the people who gave the most trouble to the friars, although they did it secretly, were the secular clergy; as was natural enough for people who had lost their positions and the profits from them.

The plan which they adopted to teach the religious doctrines to the Indians was to get together the little children of the lords and of the principal men of the place, and they established them around the monastery in the houses which each town made for its people, where those who came from each place lived all together and their fathers and relatives brought them food. To these children were added those who came to the *Doctrina,* and as a result of this attendance, many of them asked for baptism with great devotion. And these children, after being instructed, took care to notify the priests of acts of idolatry or of drunken orgies that occurred; and they broke the idols although they belonged to their own fathers. And they urged the divorced women and the orphans if they had been reduced to slavery, to complain to the friars; and though they were threatened by their own people they did not stop on this account but answered instead that they did them honor, since it was for the good of their souls. The *Adelantado* and the judges of the King have always appointed *fiscales* to the friars to bring the Indians together for the teaching of the *Doctrina,* as well as to punish those who returned to their old way of living. The lords at first sent their children unwillingly, thinking that they wished to make slaves of them as the Spaniards had done; and for this reason they frequently sent their many young slaves instead of their sons. But when they understood what the purpose was, they let them go willingly.

Thus the young people made such progress in the schools and the rest of the people in the Christian doctrine, that it was an admirable thing to see.

They (the friars) learned to read and write in the language of the Indians, which was brought so well into the form of a grammar that it was studied like Latin. And it was found that they did not use six of our letters, which are: D, F, G, Q, R, S, which they did not need for any purpose. But they are obliged to double others and to add others in order to understand the varied significance of certain words. Thus *pa* means "to open," and *ppa* (compressing the lips hard) (means) "to break." *Tan* is "lime" or "ashes," and *tan,* uttered with force between the tongue and the upper teeth, means "word" or "to speak"; and so with other expressions. And considering that they had different characters for these things, there was no necessity of inventing new forms of letters, but rather to make use of the Latin letters, so that the use of them should be common to all. Commands were given to them also to leave the habitations which they had in the woods, and to gather as before in good villages, so that they could be taught more easily, and that the friars should not have so much trouble, for whose support they gave alms at the *Pascuas* and other festivals. And they gave alms for the churches through two old Indians, appointed for this purpose; and in this way they gave what was needed to the friars, when the latter went to visit them, and also furnished the churches with vestments.

This people, after having been instructed in religion, and the young boys having advanced in their studies as we have said, were perverted by the priests whom they had at the time of their idolatry and by their chiefs. And they returned to the worship of their idols and to offer them sacrifices not only of incense but also of human blood. The friars made an Inquisition about this and asked the aid of the *alcade mayor,* and they arrested a great number and put them on trial, after which an *auto (de fe)* was celebrated, at which they placed many upon the scaffold wearing a (*coroza*) of paper, and scourged and shorn, while others were clothed with the *sambenito* for a time. And some, deceived by the devil, hanged themselves for grief, and in general they all showed deep repentance and a willingness to become good Christians.

At this time, there arrived at Campeche Fray Francisco Toral, a Franciscan friar, a native of Ubeda, who had been for twenty years in the (bishopric) of Mexico, and who came now as Bishop of Yucatan. He, on the information given him by the Spaniards and on the complaints of the Indians, undid what the friars had done and ordered the prisoners to be set at liberty. And the *provincial* (Landa) took offense at this and determined to go to Spain, carrying his complaints in the first place to Mexico. And so he came to Madrid, where the members of the Council of the Indies censured him severely on account of his having usurped the office of Bishop and Inquisitor.

3. *THE JESUIT RELATIONS*

The Jesuits did not lag far behind the Franciscans and Dominicans in making their way to the New World. By the end of the seventeenth century, these black-robed priests were a familiar presence in the northern wilderness regions of New France, as well as the jungles of Brazil. Although the Jesuits who worked in the New World during the sixteenth and seventeenth centuries were few in number, they produced a surprisingly vast number of accounts of their missionary activities. During the 1890s, these accounts, which took the form mostly of correspondence, were gathered together in a thirty-seven volume collection entitled *The Jesuit Relations*. Originally these relations were circulated individually throughout Europe by the Jesuit administration in order to raise European awareness about the spread of Christianity in the New World and to highlight the success of the Jesuits as Christian evangelists. The Jesuit administration hoped that publishing the missionary experiences of their members would stimulate European financial and political support for their spiritual work at a time when the rapid expansion of the order after 1534 had won them many enemies, Catholic as well as Protestant. Among their most ardent opponents were the Franciscans and Dominicans, two of the older missionary orders that viewed the Jesuits and other recently established missionary orders as unwelcome competition. To incite European support for their work, many of the Jesuit relations focus on conversion tales and heroic martyrdoms of individual Jesuits. The following letter describes the martyrdom of Antoine Daniel in 1649. However, the letter also describes in some detail the state of the Jesuit mission in the colony at the time.

The Jesuit Relations

LETTER OF FATHER PAUL RAGUENEAU TO THE VERY REVEREND FATHER VINCENT CARAFFA, GENERAL OF THE SOCIETY OF JESUS, AT ROME (1649)

[This is a letter, written by Ragueneau, in the Huron country, March 1, 1649, to the father general of the Jesuits, giving in response to the latter's request, many details of the Huron mission. Affairs temporal are in a dangerous condition; for the constant attacks of the Iroquois have destroyed all the outlying Huron villages, and the mission is now forced to rely on its own strength for defense. So well has the mission been conducted, that it produces most of its own food. . . . It has every prospect of success, were it not for the raids of the Iroquois. In one of these (occurring in July, 1648), they take by storm the mission village of St. Joseph, which they burn down, and Father Antoine Daniel is slain by the enemy, while encouraging his flock,—the first martyr in that mission.]

OUR VERY REVEREND FATHER IN CHRIST:
  Pax Christi
  I have received, very Reverend Paternity, your letter dated January 20, 1647. If you wrote us last year, 1648, we have not yet received that letter. Your Paternity evinces pleasure in the news of the state of our Huron mission. Indeed (such is your Paternal love toward us), you even stoop to details and bid us inform you of everything.
  There are here eighteen Fathers, four coadjutors, twenty-three Données, seven servants (two whom alone wages are paid), four boys and eight soldiers. Truly, we are so threatened by the hostile rage of our savage enemies that, unless we wish our enterprise and ourselves to perish in an hour, it was quite necessary for us to seek the protection of these men, who devote themselves to both domestic duties and farm work, and also to building fortifications, and to military service. For since, until late years, our abode, which we call the Residence of Ste. Marie, was surrounded on every side by the numerous villages of our friends, the Hurons, we feared more for them than for ourselves from hostile attack: so during that time, however small our number, we lived in safety, without anxiety. But now, far different is the aspect of our affairs and of this whole region; for so crushed are our Hurons by disasters, that, their outposts being taken and laid waste with fire and sword, most of them have been forced to change their abodes, and retreat elsewhere; hence it has come to pass that at last we are devoid of the protection of others; and now we, stationed at the front, must defend ourselves with our own strength, our own courage, and our own numbers.
  This our dwelling—or shall I say our fort?—of Sainte Marie, the French who are with us defend, while our Fathers sally forth, far and wide, scattered among the villages of the Hurons, and through the Algonquin tribes far distant from us,—each one watching over his own mission, and intent only upon the ministry of the word, leaving all temporal cares to those who remain at home. In truth, domestic matters keep so fortunate a course that, although our number has increased, and we greatly desire new help to be sent us,—both of laymen and, especially, of our own fathers,—still in no wise is it necessary to increase expenses. On the contrary, they are lessening daily, and each year we ask for less temporal aid to be sent us—so much so that we can, for the most part, support ourselves upon that which is here produced. Verily, there is not one of our brethren who does not feel in this respect great relief from those distresses which were in former years very burdensome, and seemed insurmountable. For we have larger supplies from fishing and hunting than formerly; and we have not merely fish and eggs, but also pork, and milk products, and even cattle, from which we hope for great addition to our store. I write of these particulars, because your Paternity so desired.
  Christianity has certainly made progress here, in many ways, beyond our expectation. We baptized, the past year, about one thousand seven hundred,—not counting many whom we shall mention below as baptized by Father Antoine Daniel, the number of whom could not be accurately given. Nor are these, albeit barbarians, such Christians as one might be inclined to suppose, ignorant of things divine and not sufficiently quali-

fied for our mysteries. Many indeed understand religion, and that profoundly; and there are some whose virtue, piety, and remarkable holiness even the most holy Religious might without sin envy. One who is an eye-witness of these things cannot sufficiently admire the finger of God, and congratulate himself that so fortunate a field of labor, so rich in divine blessing, had fallen to his lot.

We maintain eleven missions—eight in the Huron language and three Algonquin. The work is divided between an equal number of Fathers who have had experience. Four, sent to us last year, devote their time to learning the language; and these we have assigned as helpers to the chief missionaries. Thus only three Fathers remain at home— one as spiritual Director, another as Procurator and minister, the third to look after the needs of the Christians, who come to us from every quarter. For out of our own poverty we minister to the poverty of the Christians, and heal their diseases both of soul and body, surely to the great advancement of Christianity. Last year, nearly six thousand partook of our hospitality. How strange it is that *in terra alienda, in loco horroris et vastae solitudinis,* we should seem to draw *mel de petra, oleumque de saxo durissimo*—thence to supply the needs, not merely of us who are strangers, but also of the natives themselves. I say these things that your Paternity may know the abundance of God's goodness toward us. For, while during this year famine has been heavy upon the villages on all sides of us, and now weighs upon them even more heavily, no blight of evil has fallen upon us; nay, we have enough provisions upon which to live comfortably during three years.

But one thing—the fear of war and the rage of foes—seems able to overthrow the happy state of this infant church, and stay the advance of Christianity; for it grows yearly, and it is clear that no help can come to us save from God alone. The latest disaster that befell our Hurons—in July of last year, 1648—was the severest of all. Many of them had made ready to visit our French people in the direction of Quebec, to trade; other tasks had drawn some away from their villages; while many had undertaken a hostile expedition in another direction; when suddenly the enemy came upon them, stormed two villages, rushed into them, and set them on fire. With their wonted cruelty they dragged into captivity mothers with their children, and showed no mercy to any age.

Of these villages, one was called Saint Joseph; this was one of our principal missions, where a church had been built, where the people had been instructed in Christian rites, and where the faith had taken deep root. In charge of this Church was Father Antoine Daniel, a man of great courage and endurance, whose gentle kindness was conspicuous among his great virtues. He had hardly finished the usual mass after sunrise; and the Christians, who had assembled in considerable numbers, had not yet left the sacred house, when, at the war cry of the enemy, in haste and alarm they seized their weapons. Some rush into the fight, others flee headlong; everywhere is terror, everywhere lamentation.

Antoine hastened wherever he saw the danger most threatening and bravely encouraged his people—inspiring not only the Christians with Christian strength, but many unbelievers with faith. He was heard to speak of contempt for death, and of the joys of Paradise, with such ardor of soul that he seemed already to enjoy his bliss. Indeed, many sought baptism; and so great was the number that he could not attend to each one separately; but was forced to dip his handkerchief in the water and baptize by sprinkling the multitude who thronged around him.

Meantime, there was no cessation in the ferocious attack of the enemy, and everywhere resounded the noise of muskets. Many fell around him who received at the same instant the life-giving water of baptism, and the stroke of death. When he saw that his people had fled, he himself, intent upon the gain of souls,—mindful of the safety of others, but forgetful of his own,—hurried into the cabins to baptize the sick, the aged, and children, and filled them with his own zeal. At last, he betook himself to the church, whither the hope of eternal glory had brought many Christians, and the fear of hell-fire many catechumens. Never were there more earnest prayers, never stronger proofs of true faith and real penitence. To these he gives new life of baptism, those he releases from the bonds of sin; he sets all on fire with divine love. Almost his only words were: "Brothers, today we shall be in Paradise; believe this, hope this, that God may forever love you."

Already the foe had scaled the rampart, and throughout the village the torch had been applied, and the cabins were burning. The victors are informed that there is rich plunder, easy to get, if they will hasten to the church; that there numbers of old people, and women, and a band of children, are gathered. Thither they hurry with discordant shouts, after their manner. The Christians see the enemy approaching. Antoine bids them flee wherever escape is yet possible.

That he may delay the enemy, and, like a good shepherd, aid the escape of his flock, he blocks the way of the armed men and breaks their onset; a single man against the foe, but verily filled with divine strength, he, who during all his life had been as the gentlest dove, was brave as a Lion while he met death. Truly, I might apply to him that saying of Jeremias: "He hath forsaken his covert as the Lion, for the land is laid waste because of the wrath of the dove, and because of the fierce anger of the Lord." At last he fell, mortally wounded by a musket shot; and, pierced with arrows, he yielded to God the blessed life which he laid down for his flock, as a good Shepherd, calling upon the name of Jesus. Savagely enraged against his lifeless body, hardly one of the enemy was there who did not add a new wound to his corpse; until at length, the church having been set on fire, his naked body cast into the flames was so completely consumed that not even a bone was left: indeed, he could not have found a more glorious funeral pyre.

In thus delaying the enemy, he was serviceable to his flock, even after his death. Many reached places of safety; others the victors overtook, especially mothers—at every step delayed by the babes at their breasts, or by those whose childish years—as yet unaccustomed to prudent fear—betrayed their hiding places.

Antoine had just finished his fourteenth year at the Huron mission, everywhere a useful man, and assuredly raised up for the salvation of those tribes; but certainly ripe for heaven, and the first man of our society to be taken from us. True, his death was sudden, but did not find him unprepared: for he had always so lived that he was ever ready for death. Yet the Divine Goodness toward him seems to have been remarkable; for he had finished, only the first day of July, eight days of continuous spiritual Exercises of the Society in this house of Sainte Marie; and on the very next day, without any delay, or even one day's rest, he hastened to his own mission. Verily he burned with a zeal for God more intense than any flame that consumed his body.

He was a native of Dieppe, born of worthy and pious Parents. He had entered the Society in 1621, at the age of twenty one years; he was admitted to the Profession of the four vows in 1640; and at last ended his life July fourth, 1648. He was indeed a remarkable man; and a truly worthy son of the society—humble, obedient, united with God, of never failing patience, and indomitable courage in adversity. Thus he left to us a shining example of all the virtues; to the savage Christians, an impression of exalted faith and piety; to all, even the unbelievers, heavy grief at his death. Now at last, he will be granted, we certainly hope, as a most powerful Advocate in heaven for all this country.

In fact, by one of our number (a man of eminent piety and of well-attested humility, Father Joseph Marie Chaumonot) he was seen once and again after death. But when first our Fathers were gathered in council, and planning, as is their wont, for the promotion of Christianity, father Antoine was seen to appear in their midst, to revive us all with his strong counsel, and with the divine spirit which filled him. He seemed to be about thirty, as far as could be judged by his face; which presented to the Fathers a noble aspect, quite unlike anything human. The Father was asked how the Divine Goodness could suffer the body of his servant to be so shamefully treated after death,—disfigured as if by disgraceful wounds,—and to be so consumed by fire that nothing, not even a handful of ashes, was left to us. "Great is the Lord," replied he, "and most worthy of Praise. He beheld this reproach of his servant; and, to compensate for this in Divine fashion, he granted me many souls from purgatory, to accompany my triumph in heaven."

To make an end of writing, without exceeding the limit of a letter, I will add—what should have been written first of all to Your Paternity—that such is the condition of this house, and indeed of the whole mission, that I think hardly anything could be added to the piety, obedience, humility, patience, and charity of our brethren, and to their scrupulous observance of the rules. We are all of one heart, one soul, one spirit of the society. Nay, what must seem more wonderful, out of all the men attached to the house, of condition and nature so varied,—servants, boys, données, soldiers,—there is not one who does not seriously attend to his soul's salvation; so that clearly vice is banished hence, here virtue rules, and this is seen to be the home of holiness. This surely is our rejoicing, our peace in war, and our great security; for, whatever may be the dispensation of divine Providence, in life or in death this will be our consolation, that we are the Lord's and ever shall be, as we are permitted to hope. That so it may be, we implore your Paternity's Benediction upon us and our mission; and I chiefly, though unworthiest of all,—

Your most Reverend Paternity's
Most humble and obedient son,
PAUL RAGUENEAU

From the Residence of Sainte Marie,
among the Hurons, new France,
March 1, 1649.
To our Most Reverend Father in Christ,
  Vincent Caraffa, General of the
  Society of Jesus, Rome.

4. JOHN WINTHROP, *A MODEL OF CHRISTIAN CHARITY*

The division of the European world into Catholic and Protestant communities following Luther's split with the Church in 1521 ensured that the Catholic faith would not long continue its monopoly over European religious life in the New World. By 1550, England was a Protestant nation, and it was eagerly participating in Atlantic exploration and colonization. The Dutch were also becoming increasingly important commercial competitors with

Spain and Portugal by the end of the sixteenth century, and many of these merchant adventurers were also Protestant in faith. Among the first Protestant communities to make their mark in North America were the Puritan settlements of New England. The Puritans were English followers of John Calvin, the famous sixteenth-century Protestant thinker who transformed the city of Geneva into a model of the ideal Christian community. The close-knit nature of Puritan communities and their rejection of many facets of secular life as sinful made them popular targets of religious intolerance by the seventeenth century because they seemed to be separating themselves from English society. The following excerpt is taken from a sermon given by John Winthrop (1588–1649) on board the ship *Arabella*. Entitled *A Model of Christian Charity* (1630), this sermon is one of the most famous texts from the early colonial period in New England. Winthrop was a longtime governor of Massachusett's Bay Colony. For early Puritan settlers in Massachusetts Bay, the New World gave them an opportunity to re-create an ideal Christian community in a setting far removed from English persecution. As the following excerpt shows, many of these early settlers believed that their voyage to the New World was destined by God. It was providential.

A Model of Christian Charity

From the former Considerations ariseth these Conclusions.

1 First, This loue among Christians is a reall thing not Imaginarie.

2ly This loue is as absolutely necessary to the being of the body of Christ, as the sinewes and other ligaments of a naturall body are to the being of that body.

3ly. This loue is a divine spirituall nature free, actiue strong Couragious permanent vnder valueing all things beneathe its proper object, and of all the graces this makes vs nearer to resemble the virtues of our heavenly father.

4ly, It restes in the loue and wellfare of its beloued, for the full and certaine knowledge of these truthes concerning the nature vse, [and] excellency of this grace, that which the holy ghost hath left recorded 1. Cor. 13. may giue full satisfaccion which is needfull for every true member of this louely body of the Lord Jesus, to worke vpon theire heartes, by prayer meditacion continuall exercise at least of the speciall [power] of this grace till Christ be formed in them and they in him all in eache other knitt together by this bond of loue.

It rests now to make some applicacion of this discourse by the present designe which gaue the occasion of writeing of it. Herein are 4 things to be propounded: first the persons, 2ly, the worke, 3ly, the end, 4ly the meanes.

1. For the persons, wee are a Company professing our selues fellow members of Christ, In which respect onely though wee were absent from eache other many miles, and had our imploymentes as farre distant, yet wee ought to account our selues knitt together by this bond of loue, and liue in the exercise of it, if wee would haue comforte of our being in Christ, this was notorious in the practise of the Christians in former times, as is testified of the Waldenses from the mouth of one of the adversaries Aeneas Syluius,

mutuo [solent amare] pene antequam norint, they vse to loue any of theire owne religion even before they were acquainted with them.

2ly. for the worke wee haue in hand, it is by a mutuall consent through a speciall overruleing providence, and a more then an ordinary approbation of the Churches of Christ to seeke out a place of Cohabitation and Consorteshipp vnder a due forme of Government both ciuill and ecclesiasticall. In such cases as this the care of the publique must oversway all private respects, by which not onely conscience, but meare Ciuill pollicy doth binde vs; for it is a true rule that perticuler estates cannott subsist in the ruine of the publique.

3ly. The end is to improue our liues to doe more seruice to the Lord the comforte and encrease of the body of christe whereof wee are members that our selues and posterity may be the better preserued from the Common corrupcions of this euill world to serue the Lord and worke out our Salvacion vnder the power and purity of his holy Ordinances.

4ly for the meanes whereby this must bee effected, they are 2fold, a Conformity with the worke and end wee aime at, these wee see are extraordinary, therefore wee must not content our selues with vsuall ordinary meanes whatsoever wee did or ought to haue done when wee liued in England, the same must wee doe and more allsoe where wee goe: That which the most in theire Churches maineteine as a truthe in profession onely, wee must bring into familiar and constant practise, as in this duty of loue wee must loue brotherly without dissimulation, wee must loue one another with a pure hearte feruently wee must beare one anothers burthens, wee must not looke onely on our owne things, but allsoe on the things of our brethren, neither must wee think that the lord will beare with such faileings at our hands as hee dothe from those among whome wee haue liued, and that for 3 Reasons.

1. In regard of the more neare bond of mariage, betweene him and vs, wherein he hath taken vs to be his after a most strickt and peculiar manner which will make him the more Jealous of our loue and obedience soe he tells the people of Israell, you onely haue I knowne of all the families of the Earthe therefore will I punishe you for your Transgressions.

2ly, because the lord will be sanctified in them that come neare him. Wee know that there were many that corrupted the seruice of the Lord some setting vpp Alters before his owne, others offering both strange fire and strange Sacrifices allsoe; yet there came noe fire from heaven, or other sudden Judgement vpon them as did vpon Nadab and Abihu whoe yet wee may thinke did not sinne presumptuously.

3ly When God giues a speciall Commission he lookes to haue it strictly obserued in every Article, when hee gaue Saule a Commission to destroy Amaleck hee indented with him vpon certaine Articles and because hee failed in one of the least, and that vpon a faire pretence, it lost him the kingdome, which should haue beene his reward, if hee had obserued his Commission: Thus stands the cause betweene God and vs, wee are entered into Covenant with him for this worke, wee haue taken out a Commission, the Lord hath giuen vs leaue to drawe our owne Articles wee haue professed to enterprise these Accions vpon these and these ends, wee haue herevpon besought him of favour and blessing: Now if the Lord shall please to heare vs, and bring vs in peace to the place wee desire, then hath hee ratified this Covenant and sealed our Commission, [and] will expect a strickt performance of the Articles contained in it, but if wee shall neglect the observacion of these Articles which are the ends wee haue propounded, and dissembling with our God, shall fall to embrace this present world and prosecute our carnall intencions, seekeing greate things for our selues and our posterity, the Lord will surely breake out in wrathe against vs be revenged of such a periured people and make vs knowe the price of the breache of such a Covenant.

Now the onely way to avoyde this shipwracke and to provide for our posterity is to followe the Counsell of Micah, to doe Justly, to loue mercy, to walk humbly with our God, for this end, wee must be knitt together in this worke as one man, wee must entertaine each other in brotherly Affeccion, wee must be willing to abridge our selues of our superfluities, for the supply of others necessities, wee must vphold a familiar Commerce together in all meekenes, gentlenes, patience and liberallity, wee must delight in eache other, make others Condicions our owne reioyce together, mourne together, labour, and suffer together, allwayes haueing before out eyes our Commission and Community in the worke, our Community as members of the same body, soe shall wee keepe the vnitie of the spirit in the bond of peace, the Lord will be our God and delight to dwell among vs, as his owne people and will commaund a blessing vpon vs in all our wayes, soe that wee shall see much more of his wisdome power goodnes and truthe then formerly wee haue beene acquainted with, wee shall finde that the God of Israell is among vs, when tenn of vs shall be able to resist a thousand of our enemies, when hee shall make vs a prayse and glory, that men shall say of succeeding plantacions: the lord make it like that of New England: for wee must Consider that wee shall be as a Citty vpon a Hill, the eies of all people are vppon vs; soe that if wee shall deale falsely with our god in this worke wee haue vndertaken and soe cause him to withdrawe his present help from vs, wee shall be made a story and a by-word through the world, wee shall open the mouthes of enemies to speake euill of the wayes of god and professours for Gods sake; wee shall shame the faces of many of gods worthy seruants, and cause theire prayers to be turned into Cursses vpon vs till wee be consumed out of the good land whether wee are goeing: And to shutt vpp this discourse with that exhortacion of Moses that faithfull seruant of the Lord in his last farewell to Israell Deut. 30. Beloued there is now sett before vs life, and good, deathe and euill in that wee are Commaunded this day to loue the Lord our God, and to loue one another to walke in his wayes and to keepe his Commaundements and his Ordinance, and his lawes, and the Articles of our Covenant with him that wee may liue and be multiplyed, and that the Lord our God may blesse vs in the land whether wee goe to possesse it: But if our heartes shall turne away soe that wee will not obey, but shall be seduced and worshipp [serue *cancelled*] other Gods our pleasures, and proffitts, and serue them; it is propounded vnto vs this day, wee shall purely perishe out of the good Land whether wee passe over this vast Sea to possesse it;

> Therefore lett vs chose life,
> that wee, and our Seede,
> may liue; by obeying his
> voyce, and cleaueing to him,
> for hee is our life, and
> our prosperity.

Figure 10.1 Engraving taken from Casas, Bartolomé de las. *An Account of the first voyage and discoveries made by the Spaniards in America.* London: Printed by J. Darby for D. Brown, 1699. Rare Books Division, J. Willard Marriott Library, University of Utah.

Note: This engraving depicts the burning of an Amerindian by Spanish soldiers with the blessing of a European missionary. Burning was a form of judicial punishment typically used in the crime of heresy. As the depiction shows, the state often lent its support to the persecution and punishment of the more serious spiritual crimes such as heresy. The burning of this individual suggests that the ruling colonial government believed he had turned away from Christianity to his former beliefs. In other words, he was no longer simply ignorant of Christianity but willfully rejecting the "true" faith.

Study Questions

1. According to Diego de Landa, why did the Franciscans torture and kill many of the Mayan peoples in 1562? Does he consider this treatment legitimate?
2. According to Landa, why were the Spanish settlers hostile to the Franciscans?
3. Compare the missionary strategies employed by Matteo Ricci and the Jesuits working in the Americas. How were these strategies the same? Different? Explain.
4. According to *The Jesuit Relations,* what was the state of the Jesuit mission in New France?
5. According to Winthrop, what was the nature and purpose of the Puritan community in the New World? How would this perspective affect Puritan relations with native peoples?
6. Regarding the illustration, why was burning considered the appropriate punishment in Europe for heresy? What is the definition of heresy?

Suggested Readings

Bozeman, Theodore Dwight. *To Live Ancient Lives: The Primitivist Dimension in Puritanism.* Chapel Hill: The Institute of Early Modern History and Culture, 1988.

Miller, Perry. *Errand into the Wilderness.* Cambridge: Belknap Press,1956.

Phelan, John Leddy. *The Millennial Kingdom of the Franciscans in the New World.* Berkeley: University of California Press, 1970.

Rafael, Vincente L. *Contracting Colonialism: Translation and Christian Conversion in Tagalog Society under Early Spanish Rule.* Durham and London: Duke University Press, 1993.

Web Sites

1. John Calvin

   http://crh.choate.edu/histsources/Europe/fourth%20level/Ref.do.calvin.htm

2. *Jesuit Relations*

   http://vc.lemoyne.edu/relations/relations_38.html

3. John Winthrop, *A Model of Christian Charity*

   http://www.Demog.berkeley.edu/145/documents/winthrop.modell.htm

11

The Influence of Exploration on Europe 1500–1700 A.D.

TEXTS

1. Richard Hakluyt, *Voyages*

2. Galileo Galilei, *Dialogues on Two New Sciences*

3. John Locke, *An Essay Concerning Human Understanding*

4. *Mercure de France,* Relation of the Arrival in France of Four Savages of Mississippi (1725)

5. Maize depicted in the sixteenth-century herbal by Leonhart Fuchs, *De historia stirpium commentarii insignes . . .* (1542).

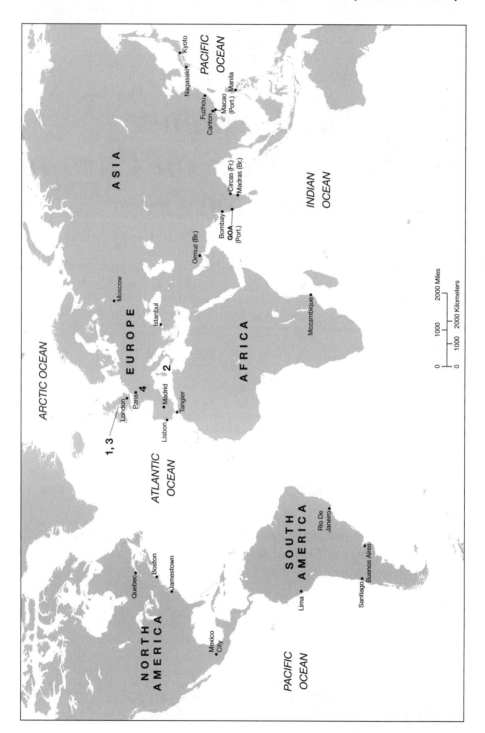

Europeon fascination with the native cultures encountered across the Atlantic only continued to grow during the sixteenth and seventeenth centuries, stimulating the printing of travel accounts, the consumption of products from the New World, and even European collection of such exotic indigenous artifacts as Brazilian and Mexican featherwork and weapons. Rare visits by native peoples to European centers such as the Iroquois delegation to the French court in 1725 [4] became important and popular public occasions, their every move recorded and printed for public consumption. Despite this obvious enthusiasm for all things native, historians have debated the degree to which European culture was changed through its exploration of the Atlantic world. Those who minimize its effects during the Early Modern period point out that Europeans continued to filter their experiences through long-established categories of analysis. The Bible and the writings of the ancient Greeks provided the most important models for interpreting native cultures, the natural world, and the cosmos throughout the sixteenth century even as the voyages of exploration were raising questions about the use of these ancient authorities. Yet there is no question that exploration of the Atlantic did profoundly affect European society in a number of ways. Societies encountered in the New World became important economic resources of European nations from very early on. By the end of the sixteenth century, trading companies such as the Dutch East India Company were forming in France, England, and the Netherlands to capitalize on trade in the New World. Many of these institutions came to play important political, judicial, and economic roles in the colonies because of the extensive privileges granted them by royal authorities.

European knowledge of the world expanded alongside the expansion of the economy as observation and experience came to take increasingly important roles in scholarly study. Geography [1] was perhaps the fastest changing field of knowledge of all. Every exploratory voyage brought back to Europe current information on distant lands, and stimulated the constant and rapid production of more accurate maps to reflect the new contours of the known world. Changing knowledge about the shape of the world went hand in hand with the development of astronomy as first Portuguese and later other European explorers relied on the stars to navigate the Atlantic Ocean. The Islamic world was far advanced in the field of mathematics and astronomy at this time, and Europeans used not only Islamic texts but also the astrolabe and other Islamic-devised implements in navigation. The work of individuals such as Galileo [2] in the fields of astronomy, physics, and mathematics, for example, was heavily indebted to knowledge coming from the East, as well as from European sailors.

Travel and scientific books also disseminated detailed descriptions of the wildlife and plants found in the New World. Although many Europeans believed that these plants were the exotic species mentioned in Mandeville's *Travels* and Pliny's *Natural History*, increasingly scholars came to realize that what they were encountering was altogether unknown in Europe. To give some idea of the expansion in European knowledge of plant life, we can compare German herbalist Leonhart Fuchs's famous sixteenth-century catalog of plants (*see* illustration) with that of the English botanist John Ray. Compiled at the end of the seventeenth century, Ray's catalog includes almost twenty thousand species of plants compared with the five hundred found in that of Fuchs. Needless to say, this rapid influx of information on new species from Asia, Africa, and the Americas placed additional pressure on botanists by the seventeenth century to develop a more complex taxonomy for classifying plants, as well as more systemized methods for collecting, describing, and cultivating specimens. Yet another area that was greatly affected by the exploratory voyages was that of moral philosophy. The early Spanish debates on the nature of the indigenous populations of the New World continued into the next centuries and sparked ongoing discussions about the true character of humanity and human society. The moral philosophers of the seventeenth century such as John Locke, [3] however, by this time relied as much on human observation and experience as they did on classical theories of society in developing their own interpretations. Not surprisingly, these debates also fed into discussions on the nature of imperial rule and its role with respect to indigenous peoples.

1. RICHARD HAKLUYT, *VOYAGES*

Medieval maps took mostly two recognized forms: the T-O map and the portolan chart. A T-O map was legacy of classical geographic knowledge. Asia lay at the top of the map, and Europe and Africa divided the bottom part of the world on the left and right, respectively. Dividing Europe from Africa was the Mediterranean Sea; lying horizontally was the Nile River. With the rise of Christianity, the standard T-O map by the fifth century A.D. placed Jerusalem, the Holy Land, at the center of the world, and the bodies of water came to resemble arms of the cross. The T-O map remained influential into the fifteenth century, but it was far from accurate. For example, this map lacked any perception of a directional "east" or "west" unlike modern maps. More accurate, if regional, maps were the portolan charts used by merchants to show the coastline and ports of the lands where they traded merchandise. Already by the fourteenth century, the circulation of Ptolemy's *Geographia* was affecting how Europeans portrayed their world and led to the rejection during the mid–fifteenth century of the T-O map formation. It was the influx of new information from the fifteenth- and sixteenth-century European explorers of the Atlantic ocean, however, and its rapid transmission through the new medium of printing, that led to the dramatic transformation of map making. By the end of the sixteenth century, the maps emanating from the presses of Europe much more closely reflect the contours of the world as it is known today. The increasing accuracy of European geographic knowledge, however, is only one of the reasons why historians are fascinated by cartography during the Early Modern period. Maps were an educational tool throughout European history, providing Europeans with a shared understanding of the world. Moreover, kings and princes collected and commissioned maps to illustrate the extent of their domains and political and economic influence. Maps, therefore, provide valuable insight into the cultural assumptions of a society and that society's understanding of its place in the world. The following excerpt is taken from Hakluyt's *Voyages*. Richard Hakluyt (ca. 1553–1616) is best known as a publisher of early English voyages of exploration. Printed here is a letter from Robert Thorne to the ambassador of Henry VIII of England to Charles V, the Holy Roman emperor, in 1527. Thorne is responding to request from the ambassador for information on the recent discoveries of Spain and Portugal. Beyond the information he provides on the discoveries themselves, what is fascinating about this excerpt is that Thorne spends substantial time describing how to read a map.

The English Voyages

Right noble and reverend in &c. I have received your letters, and have procured and sent to know of your servant, who, your Lordship wrote, should be sicke in Merchena. I cannot there or els where heare of him, without he be returned to you, or gone to S. Lucar, and shipt. I cannot judge but that of some contagious sicknesse hee died, so that the owner of the house for defaming his house would bury him secretly, and not be knowen of it. For such things have often times happened in this countrey.

Also to write unto your Lordshippe of the new trade of Spicery of the Emperour, there is no doubt but that the Islands are fertile of Cloves, Nutmegs, Mace, and Cinnamom: and that the said Islands, with other there about, abound with golde, Rubies, Diamondes, Balasses, Granates, Jacincts, and other stones & pearles, as all other lands, that are under and neere the Equinoctiall. For we see, where nature giveth any thing, she is no nigard. For as with us and other, that are aparted from the said Equinoctiall, our mettals be Lead, Tinne, and Iron, so theirs be Gold, Silver, and Copper. And as our fruits and graines bee Apples, Nuts, and Corne, so theirs be Dates, Nutmegs, Pepper, Cloves, and other Spices. And as we have Jeat, Amber, Cristall, Jasper, and other like stones, so have they Rubies, Diamonds, Balasses, Saphyres, Jacincts, and other like. And though some say that of such precious mettals, graines, or kind of spices, and precious stones, the abundance and quantity is nothing so great, as our mettals, fruits or stones above rehearsed: yet if it be well considered, how the quantitie of the earth under the Equinoctiall to both the Tropicall lines, (in which space is found the sayd Golde, spices and precious stones) is as much in quantity, as almost all the earth from the Tropickes to both the Poles; it cannot be denied but there is more quantity of the sayd mettals, fruites, spices, and precious stones, then there is of the other mettals and other things before rehearsed. And I see that the preciousnes of these things is measured after the distance that is between us, and the things that we have appetite unto. For in this navigation of the Spicerie was discovered, that these Islands nothing set by golde, but set more by a knife and a nayle of iron, then by his quantitie of Golde: and with reason, as the thing more necessary for mans service. And I doubt not but to them should be as precious our corne and seedes, if they might have them, as to us their spices: & likewise the pieces of glasse that here we have counterfeited are as precious to them, as to us their stones: which by experience is seene daylie by them that have trade thither. This of the riches of those countries is sufficient.

Touching that your Lordship wrote, whether it may bee profitable to the Emperor or no? it may be without doubt of great profite: if, as the king of Portingal doth, he would become a merchant, and provide shippes and their lading, and trade thither alone, and defend the trade of these Islands for himselfe. But other greater businesse withholdeth him from this. But still, as now it is begunne to be occupied, it would come to much. For the shippes coming in safetie, there would thither many every yere, of which to the Emperour is due of all the wares and jewels that come from thence the fift part for his custome cleare without any cost. And besides this hee putteth in every flote a certaine quantitie of money, of which hee enjoyeth of the gaines pound and pounds like as other adventurers doe. In a fleete of three shippes and a Caravel that went from this citie armed by the marchants of it, which departed in Aprill last past, I and my partener have one thousand foure hundred duckets that we employed in the sayd fleete, principally for that two English men, friends of mine, which are somewhat learned in Cosmographie, should goe in the same shippes, to bring me certaine relation of the situation of the countrey, and to be expert in the navigation of those seas, and there to have informations of many other things, and advise that I desire to knowe especially. Seeing in these quarters are shippes, and mariners of that countrey, and cardes by which they saile, though much unlike ours, that they should procure to have the said cards, and learne how they understand them, and especially to know what navigation they have for those Islands Northwards, and Northeastward.

For if from the sayd Islands the sea did extend, without interposition of land, to saile from the North point to the Northeast poynt one thousand seven hundred or one thousand eight hundred leagues, they should come to the New found Islands that we discovered, and so we should be neerer to the sayd Spicerie by almost two thousand leagues then the Emperour, or the king of Portingal are. And to advise your Lordship, whether of these Spiceries of the king of Portingal or the Emperours is neerer, and also of the titles that either of them hath, and howe our New found lands are parted from it, (for that by writing some demonstration, it were hard to give any declaration of it) I have caused that your Lordship shall receive herewith a little Mappe or Carde of the world: the which, I feare me, shall put your Lordship to more labour to understand, then me to make it, onely for that it is made in so litle roome that it cannot be but obscurely set out, that is desired to be seene in it, and also for that I am in this science little expert: Yet to remedy in part this difficultie, it is necessary to declare to your Lordship my intent, with which I trust you shall perceive in this Card part of your desire, if, for that I cannot expresse mine intent, with my declaration I doe not make it more obscure.

First, your Lordship knoweth that the Cosmographers have divided the earth by 360 degrees in latitude, and as many in longitude, under the which is comprehended all the roundnes of the earth: the latitude being divided into foure quarters, ninetie degrees amount to every quarter, which they measure by the altitude of the Poles, that is the North and South starres, being from the line Equinoctiall till they come right under the North starre the said ninetie degrees: and as much from the sayd line Equinoctiall to the South starre be other ninety degrees. And as much more is also from either of the sayd starres agayne to the Equinoctiall. Which imagined to bee round, is soone perceived thus, 360 degrees of latitude to be consumed in the said foure quarters of ninetie degrees a quarter: so that this latitude is the measure of the worlde from North to South, and from South to North. And the longitude, in which are also counted other 360, is counted from West to East, or from East to West, as in the Card is set.

The sayd latitude your Lordship may see marked and divided in the ende of this Card on the left hand: so that if you would know in what degrees of latitude any region or coast standeth, take a compasse, and set the one foot of the same in the Equinoctial line right against the said region, & apply the other foote of the compasse to the said region or coast, & then set the sayd compasse at the end of the Card, where the degrees are divided. And the one foote of the compasse standing in the line Equinoctial, the other will shew in the scale the degrees of altitude or latitude that the said region is in. Also the longitude of the world I have set out in the nether part of the Card, conteining also 360 degrees: which begin to be counted after Ptoleme and other Cosmographers from an headland called Capo Verde, which is over against a little crosse made in the part Occidental, where the division of the degrees beginneth, and endeth in the same Capo Verde.

Now to know in what longitude any land is, your Lordship must take a ruler or a compasse, and set the one foot of the compasse upon the land or coast whose longitude you would know, and extend the other foot of the compasse to the next part of one of the transversall lines in the Orientall or Occidental part: which done, set the one foot of the compasse in the said transversal line at the end of the nether scale, the scale of longitude, and the other foot sheweth the degree of longitude that the region is in. And your Lordship must understand that this Card, though little, conteineth the universall whole world betwixt two collaterall lines, the one in the Occidentall part descendeth perpendicular upon the 175 degree, & the other in the Orientall on the 170 degree, whose distance measureth the scale of longitude. And that which is without the two said transversall lines, is onely to shew how the Orientall part is joined with the Occident, and Occident with the Orient. For that that is set without the line in the Oriental part, is the same that is set within the other line in the Occidentall part: and that that is set without the line in the Occidentall part, is the same that is set within the line in the Orientall part, to shew that though this figure of the world in plaine or flatte seemeth to have an end, yet one imagining that this sayd Card were set upon a round thing, where the endes should touch by the lines, it would plainely appeare howe the Orient part joyneth with the Occident, as there without the lines it is described and figured.

And for more declaration of the said Card, your Lordship shall understand, that beginning on the part Occidental within the line, the first land that is set out, is the maine land and Islands of the Indies of the Emperour. Which maine land or coast goeth Northward, and finisheth in the land that we found, which is called here Terra de Labrador. So that it appeareth the sayd land that we found, and the Indies to be all one maine land.

The sayd coast from the sayd Indies Southward, as by the Card your Lordshippe may see, commeth to a certaine straight Sea, called Estrecho de todos Santos: by which straight Sea the Spaniards goe to the Spiceries, as I shall declare more at large: the which straight Sea is right against three hundred fifteene degrees of longitude, and is of latitude or altitude from the Equinoctiall three and fifty degrees. The first land from the sayd beginning of the Card toward the Orient are certaine Islands of the Canaries, and Islandes of Capo Verde. But the first maine land next to the line Equinoctial is the sayd Capo

Verde, and from thence Northward by the straight of this sea of Italie. And so followeth Spayne, France, Flanders, Almaine, Denmarke, and Norway, which is the highest parte toward the North. And over against Flanders are our Islands of England and Ireland. Of the landes and coastes within the streights I have set out onely the Regions, dividing them by lines of their limits, by which plainely I thinke your Lordship may see, in what situation everie region is, and of what highnesse, and with what regions it is joyned. I doe thinke few are left out of all Europe. In the parts of Asia and Affrica I could not so wel make the sayd divisions: for that they be not so wel knowen, nor need not so much. This I write because in the said Card be made the said lines & strikes, that your Lordship should understand wherefore they doe serve. Also returning to the foresaid Capo verde, the coast goeth Southward to a Cape called Capo de buona speransa: which is right over against the 60. & 65. degree of longitude. And by this Cape go the Portingals to their Spicerie. For from this Cape toward the Orient, is the land of Calicut, as your Lordship may see in the headland over against the 130. degree. From the sayd Cape of Buona speransa the coast returneth toward the line Equinoctial, and passing forth entreth the red sea, & returning out, entreth again into the gulfe of Persia, and returneth toward the Equinoctiall line, till that it commeth to the headland called Calicut aforesayd, and from thence the coast making a gulfe, where is the river of Ganges, returneth toward the line to a headland called Malaca, where is the principall Spicerie: & from this Cape returneth and maketh a great gulfe, and after the coast goeth right toward the Orient, and over against this last gulfe and coast by many Islands, which be Islandes of the Spiceries of the Emperour. Upon which the Portingals and he be at variance.

The sayd coast goeth toward the Orient, and endeth right against the 155. degrees, and after returneth toward the Occident Northward: which coast not yet plainely knowen, I may joine to the New found lande found by us, that I spake of before. So that I finish with this briefe declaration of the Card aforesayd. Well I know I should also have declared how the coasts within the straights of the Sea of Italie runne. It is playne that passing the streights on the North side of that Sea after the coast of Granado, and with that which pertaines to Spaine, is the coast of that which France hath in Italie. And then followeth in one piece all Italie, which land hath an arme of the Sea, with a gulfe which is called Mare Adriaticum. And in the bottome of this gulfe is the citie of Venice. And on the other part of the sayd gulfe is Sclavonia, and next Grecia, then the streits of Constantinople, and then the sea called Euxinus, which is within the sayd streights: and coming out of the sayd streights, followeth Turcia major (though now on both sides it is called Turcia.) And so the coast runneth Southward to Syria, and over against the sayd Turcia are the Islands of Rhodes, Candie, and Cyprus. And over against Italie are the Islands of Sicilia and Sardinia. And over against Spaine is Majorca and Minorca. In the ende of the gulfe of Syria is Judea. And from thence returneth the coast toward the Occident, till it commeth to the streights where we began, which all is the coast of Affrike and Barbarie. Also your Lordship shall understand that the coastes of the Sea throughout all the world, I have coloured with yellow, for that it may appeare that all that is within the line coloured yellow, is to be imagined to be maine land or Islands: and all without the line so coloured to bee Sea: whereby it is easie and light to know it. Albeit in this little roome any other description would rather have made it obscure then cleere. And the sayd coasts of the Sea are all set justly after the manner and forme as they lie, as the navigation approveth them throughout all the Card, save onely the coastes and Isles of the Spicerie of the Emperour which is from over against the 160. to the 215. degrees of longitude, For these coastes and situations of the Islands, every of the Cosmographers and pilots of Portingal & Spayne do set after their purpose. The Spaniards more towards the Orient, because they should appeare to appertain to the Emperour: & the Portingals more toward the Occident, for that they should fal within their jurisdiction. So that the pilots and navigants thither, which in such cases should declare the truth, by their industrie do set them falsly every one to favour his prince. And for this cause can be no certaine situation of that coast and Islands, till this difference betwixt them be verified.

In the yeere 1484 the king of Portingal minded to arme certaine Carvels to discover this Spicerie. Then forasmuch as he feared that being discovered, every other prince woulde sende and trade thither, so that the cost and perill of discovering should be his, and the profite common: wherefore first hee gave knowledge of this his minde to all princes Christened, saying that hee would seeke amongst the infidels newe possessions of regions, and therefore would make a certaine armie: and that if any of them would helpe in the cost of the sayd armie, he should enjoy his part of the profite or honour that should come of it. And as then this discovering was holden for a strange thing and uncertaine. Nowe they say, that all the Princes of Christendome answered, that they would be no part of such an armie, nor yet of the profit that might come of it. After the which he gave knowledge to the Pope of his purpose, and of the answere of all the Princes, desiring him that seeing that none would helpe in the costes, that he would judge all that should bee found and discovered to be of his jurisdiction, and commannd that none other princes should intermeddle therewith. The Pope sayd not as Christ saith, Quis me constituit judicem inter vos? He did not refuse, but making himselfe as Lord and Judge of all, not onely granted that all that should be discovered from Orient to Occident, should be the kings of Portingal, but also, that upon great censures no other Prince should discover but he. And if they did, all to bee the kings of Portingal. So he armed a fleete, and in the yeere 1497 were discovered the Islands of Calicut, from whence is brought all the spice he hath.

After this in the yere 1492 the king of Spaine willing to discover lands toward the Occident without making any such diligence, or taking licence of the king of Portingal, armed certaine Carvels, and then discovered this India Occidentall, especially two Islands of the sayd India, that in this Card I set forth, naming the one la Dominica, and the other Cuba, and brought certaine golde from thence. Of the which when the king of Portingal had knowledge, he sent to the king of Spaine, requiring him to give him the sayd Islands. For that by the sentence of the Pope all that should be discovered was his, and that hee should not proceede further in the discoverie without his licence. And at the same time it seemeth that out of Castil into Portingal had gone for feare of burning infinite number of Jewes that were expelled out of Spaine, for that they would not turne to be Christians, and carried with them infinite number of golde and silver. So that it seemeth that the king of Spaine answered, that it was reason that the king of Portingal asked, and that to be obedient to that which the Pope had decreed, he would give him the sayd Islands of the Indies. Nowe for as much as it was decreed betwixt the sayde kings, that none should receive the others subjects fugitives, nor their goods, therfore the king of Portingal should pay and returne to the king of Spaine a million of golde or more, that the Jewes had caryed out of Spaine to Portingal, & that in so doing he would give these Islands, and desist from any more discovering. And not fulfilling this, he would not onely not give these Islands, but procure to discover more where him thought best. It seemeth that the king of Portingal would not, or could not with his ease pay this money. And so not paying, that he could not let the king of Spaine to discover: so that he enterprised not toward the Orient where he had begun & found the Spicerie. And consented to the king of Spaine, that touching this discovering they should divide the worlde betweene them two. And that all that should be discovered from Cape Verde, where this Card beginneth to be counted in the degrees of longitude, to 180 of the sayd scale of longitude, which is halfe the world toward the Orient, & finisheth in this Card right over against a little crosse made at the said 180 degrees, to be the king of Portingals. And all the land from the said Crosse towarde the Occident, until it joyneth with the other Crosse in the Orient, which conteineth the other hundreth and eightie degrees, that is the other halfe of the worlde, to be the king of Spaines. So that from the land over against the said hundreth & eighty degrees untill it finish in the three hundred and sixtie on both the ends of the Card, is the jurisdiction of the king of Spaine. So after this maner they divided the world betweene them.

Now for that these Islands of Spicery fall neere the terme and limites betweene these princes (for as by the sayd Card you may see they begin from one hundred and sixtie degrees of longitude, and ende in 215) it seemeth all that falleth from 160 to 180 degrees, should be of Portingal: and all the rest of Spaine. And for that their Cosmographers and Pilots coulde not agree in the situation of the sayde Islandes (for the Portingals set them all within their 180 degrees, and the Spaniards set them all without:) and for that in measuring, all the Cosmographers of both partes, or what other that ever have bene cannot give certaine order to measure the longitude of the worlde, as they doe of the latitude: for that there is no starre fixed from East to West, as are the starres of the Poles from North to South, but all mooveth with the moving divine: no maner can bee founde howe certainly it may bee measured, but by conjectures, as the Navigants have esteemed the way they have gone. But it is manifest that Spaine had the situation of al the lands from Cape Verde, toward the Orient of ye Portingals to their 180 degrees. And in all their Cardes they never hitherto set the saide Islands within their limitation of the sayd 180 degrees, (though they knewe very well of the Islands,) till now that the Spaniards discovered them. And it is knowen that the king of Portingal had trade to these Islands afore, but would never suffer Portingal to go thither from Calicut: for so much as he knew that it fell out of his dominion: least by going thither there might come some knowledge of those other Islands of the king of Spaine, but bought the cloves of Marchants of that countrey, that brought them to Calicut, much deerer then they would have cost, if he had sent for them, thinking after this maner it would abide alwayes secret. And now that it is discovered he sendes and keepes the Spaniards from the trade all that he can.

Also it should seeme that when this foresaid consent of the division of the worlde was agreed of betweene them, the king of Portingal had already discovered certaine Islandes that lie over against Cape Verde, and also certaine part of the maine land of India toward the South, from whence he fette Brasill, and called it the land of Brasil. So for that all should come in his terme and limites, hee tooke three hundred and seventie leagues beyond Cape Verde: and after this, his 180 degrees, being his part of the worlde, should begin in the Carde right over against the 340 degrees, where I have made a little compasse with a crosse, and should finish at the 160 degree, where also I have made another little marke. And after this computation without any controversie, the Islands of the spicery fal out of the Portingals domination. So that nowe the Spaniards say to the Portingals, that if they would beginne their 180 degrees from the sayde Cape Verde, to the intent they should extende more toward the Orient, and so to touch those Islandes of the Spicerie of the Emperour, which is al that is betweene the two crosses made in this Card, that then the Islands of Cape Verde and the lande of Brasil that the Portingals nowe obtaine, is out of the sayd limitation, and that they are of the Emperours. Or if their 180 degrees they count from the 370 leagues beyond the said Cape Verde, to include in it the said Islands and lands of Brasil, then plainely appeareth the said 180 degrees should finish long before they come to these Islands of the Spicerie of the Emperour: As by this Carde your Lordship may see. For their limits should begin at the 340 degrees of this Carde, and ende at the 160 degrees, where I have made two little markes of the compasse with crosses in them.

So that plainely it should appeare by reason, that the Portingals should leave these Islands of Cape Verde and land of Brasil, if they would have part of the Spicerie of the Emperours: or els holding these, they have no part there. To this the Portingals say, that they will beginne their 180 degrees from the selfe same Cape Verde: for that it may extende so much more toward the Orient, and touch these Islandes of the Emperours: and would winne these Islandes of Cape Verde and land of Brasil neverthelesse, as a thing that they possessed before the consent of this limitation was made.

So none can verely tell which hath the best reason. They be not yet agreed, Quare sub Judice lis est.

But without doubt (by all conjectures of reason) the sayd Islands fall all without the limitation of Portingal, and pertaine to Spaine, as it appeareth by the most part of all the Cardes made by the Portingals, save those which they have falsified of late purposely.

But now touching that your Lordship wrote, whether that which we discovered toucheth any thing the foresayd coastes: once it appeareth plainely, that the Newefound land that we discovered, is all a maine land with the Indies Occidentall, from whence the Emperour hath all the gold and pearles: and so continueth of coast more then 5000 leagues of length, as by this Carde appeareth. For from the said New lands it proceedeth toward the Occident to the Indies, and from the Indies returneth toward the Orient, and after turneth Southward up till it come to the Straits of Todos Santos, which I reckon to be more then 5000 leagues.

So that to the Indians it should seeme that we have some title, at least that for our discovering we might trade thither as other doe. But all this is nothing neere the Spicerie.

Now then if from the sayd New found lands the Sea be navigable, there is no doubt, but sayling Northward and passing the Pole, descending to the Equinoctial line, we shall hit these Islands, and it should be a much shorter way, then either the Spaniards or the Portingals have. For we be distant from the Pole but thirty and nine degrees, and from the Pole to the Equinoctiall be ninetie, the which added together, bee an hundred twenty and nine degrees, leagues 2489. and miles 7440: Where we should find these islands. And the Navigation of the Spaniards to the Spicerie is, as by this Carde you may see, from Spaine to the Islandes of Canarie, and from these Islandes they runne over the line Equinoctiall Southwarde to the Cape of the maine land of the Indians, called the Cape of Saint Augustine, and from this Cape Southwards to the straites of Todos Santos, in the which navigation to the said straites is 1700. or 1800 leagues; and from these Straites being past them, they returne towarde the line Equinoctiall to the Islands of Spicerie, which are distant from the saide Straites 4200. or 4300. leagues.

The navigation of the Portingals to the said Islandes is departing from Portingall Southward towarde the Cape Verde, and from thence to another Cape passing the line Equinoctial called Capo de bona speransa, and from Portingal to the Cape is 1800 leagues, and from this Cape to the Islands of Spicerie of the Emperour is 2500. leagues.

So that this navigation amounteth all to 4300. leagues. So that (as afore is sayd,) if between our New found lands or Norway, or Island, the seas toward the North be navigable, we should goe to these Islands a shorter way by more then 2000. leagues.

And though we went not to the sayd Islandes, for that they are the Emperours or kings of Portingal, wee shoulde by the way and comming once to the line Equinoctiall, finde landes no lesse riche of golde and Spicerie, as all other landes are under the sayd line Equinoctiall: and also should, if we may passe under the North, enjoy the navigation of all Tartarie. Which should be no lesse profitable to our commodities of cloth, then these Spiceries to the Emperour, and king of Portingal.

But it is a generall opinion of all Cosmographers, that passing the seventh clime, the sea is all ice, and the colde so much that none can suffer it. And hitherto they had all the like opinion, that under the line Equinoctiall for much heate the land was unhabitable.

Yet since (by experience is proved) no land so much habitable nor more temperate. And to conclude, I thinke the same should be found under the North, if it were experimented. For as all judge, Nihil fit vacuum in rerum natura: So I judge, there is no land unhabitable, nor Sea innavigable. If I should write the reason that presenteth this unto me, I should be too prolixe, and it seemeth not requisite for this present matter. God knoweth that though by it I should have no great interest, yet I have had and still have no litle mind of this businesse: So that if I had facultie to my will, it should be the first thing that I woulde understand, even to attempt, if our Seas Northward be navigable to the Pole, or no. I reason, that as some sickenesses are hereditarious, and come from the father to the sonne, so this inclination or desire of this discoverie I inherited of my father, which with another marchant of Bristow named Hugh Eliot, were the discoveries of the New found lands, of the which there is no doubt, (as nowe plainely appeareth) if the mariners would then have bene ruled, and followed their Pilots minde, the lands of the West Indies (from whence all the gold commeth) had bene ours. For all is one coast, as by the Carde appeareth, and is aforesayd.

Also in this Carde by the coastes where you see C. your Lordship shall understand it is set for Cape or headland, where I. for Iland, where P. for Port, where R. for River. Also in all this little Carde I thinke nothing be erred touching the situation of the land, save onely in these Ilands of Spicerie: which, for that (as afore is sayd) every one setteth them after his minde, there can be no certification how they stand. I doe not denie, that there lacke many things, that a consummate Carde should have, or that a right good demonstration desireth. For these should be expressed all the mountains and Rivers that are principall of name in the earth, with the names of Portes of the sea, the names of all principall cities, which all I might have set, but not in this Carde, for the litle space would not consent.

Your Lordship may see that setting onely the names almost of every Region, and yet not of all, the roome is occupied. Many Islands are also left out, for the said lack of roome, the names almost of all Portes put to silence, with the roses of the windes or points of the compasse: For that this is not for Pilots to sayle by, but a summary declaration of that which your Lordship commanded. And if by this your Lordship cannot wel perceive the meaning of this Card, of the which I would not marveile, by reason of the rude composition of it, will it please your Lordship to advise mee to make a bigger and a better Mappe, or els that I may cause one to be made. For I know my selfe in this and all other nothing perfect, but Licet semper discens, nunquam tamen ad perfectam scientiam pervenines. Also I know, to set the forme Sphericall of the world in Plano after the true rule of Cosmographie, it would have bene made otherwise then this is: howbeit the demonstration should not have bene so plaine.

And also these degrees of longitude, that I set in the lower part of this card, should have bin set along by the line Equinoctiall, & so then must be imagined. For the degrees of longitude neere either of the poles are nothing equall in bignesse to them in the Equinoctiall. But these are set so, for that setting them a long the Equinoctial, it would have made obscure a great part of the map. Many other curiosities may be required, which for the nonce I did not set downe, as well for that the intent I had principally was to satisfie your doubt touching the spicerie, as for that I lack leasure and time. I trust your Lordship correcting that which is erred, will accept my good will, which is to doe any thing that I may in your Lordships service. But from henceforth I knowe your Lordship will rather commaund me to keepe silence, then to be large, when you shall be wearied with the reading of this discourse. Jesus prosper your estate and health.

Your Lordships
Robert Thorne 1527.

Also this Carde and that which I write touching the variance betweene the Emperour and the king of Portingall, is not to be shewed or communicated there with many of that court. For though there is nothing in it prejudiciall to the Emperour, yet it may be a cause of paine to the maker: as well for that none may make these Cardes, but certaine appointed and allowed for masters, as for that peradventure it would not sound well to them, that a stranger should know or discover their secretes: and would appeare worst of all, if they understand that I write touching the short way to the spicerie by our Seas. Though peradventure of troth it is not to be looked to, as a thing that by all opinions is unpossible, and I thinke never will come to effect: and therefore neither here nor else where is it to be spoken of. For to move it amongst wise men, it should bee had in derision. And therefore to none I would have written nor spoken of such things, but to your Lordship, to whom boldly I commit in this all my foolish fantasie as to my self. But if it please God that into England I may come with your Lordship, I will shew some conjectures of reason, though against the generall opinion of Cosmographers, by which shall appeare this that I say not to lacke some foundation. And till that time I beseeche your Lordship let it be put to silence: and in the meane season it may please God to send our two Englishmen, that are gone to the Spicerie, which may also bring more plaine declaration of that which in this case might be desired.

Also I knowe I needed not to have beene so prolixe in the declaration of this Carde to your Lordship, if the sayd Carde had bene very well made after the rules of Cosmographie. For your Lordship would soone understand it better then I, or any other that could have made it: and so it should appeare that I shewed Delphinum natare. But for that I have made it after my rude maner, it is necessary that I be the declarer or gloser of mine own worke, or els your Lordship should have had much labour to understand it, which now with it also cannot be excused, it is so grossely done. But I knew you looked for no curious things of mee, and therefore I trust your Lordship will accept this, and hold me for excused. In other mens letters that they write they crave pardon that at this present they write no larger: but I must finish, asking pardon that at this present I write so largely. Jesus preserve your Lordship with augmentation of dignities.

Your servant Robert
Thorne, 1527.

Epitaphium M. Roberti Thorni, sepulti in Ecclesia
  Templariorum Londini.
Robertus jacet hîc Thorne, quem Bristolia quondam
  Prætoris meritò legit ad officium.

Huic etenim semper magnæ Respublica curæ,
  Charior & cunctic patria divitiis.
Ferre inopi auxilium, tristes componere lites,
  Dulce huic consilio quósque juvare fuit.
Qui pius exaudis miserorum voto precésque,
  Christe huic cœli des regione locum.

2. GALILEO GALILEI, *DIALOGUES ON TWO NEW SCIENCES*

Arguably the most important scientific thinker of the Early Modern period, the Italian born, humanist-educated Galileo Galilei (1564–1642) is perhaps best known today for his work in the field of astronomy. Galileo's controversial text, *Dialogue on the Two Chief World Systems: Ptolemaic and Copernican,* led to his first trial before the Roman Inquisition on the charge of heresy in 1632. The *Dialogue* argues in favor of the heliocentric universe, a theory that was first articulated by Nicholaus Copernicus (1473–1543) in his treatise *On the Revolutions of the Heavenly Spheres.* The notion of a heliocentric universe ran contrary to the then widely accepted belief that the earth lay at the center of the universe. Galileo's influence on the fields of mathematics and physics was as significant as it was on the field of astronomy. It is important to realize, however, that his work and that of other early modern scientific thinkers owed an enormous debt to the data collected by early modern sailors and to Islamic scientific scholarship. It was Medieval Islamic thinkers, for example, who developed algebra and the Arabic numerical system. Without these innovations in mathematics, Galileo could not have devised his law of falling bodies. The following excerpt is taken from the first book of his *Dialogues Concerning Two New Sciences* (1637).

The Two New Sciences of Galileo

First Day
Interlocutors: Salviati, Sagredo and Simplicio

SALV. The constant activity which you Venetians display in your famous arsenal suggests to the studious mind a large field for investigation, especially that part of the work which involves mechanics; for in this department all types of instruments and machines are constantly being constructed by many artisans, among whom there must be some who, partly by inherited experience and partly by their own observations, have become highly expert and clever in explanation.

SAGR. You are quite right. Indeed, I myself, being curious by nature, frequently visit this place for the mere pleasure of observing the work of those who, on account of their superiority over other artisans, we call "first rank men." Conference with them has often helped me in the investigation of certain effects including not only those which are striking, but also those which are recondite and almost incredible. At times also I have been put to confusion and driven to despair of ever explaining something for which I could not account, but which my senses told me to be true. And notwithstanding the fact that what the old man told us a little while ago is proverbial and commonly accepted, yet it seemed to me altogether false, like many another saying which is current among the ignorant; for I think they introduce these expressions in order to give the appearance of knowing something about matters which they do not understand.

SALV. You refer, perhaps, to that last remark of his when we asked the reason why they employed stocks, scaffolding and bracing of larger dimensions for launching a big vessel than they do for a small one; and he answered that they did this in order to avoid the danger of the ship parting under its own heavy weight [*vasta mole*], a danger to which small boats are not subject?

SAGR. Yes, that is what I mean; and I refer especially to his last assertion which I have always regarded as a false, though current, opinion; namely, that in speaking of these and other similar machines one cannot argue from the small to the large, because many devices which succeed on a small scale do not work on a large scale. Now, since mechanics has its foundation in geometry, where mere size cuts no figure, I do not see that the properties of circles, triangles, cylinders, cones and other solid figures will change with their size. If, therefore, a large machine be constructed in such a way that its parts bear to one another the same ratio as in a smaller one, and if the smaller is sufficiently strong for the purpose for which it was designed, I do not see why the larger also should not be able to withstand any severe and destructive tests to which it may be subjected.

SALV. The common opinion is here absolutely wrong. Indeed, it is so far wrong that precisely the opposite is true, namely, that many machines can be constructed even more perfectly on a large scale than on a small; thus, for instance, a clock which indicates and strikes the hour can be made more accurate on a large scale than on a small. There are some intelligent people who maintain this same opinion, but on more reasonable grounds, when they cut loose from geometry and argue that the better performance of the large machine is owing to the imperfections and variations of the material. Here I trust you will not charge me with arrogance if I say that imperfections in the material, even those which are great enough to invalidate the clearest mathematical proof, are not sufficient to explain the deviations observed between machines in the concrete and in the abstract. Yet I shall say it and will affirm that, even if the imperfections did not exist and matter were absolutely perfect, unalterable and free from all accidental variations, still the mere fact that it is matter makes the larger machine, built of the same material and in the same proportion as the smaller, correspond with exactness to the smaller in every respect except that it will not be so strong or so resistant against violent treatment; the larger the machine, the greater its weakness. Since I assume matter to be unchangeable and always the same, it is clear that we are no less able to treat this constant and invariable property in a rigid manner than if it belonged to simple and pure mathematics. Therefore, Sagredo, you would do well to change the opinion which you, and perhaps also many other students of mechanics, have entertained concerning the ability of machines and structures to resist external disturbances, thinking that when they are built of the same material and maintain the same ratio between parts, they are able equally, or rather proportionally, to resist or yield to such external disturbances and blows. For we can demonstrate by geometry that the large machine is not proportionately stronger than the small. Finally, we may say that, for every machine and structure, whether artificial or natural, there is set a necessary limit beyond which neither art nor nature can pass; it is here understood, of course, that the material is the same and the proportion preserved.

SAGR. My brain already reels. My mind, like a cloud momentarily illuminated by a lightning-flash, is for an instant filled with an unusual light, which now beckons to me and which now suddenly mingles and obscures strange, crude ideas. From what you have said it appears to me impossible to build two similar structures of the same material, but of different sizes and have them proportionately strong; and if this were so, it would not be possible to find two single poles of the same wood which shall be alike in strength and resistance but unlike in size.

SALV. So it is, Sagredo. And to make sure that we understand each other, I say that if we take a wooden rod of a certain length and size, fitted, say, into a wall at right angels, i.e., parallel to the horizon, it may be reduced to such a length that it will just support itself; so that if a hair's breadth be added to its length it will break under its own weight and will be the only rod of the kind in the world. Thus if, for instance, its length be a hundred times its breadth, you will not be able to find another rod whose length is also a hundred times its breadth and which, like the former, is just able to sustain its own weight and no more: all the larger ones will break while all the shorter ones will be strong enough to support something more than their own weight. And this which I have said about the ability to support itself must be understood to apply also to other tests; so that if a piece of scantling [corrente] will carry the weight of ten similar to itself, a beam [trave] having the same proportions will not be able to support ten similar beams.

Please observe, gentlemen, how facts which at first seem improbable will, even on scant explanation, drop the cloak which has hidden them and stand forth in naked and simple beauty. Who does not know that a horse falling from a height of three or four cubits will break his bones, while a dog falling from the same height or a cat from a height of eight or ten cubits will suffer no injury? Equally harmless would be the fall of a grasshopper from a tower or the fall of an ant from the distance of the moon. Do not children fall with impunity from heights which would cost their elders a broken leg or perhaps a fractured skull? And just as smaller animals are proportionately stronger and more robust than the larger, so also smaller plants are able to stand up better than larger. I am certain you both know that an oak two hundred cubits [braccia] high would not be able to sustain its own branches if they were distributed as in a tree of ordinary size; and that nature cannot produce a horse as large as twenty ordinary horses or a giant ten times taller than an ordinary man unless by miracle or by greatly altering the proportions of his limbs and especially of his bones, which would have to be considerably enlarged over the ordinary. Likewise the current belief that, in the case of artificial machines the very large and the small are equally feasible and lasting is a manifest error. Thus, for example, a small obelisk or column or other solid figure can certainly be laid down or set up without danger of breaking, while the very large ones will go to pieces under the slightest provocation, and that purely on account of their own weight. And here I must relate a circumstance which is worthy of your attention as indeed are all events which happen contrary to expectation, especially when a precautionary measure turns out to be a cause of disaster. A large marble column was laid out so that its two ends rested each upon a piece of beam; a little later it occurred to a mechanic that, in order to be doubly sure of its not breaking in the middle by its own weight, it would be wise to lay a third support midway; this seemed to all an excellent idea; but the sequel showed that it was quite the opposite, for not many months passed before the column was found cracked and broken exactly above the new middle support.

SIMP. A very remarkable and thoroughly unexpected accident, especially if caused by placing that new support in the middle.

SALV. Surely this is the explanation, and the moment the cause is known our surprise vanishes; for when the two pieces of the column were placed on level ground it was observed that one of the end beams had, after a long while, become decayed and sunken, but that the middle one remained hard and strong, thus causing one half of the column to project in the air without any support. Under these circumstances the body therefore behaved differently from what it would have done if supported only upon the first beams; because no matter how much they might have sunken the column would have gone with them. This is an accident which could not possibly have happened to a small column, even though made of the same stone and having a length corresponding to its thickness, i.e., preserving the ratio between thickness and length found in the large pillar.

SAGR. I am quite convinced of the facts of the case, but I do not understand why the strength and resistance are not multiplied in the same proportion as the material; and I am the more puzzled because, on the contrary, I have noticed in other cases that the strength and resistance against breaking increase in a larger ratio than the amount of material. Thus, for instance, if two nails be driven into a wall, the one which is twice as big as the other will support not only twice as much weight as the other, but three or four times as much.

SALV. Indeed you will not be far wrong if you say eight times as much; nor does this phenomenon contradict the other even though in appearance they seem so different.

SAGR. Will you not then, Salviati, remove these difficulties and clear away these obscurities if possible: for I imagine that this problem of resistance opens up a field of beautiful and useful ideas; and if you are pleased to make this the subject of to-day's discourse you will place Simplicio and me under many obligations.

SALV. I am at your service if only I can call to mind what I learned from our Academician who had thought much upon this subject and according to his custom had demonstrated everything by geometrical methods so that one might fairly call this a new science. For, although some of his conclusions had been reached by others, first of all by Aristotle, these are not the most beautiful and, what is more important, they had not been proven in a rigid manner from fundamental principles. Now, since I wish to convince you by demonstrative reasoning rather than to persuade you by mere probabilities, I shall suppose that you are familiar with present-day mechanics so far as it is needed in our discussion. First of all it is necessary to consider what happens when a piece of wood or any other solid which coheres firmly is broken; for this is the fundamental fact, involving the first and simple principle which we must take for granted as well known.

To grasp this more clearly, imagine a cylinder or prism, AB, made of wood or other solid coherent material. Fasten the upper end, A, so that the cylinder hangs vertically. To the lower end, B, attach the weight C. It is clear that however great they may be, the tenacity and coherence [tenacitá e coerenza] between the parts of this solid, so long as they are not infinite, can be overcome by the pull of the weight C, a weight which can be increased indefinitely until finally the solid breaks like a rope. And as in the case of the rope whose strength we know to be derived from a multitude of hemp threads which compose it, so in the case of the wood, we observe its fibres and filaments run lengthwise and render it much stronger than a hemp rope of the same thickness. But in the case of a stone or metallic cylinder where the coherence seems to be still greater the cement which holds the parts together must be something other than filaments and fibres; and yet even this can be broken by a strong pull.

SIMP. If this matter be as you say I can well understand that the fibres of the wood, being as long as the piece of wood itself, render it strong and resistant against large forces tending to break it. But how can one make a rope one hundred cubits long out of hempen fibres which are not more than two or three cubits long, and still give it so much strength? Besides, I should be glad to hear your opinion as to the manner in which the parts or metal, stone, and other materials not showing a filamentous structure are put together; for, if I mistake not, they exhibit even greater tenacity.

SALV. To solve the problems which you raise it will be necessary to make a digression into subjects which have little bearing upon our present purpose.

SAGR. But if, by digressions, we can reach new truth, what harm is there in making one now, so that we may not lose this knowledge, remembering that such an opportunity, once omitted, may not return; remembering also that we are not tied down to a fixed and brief method but that we meet solely for our own entertainment? Indeed, who knows but that we may thus frequently discover something more interesting and beautiful than the solution originally sought? I beg of you, therefore, to grant the request of Simplicio, which is also mine; for I am no less curious and desirous than he to learn what is the binding material which holds together the parts of solids so that they can scarcely be separated. This information is also needed to understand the coherence of the parts of fibres themselves of which some solids are built up.

SALV. I am at your service, since you desire it. The first question is, How are fibres, each not more than two or three cubits in length, so tightly bound together in the case of a rope one hundred cubits long that great force [violenza] is required to break it?

Now tell me, Simplicio, can you not hold a hempen fibre so tightly between your fingers that I, pulling by the other end, would break it before drawing it away from you? Certainly you can. And now when the fibres of hemp are held not only at the ends, but are grasped by the surrounding medium throughout their entire length is it not manifestly more difficult to tear them loose from what holds them than to break them? But in the case of the rope the very act of twisting causes the threads to bind one another in such a way that when the rope is stretched with a great force the fibres break rather than separate from each other.

At the point where a rope parts the fibres are, as everyone knows, very short, nothing like a cubit long, as they would be if the parting of the rope occurred, not by the breaking of the filaments, but by their slipping one over the other.

SAGR. In confirmation of this it may be remarked that ropes sometimes break not by a lengthwise pull but by excessive twisting. This, it seems to me, is a conclusive argument because the threads bind one another so tightly that the compressing fibres do not permit those which are compressed to lengthen the spirals even that little bit by which it is necessary for them to lengthen in order to surround the rope which, on twisting, grows shorter and thicker.

SALV. You are quite right. Now see how one fact suggests another. The thread held between the fingers does not yield to one who wishes to draw it away even when pulled with considerable force, but resists because it is held back by a double compression, seeing that the upper finger presses against the lower as hard as the lower against the upper. Now, if we could retain only one of these pressures there is no doubt that only half the original resistance would remain; but since we are not able, by lifting, say, the upper finger, to remove one of these pressures without also removing the other, it becomes necessary to preserve one of them by means of a new device which causes the thread to press itself against the finger or against some other solid body upon which it rests; and thus it is brought about that the very force which pulls it in order to snatch it away compresses it more and more as the pull increases. This is accomplished by wrapping the thread around the solid in the manner of a spiral; and will be better understood by means of a figure. Let AB and CD be two cylinders between which is stretched the thread EF: and for the sake of greater clearness we will imagine it to be a small cord. If these two cylinders be pressed strongly together, the cord EF, when drawn by the end F, will undoubtedly stand a considerable pull before it slips between the two compressing solids. But if we remove one of these cylinders the cord, though remaining in contact with the other, will not thereby be prevented from slipping freely. On the other hand, if one holds the cord loosely against the top of the cylinder A, winds it in the spiral form AFLOTR, and then pulls it by the end R, it is evident that the cord will begin to bind the cylinder; the greater the number of spirals the more tightly will the cord be pressed against the cylinder by any given pull.

3. JOHN LOCKE, *AN ESSAY CONCERNING HUMAN UNDERSTANDING*

The Englishman John Locke (1632–1704) was one of the most influential thinkers of the Early Modern Period. His work, along with that of Isaac Newton (1642–1727) and René Descartes (1596–1648), laid the groundwork for the Enlightenment thought of the eighteenth century. Locke's famous treatise *An Essay Concerning Human Understanding* (1690) examines human learning processes. His intent, however, was not simply to examine human nature but to effect societal change. His insistence that all men were born with natural abilities led him to argue in another work from the same year entitled *Two Treatises on Civil Government* (1690) for a society that could best foster individual talents. The following excerpt shows that Locke's philosophical approach was very much influenced by contemporary scientific methodology. Locke was influenced in particular by Francis Bacon (1561–1626), who developed a method of inductive reasoning based on observation and experimentation, which remains an important foundation of scientific investigation to this day. Locke's work shows that scientific methods emphasizing observation and experience as important stages in expanding knowledge were filtering into texts examining the human mind and human society.

Essay Concerning Human Understanding

1. Since it is the *understanding* that sets man above the rest of sensible beings, and gives him all the advantage and dominion which he has over them; it is certainly a subject, even for its nobleness, worth our labour to inquire into. The understanding, like the eye, whilst it makes us see and perceive all other things, takes no notice of itself; and it re-

quires art and pains to set it at a distance and make it its own object. But whatever be the difficulties that lie in the way of this inquiry; whatever it be that keeps us so much in the dark to ourselves; sure I am that all the light we can let in upon our minds, all the acquaintance we can make with our own understandings, will not only be very pleasant, but bring us great advantage, in directing our thoughts in the search of other things.

2. This, therefore, being my purpose—to inquire into the original, certainty, and extent of *human knowledge,* together with the grounds and degrees of *belief, opinion,* and *assent;*—I shall not at present meddle with the physical consideration of the mind; or trouble myself to examine wherein its essence consists; or by what motions of our spirits or alterations of our bodies we come to have any *sensation* by our organs, or any *ideas* in our understandings; and whether those ideas do in their formation, any or all of them, depend on matter or not. These are speculations which, however curious and entertaining, I shall decline, as lying out of my way in the design I am now upon. It shall suffice to my present purpose, to consider the discerning faculties of a man, as they are employed about the objects which they have to do with. And I shall imagine I have not wholly misemployed myself in the thoughts I shall have on this occasion, if, in this historical, plain method, I can give any account of the ways whereby our understandings come to attain those notions of things we have; and can set down any measures of the certainty of our knowledge; or the grounds of those persuasions which are to be found amongst men, so various, different, and wholly contradictory; and yet asserted somewhere or other with such assurance and confidence, that he that shall take a view of the opinions of mankind, observe their opposition, and at the same time consider the fondness and devotion wherewith they are embraced, the resolution and eagerness wherewith they are maintained, may perhaps have reason to suspect, that either there is no such thing as truth at all, or that mankind hath no sufficient means to attain a certain knowledge of it.

3. It is therefore worth while to search out the bounds between opinion and knowledge; and examine by what measures, in things whereof we have no certain knowledge, we ought to regulate our assent and moderate our persuasion. In order whereunto I shall pursue this following method:—

First, I shall inquire into the original of those *ideas,* notions, or whatever else you please to call them, which a man observes, and is conscious to himself he has in his mind; and the ways whereby the understanding comes to be furnished with them.

Secondly, I shall endeavour to show what *knowledge* the understanding hath by those ideas; and the certainty, evidence, and extent of it.

Thirdly, I shall make some inquiry into the nature and grounds of *faith* or *opinion:* whereby I mean that assent which we give to any proposition as true, of whose truth yet we have no certain knowledge. And here we shall have occasion to examine the reasons and degrees of *assent.*

4. If by this inquiry into the nature of the understanding, I can discover the powers thereof; how far they reach; to what things they are in any degree proportionate; and where they fail us, I suppose it may be of use to prevail with the busy mind of man to be more cautious in meddling with things exceeding its comprehension; to stop when it is at the utmost extent of its tether; and to sit down in a quiet ignorance of those things which, upon examination, are found to be beyond the reach of our capacities. We should not then perhaps be so forward, out of an affectation of an universal knowledge, to raise questions, and perplex ourselves and others with disputes about things to which our understandings are not suited; and of which we cannot frame in our minds any clear or distinct perceptions, or whereof (as it has perhaps too often happened) we have not any

notions at all. If we can find out how far the understanding can extend its view; how far it has faculties to attain certainty; and in what cases it can only judge and guess, we may learn to content ourselves with what is attainable by us in this state.

5. For though the comprehension of our understandings comes exceeding short of the vast extent of things, yet we shall have cause enough to magnify the bountiful Author of our being, for that proportion and degree of knowledge he has bestowed on us, so far above all the rest of the inhabitants of this our mansion. Men have reason to be well satisfied with what God hath thought fit for them, since he hath given them whatsoever is necessary for the conveniences of life and information of virtue; and has put within the reach of their discovery, the comfortable provision for this life, and the way that leads to a better. How short soever their knowledge may come of an universal or perfect comprehension of whatsoever is, it yet secures their great concernments, that they have light enough to lead them to the knowledge of their Maker, and the sight of their own duties. Men may find matter sufficient to busy their heads, and employ their hands with variety, delight, and satisfaction, if they will not boldly quarrel with their own constitution, and throw away the blessings their hands are filled with, because they are not big enough to grasp everything. We shall not have much reason to complain of the narrowness of our minds, if we will but employ them about what may be of use to us; for of that they are very capable. And it will be an unpardonable, as well as childish peevishness, if we undervalue the advantages of our knowledge, and neglect to improve it to the ends for which it was given us, because there are some things that are set out of the reach of it. It will be no excuse to an idle and untoward servant, who would not attend his business by candle light, to plead that he had not broad sunshine. The Candle that is set up in us shines bright enough for all our purposes. The discoveries we can make with this ought to satisfy us; and we shall then use our understandings right, when we entertain all objects in that way and proportion that they are suited to our faculties, and upon those grounds they are capable of being proposed to us; and not peremptorily or intemperately require demonstration, and demand certainty, where probability only is to be had, and which is sufficient to govern all our concernments. If we will disbelieve everything, because we cannot certainly know all things, we shall do muchwhat as wisely as he who would not use his legs, but sit still and perish, because he had no wings to fly.

6. When we know our own strength, we shall the better know what to undertake with hopes of success; and when we have well surveyed the *powers* of our own minds, and made some estimate what we may expect from them, we shall not be inclined either to sit still, and not set our thoughts on work at all, in despair of knowing anything; nor on the other side, question everything, and disclaim all knowledge, because some things are not to be understood. It is of great use to the sailor to know the length of his line, though he cannot with it fathom all the depths of the ocean. It is well he knows that it is long enough to reach the bottom, at such places as are necessary to direct his voyage, and caution him against running upon shoals that may ruin him. Our business here is not to know all things, but those which concern our conduct. If we can find out those measures, whereby a rational creature, put in that state in which man is in this world, may and ought to govern his opinions, and actions depending thereon, we need not to be troubled that some other things escape our knowledge.

7. This was that which gave the first rise to this *Essay* concerning the understanding. For I thought that the first step towards satisfying several inquiries the mind of man was very apt to run into, was, to take a survey of our own understandings, examine our own powers, and see to what things they were adapted. Till that was done I suspected we

began at the wrong end, and in vain sought for satisfaction in a quiet and sure possession of truths that most concerned us, whilst we let loose our thoughts into the vast
ocean of Being; as if all that boundless extent were the natural and undoubted possession of our understandings, wherein there was nothing exempt from its decisions, or that
escaped its comprehension. Thus men, extending their inquiries beyond their capacities,
and letting their thoughts wander into those depths where they can find no sure footing,
it is no wonder that they raise questions and multiply disputes, which, never coming to
any clear resolution, are proper only to continue and increase their doubts, and to confirm them at last in perfect skepticism. Whereas, were the capacities of our understandings well considered, the extent of our knowledge once discovered, and the horizon
found which sets the bounds between the enlightened and dark parts of things; between
what is and what is not comprehensible by us, men would perhaps with less scruple ac-
quiesce in the avowed ignorance of the one, and employ their thoughts and discourse
with more advantage and satisfaction in the other.

    8. Thus much I thought necessary to say concerning the occasion of this Inquiry
into human Understanding. But, before I proceed on to what I have thought on this subject, I must here in the entrance beg pardon of my reader for the frequent use of the
word *idea,* which he will find in the following treatise. It being that term which, I think,
serves best to stand for whatsoever is the *object* of the understanding when a man
thinks, I have used it to express whatever is meant by *phantasm, notion, species,* or *whatever it is which the mind can be employed about in thinking;* and I could not avoid frequently using it.

    I presume it will be easily granted me, that there are such *ideas* in men's minds:
every one is conscious of them in himself; and men's words and actions will satisfy him
that they are in others.

    Our first inquiry then shall be,—how they come into the mind.

No Innate Speculative Principles

1. It is an established opinion amongst some men, that there are in the understanding
certain *innate principles;* some primary notions, characters, as it were stamped upon the
mind of man; which the soul receives in its very first being, and brings into the world
with it. It would be sufficient to convince unprejudiced readers of the falseness of this
supposition, if I should only show (as I hope I shall in the following parts of this Discourse) how men, barely by the use of their natural faculties, may attain to all the knowledge they have, without the help of any innate impressions; and may arrive at certainty,
without any such original notions or principles. For I imagine any one will easily grant
that it would be impertinent to suppose the ideas of colours innate in a creature to
whom God hath given sight, and a power to receive them by the eyes from external objects: and no less unreasonable would it be to attribute several truths to the impressions
of nature, and innate characters, when we may observe in ourselves faculties fit to attain
as easy and certain knowledge of them as if they were originally imprinted on the mind.

    But because a man is not permitted without censure to follow his own thoughts in
the search of truth, when they lead him ever so little out of the common road, I shall set
down the reasons that made me doubt of the truth of that opinion, as an excuse for my
mistake, if I be in one; which I leave to be considered by those who, with me, dispose
themselves to embrace truth wherever they find it.

    2. There is nothing more commonly taken for granted than that there are certain
principles, both *speculative* and *practical,* (for they speak of both), universally agreed

upon by all mankind: which therefore, they argue, must needs be the constant impressions which the souls of men receive in their first beings, and which they bring into the world with them, as necessarily and really as they do any of their inherent faculties.

3. This argument, drawn from universal consent, has this misfortune in it, that if it were true in matter of fact, that there were certain truths wherein all mankind agreed, it would not prove them innate, if there can be any other way shown how men may come to that universal agreement, in the things they do consent in, which I presume may be done.

4. But, which is worse, this argument of universal consent, which is made use of to prove innate principles, seems to me a demonstration that there are none such: because there are none to which all mankind give an universal assent. I shall begin with the speculative, and instance in those magnified principles of demonstration, 'Whatsoever is, is,' and 'It is impossible for the same thing to be and not to be'; which, of all others, I think have the most allowed title to innate. These have so settled a reputation of maxims universally received, that it will no doubt be thought strange if any one should seem to question it. But yet I take liberty to say, that these propositions are so far from having an universal assent, that there are a great part of mankind to whom they are not so much as known.

5. For, first, it is evident that all children and idiots have not the least apprehension or thought of them; and the want of that is enough to destroy that universal assent which must needs be the necessary concomitant of all innate truths: it seeming to me near a contradiction to say that there are truths imprinted on the soul which it perceives or understands not; imprinting, if it signify anything. being nothing else but the making certain truths to be perceived. For to imprint anything on the mind without the mind's perceiving it, seems to me hardly intelligible. If therefore children and idiots have souls, have minds, with those impressions upon them, they must unavoidably perceive them, and necessarily know and assent to these truths; which since they do not, it is evident that there are no such impressious. For if they are not notions imprinted, how can they be innate? and if they are notions naturally imprinted, how can they be unknown? To say a notion is imprinted on the mind, and yet at the same time to say that the mind is ignorant of it, and never yet took notice of it, is to make this impression nothing. No proposition can be said to be in the mind which it never yet knew, which it was never yet conscious of. For if any one may, then, by the same reason, all propositions that are true, and the mind is capable of ever assenting to, may be said to be in the mind, and to be imprinted: since, if any one can be said to be in the mind, which it never yet knew, it must be only because it is capable of knowing it, and so the mind is of all truths it ever shall know. Nay, thus truths may be imprinted on the mind which it never did nor ever shall know; for a man may live long, and die at last in ignorance of many truths which his mind was capable of knowing, and that with certainty. So that if the capacity of knowing, be the natural impression contended for, all the truths a man ever comes to know will, by this account, be every one of them innate; and this great point will amount to no more, but only to a very improper way of speaking; which, whilst it pretends to assert the contrary, says nothing different from those who deny innate principles. For nobody, I think, ever denied that the mind was capable of knowing several truths. The capacity, they say, is innate, the knowledge acquired. But then to what end such contest for certain innate maxims? If truths can be imprinted on the understanding without being perceived, I can see no difference there can be between any truths the mind is capable of knowing in respect of their original: they must all be innate or all adventitious; in vain shall a man go about to distinguish them. He therefore that talks of innate notions in the

understanding, cannot (if he intend thereby any distinct sort of truths) mean such truths to be in the understanding as it never perceived, and is yet wholly ignorant of. For if these words (to be in the understanding) have any propriety, they signify to be understood; so that to be in the understanding and not to be understood, to be in the mind and never to be perceived, is all one as to say anything is and is not in the mind or understanding. If therefore these two propositions, "Whatsoever is, is," and "it is impossible for the same thing to be and not to be," are by nature imprinted, children cannot be ignorant of them; infants, and all that have souls, must necessarily have them in their understandings, know the truth of them, and assent to it.

6. To avoid this, it is usually answered, that all men know and assent to them, *when they come to the use of reason;* and this is enough to prove them innate. I answer:

7. Doubtful expressions, that have scarce any signification, go for clear reasons to those who, being prepossessed, take not the pains to examine even what they themselves say. For, to apply this answer with any tolerable sense to our present purpose, it must signify one of these two things: either that as soon as men come to the use of reason these supposed native inscriptions come to be known and observed by them; or else, that the use and exercise of men's reason, assists them in the discovery of these principles, and certainly makes them known to them.

8. If they mean, that by the use of reason men may discover these principles, and that this is sufficient to prove them innate; their way of arguing will stand thus, viz. that whatever truths reason can certainly discover to us, and make us firmly assent to, those are all naturally imprinted on the mind; since that universal assent, which is made the mark of them, amounts to no more but this,—that by the use of reason we are capable to come to a certain knowledge of and assent to them; and, by this means, there will be no difference between the maxims of the mathematicians, and theorems they deduce from them: all must be equally allowed innate; they being all discoveries made by the use of reason, and truths that a rational creature may certainly come to know, if he apply his thoughts rightly that way.

4. *Mercure de France*, Relation of the Arrival in France of Four Savages of Mississippi (1725)

The journey of the four native chiefs in 1725 to the court of Louis XV was not the first appearance of native Americans in Europe, but such visitations were rare enough in the Early Modern period to generate enormous public interest. A visit by four chiefs to the court of Queen Anne in 1710 resulted in an outpouring of published broadsides, pamphlets, and treatises from the English presses; a similar publishing flurry took place during a visit by four other chiefs to France fifteen years later in 1725. The *Mercure de France* and other popular presses published detailed descriptions of the dress and comportment of the Indian visitors, as well as their reaction to the very different sights and sounds of French society. The true opinions of the native visitors are all but obscured in these Eurocentric accounts. The following excerpt from the *Mercure de France* includes speeches given by the chiefs before the king. These speeches express sentiments that were very much in tune with paternalistic

French perceptions of its role as a colonizing nation: native awe of French authority and cultural sophistication and a desire to be Christianized. The speeches express an emerging conception of "empire" in French popular discourse, a conception that married French cultural superiority with a duty to care for culturally "inferior" peoples under French protection. The following speeches suggest that this imperial role was welcomed, even invited, by the subject native peoples. Of course, this was the perspective of the French and not of the native peoples.

Speech of Chicagou, Chief of the Metchigamias to the King, Chief of Chiefs, and the Father of the French:

"I no longer regret having suffered, having to leave my wife, my children and my entire nation, because I see today the father of all of the French surrounded by his chiefs. I am a chief myself, and considered so in my nation. But I see well now that I am nothing before you, to whom as many chiefs and people in the world obey as there are trees in our forests. I should fear speaking to you, however my heart is reassured. And here is what I say to you, Sire, my father. You are like a beautiful star which rises and which glitters in the beautiful sky when there are no clouds, and I have as great a pleasure in seeing you after such a long voyage as our wives have in seeing the sun appear after several days of rain in the Spring when they clear our lands. You warm us with your rays, me and all of the my fellow Illinois. We love the prayer, we have a French heart, and we want always to listen to your words. Speak when you wish, we will obey. The Foxes are our enemies as they are yours. Order the French to go with all of the Nations to fight them and I Chicagou, I will show them the way, & I will show them how to raise their tails. . . . Regard us as your children, be greater than your ancestors. Finally, that we children, who are at the breasts of their mothers, are able still to call their father, when they are in extreme old age. Here speaks to you today your son Chicagou."

Speech of the Chiefs of the Three Savage Nations, Missouri, Osaga, and Otoptata, Brought to France by the Order of the King:

Great Chief of the French.

"The great spirit, master of your life, brought us to your country and gave us the courage to cross the seas to see you. Your name alone was known to us. We recognize you today, because we see that you brighten the earth much as the Sun, and a ray fell upon us, which we have followed. We tremble, and our eyes dare not to look upon your face. Your officers and soldiers informed us with what care they protect your person. We will carry back in our heads your person, your magnificence, the beauty of your homes, your villages, your lands, and the manner in which we were treated, images which our old people await, observing as they do from afar where we have walked. We wish that their eyes could see here.

"We offer you the tree of peace from the three nations, from our arms, armed with arrows, and we will plant it where you would like. Those which you choose will be our shelter. Our lands have been yours for a long time, do not abandon them. Plant there French people, protect us as your true soldiers, and give us the white collars, the chiefs of prayer, to instruct us. Have pity on us here and furthermore, we are in your arms. You have big heart. We place at your feet our crowns and the pipes of peace as a pledge of alliance."

Having paid their compliments, the savages removed from themselves all of the emblems of their status as chiefs and warriors, that is to say, their plumed helmets, which are not the least of their ornaments and which everyone admires, and their tomahawks, their bows and quivers, and so on. This homage, which could not have been more complete nor more submissive, accompanied by oaths in the name of all of their nations, was considered both singular and new, and it was widely discussed as something well-contrived and well-undertaken. The King spoke on this occasion with the vivacity of his spirit, and the thousands of questions which he made to father de Beaubois and the Chevalier de Bourgmont on the manners, morals, and different religions of the savages showed his close attention to these matters. One acknowledges above all the excess of goodwill and affability with which he honored these two people by speaking to them for more than an hour, in the presence of the lords of his court. The audience would have lasted longer if the King had not remarked himself that the hour of Council had arrived. His majesty promised in particular that he would ensure that those Nations which assured him that they were docile and easily governed would not lack for missionaries who were achieving such wonderful results for the Religion.

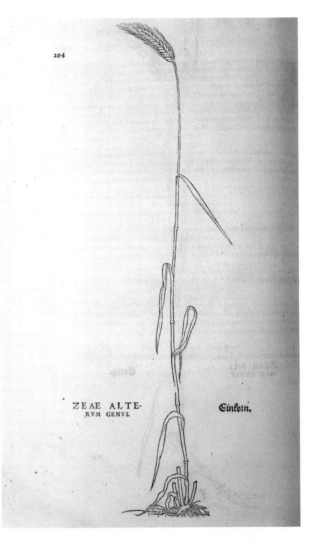

Figure 11.1 Engraving of the New World plant maize (corn). Fuchs, Leonhart. *De historia stirpium commentarii insignes* . . . Basileae: In officinum Isingriniana, 1542. Rare Books Division, J. Willard Marriott Library, University of Toronto.

Note: This famous Herbal established a new standard of scientific observation and illustration. It is also the first European book to include discussion and illustration of New World plants. Among the New World plants included here are the pumpkin, marigold, maize, potato, and tobacco. Within a century, European knowledge of plant life would vastly exceed that of Fuchs. However, his work represents an important early stage in the expansion of European knowledge about the natural world as a result of European voyages of exploration.

Study Questions

1. Why is John Thorne eager to explain how one reads a map to the ambassador, and why does he think that the ambassador would be interested?
2. How did Early Modern exploration transform the study of the natural world? Do you see similarities in the work of Galileo Galilei and John Locke?
3. According to the *Mercure de France,* how did the native chiefs perceive the role of France in their own society? What does this tell us about French perceptions of empire and colonization?
4. Does John Locke's interest in understanding human nature reflect contemporary currents of debate? How is it different from the debates of the sixteenth century?

Suggested Readings

Elliott, J. H. *The Old World and the New, 1492–1650.* Cambridge: Cambridge University Press, 1970; rev. ed. 1992.

Grafton, Anthony. *New World, Ancient Texts: The Power of Tradition and the Shock of Discovery.* Cambridge, MA: Belknap Press of Harvard University Press, 1992.

Hinderaker, Eric. The "Four Indian Kings" and the Imaginative Construction of the First British Empire. *The William and Mary Quarterly* 3rd series, 53, no. 3 (July 1996): 487–526.

Kupperman, Karen Ordahl, ed. *American in European Consciousness 1493–1750.* Chapel Hill: University of North Carolina Press, 1995.

Lawson, Philip. *The East India Company: A History.* London and New York: Longmans, 1993.

Web Sites

1. René Descartes' Epistemology

   http://plato.stanford.edu/entries/descartes-epistemology

2. Galileo Galilei

   http://www-isds.jpl.nasa.gov/cwo/cwo_54ga/html/cd/galileo.htm

3. John Locke, *On Human Understanding*

   http://www.ilt.columbia.edu/academic/digitexts/locke/understanding/title.html

12

Fictionalizing the World
1500–1700 A.D.

TEXTS

1. Thomas More, *Utopia*
2. William Shakespeare, *The Tempest*
3. Cyrano de Bergerac, *Voyage to the Moon*
4. Jonathon Swift, *Gulliver's Travels*
5. Cyrano de Bergerac, Flying to the Moon

From the time of the ancient Greeks to the present day, literary authors have seen rich possibilities in the travel literature genre for educating, reforming, and entertaining their respective societies. Well-known ancient and Medieval examples include Homer's *Odyssey* and Chretien de Troyes's *Arthurian Romances*. During the Early Modern period, travel literature became a particularly popular literary vehicle as the expansion of European knowledge about the world fueled thirst for tales of exotic lands. Renaissance authors such as William Shakespeare (1564–1616) and John Donne (1572–1631) in England and François Rabelais (1490–1553?) and Cyrano de Bergerac in France viewed exploration of the known world as a part of the human quest for self-knowledge. Humans and the world were all divine creations, but humans were uniquely chosen to rule over the earth in much the way that God ruled in the heavens. Humans were made in the image and likeness of God. Moreover, individuals were free to determine their own destiny because they possessed free will and limitless abilities. For these men, exploration celebrated humanity because it was a voyage in pursuit of self-knowledge, and the explorer easily translated into a literary archetype of knowledge achieved through experience. However, early modern authors also viewed the explorer as an immediately accessible metaphorical vehicle for examining the values, beliefs, and character of European culture. Fictional foreign societies encountered on the journey functioned as mirrors upon the European soul, described in terms that made them relatable to European societies of the time. These fictional lands were not always more perfect representations of European societies. Whereas Thomas More's *Utopia* does portray an ideal society, [1] the kingdoms encountered in *Gulliver's Travels* [4] exhibit many of the worst characteristics of English society. For Shakespeare, [2] distant lands were potential sites of magical, mystical encounters in which European societal roles and values were easily overturned. *A Voyage to the Moon* [3, 5] in contrast, provides Cyrano de Bergerac an excuse for critiquing the intellectual and political foibles of French society.

1. THOMAS MORE, *UTOPIA*

The son of a successful London lawyer, Thomas More (1478–1535) also practiced law before obtaining a seat in the English Parliament. More's oratorical brilliance soon won the attention of the chancellor of England, Cardinal Thomas Wolsey (1473–1530), who brought More into the royal administration. More's refusal to publicly condone Henry VIII's divorce from his first wife, Catherine of Aragon, led to his execution in 1535. However, his stance earned him a lasting reputation as a devout Catholic and a man of rigorous ethical conviction. Thomas More was already highly respected in England as a humanist scholar by the time *Utopia* was published in 1516. However, it is this work that earned him international renown during his own lifetime. It was More who coined the term "utopia," a word which means "no place" in Latin. To this day, a *utopian* society refers to an idealized society. The following excerpt recounts the journey of Raphael to the kingdom of Utopia. More's Christian humanist formation is very much in evidence throughout the text. Utopia is a land governed by reason, a land where necessity rather than greed determines the nature of social relations and the sharing of material resources.

Utopia

"The island of Utopia in the middle, where it is broadest, is two hundred miles broad, and holds almost at the same breadth over a great part of it, but grows narrower towards both ends. Its figure is not unlike a crescent; between its horns the sea comes in eleven miles broad, and spreads itself into a great bay, which is environed with land to the compass of about five hundred miles, and is well secured from winds. There is no great current in the bay, and the whole coast is, as it were, one continued harbour, which gives all that live in the island great convenience for mutual commerce: but the entry into the bay, what by rocks on one hand, and shallows on the other, is very dangerous. In the middle of it there is one single rock which appears above water, and so is not dangerous: on the top of it there is a tower built, in which a garrison is kept. The other rocks lie under water, and are very dangerous. The channel is known only to the natives; so that if any stranger should enter into the bay, without one of their pilots, he would run a great danger of shipwreck; for even they themselves could not pass it safe, if some marks that are on their coast did not direct their way; and if these should be but a little shifted, any fleet that might come against them, how great soever it were, would be certainly lost. On the other side of the island there are likewise many harbours; and the coast is so fortified, both by nature and art, that a small number of men can hinder the descent of a great army. But they report (and there remain good marks of it to make it credible) that this was no island at first, but a part of the continent. Utopus that conquered it (whose name it still carries, for Abraxa was its first name,) and brought the rude and uncivilized inhabitants into such a good government, and to that measure of politeness that they do now far excel all the rest of mankind; having soon subdued them, he designed to separate them from the continent, and to bring the sea quite about them; and in order to that, he made a deep channel to be digged, fifteen miles long. He not only forced the inhabitants to work at it, but likewise his own soldiers, that the natives might not think he treated them like slaves; and, having set vast numbers of men to work, he brought it to a speedy conclusion, beyond all men's expectations. By this their neighbours, who laughed at the folly of the undertaking at first, were struck with admiration and terror, when they saw it brought to perfection.

"There are fifty-four cities in the island, all large and well-built. The manners, customs, and laws of all their cities are the same, and they are all contrived as near in the same manner as the ground on which they stand will allow; the nearest lie at least twenty-four miles distance from one another, and the most remote are not so far distant but that a man can go on foot in one day from it to that which lies next it. Every city sends three of their wisest senators once a year to Amaurot, for consulting about their common concerns; for that is the chief town of the island, being situated near the centre of it, so that it is the most convenient place for their assemblies. Every city has so much ground set off for its jurisdiction that there is twenty miles of soil round it, assigned to it; and where the towns lie wider, they have much more ground. No town desires to enlarge their bounds; for they consider themselves rather as tenants than landlords of their soil.

"They have built over all the country, farmhouses for husbandmen, which are well-contrived, and are furnished with all things necessary for country labour. Inhabitants are sent by turns from the cities to dwell in them; no country family has fewer than forty men and women in it, besides two slaves. There is a master and a mistress set over every family; and over thirty families there is a magistrate settled. Every year, twenty of this family come back to the town, after they have stayed out two years in the country; and, in their room, there are other twenty sent from the town, that they may learn country work from those that have been already one year in the country, which they must teach those that come to them the next year from the town. By this means such as dwell in those country farms are never ignorant of agriculture, and so commit no errors in it, which might otherwise be fatal to them, and bring them under a scarcity of corn. But though there is every year such a shifting of the husbandmen, that none may be forced against his mind to follow that hard course of life too long, yet many among them take such pleasure in it, that they desire leave to continue many years in it. These husbandmen labour the ground, breed cattle, hew wood, and convey it to the towns, either by land or water, as is most convenient. They breed an infinite multitude of chickens in a very curious manner; for the hens do not sit and hatch them, but they lay vast numbers of eggs in a gentle and equal heat, in which they are hatched; and they are no sooner out of the shell, and able to stir about, but they seem to consider those that feed them as their mothers, and follow them as other chickens do the hen that hatched them. They breed very few horses, but those they have are full of mettle, and are kept only for exercising their youth in the art of sitting and riding of them; for they do not put them to any work, either of ploughing or carriage, in which they employ oxen; for, though horses are stronger, yet they find oxen can hold out longer; and, as they are not subject to so many diseases, so they are kept upon a less charge, and with less trouble; and when they are so worn out that they are no more fit for labour, they are good meat at last. They sow no corn but that which is to be their bread; for they drink either wine, cider, or perry, and often water,—sometimes pure, and sometimes boiled with honey or liquorice, with which they abound. And, though they know exactly well how much corn will serve every town, and all that tract of country which belongs to it, yet they sow much more, and breed more cattle than are necessary for their consumption; and they give that overplus of which they make no use to their neighbours. When they want anything in the country which it does not produce, they fetch that from the town, without carrying anything in exchange for it; and the magistrates of the town take care to see it given them; for they meet generally in the town once a month, upon a festival day. When the time of harvest comes, the magistrates in the country send to those in the towns, and let them know how many hands they will need for reaping the harvest; and the number they call for being sent to them, they commonly dispatch it all in one day.

Of Their Towns, Particularly of Amaurot.

"He that knows one of their towns knows them all, they are so like one another, except where the situation makes some difference. I shall therefore describe one of them, and it is no matter which; but none is so proper as Amaurot; for, as none is more eminent, all the rest yielding in precedence to this, because it is the seat of their supreme council, so there was none of them better known to me, I having lived for five years altogether in it.

"It lies upon the side of a hill, or rather a rising ground. Its figure is almost square; for from the one side of it, which shoots up almost to the top of the hill, it runs down in a descent for two miles to the river Anider; but it is a little broader the other way that runs along by the bank of that river. The Anider rises about eighty miles above Amaurot, in a small spring at first; but, other brooks falling into it, of which two are more considerable, as it runs by Amaurot it is grown half-a-mile broad; but it still grows larger and larger till, after sixty miles' course below it, it is buried in the ocean. Between the town and the sea, and for some miles above the town, it ebbs and flows every six hours, with a strong current. The tide comes up for about thirty miles so full that there is nothing but salt water in the river, the fresh water being driven back with its force; and above that for some miles the water is brackish, but a little higher, as it runs by the town, it is quite fresh; and when the tide ebbs, it continues fresh all along to the sea. There is a bridge cast over the river, not of timber, but of fair stone, consisting of many stately arches; it lies at that part of the town which is furthest from the sea, so that ships without any hindrance lie all along the side of the town. There is likewise another river that runs by it, which though it is not great, yet it runs pleasantly, for it rises out of the same hill on which the town stands, and so runs down through it, and falls in the Anider. The inhabitants have fortified the fountain-head of this river, which springs a little without the town; that so, if they should happen to be besieged, the enemy might not be able to stop or divert the course of the water, nor poison it; from thence it is carried in earthen pipes to the lower streets; and for those places of the town to which the water of that small river cannot be conveyed, they have great cisterns for receiving the rain-water, which supplies the want of the other. The town is compassed with a high and thick wall, in which there are many towers and forts; there is also a broad and deep dry ditch, set thick with thorns, cast round three sides of the town, and the river is instead of a ditch on the fourth side. The streets are made very convenient for all carriages, and are well sheltered from the winds. Their buildings are good, and are so uniform that a whole side of a street looks like one house. The streets are twenty feet broad; there lie gardens behind all their houses; these are large, but inclosed with buildings that on all hands face the streets; so that every house has both a door to the street, and a back-door to the garden; their doors have all two leaves, which as they are easily opened, so they shut of their own accord; and, there being no property among them, every man may freely enter into any house whatsoever. At every ten years' end they shift their houses by lots. They cultivate their gardens with great care, so that they have both vines, fruits, herbs, and flowers in them; and all is well ordered and so finely kept, that I never saw gardens anywhere that were so fruitful as theirs are. And this humour of ordering their gardens so well, is not only kept up by the pleasure they find in it, but also by an emulation between the inhabitants of the several streets, who vie with one another in this matter; and there is, indeed, nothing belonging to the whole town that is both more useful and more pleasant. So that he who founded the town seems to have care of nothing more than of their gardens; for they say the whole scheme of the town was designed at first by Utopus; but he left all that belonged to the ornament and improvement of it, to be added by those that should come after him, that being too much for one man to bring to perfection. Their records, that contain the history of their town and state, are preserved with an exact care, and run backwards seventeen hundred and sixty years. From these it appears, that their houses were at first low and mean, like cottages, made of any sort of timber, and were built with mud walls, and thatched with straw. But now their houses are three stories high, the fronts of them are faced either with stone, plastering, or brick; and between the facings of their walls they throw in their rubbish; their roofs are flat, and on them they lay a sort of plaster which costs very little, and yet it is so tempered that it is not apt to take fire, so it resists the weather more than lead does. They have abundance of glass among them, with which they glaze their windows; they use also in their windows a thin linen cloth that is so oiled or gummed, that by that means it both lets in the light more freely to them, and keeps out the wind the better.

Of Their Magistrates.

"Thirty families choose every year a magistrate, who was called anciently the Syphogrant, but is now called the Philarch; and over every ten syphogrants, with the families subject to them, there is another magistrate, who was anciently called the Tranibore, but of late the Archphilarch. All the syphogrants, who are in number two hundred, choose the prince out of a list of four, whom the people of the four divisions of the city name to them, but they take an oath before they proceed to an election, that they will choose him whom they think meetest for the office; they give their voices secretly, so that it is not known for whom every one gives his suffrage. The prince is for life, unless he is removed upon suspicion of some design to enslave the people. The tranibors are newly chosen every year, but they are for the most part still continued. All their other magistrates are only annual.

"The tranibors meet every third day, and oftener if need be, and consult with the prince, either concerning the affairs of the state in general, or such private differences as may arise sometimes among the people; though that falls out but seldom. There are always two syphogrants called into the council-chamber, and these are changed every day. It is a fundamental rule of their government, that no conclusion can be made in anything that relates to the public, till it has been first debated three several days in their council. It is death for any to meet and consult concerning the state, unless it be either in their ordinary council, or in the assembly of the whole body of the people.

"These things have been so provided among them, that the prince and the tranibors may not conspire together to change the government, and enslave the people; and, therefore, when anything of great importance is set on foot, it is sent to the syphogrants, who, after they have communicated it with the families that belong to their divisions, and have considered it among themselves, make report to the senate; and upon great occasions, the matter is referred to the council of the whole island. One rule observed in their council is, never to debate a thing on the same day in which it is first proposed; for that is always referred to the next meeting, that so men may not rashly, and in the heat of discourse engage themselves too soon, which may bias them so much that, instead of considering the good of the public, they will rather study to maintain their own notions; and, by a perverse and preposterous sort of shame, hazard their country, rather than endanger their own reputation, or venture the being suspected to have wanted foresight in the expedients that they proposed at first. And, therefore, to prevent this they take care that they may rather be deliberate than sudden in their motions.

Of Their Trades, and Manner of Life.

"Agriculture is that which is so universally understood among them all, that no person, either man or woman, is ignorant of it; from their childhood they are instructed in it, partly by what they learn at school, and partly by practice, they being led out often into the fields about the town, where they not only see others at work, but are likewise exercised in it themselves.

"Besides agriculture, which is so common to them all, every man has some peculiar trade to which he applies himself, such as the manufacture of wool, or flax, masonry, smiths' work, or carpenters' work; for there is no other sort of trade that is in great esteem among them.

"All the island over they wear the same sort of clothes, without any other distinction except that which is necessary for marking the difference between the two sexes, and the married and unmarried. The fashion never alters; and, as it is not ungraceful, not uneasy, so it is fitted for their climate, and calculated both for their summers and winters. Every family makes their own clothes; but all among them, women as well as men, learn one or other of the trades formerly mentioned. Women, for the most part, deal in wool and flax, which suit better with their feebleness, leaving the other ruder trades to the men. Generally the same trade passes down from father to son, inclinations often following descent; but if any man's genius lies another way, he is by adoption translated into a family that deals in the trade to which he is inclined; and when that is to be done, care is taken, not only by his father but by the magistrate, that he may be put to a discreet and good man. And if, after a man has learned one trade, he desires to acquire another, that is also allowed, and is managed in the same manner as the former. When he has learned both, he follows that which he likes best, unless the public has more occasion for the other.

"The chief, and almost the only business of the syphogrants is, to take care that no man may live idle, but that every one may follow his trade diligently. Yet they do not wear themselves out with perpetual toil from morning to night, as if they were beasts of burden, which as it is indeed a heavy slavery, so it is the common course of life of all tradesmen everywhere, except among the Utopians; but they, driving the day and night into twenty-four hours, appoint six of these for work, three of them are before dinner; and after that they dine, and interrupt their labour for two hours, and then they go to work again for other three hours, and after that they sup, and at eight o'clock, counting from noon, they go to bed, and sleep eight hours; and for their other hours, besides those of work, and those that go for eating and sleeping, they are left to every man's discretion: yet they are not to abuse that interval to luxury and idleness, but must employ it in some proper exercise, according to their various inclinations, which is for the most part reading.

2. WILLIAM SHAKESPEARE, *THE TEMPEST*

William Shakespeare (1564–1616) is the most famous and perhaps the most brilliant of the English playwrights. Born in the town of Stratford-upon-Avon, Shakespeare's father was a glover by profession. As early as 1592, Shakespeare was working as an actor in London. It was as a poet and playwright, however, that Shakespeare is known today. His enormous corpus of work reflects a consuming fascination with many of the intellectual and cultural developments of his age, including the European voyages of exploration. Although he never left England, Shakespeare frequently situated his plays in foreign lands such as Italy and France and populated his works with travelers. He also constructed fictional societies. One of the most famous of these is the fictional island on which the *Tempest* takes place. Shakespeare's island is a land imbued with magic and magical beings. Here on this distant land, traditional European social rules do not apply.

The Tempest

SCENE II. *The island. Before* PROSPERO'S *cell.*

Enter PROSPERO *and* MIRANDA.

> *Mir.* If by your art, my dearest father, you have
> Put the wild waters in this roar, allay them.
> The sky, it seems, would pour down stinking pitch,
> But that the sea, mounting to the welkin's cheek,
> Dashes the fire out. O, I have suffer'd
> With those that I saw suffer: a brave vessel,
> Who had, no doubt, some noble creature in her,
> Dash'd all to pieces. O, the cry did knock
> Against my very heart. Poor souls, they perish'd.
> Had I been any god of power, I would
> Have sunk the sea within the earth or ere
> It should the good ship so have swallow'd and
> The fraughting souls within her.
>   *Pros.*   Be collected:
> No more amazement: tell your piteous heart
> There's no harm done.
>   *Mir.*   O, woe the day!
>   *Pros.*   No harm.
> I have done nothing but in care of thee,
> Of thee, my dear one, thee, my daughter, who
> Art ignorant of what thou art, nought knowing
> Of whence I am, nor that I am more better
> Than Prospero, master of a full poor cell,
> And thy no greater father.
>   *Mir.*   More to know
> Did never meddle with my thoughts.
>   *Pros.*   'T is time
> I should inform thee farther. Lend thy hand,
> And pluck my magic garment from me. So:
>   *[Lays down his mantle.*
> Lie there, my art. Wipe thou thine eyes; have comfort.
> The direful spectacle of the wreck, which touch'd
> The very virtue of compassion in thee,
> I have with such provision in mine art
> So safely ordered that there is no soul—

No, not so much perdition as an hair
Betid to any creature in the vessel
Which thou heard'st cry, which thou saw'st sink. Sit down;
For thou must now know farther.
    Mir.   You have often
Begun to tell me what I am, but stopp'd
And left me to a bootless inquisition,
Concluding 'Stay: not yet.'
    Pros.   The hour's now come;
The very minute bids thee ope thine ear;
Obey and be attentive. Canst thou remember
A time before we came unto this cell?
I do not think thou canst, for then thou wast not
Out three years old.
    Mir.   Certainly, sir, I can.
Pros. By what? by any other house or person?
Of any thing the image tell me that
Hath kept with thy remembrance.
    Mir.   'T is far off
And rather like a dream than an assurance
That my remembrance warrants. Had I not
Four or five women once that tended me?
    Pros. Thou hadst, and more, Miranda. But how is it
That this lives in thy mind? What seest thou else
In the dark backward and abysm of time?
If thou remember'st aught ere thou camest here,
How thou camest here thou mayst.
    Mir.   But that I do not.
Pros. Twleve year since, Miranda, twelve year since,
Thy father was the Duke of Milan and
A prince of power.
    Mir.   Sir, are not you my father?
    Pros. Thy mother was a piece of virtue, and
She said thou wast my daughter; and thy father
Was Duke of Milan; and thou his only heir
And princess no worse issued.
    Mir.   O the heavens!
What foul play had we, that we came from thence?
Or blessed was't we did?
    Pros.   Both, both, my girl:
By foul play, as thou say'st, were we heaved thence,
But blessedly help hither.
    Mir.   O, my heart bleeds
To think o' the teen that I have turn'd you to,
Which is from my remembrance! Please you, farther.
    Pros. My bother and thy uncle, call'd Antonio—
I pray thee, mark me—that a brother should
Be so perfidious!—he whom next thyself

Of all the world I loved and to him put
The manage of my state; as at that time
Through all the signories it was the first
And Prospero the prime duke, being so reputed
In dignity, and for the liberal arts
Without a parallel; those being all my study,
The government I cast upon my brother
And to my state grew stranger, being transported
And rapt in secret studies. Thy false uncle—
Dost thou attend me?
    Mir.   Sir, most heedfully.
    Pros. Being once perfected how to grant suits,
How to deny them, who to advance and who
To trash for over-topping, new created
The creatures that were mine, I say, or changed 'em,
Or else new form'd em; having both the key
Of officer and office, set all hearts i' the state
To what tune pleased his ear; that now he was
The ivy which had hid my princely trunk,
And suck'd my verdure out on't. Thou attend'st not.
    Mir. O, good sir, I do.
    Pros.   I pray thee, mark me.
I, thus neglecting worldy ends, all dedicated
To closeness and the bettering of my mind
With that which, but by being so retired,
O'er-prized all popular rate, in my false brother
Awaked an evil nature; and my trust,
Like a good parent, did beget of him
A falsehood in its contrary as great
As my trust was; which had indeed no limit,
A confidence sans bound. He being thus lorded,
Not only with what my revenue yielded,
But what my power might else exact, like one
Who having into truth, by telling of it,
Made such a sinner of his memory,
To credit his own lie, he did believe
He was indeed the duke; out o' the substitution,
And executing the outward face of royalty,
With all prerogative: hence his ambition growing—
Dost thou hear?
    Mir.   Your tale, sir, would cure deafness.
    Pros. To have no screen between this part he play'd
And him he play'd it for, he needs will be
Absolute Milan. Me, poor man, my library
Was dukedom large enough: of temporal royalties
He thinks me now incapable; confederates—
So dry he was for sway—wi' the King of Naples
To give him annual tribute, do him homage,

Subject his coronet to his crown, and bend
The dukedom yet unbow'd—alas, poor Milan!—
To most ignoble stooping.
    Mir.   O the heavens!
    Pros. Mark his condition and the event; then tell me
If this might be a brother.
    Mir.   I should sin
To think but nobly of my grandmother:
Good wombs have borne bad sons.
    Pros.   Now the condition.
This King of Naples, being an enemy
To me inveterate, hearkens my brother's suit;
Which was, that he, in lieu o' the premises
Of homage and I know not how much tribute,
Should presently extirpate me and mine
Out of the dukedom and confer fair Milan
With all the honours on my brother: whereon,
A treacherous army levied, one midnight
Fated to the purpose did Antonio open
The gates of Milan, and, i' the dead of darkness,
The ministers for the purpose hurried thence
Me and thy crying self.
    Mir.   Alack, for pity!
I, not remembering how I cried out then,
Will cry it o'er again: it is a hint
That wrings mine eyes to't.
    Pros.   Hear a little further
And then I'll bring thee to the present business
Which now's upon's; without the which this story
Were most impertinent.
    Mir.   Wherefore did they not
That hour destroy us?
    Pros.   Well demanded, wench:
My tale provokes that question. Dear, they durst not,
So dear the love my people bore me, nor set
A mark so bloody on the business, but
With colours fairer painted their foul ends.
In few, they hurried us aboard a bark,
Bore us some leagues to sea; where they prepared
A rotten carcass of a butt, not rigg'd,
Nor tackle, sail, nor mast; the very rats
Instinctively have quit it: there they hoist us,
To cry to the sea that roar'd to us, to sigh
To the winds whose pity, sighing back again,
Did us but loving wrong.
    Mir.   Alack, what trouble
Was I then to you!
    Pros.   O, a cherubin

Thou wast that did preserve me. Thou didst smile,
Infused with a fortitude from heaven,
When I have deck'd the sea with drops full salt,
Under my burthern groan'd; which raised in me
An undergoing stomach, to bear up
Against what should ensue.

  Mir.   How came we ashore?
  Pros. By Providence divine.
Some food we had and some fresh water that
A noble Neapolitan, Gonzalo,
Out of his charity, who being then appointed
Master of this design, did give us, with
Rich garments, linens, stuffs and necessaries,
Which since have steaded much; so, of his gentleness,
Knowing I loved my books, he furnish'd me
From mine own library with volumes that
I prize above my dukedom.

  Mir.   Would I might
But ever see that man!
  Pros.   Now I arise: *[Resumes his mantle.*
Sit still, and hear the last of our sea-sorrow.
Here in this island we arrived; and here
Have I, thy schoolmaster, made thee more profit
Than other princesses can that have more time
For vainer hours and tutors not so careful.

  Mir. Heavens thank you for 't! And now, I pray you, sir,
For still 't is beating in my mind, your reason.
For raising this sea-storm?
  Pros.   Know thus far forth.
By accident most strange, bountiful Fortune,
Now my dear lady, hath mine enemies
Brought to this shore; and by my prescience
I find my zenith doth depend upon
A most auspicious star, whose influence
If now I court not but omit, my fortunes
Will ever after droop. Here cease more questions:
Thou art inclined to sleep: 't is a good dulness,
And give it way: I know thou canst not choose.

             [Miranda sleeps.
Come away, servant, come. I am ready now.
Approach, my Ariel, come.

        Enter ARIEL.

  Ari. All hail, great master! grave sir, hail! I come
To answer thy best pleasure; be 't to fly,
To swim, to dive into the fire, to ride
On the curl'd clouds, to thy strong bidding task

Ariel and all his quality.
  Pros.   Hast thou, spirit,
Perform'd to point the tempest that I bade thee?
  Ari. To every article.
I boarded the king's ship; now on the beak,
Now in the waist, the deck, in every cabin,
I flamed amazement: sometime I'ld divide,
And burn in many places; on the topmast,
The yards and bowsprit, would I flame distinctly,
Then meet and join. Jove's lightnings, the precursors
O' the dreadful thunder-claps, more momentary
And sight-outrunning were not; the fire and cracks
Of sulphurous roaring the most mighty Neptune
Seem to besiege and make his bold waves tremble,
Yea, his dread trident shake.
  Pros.   My brave spirit!
Who was so firm, so constant, that this coil
Would not infect his reason?
  Ari.   Not a soul
But felt a fever of the mad and play'd
Some tricks of desperation. All but mariners
Plunged in the foaming brine and quit the vessel,
Then all afire with me: the king's son, Ferdinand,
With hair up-staring,—then like reeds, not hair,—
Was the first man that leap'd; cried, 'Hell is empty,
And all the devils are here'.
  Pros.   Why, that's my spirit!
But was not this nigh shore?
  Ari.   Close by, my master.
  Pros. But are they, Ariel, safe?
  Ari.   Not a hair perish'd;
On their sustaining garments not a blemish,
But fresher than before: and, as thou badest me,
In troops I have dispersed them 'bout the isle.
The king's son have I landed by himself;
Whom I left cooling of the air with sighs
In an odd angle of the isle, and sitting,
His arms in this sad knot.
  Pros.   Of the king's ship,
The mariners, say how thou hast disposed
And all the rest o' the fleet.
  Ari.   Safely in harbour
Is the king's ship; in the deep nook, where once
Thou call'dst me up at midnight to fetch dew
From the still-vex'd Bermoothes, there she's hid:
The mariners all under hatches stow'd;
Who, with a charm join'd to their suffer'd labour,
I have left asleep: and for the rest o' the fleet
Which I dispersed, they all have met again

And are upon the Mediterranean flote,
Bound sadly home for Naples,
Supposing that they saw the king's ship wreck'd
And his great person perish.
  Pros.   Ariel, thy charge
Exactly is perform'd: but there's more work.
What is the time o' the day?
  Ari.   Past the mid season.
  Pros. At least two glasses. The time 'twixt six and now
Must by us both be spent most preciously.
  Ari. Is there more toil? Since thou dost give me pains,
  Let me remember thee what thou hast promised,
Which is not yet perform'd me.
  Pros.   How now? moody?
What is 't thou canst demand?
  Ari.   My liberty.
  Pros. Before the time be out? no more!
  Ari.   I prithee,
Remember I have done thee worthy service;
Told thee no lies, made thee no mistakings, served
Without or grudge or grumblings: thou didst promise
To bate me a full year.
  Pros.   Dost thou forget
From what a torment I did free thee?
  Ari.   No.
  Pros. Thou dost, an think'st it much to tread the ooze
  Of the salt deep,
To run upon the sharp wind of the north,
To do me business in the veins o' the earth
When it is baked with frost.
  Ari.   I do not, sir.
  Pros. Thou liest, malignant thing! Hast thou forgot
The foul witch Sycorax, who with age and envy
Was grown into a hoop? hast thou forgot her?
  Ari. No, sir.
  Pros. Thou hast. Where was she born? speak;
tell me.
  Ari. Sir, in Argier.
  Pros. O, was she so? I must
Once in a month recount what thou hast been,
Which thou forget'st. The damn'd witch Sycorax,
For mischiefs manifold and sorceries terrible
To enter human hearing, from Argier,
Thou know'st, was banish'd: for one thing she did
They would not take her life. Is not this true?
  Ari. Ay, sir.
  Pros. This blue-eyed hag was hither brought with child
And here was left by the sailors. Thou, my slave,
As thou report'st thyself, wast then her servant;

And, for thou wast a spirit too delicate
To act her earthy and abhorr'd commands,
Refusing her grand hests, she did confine thee,
By help of her more potent ministers
And in her most unmitigable rage,
Into a cloven pine; within which rift
Imprison'd thou didst painfully remain
A dozen years; within which space she died
And left thee there; where thou didst vent thy groans
As fast as mill-wheels strike. Then was this island—
Save for the son that she did litter here,
A freckled whelp hag-born—not hour'd with
A human shape.
    Ari.   Yes, Caliban her son.
    Pros. Dull thing, I say so; he, that Caliban
Whom now I keep in service. Thou best know'st
What torment I did find thee in; thy groans
Did make wolves howl and penetrate the breasts
Of ever angry bears: it was a torment
To lay upon the damn'd, which Sycorax
Could not again undo: it was mine art,
When I arrived and heard thee, that made gape
The pine and let thee out.
    Ari.   I thank thee, master.
    Pros. If thou more murmur'st, I will rend an oak
And peg thee in his knotty entrails till
Thou hast howl'd away twelve winters.
    Ari.   Pardon, master;
I will be correspondent to command
And do my spiriting gently.
    Pros.   Do so, and after two days
I will discharge thee.
    Ari.   That's my noble master!
What shall I do! say what; what shall I do?
    Pros. Go make thyself like a nymph o' the sea: be subject
To no sight but thine and mine, invisible
To every eyeball else. Go take this shape
And hither come in't: go, hence with diligence!
                                          [Exit Ariel.
Awake, dear heart, awake! thou hast slept well;
Awake!
    Mir. The strangeness of your story put
Heaviness in me.
    Pros.   Shake it off. Come on;
We'll visit Caliban my slave, who never
Yields us kind answer.
    Mir.   'T is a villain, sir,
I do not love to look on.

Pros. But, as 't is,
We cannot miss him: he does make our fire,
Fetch in our wood and serves in offices
That profit us. What, ho! slave! Caliban!
Thou earth, thou! speak.
    Cal.   *[Within]* There's wood enough within.
    Pros. Come forth, I say! there's other business for thee:
Come, thou tortoise! when?
               re-enter ARIEL *like a water-nymph.*
Fine apparition! My quaint Ariel,
Hark in thine ear.
    Ari.   My lord, it shall be done. *[Exit.*
    Pros. Thou poisonous slave, got by the devil himself
Upon thy wicked dam, come forth!

              Enter CALIBAN.

    Cal. As wicked dew as e'er my mother brush'd
With raven's feather from unwholesome fen
Drop on you both! a south-west blow on ye
And blister you all o'er!
    Pros. For this, be sure, to-night thou shalt have cramps,
Side-stitches that shall pen thy breath up; urchins
Shall, for that vast of night that they may work,
All exercise on thee; thou shalt be pinch'd
As thick as honeycomb, each pinch more stinging
Than bees that made 'em.
    Cal.   I must eat my dinner.
This island's mine, by Sycorax my mother,
Which thou takest from me. When thou camest first,
Thou strok'dst me and mad'st much of me, wouldst give me
Water with berries in't, and teach me how
To name the bigger light, and how the less,
That burn by day and night: and then I loved thee
And show'd thee all the qualities o' the isle,
The fresh springs, brine-pits, baren place and fertile:
Cursed be I that did so! All the charms
Of Sycorax, toads, beetles, bats, light on you!
For I am all the subjects that you have,
Which first was mine own king: and here you sty me
In this hard rock, whiles you do keep from me
The rest o' the island.
    Pros.   Thou most lying slave,
Whom stripes may move, not kindness! I have used thee,
Filth as thou art, with human care, and lodged thee
In mine own cell, till thou didst seek to violate
The honour of my child.
    Cal. O ho, O ho! would 't had been done!

Thou didst prevent me; I had peopled else
This isle with Calibans.
    Pros.   Abhorred slave,
Which any print of goodness wilt not take,
Being capable of all ill! I pitied thee,
Took pains to make thee speak, taught thee each hour
One thing or other: when thou didst not, savage,
Know thine own meaning, but wouldst gabble like
A thing most brutish, I endow'd thy purposes
With words that made them known. But they vile race,
Though thou didst learn, had that in 't which good natures
Could not abide to be with; therefore wast thou
Deservedly confined into this rock,
Who hadst deserved more than a prison.
    Cal. You taught me language; and my profit on 't
Is, I know how to curse. The red plague rid you
For learning me your language!
    Pros.   Hag-seed, hence!
Fetch us in fuel; and be quick, thou 'rt best,
To answer other business. Shrug'st thou, malice?
If thou neglect'st or dost unwillingly
What I command, I 'll rack thee with old cramps,
Fill all thy bones with aches, make thee roar
That beasts shall tremble at thy din.
    Cal.   No, pray thee.
[Aside] I must obey: his art is of such power,
It would control my dam's god, Setebos,
And make a vassal of him.
    Pros.   So, slave; hence! *[Exit Caliban.*

Re-enter ARIEL, *invisible, playing and singing;* FERDINAND *following.*

                ARIEL'S *song.*

                Come unto these yellow sands,
                And then take hands:
                Curtsied when you have and kiss'd
                The wild waves whist,
                Foot it featly here and there;
                And, sweet sprites, the burthen bear.
Burthen [dispersedly]. Hark, hark!
                        Bow-wow.
                The watch-dogs bark:
                        Bow-wow.
    Ari.   Hark, hark! I hear
                The stain of strutting chanticleer
                Cry, Cock-a-diddle-dow.

Fer. Where should this music be? i' the air or the earth?

It sounds no more: and, sure, it waits upon
Some god o' the island. Sitting on a bank,
Weeping again the king my father's wreck,
This music crept by me upon the waters,
Allaying both their fury and my passion
With its sweet air: thence I have follow'd it,
Or it hath drawn me rather. But 't is gone.
No, it begins again.

ARIEL sings.

Full fathom five thy father lies;
Of his bones are coral made;
Those are pearls that were his eyes:
Nothing of him that doth fade
But doth suffer a sea-change
Into something rich and strange.
Sea-nymphs hourly ring his knell:
                                    Burthen. Ding-dong.

Ari. Hark! now I hear them,—Ding-dong, bell.
Fer. The ditty does remember my drown'd father.
This is no mortal business, nor no sound
That the earth owes. I hear it now above me.
Pros. The fringed curtains of thine eye advance
And say what thou seest yond.
Mir.   What is 't? a spirit?
Lord, how it looks about! Believe me, sir,
It carries a brave form. But 't is a spirit.
Pros. No, wench; it eats and sleeps and hath such senses
As we have, such. This gallant which thou seest
Was in the wreck; and, but he's something stain'd
With grief, that's beauty's canker, thou mightst call him
A goodly person: he hath lost his fellows
And strays about to find 'em.
Mir.   I might call him
A thing divine, for nothing natural
I ever saw so noble.
Pros.   *[Aside]* It goes on, I see,
As my soul prompts it. Spirit, fine spirit! I'll free thee
Within two days for this.
Fer.   Most sure, the goddess
On whom these airs attend! Vouchsafe my prayer
May know if you remain upon this island;
And that you will some good instruction give
How I may bear me here: my prime request,
Which I do last pronounce, is, O you wonder!
If you be maid or no?
Mir.   No wonder, sir;

But certainly a maid.
    Fer.   My language! heavens!
I am the best of them that speak this speech,
Were I but where 't is spoken.
    Pros.   How? the best?
What wert thou, if the King of Naples heard thee?
    Fer. A single thing, as I am now, that wonders
To hear thee speak of Naples. He does hear me;
And that he does I weep: myself am Naples,
Who with mine eyes, never since at ebb, beheld
The king my father wreck'd.
    Mir.   Alack, for mercy!
    Fer. Yes, faith, and all his lords; the Duke of Milan
And his brave son being twain.
    Pros.   *[Aside]* The Duke of Milan
And his more braver daughter could control thee,
If now 't were fit to do 't. At the first sight
They have changed eyes. Delicate Ariel,
I'll set thee free for this. *[To Fer.]* A word, good sir;
I fear you have done yourself some wrong: a word.
    Mir. Why speaks my father so urgently? This
Is the third man that e'er I saw, the first
That e'er I sigh'd for: pity move my father
To be inclined my way!
    Fer.   O, if a virgin,
And your affection not gone forth, I' ll make you
The queen of Naples.
    Pros.   Soft, sir! one word more.
[Aside] They are both in either's powers; but this swift
    business
I must uneasy make, lest too light winning
Make the prize light. *[To Fer.]* One word more: I charge
    thee.
That thou attend me: thou dost here usurp
The name thou owest not; and hast put thyself
Upon this island as a spy, to win it
From me, the lord on 't.
    Fer.   No, as I am a man.
    Mir. There's nothing ill can dwell in such a temple:
If the ill spirit have so fair a house,
Good things will strive to dwell with 't.
    Pros.   Follow me.
Speak not you for him; he's a traitor. Come;
I'll manacle thy neck and feet together:
Sea-water shalt thou drink; thy food shall be
The fresh-brook mussels, wither'd roots and husks
Wherein the acorn cradled. Follow.
    Fer.   No;
I will resist such entertainment till

Mine enemy has more power.
                    [Draws, and is charmed from moving.
  Mir.   O dear father,
Make not too rash a trial of him, for
He's gentle and not fearful.
  Pros.   What? I say,
My foot my tutor! Put thy sword up, traitor;
Who makest a show but darest not strike, thy conscience
Is so possess'd with guilt: come from thy ward,
For I can here disarm thee with this stick
And make thy weapon drop.
  Mir.   Beseech you, father.
  Pros. Hence! hang not on my garments.
  Mir.   Sir, have pity;
I'll be his surety.
  Pros.   Silence! one word more
Shall make me chide thee, if not hate thee. What!
An advocate for an impostor! hush!
Thou think'st there is no more such shapes as he,
Having seen but him and Caliban: foolish wench!
To the most of men this is a Caliban
And they to him are angels.
  Mir.   My affections
Are then most humble; I have no ambition
To see a goodlier man.
  Pros.   Come on; obey:
Thy nerves are in their infancy again
And have no vigour in them.
  Fer.   So they are;
My spirits, as in a dream, are all bound up.
My father's loss, the weakness which I feel,
The wreck of all my friends, nor this man's threats,
To whom I am subdued, are but light to me,
Might I but through my prison once a day
Behold this maid: all corners else o' the earth
Let liberty make use of; space enough
Have I in such a prison.
  Pros.   *[Aside]* It works. *[To Fer.]* Come on.
Thou hast done well, fine Ariel! *[To Fer.]* Follow me.
[To Ari.] Hark what thou else shalt do me.
  Mir.   Be of comfort;
My father's of a better nature, sir,
Than he appears by speech: this is unwonted
Which now came from him.
  Pros.   Thou shalt be as free
As mountain winds: but then exactly do
All points of my command.
  Ari.   To the syllable.
  Pros. Come, follow. Speak not for him. *[Exeunt.*

3. Cyrano de Bergerac, *Voyage to the Moon*

Savinien Cyrano de Bergerac (1619–1655) is perhaps best known as the witty, large-nosed soldier protagonist of Edmond Rostand's work *Cyrano*. The real Cyrano was a well-born and well-educated Frenchman who also enjoyed a brief stint as an officer in a French regiment before settling down to a literary career. He wrote several novels and plays, usually satirical, and his work influenced the famous Irish satirist Jonathan Swift. The following excerpt is taken from his work, *Voyage to the Moon*—a text that relies on European fascination with travel and travel literature to critique French society. Here Cyrano takes specific aim at the scientific learning of his age.

Voyage to the Moon

The moon was full, the sky clear, and the clocks had just struck nine as I was returning with four of my friends from a house near Paris. Our wit must have been sharpened on the cobbles of the road for it thrust home whichever way we turned it; distant as the moon was she could not escape it. The various thoughts provoked in us by the sight of that globe of saffron diverted us on the road and our eyes were filled by this great luminary. Now one of us likened her to a window in Heaven through which the glory of the blessed might be faintly seen; then another, inspired by ancient fables, imagined that Bacchus kept a tavern in Heaven and had hung out the Full Moon for his sign; then another vowed that it was the block where Diana set Apollo's ruffs; another exclaimed that it might well be the Sun himself who, having put off his rays at night, was watching through a hole what the world did when he was not there. For my part, said I, I am desirous to add my fancies to yours and without amusing myself with the witty notions you use to tickle time to make it run the faster, I think that the Moon is a world like this and that our world is their Moon. The company gratified me with a great shout of mirth.

"Perhaps in the same way", said I, "at this moment in the Moon they jest at some one who there maintains that this globe is a world."

But though I showed them that Pythagoras, Epicurus, Democritus and, in our own age, Copernicus and Kepler had been of this opinion, I did but cause them to strain their throats the more heartily.

This thought, whose boldness jumped with my humour, was strengthened by contradiction and sank so deep in me that all the rest of the way I was pregnant with a thousand definitions of the Moon of which I could not be delivered. By supporting this fantastic belief with serious reasoning I grew well-nigh persuaded of it. But hearken, reader, the miracle or accident used by Providence or Fortune to convince me of it:

I returned home and scarcely had I entered my room to rest after the journey when I found on my table an open book which I had not put there. I recognised it as mine, which made me ask my servant why he had taken it out of the book-case. I asked him but perfunctorily, for he was a fat Lorrainer, whose soul admitted of no exercises more noble than those of an oyster. He swore to me that either the Devil or I had put it there. For my own part I was sure I had not handled it for more than a year.

I glanced at it again; it was the works of Cardan; and though I had no idea of reading it I fell, as if directed to it, precisely upon a story told by this philosopher. He says that, reading one evening by candle-light, he perceived two tall old men enter through the closed door of his room and after he had asked them many questions they told him they were inhabitants of the Moon; which said, they disappeared. I remained so amazed to see a book brought there by itself as well as at the time and the leaf at which I found it open that I took this whole train of events to be an inspiration of God urging me to make known to men that the Moon is a world.

"What!" quoth I to myself, "after I have talked of a matter this very day, a book, which is perhaps the only one in a world that treats of this subject, flies down from the shelf on to my table, becomes capable of reason to the extent of opening at the very page of so marvellous an adventure and thereby supplies meditations to my fancy and an object to my resolution. Doubtless", I continued, "the two old men who appeared to that great man are the same who have moved my book and opened it at this page to spare themselves the trouble of making me the harangue they made Cardan. But", I added, "how can I clear up this doubt if I do not go there? And why not?" I answered myself at once, "Prometheus of old went to Heaven to steal fire!"

These feverish outbursts were followed by the hope of making successfully such a voyage.

I shut myself up to achieve my purpose in a rather lonely country-house where, after I had flattered my fancy with several methods which might have borne me up there, I committed myself to the heavens in this manner:

I fastened all about me a number of little bottles filled with dew, and the heat of the Sun drawing them up carried me so high that at last I found myself above the loftiest clouds. But, since this attraction caused me to rise too rapidly and instead of my drawing nearer the Moon, as I desired, she seemed to me further off than when I started, I broke several of my bottles until I felt that my weight overbore the attraction and that I was falling towards the earth. My opinion was not wrong; for I reached ground sometime later when, calculating from the hour at which I had started, it ought to have been midnight. Yet I perceived that the Sun was then at the highest point above the horizon and that it was midday. I leave you to conjecture my surprise; indeed it was so great that not knowing how to explain this miracle I had the insolence to fancy that in compliment to my boldness God had a second time fixed the Sun in Heaven to light so glorious an enterprise. My astonishment increased when I found I did not recognise the country I was in, for it appeared to me that, having risen straight up, I ought to have landed in the place from which I had started. Encumbered as I was I approached a hut where I perceived some smoke and I was barely a pistol-shot from it when I found myself surrounded by a large number of savages. They appeared mightily surprised at meeting me; for I was the first, I think, they had ever seen dressed in bottles. And, to overthrow still more any explanation they might have given of this equipment, they saw that as I walked I scarcely touched the ground. They did not know that at the least movement I gave my body the heat of the midday sun-beams lifted me up with my dew; and if my bottles had been more numerous I should very likely have been carried into the air before their eyes. I tried to converse with them; but, as if terror had changed them into birds, in a twinkling they were lost to sight in the neighbouring woods. Nevertheless I caught one whose legs without doubt betrayed his intention. I asked him with much difficulty (for I was out of breath) how far it was from there to Paris, since when people went naked in France and why they fled from me in such terror. This man to whom I spoke was an old man, yellow as an olive, who cast himself at my knees, joined his hands above his head, opened his mouth and shut his eyes. He muttered for some time but as I could not perceive that he said anything I took his language for the hoarse babble of a dumb man.

Sometime afterwards I saw coming towards me a band of soldiers with drums beating and I noticed that two left the main body to reconnoitre me. When they were near enough to hear I asked them where I was.

"You are in France", replied they, "but who the Devil put you in this condition? How does it happen that we do not know you? Has the fleet arrived? Are you going to warn the Governor of it? Why have you divided your brandy into so many bottles?"

To all this I replied that the Devil had not put me in that condition; that they did not know me because they could not know all men; that I did not know there were ships on the Seine; that I had no information to give Monsieur de Montbazon and that I was not carrying any brandy.

"Oh! Ho!" said they taking me by the arm, "you are pleased to be merry! The Governor will understand you!"

They carried me towards their main body as they spoke these words and I learned from them that I was indeed in France, but not in Europe, for I was in New France.

I was brought before the Viceroy, Monsieur de Montmagnie. He asked me my country, my name and my rank, and when I had satisfied him by relating the happy success of my voyage, whether he believed it or only feigned to believe it, he had the kindness to allot me a room in his house. I was happy to fall in with a man capable of lofty ideas, who was not scandalised when I said that the earth must have turned while I was above it, seeing that I had begun to rise two leagues from Paris and had fallen by an almost perpendicular line in Canada.

That evening just as I was going to bed he came into my room.

"I should not have interrupted your rest", said he, "had I not believed that a man who travels nine hundred leagues in half a day can easily do so without being weary. But you do not know", added he, "the merry dispute I have just had on your behalf with our Jesuit Fathers? They are convinced that you are a magician and the greatest mercy you can obtain from them is to pass for no more than an impostor. And, after all, this movement you assign to the Earth is surely some neat paradox? The reason I am not of your opinion is that although you may have left Paris yesterday you could still have reached this country to-day without the Earth having turned. For the Sun, which bore you up by means of your bottles, must have drawn you hither since, according to Ptolemy, Tycho Brahe, and modern philosophers it moves in a direction opposite to that in which you say the Earth moves. And then what probability have you for asserting that the Sun is motionless when we see it move, and that the Earth turns about its centre with such rapidity when we feel it firm beneath us?"

"Sir", replied I, "here are the reasons which oblige us to suppose so: First it is a matter of common sense to think that the Sun is placed in the centre of the Universe, since all bodies in Nature need this radical fire, which dwells in the heart of the Kingdom to be in a position to satisfy their necessities promptly; and that the cause of procreation should be placed in the midst of all bodies to act equally upon them: In the same way wise Nature placed the genitals in the centre of man, pips in the centre of apples, kernels in the centre of their fruit; and in the same way the onion shelters within a hundred surrounding skins the precious germ whence ten million others must draw their essence. The apple is a little universe by itself whose core, which is warmer than the other parts, is a Sun spreading about it the preserving heat of its globe; and the germ in the onion is the little Sun of that little world which heats and nourishes the vegetable salt of the mass. Granted this, I say that since the Earth needs the light, the heat and the influence of this great fire, she turns about it to receive equally in every part this strength which conserves her. For it would be as ridiculous to hold that this great luminous body turns about a point of no importance to it as to imagine when we see a roasted lark that it has been cooked by turning the hearth about it. Otherwise, if the Sun were made to perform this labour it would seem that the doctor needs the patient, that the strong must yield to the weak, the great serve the small, and that instead of a ship coasting the shores of a county we must make the country move around the vessel. And if you find it hard to believe that so heavy a mass can move, tell me, I pray you, are the stars and the Heavens that you make so solid any lighter? And it is easy for us who are convinced of the roundness of the earth to deduce its movements from its shape; but why suppose the sky to be round since you cannot know it and since if, of all possible shapes it has not this shape, it certainly cannot move? I do not reproach you with your eccentrics, your concentrics and your epicycles, all of which you can only explain very confusedly and from which my system is free. Let us speak only of the natural causes of this movement. On your side you are compelled to invoke the aid of intelligences to move and direct your globes! But without disturbing the tranquillity of the Sovereign Being, who doubtless created Nature quite perfect and whose wisdom completed it in such a way that by fitting it for one thing He has not rendered it unfit for another—I, on my part, find in the Earth herself the power which makes it move. I declare then that the sun-beams, together with the Sun's influence, striking upon the Earth in their motion, make it turn as we turn a globe by striking it with the hand, or that the vapours which continually evaporate from the Earth's bosom on that side where the Sun shines, are repulsed by the cold of the middle regions, rush back on the Earth and, of necessity being only able to strike it obliquely, make it dance in this fashion.

"The explanation of the two other movements is still less intricate. Consider I beg of you . . ."

At these words the Viceroy interrupted me.

"I prefer", he said, "to excuse you from that trouble (I have myself read several books of Gassendi on the subject) provided that you will listen to what I heard one day from one of our Fathers who shared your opinion. 'Truly', said he, 'I imagine that the Earth turns, not for the reasons alleged by Copernicus but because the fire of Hell (as we learn from Holy Scripture) being enclosed in the centre of the Earth, the damned souls, flying from the heat of the fire to avoid it, clamber upwards and thus make the Earth turn, as a dog makes a wheel turn when he runs round inside it.'"

We praised the good Father's zeal and, having finished the panegyric, the Viceroy said he greatly wondered the system of Ptolemy should be so generally received, considering how little probable it is.

"Sir", I replied, "most men judge only by their senses, are convinced only by their eyes; and just as a man in a ship sailing by the coast thinks himself stationary and the shore moving, so men, turning with the Earth around the sky, believe that the sky itself turns around them. Add to this the intolerable pride of humans beings, who are convinced that Nature was made for them alone—as if it were probable that the Sun, a vast body four hundred and thirty-four times greater than the Earth, should have been lighted only to ripen its medlars and to head its cabbages. For my part, far from yielding to their impertinence, I believe that the planets are worlds around the Sun and that the fixed stars are suns too with planets around them, that is to say, worlds, which we cannot see from here because they are too small and because their borrowed light cannot reach us. For, in good faith, how can we suppose that globes so spacious are only huge desert countries and that ours, because we grovel on it before a dozen proud-stomached rogues, should have been made to command them all?

4. JONATHON SWIFT, *GULLIVER'S TRAVELS*

Cousin of the playright Dryden and friend of Alexander Pope, the Irish-born Swift (1667–1745) was already a famous political activist and satirist in England by the time of his publication of *Gulliver's Travels* in 1726. His active defense of Irish rights fueled many of his most important works, among them the controversial essay *A Modest Proposal*. Imitating the style of the scientific writing of the day, *A Modest Proposal* recommends English cannibalism of the Irish as an efficient means to utilize the resources of the subject nation. In his most famous work, *Gulliver's Travels*, Swift critiques the political foibles of English society. Both in form and in tone, the *Travels* reflects the influence of the work of Cyrano de Bergerac. The following excerpt is taken from Gulliver's journey to the kingdom of Lilliput. His satirical examination of the Lilliputian government is a barely concealed attack on the government of George I (1714–1727) of England and the political wranglings of the two main parties, the Whigs and Tories.

Gulliver's Travels

Chapter IV

Mildendo, the Metropolis of Lilliput, Described, Together with the Emperor's Palace. A Conversation between the Author and Principal Secretary, Concerning the Affairs of That Empire. The Author's Offers to Serve the Emperor in His Wars.

The first request I made, after I had obtained my liberty, was, that I might have licence to see Mildendo, the metropolis; which the emperor easily granted me, but with a special charge to do no hurt either to the inhabitants or their houses. The people had notice, by proclamation, of my design to visit the town. The wall, which encompasses it, is two feet and a half high, and at least eleven inches broad, so that a coach and horses may be driven very safely round it; and it is flanked with strong towers, at ten feet distance. I stepped over the great western gate, and passed very gently and sideling through the two principal streets, only in my short waistcoat, for fear of damaging the roofs and eaves of the houses with the skirts of my coat.

The emperor's palace is in the centre of the city, where the two great streets meet. It is enclosed by a wall of two feet high, and twenty feet distance from the buildings. I had his majesty's permission to step over this wall; and the space being so wide between that and the palace, I could easily view it on every side. The outward court is a square of forty feet, and includes two other courts: in the inmost are the royal apartments, which I was very desirous to see, but found it extremely difficult: for the great gates, from one square into another, were but eighteen inches high, and seven inches wide. Now the buildings of the outer court were at least five feet high, and it was impossible for me to stride over them without infinite damage to the pile, though the walls were strongly built of hewn stone, and four inches thick. At the same time the emperor had a great desire that I should see magnificence of his palace; but this I was not able to do till three days after, which I spent in cutting down with my knife some of the largest trees in the royal park, about a hundred yards' distance from the city. Of these trees I made two stools, each about three feet high, and strong enough to bear my weight. The people having received notice a second time, I went again through the city to the palace with my two stools in my hands. When I came to the side of the outer court, I stood upon one stool, and took the other in my hand; this I lifted over the roof, and gently set it down on the space between the first and second court, which was eight feet wide. I then stept over the building very conveniently from one stool to the other, and drew up the first after me with a hooked stick. By this contrivance I got into the inmost court; and, lying down upon my side, I applied my face to the windows of the middle stories, which were left open on purpose, and discovered the most splendid apartments that can be imagined. There I saw the empress and the young princes, in their several lodgings, with their chief attendants about them. Her imperial majesty was pleased to smile very graciously upon me, and gave me out of the window her hand to kiss.

But I shall not anticipate the reader with farther descriptions of this kind, because I reserve them for a greater work, which is now almost ready for the press; containing a general description of this empire, from its first erection, through a long series of princes; with a particular account of their wars and politics, laws, learning, and religion; their plants and animals, their peculiar manners and customs, with other matters very curious and useful; my chief design at present being only to relate such events and transactions as happened to the public or to myself during a residence of about nine months in that empire.

One morning, about a fortnight after I had obtained my liberty, Reldresal, principal secretary (as they style him) for private affairs, came to my house attended only by one servant. He ordered his coach to wait at a distance, and desired I would give him an hour's audience; which I readily consented to, on account of his quality and personal merits, as well as of the many good offices he had done me during my solicitations at court. I offered to lie down, that he might the more conveniently reach my ear; but he chose rather to let me hold him in my hand during our conversation. He began with compliments on my liberty; said, "he might pretend to some merit in it;" but, however, added, "that if it had not been for the present situation of things at court, perhaps I might not have obtained it so soon. For," said he, "as flourishing a condition as we may appear to be in to foreigners, we labour under two mighty evils; a violent faction at home, and the danger of an invasion, by a most potent enemy, from abroad. As to the first, you are to understand, that for above seventy moons past there have been two struggling parties in this empire, under the names of *Tramecksan* and *Slamecksan*, from the high and low heels of their shoes, by which they distinguish themselves. It is alleged, indeed, that the high heels are most agreeable to our ancient constitution; but, however this be, his majesty has determined to make use only of low heels in the administration of the government, and all offices in the gift of the crown, as you cannot but observe; and particularly, that his majesty's imperial heels are lower at least by a *drurr*, than any of his court: (*drurr* is a measure about the fourteenth part of an inch.) The animosities between these two parties run so high, that they will neither eat, nor drink, nor talk with each other. We compute the *Tramecksan*, or high heels, to exceed us in number; but the power is wholly on our side. We apprehend his imperial highness, the heir to the crown, to have some tendency towards the high heels; at least, we can plainly discover that one of his heels is higher than the other, which gives him a hobble in his gait. Now, in the midst of these intestine disquiets, we are threatened with an invasion from the Island of Blefuscu, which is the other great empire of the universe, almost as large and powerful as this of his majesty. For, as to what we have heard you affirm, that there are other kingdoms and states in the world, inhabited by human creatures as large as yourself, our philosophers are in much doubt, and would rather conjecture that you dropped from the moon, or one of the stars: because it is certain, that a hundred mortals of your bulk would in a short time destroy all the fruits and cattle of his majesty's dominions: besides, our histories of six thousand moons make no mention of any other regions than the two great empires of Lilliput and Blefuscu. Which two mighty powers have, as I was going to tell you, been engaged in a most obstinate war for six-and-thirty moons past. It began upon the following occasion: it is allowed on all hands, that the primitive way of breaking eggs, before we eat them, was upon the larger end; but his present majesty's grandfather, while he was a boy, going to eat an egg, and breaking it according to the ancient practice, happened to cut one of his fingers. Whereupon the emperor his father published an edict, commanding all his subjects, upon great penalties, to break the smaller ends of their eggs. The people so highly resented this law, that our histories tell us, there have been six rebellions raised on that account; wherein one emperor lost his life, and another his crown. These civil commotions were constantly fomented by the monarchs of Blefuscu; and when they were quelled, the exiles always fled for refuge to that empire. It is computed that eleven thousand persons have at several times suffered death, rather than submit to break their eggs at the smaller end. Many hundred large volumes have been published upon this controversy: but the books of the Big-endians have been long forbidden, and the whole party rendered incapable by law of holding employments. During the course of these troubles, the emperors of Blefuscu did frequently expostulate by their ambassadors, accusing us of making a schism in religion, by offending against a fundamental doctrine of our great prophet Lustrog, in the fifty-fourth chapter of the Blundecral, (which is their Alcoran.) This, however, is thought to be a mere strain upon the text; for the words are these: that all true believers break their eggs at the convenient end. And which is the convenient end, seems, in my humble opinion, to be left to every man's conscience, or at least in the power of the chief magistrate to determine. Now, the Big-endian exiles have found so much credit in the emperor of Blefuscu's court, and so much private assistance and encouragement from their party here at home, that a bloody war has been carried on between the two empires for six-and-thirty moons, with various success: during which time we have lost forty capital ships, and a much greater number of smaller vessels, together with thirty thousand of our best seamen and soldiers; and the damage received by the enemy is reckoned to be somewhat greater than ours. However, they have now equipped a numerous fleet, and are just preparing to make a descent upon us; and his imperial majesty, placing great confidence in your valour and strength, has commanded me to lay this account of his affairs before you."

I desired the secretary to present my humble duty to the emperor; and to let him know, "that I thought it would not become me, who was a foreigner, to interfere with parties; but I was ready, with the hazard of my life, to defend his person and state against all invaders."

Figure 12.1 Flying to the moon. Taken from Savinien Cyrano de Berg-erac, *Voyage to the Moon* in *A Voyage to the Moon and Sun*. New York: George Routledge & Sons, Ltd.; E.P. Dutton and Co., 1923. translated by Richard Aldington.

Study Questions

1. In what ways do we see the influence of Christian humanism in *Utopia?*
2. What function does the island serve in Shakespeare's play, *The Tempest?*
3. What does Cyrano criticize about the state of scientific knowledge during this period? How does this reflect contemporary intellectual currents? European exploration?
4. Compare the society encountered in *Gulliver's Travels* with that of *Utopia.* Do these different images of societies reflect changing European values from the sixteenth to eighteenth centuries?

Suggested Readings

Boyle, Frank. *Swift as Nemesis: Modernity and Its Satirist.* Stanford, CA: Stanford University Press, 2000.

Greenblatt, Stephen. *Marvelous Possessions: The Wonder of the New World.* New York: Clarendon Press, 1991.

Manuel, Frank E., and Fritzie P. Manuel. *French Utopias: An Anthology of Ideal Societies.* New York: Free Press, 1966.

Motooka, Wendy. *The Age of Reasons: Quixotism, Sentimentalism, and Political Economy in Eighteenth-Century Britain.* London and New York: Routledge, 1998.

Web Sites

1. John Milton

   http://www.luminarium.org/sevenlit/milton/

2. Thomas Roper, *Life of Sir Thomas More*

   http://www.fordham.edu/halsall/mod/16Croper-more.html

3. A Shakespeare Timeline

   http://daphne.palomar.edu/shakespeare/timeline/timeline.htm

13

Women and Colonization
1500–1700 A.D.

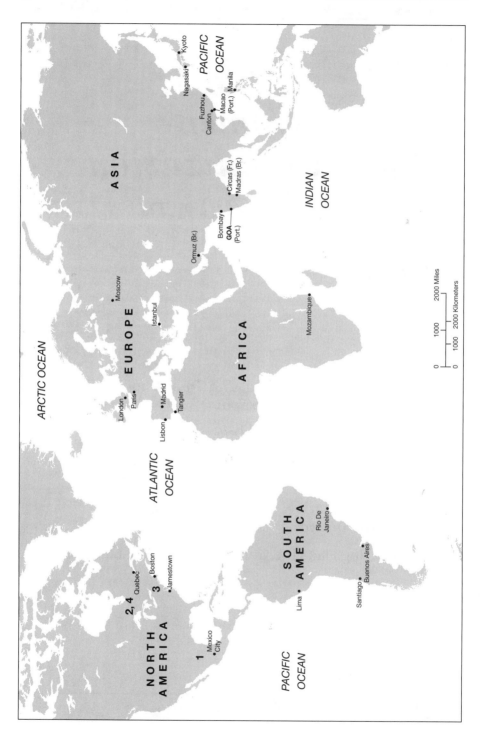

The colonial experience was a transformative one for both European and indigenous women though it is fair to say that for indigenous women, the experience was largely negative. European men had always regarded women as the natural spoils of war, and native women were subject to rape, enslavement, and other abuses by their European conquerors. Even when not enslaved or physically abused, indigenous women also had to live under the rule of the Europeans. For the native women of North America, this would over time subject them to European conceptions of the economic, political, social, and spiritual roles of women. Early chroniclers of the native communities in North America such as John Morton, Thomas Hariot, and Pierre de Charlevoix were surprised by the political authority wielded by native women in their own communities. Men still ruled, but native women could influence communal decisions to a much greater degree than women in Europe. Lineage also often passed through the female line, making women an important transmitter of property in these northern societies. Colonial rule, however, threatened native political, economic, and social structures. The more native cultures were influenced by European culture, the more native women lost power in their own society.

The colonial experience for female settlers was very different from that of indigenous women. Members of the conquering society, European women enjoyed a more protected existence in general. Even so, life in the early colonial settlements could be very difficult. Many of the European women who went to New England, Virginia, and Maryland, for example, arrived as indentured servants of wealthier colonists. These women worked very hard, usually doing labor both in the fields and in the household. More fortunate were the wives and daughters of landowners and merchants, but they too worked extremely hard. The women made butter and cheese from cow's milk, brewed beer, manufactured linens and wools, helped as occasional labor on the land, and worked in the family shop among other forms of labor, and they did all of this while caring for the children. Other realities of colonial life were disease, crop failures, and native Indian attacks. Of six thousand settlers who arrived in Virginia between 1607–1624, for example, only twelve hundred were there by 1625.

The demanding nature of life in the colonies meant that for many European women, the colonies were as much a frontier in terms of gender roles as they were of European civilization. Imbued with European conceptions about masculine and feminine nature, colonial men and women accepted that women were physically and intellectually weaker and more sexually licentious than men. They accepted that women should be submissive and chaste and that the proper sphere of female activity was the home. The rigorous nature of life in the colonies, however, and the demands on women to play an equal role in supporting their families, meant that many European women enjoyed a greater freedom of movement, comportment, and expression than did their counterparts on the continent. Women traveled the roads to market and operated their own market stalls. Some women were able to own land, and in certain colonies they were also more free to speak their mind about politics, religion, and other concerns traditionally considered the arena of men.

Growing concern about female autonomy, combined with fear about blurring status distinctions, perhaps explains why so many colonial treatises concern themselves with the comportment of men and women. Early modern Europeans presumed that human society was inherently unequal and hierarchical. All men were not equal, and women were decidedly unequal to men. These treatises attacked women and men who dressed above their social stations, as well as women who behaved like men, because many contemporaries feared that transgressions against established gender and social roles would destabilize existing social structures.

The following documents represent four very different perspectives on women in the colonies. The general lack of indigenous texts written by women for the early colonial period means relying frequently on male European sources and so they must be used judiciously. The account of Diaz del Castillo discusses Doña Marina, [1] the well-known female interpreter who was instrumental in Cortes's success against the Aztec Empire in 1521. Dona Marina remains a shadowy figure in his discourse, but what is clear from Castillo's account is that she exerted enormous influence over Cortes, as well as many of the native communities in Mexico. The correspondence of Marie de l'Incarnation [2] gives us insight into the experiences of a female religious in New France during the seventeenth century. Mary Rowlandson's description of her captivity [3] reflects a Protestant Englishwoman's interpretation of native society during a time of tremendous conflict between European settlers and native communities. Pierre de Charlevoix's [4] description of female political authority among the Iroquois provides a decidedly more respectful view of naive society than that of Rowlandson, and in particular on the role of native women in their own society.

1. Bernal Diaz del Castillo, *The True History of the Conquest of New Spain*

One of the best-known chroniclers of the Spanish Conquest of Mexico is Bernal del Castillo (1496–1584). Castillo was a Spanish nobleman who followed Cortes on his early forays into the Aztec kingdom in 1521. The following excerpt discusses Doña Marina, a native woman Christianized by the Spanish conquistadors. Early accounts agree that Doña Marina was from an important Indian family. Her treatment by Cortes and his men was typical of many native women during this period, and she eventually became Cortes's mistress. This account also shows that Doña Marina's knowledge of Spanish and native languages, political connections, and evident intelligence made her a vital ally of Cortes. With her aid, Cortes won the support of several different native communities which enabled him and his men to crush ruling Aztec authority.

The Story of Doña Marina

So the talk ceased until the next day when the sacred image of Our Lady and the Cross were set up on the altar and we all paid reverence to them, and Padre Fray Bartolomé de Olmedo said mass and all the Caciques and chiefs were present and we gave the name of Santa Maria de la Victoria to the town, and by this name the town of Tabasco is now called. The same friar, with Aguilar as interpreter, preached many good things about our holy faith to the twenty Indian women who had been given us, telling them not to believe in the Idols which they had been wont to trust in, for they were evil things and not gods, and that they should offer no more sacrifices to them for they would lead them astray, but that they should worship our Lord Jesus Christ, and immediately afterwards they were baptized. One Indian lady who was given to us here was christened Doña Marina, and she was truely a great chieftainess and the daughter of great Caciques and the mistress of vassals, and this her appearance clearly showed. Later on I will relate why it was and in what manner she was brought here.

I do not clearly remember the names of all the other women, and it is not worth while to name any of them; however, they were the first women to become Christians in New Spain.

Cortés allotted one of them to each of his captains and Doña Marina, as she was good looking and intelligent and without embarrassment, he gave to Alonzo Hernández Puertocarrero, who I have already said was a distinguished gentleman, and cousin of the Count of Medellin. When Puertocarrero went to Spain, Doña Marina lived with Cortés, and bore him a son named Don Martin Cortés.

We remained five days in this town, to look after the wounded and those who were suffering from pain in the loins, from which they all recovered. Furthermore, Cortés drew the Caciques to him by kindly converse, and told them how our master the Emperor, whose vassals we were, had under his orders many great lords, and that it would be well for them also to render him obedience, and that then, whatever they might be in need of, whether it was our protection or any other necessity, if they would make it known to him, no matter where he might be, he would come to their assistance.

The Caciques all thanked him for this, and thereupon all declared themselves the vassals of our great Emperor. These were the first vassals to render submission to His Majesty in New Spain.

Cortés then ordered the Caciques to come with their women and children early the next day, which was Palm Sunday, to the altar, to pay homage to the holy image of Our Lady and to the Cross, and at the same time Cortés ordered them to send six Indian carpenters to accompany our carpenters to the town of Cintla where our Lord God was pleased to give us victory in the battle which I have described, there to cut a cross on a great tree called a Ceiba which grew there, and they did it so that it might last a long time, for as the bark is renewed the cross will show there for ever. When this was done he ordered the Indians to get ready all the canoes that they owned to help us to embark, for we wished to set sail on that holy day because the pilots had come to tell Cortés that the ships ran a great risk from a *Norther* which is a dangerous gale.

The next day, early in the morning, all the Caciques and chiefs came in their canoes with all their women and children and stood in the court where we had placed the church and cross, and many branches of trees had already been cut ready to be carried in the procession. Then the Caciques beheld us all, Cortés, as well as the captains, and every one of us marching together with the greatest reverence in a devout procession, and the Padre de la Merced and the priest, Juan Diaz, clad in their vestments, said mass, and we paid reverence to and kissed the Holy Cross, while the Caciques and Indians stood looking on at us.

When our solemn festival was over the chiefs approached and offered Cortés ten fowls, and baked fish and vegetables, and we took leave of them, and Cortés again commended to their care the Holy image and the sacred crosses and told them always to keep the place clean and well swept and to deck the cross with garlands and to reverence it, and then they would enjoy good health and bountiful harvests.

It was growing late when we got on board ship and the next day, Monday, we set sail in the morning and with a fair wind laid our course for San Juan de Ulúa, keeping close in shore all the time.

As we sailed along in the fine weather, we soldiers who knew the coast would say to Cortés, "Señor, over there is La Rambla, which the Indians call Ayagualulco," and soon afterwards we arrived off Tonalá which we called San Antonio, and we pointed it out to him. Further on we showed him the great river of Coatzacoalcos, and he saw the lofty snow capped mountains, and then the Sierra of San Martin, and further on we pointed out the split rock, which is a great rock standing out in the sea with a mark on the top of it which gives it the appearance of a seat. Again further on we showed him the Rio de Alvarado, which Pedro de Alvarado entered when we were with Grijalva, and then we came in sight of the Rio de Banderas, where we had gained in barter the sixteen thousand dollars, then we showed him the Isla Blanca, and told him where lay the Isla Verde, and close in shore we saw the Isla de Sacrificios where we found the altars and the Indian victims in Grijalva's time; and at last our good fortune brought us to San Juan de Ulúa soon after midday on Holy Thursday.

I remember that a gentleman, Alonzo Hernández Puertocarrero came up to Cortés and said: "It seems to me, sir, that these gentlemen who have been twice before to this country are saying to you:—

Cata Francia, Montesinos.	Behold France, Montesinos.
Cata Paris la ciudad.	Look at Paris, the city.
Cata las aguas de Duero	See the waters of the Duero
Do van a dar en la Mar.	Flowing to the sea.

I say that you are looking on rich lands, may you know how to govern them well!"

Cortés knew well the purpose for which these words were said, and answered: "Let God give us the good fortune in fighting which He gave to the Paladin Roldan, and with Your Honour and the other gentlemen for leaders, I shall know well how to manage it."

Let us leave off here, for this is what took place and Cortés did not go into the Rio de Alvarado, as Gomara says he did.

Chapter XXXVII

Showing that Doña Marina Was a Cacica *and the Daughter of Persons of High Rank, and Was the Mistress of Towns and Vassals, and How It Happened That She Was Taken to Tabasco.*

Before telling about the great Montezuma and his famous City of Mexico and the Mexicans, I wish to give some account of Doña Marina, who from her childhood had been the mistress and Cacica of towns and vassals. It happened in this way:

Her father and mother were chiefs and Caciques of a town called Paynala, which had other towns subject to it, and stood about eight leagues from the town of Coatzacoalcos. Her father died while she was still a little child, and her mother married another

Cacique, a young man, and bore him a son. It seems that the father and mother had a great affection for this son and it was agreed between them that he should succeed to their honours when their days were done. So that there should be no impediment to this, they gave the little girl, Doña Marina, to some Indians from Xicalango and this they did by night so as to escape observation, and they then spread the report that she had died, and as it happened at this time that a child of one of their Indian slaves died they gave out that it was their daughter and the heiress who was dead.

The Indians of Xicalango gave the child to the people of Tabasco, and the Tabasco people gave her to Cortés. I myself knew her mother, and the old woman's son and her half-brother, when he was already grown up and ruled the town jointly with his mother, for the second husband of the old lady was dead. When they became Christians, the old lady was called Marta and the son Lázaro. I knew all this very well because in the year 1523 after the conquest of Mexico and the other provinces, when Cristóval de Olid revolted in Honduras, and Cortés was on his way there, he passed through Coatzacoalcos and I and the greater number of the settlers of that town accompanied him on that expedition as I shall relate in the proper time and place. As Doña Marina proved herself such an excellent woman and good interpreter throughout the wars in New Spain, Tlascala and Mexico (as I shall show later on) Cortés always took her with him, and during that expedition she was married to a gentleman named Juan Jaramillo at the town of Orizaba, before certain witnesses, one of whom was named Aranda, a settler in Tabasco and this man told [me] about the marriage (not in the way the historian Gomara relates it).

Doña Marina was a person of the greatest importance and was obeyed without question by the Indians throughout New Spain.

When Cortés was in the town of Coatzacoalcos he sent to summon to his presence all the Caciques of that province in order to make them a speech about our holy religion, and about their good treatment, and among the Caciques who assembled was the mother of Doña Marina and her half-brother, Lazaro.

Some time before this Doña Marina had told me that she belonged to that province and that she was the mistress of vassals, and Cortés also knew it well, as did Aguilar, the interpreter. In such a manner it was that mother, daughter and son came together, and it was easy enough to see that she was the daughter from the strong likeness she bore to her mother.

These relations were in great fear of Doña Marina, for they thought that she had sent for them to put them to death, and they were weeping.

When Doña Marina saw them in tears, she consoled them and told them to have no fear, that when they had given her over to the men from Xicalango, they knew not what they were doing, and she forgave them for doing it, and she gave them many jewels of gold, and raiment, and told them to return to their town, and said that God had been very gracious to her in freeing her from the worship of idols and making her a Christian, and letting her bear a son to her lord and master Cortés and in marrying her to such a gentleman as Juan Jaramillo, who was now her husband. That she would rather serve her husband and Cortés than anything else in the world, and would not exchange her place to be Cacica of all the provinces in New Spain.

All this which I have repeated here I know for certain (and I swear to it.)

This seems to me very much like what took place between Joseph and his brethren in Egypt when they came into his power over the matter of the wheat. It is what actually happened and not the story which was told to Gomara, who also says other things which I will leave unnoticed.

To go back to my subject: Doña Marina knew the language of Coatzacoalcos, which is that common to Mexico, and she knew the language of Tabasco, as did also Jerónimo de Aguilar, who spoke the language of Yucatan and Tabasco, which is one and the same. So that these two could understand one another clearly, and Aguilar translated into Castilian for Cortés.

This was the great beginning of our conquests and thus, thanks be to God, things prospered with us. I have made a point of explaining this matter, because without the help of Doña Marina we could not have understood the language of New Spain and Mexico.

Here I will leave off, and go on later to tell how we disembarked in the Port of San Juan de Ulúa.

2. MARIE DE L'INCARNATION, *LETTERS*

The French-born Marie de l'Incarnation (1599–1672) was already developing a reputation in France as a mystic when she undertook a voyage to New France in 1639. She went to New France with two other members of the Ursuline order to establish schools for native girls. Known mostly as a teaching order, the Ursulines were one of the many new female religious orders to emerge in Europe after 1500. At the time of Marie's arrival in Quebec, there were fewer than three hundred Europeans in all of New France. During her many years there, Marie wrote numerous letters to family, friends, and religious superiors. At times intimate in tone and always richly descriptive, these letters are an important historical source on early colonial life in New France. The following letter praises the bravery and spiritual industry of the Jesuits while detailing the spiritual progress of the native peoples under the supervision of the Jesuits and the Ursulines. Marie and her sister Ursulines worked closely with the Jesuits, as well as with native communities and European settlers. The letter is interesting for many reasons, not the least because of its somewhat contradictory description of the progress of spiritual reform in New France. Clearly not all native peoples were as receptive to Christian evangelization as such European spiritual reformers as Marie would have liked.

To the Superior of the Ursulines of Tours
My Reverend and Dearest Mother,

The lateness of the ship bearing your letters to us made me almost despair of receiving any of them, because we were convinced the ship was lost. It is prudent not to put everything in the same vessel, because if the vessel is lost, one loses both the reassurance and hope of receiving anything until the following year. Finally the ship arrived at the end of the month, bearing your blessings, without which we would be lacking a great deal. The God of Canada who inspired you to aid his Seminary will reward you with his infinite goods. The news that I sent by another means informed you about what has happened regarding the education of our seminarists, and I was prepared to tell you about the heroic actions of our reverend fathers. That is what I am going to do.

Demons have conspired to destroy, if they can, the mission of the Hurons, and they make all of the accusations leveled at the missionaries appear as though they are true. They hold large assemblies with the intent of exterminating the Jesuits, and they, far from being afraid, await death with a marvelous constancy. They even go to the places which are the most inflamed against them. One of the oldest and most important women of this nation harangued the members of one assembly, saying: "It is the Black Robes who are killing us by using their own means. Listen to me, I will prove it with evidence so that you will know that it is true. They arrive at a village where everyone is healthy. As soon as they are established, all but three or four people will have died. They change locations and the same thing happens. They visit the huts of other villages and only those who do not enter are exempt from death and illness. Do you not see that when they move their lips in what they call a prayer, other kinds of things leave their mouths? It is the same when they read their books. Furthermore, in their huts there are large wooden objects (guns) which they use to make noise and spread their magic all around. If we do not immediately kill them, they will ruin the country to such an extent that nothing small nor large will remain."

When this women finished speaking, all concluded that what she said was the truth and that it was necessary to remedy such a great evil. What further aggravated matters was that a savage encountered an unknown person while out walking and he was terrified by him. The specter said to him: "Listen to me, I am Jesus who the black robes invoke to do evil: but I am not the master of their trickery." This demon, who feigned to be Jesus, swore a thousand imprecations against the prayer and doctrine taught by the Jesuits, which strangely increased the hatred already directed at them. One can already see the effects. Some are beaten, some injured, others chased from their huts and villages. However, because death is causing strange ravages all over, it is essential to throw oneself without fear into the danger, in order to baptize the children and those found in this state. The good Joseph who follows them everywhere, performing the apostolic office, bears the opprobrium of his nation in the name of Jesus Christ. Moreover, the more evil that befalls them, the bolder they become.

The reverend father Pijart came from Quebec this year on mission. He was forced to row throughout the entire voyage, with such inhumanity that when he arrived he could barely support himself and he had difficulty saying the mass. He recounted to me the troubles experienced by the fathers on this mission. They are inconceivable, and yet his heart was filled with such ardor to return that he forgot all the difficulties of the voyage in order to find his beloved crosses which he said he would never exchange, except for the will of God, for paradise. It was impossible to convince him to take small refreshments for the road. I do not know what happened to him or the fathers who accompanied him because the accusations brought against them came at a time which made them seem true. They were regarded as sorcerers to the extent that, where they went, God permitted death to accompany them, to make the faith of those who converted more pure. They were reduced to such an extremity that they were forced to hide their breviaries and stop vocal prayers. I urge you, my dearest mother, to renew your prayers for these great servants of God. I send you, as my dearest friend, the letters which they wrote to me, so that you will see them and you will guard them with respect, coming as they do from these admirable workers of the gospel.

Regarding the sedentary savages, they live in the fervor of the first Christians in the Church. It is not possible to find souls more pure or zealous in observing the law of God. I admire them when I see them submit like children to those who instruct them. Mother Marie de Saint-Joseph, who writes to you of their fervor, gives you ample reason to praise the author of such good works, and for praying for the conversion of the errant savages, who begin to be touched by the faith and want to follow the example of their compatriots, who are sedentary since their conversion. Love above all our little seminary which lodges the most innocent souls and ones recently washed in the blood of the Lamb. They pray a lot for you and for their other benefactors, and I doubt not at all that you feel the effects, since God is pleased to fulfil the prayers of pure souls. I asked the Governor and the reverend Pere Le Jeune to send you a particular product which is like cotton, in order to show the many ways it can be used. I believe that it is necessary to beat and card it, if one wants to be able to spin it. It is more delicate than silk or beaver. I am asking you then to find those who have the ability to make it, and if they can make it and use it, to show us their efforts. We will cultivate it here if it proves to be useful for something.

Goodbye, dearest Mother, I am not so far from you in spirit as I am in body. We love an immense object in which we live, and in this also I see you and embrace you by the union which joins us to him, and which joins us there, I hope eternally.
Quebec, September 13, 1640.

3. MARY ROWLANDSON, *A NARRATIVE OF THE CAPTIVITY AND RESTORATION OF MRS. MARY ROWLANDSON*

Mary White Rowlandson was born in England around 1636, and emigrated to Massachusetts with her family in 1639. By 1676, she had married and was raising three children in Lancaster, Massachusetts, about thirty miles west of Boston. At this time, her life became entwined with a dispute known as King Philip's War between the various native American tribes of Massachusetts and the English colonists. On February 6, 1976, Lancaster was attacked, and Mary Rowlandson and her children were taken captive. Rowlandson's harsh account of the indigenous peoples who held her captive does not make her a sympathetic figure today. She shows very little concern, for example, that the English were encroaching on native lands. Her account is nevertheless historically valuable, however, because it reflects the cultural and spiritual views of many of her contemporaries.

A Narrative of the Captivity and Restauration of Mrs. Mary Rowlandson

On the tenth of February 1675, Came the Indians with great numbers upon Lancaster: Their first coming was about Sun-rising; hearing the noise of some Guns, we looked out; several Houses were burning, and the Smoke ascending to Heaven. There were five persons taken in one house, the Father, and the Mother and a sucking Child, they knockt on the head; the other two they took and carried away alive. Their were two others, who being out of their Garison upon some occasion were set upon; one was knockt on the head, the other escaped: Another their was who running along was shot and wounded, and fell down; he begged of them his life, promising them Money (as they told me) but they would not hearken to him but knockt him in head, and stript him naked, and split open his Bowels. Another seeing many of the Indians about his Barn, ventured and went out, but was quickly shot down. There were three others belonging to the same Garison who were killed; the Indians getting up upon the roof of the Barn, had advantage to shoot down upon them over their Fortification. Thus these murtherous wretches went on, burning, and destroying before them.

At length they came and beset our own house, and quickly it was the dolefullest day that ever mine eyes saw. The House stood upon the edge of a hill; some of the Indians got behind the hill, others into the Barn, and others behind any thing that could shelter them; from all which places they shot against the House, so that the Bullets seemed to fly like hail; and quickly they wounded one man among us, then another, and then a third, About two hours (according to my observation, in that amazing time) they had been about the house before they prevailed to fire it (which they did with Flax and Hemp, which they brought out of the Barn, and there being no defence about the House, only two Flankers at two opposite corners and one of them not finished) they fired it once and one ventured out and quenched it, but they quickly fired it again, and that took. Now is the dreadfull hour come, that I have often heard of (in time of War, as it was the case of others) but now mine eyes see it. Some in our house were fighting for their lives, others wallowing in their blood, the House on fire over our heads, and the bloody Heathen ready to knock us on the head, if we stirred out. Now might we hear Mothers and Children crying out for themselves, and one another, Lord, What shall we do? Then I took my Children (and one of my sisters, hers) to go forth and leave the house: but as soon as we came to the dore and appeared, the Indians shot so thick that the bulletts rattled against the House, as if one had taken an handfull of stones and threw them, so that we were fain to give back. We had six stout Dogs belonging to our Garrison, but none of them would stir, though another time, if any Indian had come to the door, they were ready to fly upon him and tear him down. The Lord hereby would make us the more to acknowledge his hand, and to see that our help is always in him. But out we must go, the fire increasing, and coming along behind us, roaring, and the Indians gaping before us with their Guns, Spears and Hatchets to devour us. No sooner were we out of the House, but my Brother in Law (being before wounded, in defending the house, in or near the throat) fell down dead, wherat the Indians scornfully shouted, and hallowed, and were presently upon him, stripping off his cloaths, the bulletts flying thick, one went through my side, and the same (as would seem) through the bowels and hand of my dear Child in my arms. One of my elder Sisters Children, named William, had then his Leg broken, which the Indians perceiving, they knockt him on head. Thus were we butchered by those merciless Heathen, standing amazed, with the blood running down to our heels. My eldest Sister being yet in the House, and seeing those wofull sights, the Infidels haling Mothers one way, and Children another, and some wallowing in their blood: and her elder Son telling her that her Son William was dead, and my self was wounded, she said, And, Lord, let me dy with them; which was no sooner said, but she was struck with a Bullet, and fell down dead over the threshold. I hope she is reaping the fruit of her good labours, being faithfull to the service of God in her place. In her younger years she lay under much trouble upon spiritual accounts, till it pleased God to make that previous

Scripture take hold of her heart, 2 Cor. 12. 9. *And he said unto me, my Grace is sufficient for thee.* More then twenty years after I have heard her tell how sweet and comfortable that place was to her. But to return: The Indians laid hold of us, pulling me one way, and the Children another, and said, Come go along with us; I told them they would kill me: they answered, If I were willing to go along with them, they would not hurt me.

Oh the dolefull sight that now was to behold at this House! *Come, behold the works of the Lord, what dissolations he has made in the Earth.* Of thirty seven persons who were in this one House, none escaped either present death, or a bitter captivity, save only one, who might say as he, Job 1. 15, *And I only am escaped alone to tell the News.* There were twelve killed, some shot, some stab'd with their Spears, some knock'd down with their Hatchets. When we are in prosperity, Oh the little that we think of such dreadfull sights, and to see our dear Friends, and Relations ly bleeding out their heart-blood upon the ground. There was one who was chopt into the head with a Hatchet, and stript naked, and yet was crawling up and down. It is a solemn sight to see so many Christians lying in their blood, some here, and some there, like a company of Sheep torn by Wolves, All of them stript naked by a company of hell-hounds, roaring, singing, ranting and insulting, as if they would have torn our very hearts out; yet the Lord by his Almighty power preserved a number of us from death, for there were twenty-four of us taken alive and carried Captive.

I had often before this said, that if the Indians should come, I should chuse rather to be killed by them then taken alive but when it came to the tryal my mind changed; their glittering weapons so daunted my spirit, that I chose rather to go along with those (as I may say) ravenous Beasts, then that moment to end my dayes; and that I may the better declare what happened to me during that grievous Captivity, I shall particularly speak of the severall Removes we had up and down the Wilderness.

The First Remove

Now away we must go with those Barbarous Creatures, with our bodies wounded and bleeding, and our hearts no less than our bodies. About a mile we went that night, up upon a hill within sight of the Town, where they intended to lodge. There was hard by a vacant house (deserted by the English before, for fear of the Indians). I asked them whither I might not lodge in the house that night to which they answered, what will you love English men still? this was the dolefullest night that ever my eyes saw. Oh the roaring, and singing and danceing, and yelling of those black creatures in the night, which made the place a lively resemblance of hell. And as miserable was the wast that was there made, of Horses, Cattle, Sheep, Swine, Calves, Lambs, Roasting Pigs, and Fowl (which they had plundered in the Town) some roasting, some lying and burning, and some boyling to feed our merciless Enemies; who were joyful enough though we were disconsolate. To add to the dolefulness of the former day, and the dismalness of the present night: my thoughts ran upon my losses and sad bereaved condition. All was gone, my Husband gone (at least separated from me, he being in the Bay; and to add to my grief, the Indians told me they would kill him as he came homeward) my Children gone, my Relations and Friends gone, our House and home and all our comforts within door, and without, all was gone, (except my life) and I knew not but the next moment that might go too. There remained nothing to me but one poor wounded Babe, and it seemed at present worse than death that it was in such a pitiful condition, bespeaking Compassion, and I had no refreshing for it, nor suitable things to revive it. Little do many think what is the savageness and bruitishness of this barbarous Enemy, I even those that seem to profess more than others among them, when the English have fallen into their hands.

Those seven that were killed at Lancaster the summer before upon a Sabbath day, and the one that was afterward killed upon a week day, were slain and mangled in a barbarous manner, by one-ey'd John, and Marlborough's Praying Indians, which Capt. Mosely brought to Boston, as the Indians told me.

The Second Remove

But now, the next morning, I must turn my back upon the Town, and travel with them into the vast and desolate Wilderness, I knew not whither. It is not my tongue, or pen can express the sorrows of my heart, and bitterness of my spirit, that I had at this departure; but God was with me, in a wonderfull manner, carrying me along, and bearing up my spirit, that it did not quite fail. One of the Indians carried my poor wounded Babe upon a horse, it went moaning all along, I shall dy, I shall dy. I went on foot after it, with sorrow that cannot be exprest. At length I took it off the horse, and carried it in my armes till my strength failed, and I fell down with it: Then they set me upon a horse with my wounded Child in my lap, and there being no furniture upon the horse back, as we were going down a steep hill, we both fell over the horses head, at which they like inhumane creatures laught, and rejoyced to see it, though I thought we should there have ended our dayes, as overcome with so many difficulties. But the Lord renewed my strength still, and carried me along, that I might see more of his Power; yea, so much that I could never have thought of, had I not experienced it.

After this it quickly began to snow, and when night came on, they stopt: and now down I must sit in the snow, by a little fire, and a few boughs behind me, with my sick Child in my lap; and calling much for water, being now (through the wound) fallen into a violent Fever. My own wound also growing so stiff, that I could scarce sit down or rise up; yet so it must be, that I must sit all this cold winter night upon the cold snowy ground, with my sick Child in my armes, looking that every hour would be the last of its life; and having no Christian friend near me, either to comfort or help me. Oh, I may see the wonderfull power of God, that my Spirit did not utterly sink under my affliction: still the Lord upheld me with his gracious and mercifull Spirit, and we were both alive to see the light of the next morning.

The Third Remove

The morning being come, they prepared to go on their way. One of the Indians got up upon a horse, and they set me up behind him, with my poor sick Babe in my lap. A very wearisome and tedious day I had of it; what with my own wound, and my Childs being so exceeding sick, and in a lamentable condition with her wound. It may be easily judged what a poor feeble condition we were in, there being not the least crumb of refreshing that came within either of our mouths, from Wednesday night to Saturday night, except only a little cold water. This day in the afternoon, about an hour by Sun, we came to the place where they intended, *viz.* an Indian Town, called Wenimesset, Norward of Quabaug. When we were come, Oh the number of Pagans (now merciless enemies) that there came about me, that I may say as David, Psal. 27. 13, *I had fainted, unless I had believed,* etc. The next day was the Sabbath: I then remembered how careless I had been of Gods holy time, how many Sabbaths I had lost and mispent, and how evily I had walked in Gods sight; which lay so close unto my spirit, that it was easie for me to see how righteous it was with God to cut off the thread of my life, and cast me out of his presence for ever. Yet the Lord still shewed mercy to me, and upheld me; and as he wounded me with one hand, so he healed me with the other. This day there came to me one Robbert Pepper (a man belonging to Roxbury) who was taken in Captain Beers his Fight, and had been now a considerable time with the Indians; and up with them almost as far as Albany, to see king Philip, as he told me, and was now very lately come into these parts. Hearing, I say, that I was in this Indian Town, he obtained leave to come and see me. He told me, he himself was wounded in the leg at Captain Beers his Fight; and was not able some time to go, but as they carried him, and as he took Oaken leaves and laid to his wound, and through the blessing of God he was able to travel again. Then I took Oaken leaves and laid to my side, and with the blessing of God it cured me also; yet before the cure was wrought, I may say, as it is in Psal. 38. 5, 6. *My wounds stink and are corrupt, I am troubled, I am bowed down greatly, I go mourning all the day long.* I sat much alone with a poor wounded Child in my lap, which moaned night and day, having nothing to revive the body, or cheer the spirits of her, but in stead of that, sometimes one Indian would come and tell me one hour, that your Master will knock your Child in the head, and then a second, and then a third, your Master will quickly knock your Child in the head.

This was the comfort I had from them, miserable comforters are ye all, as he said. Thus nine dayes I sat upon my knees, with my Babe in my lap, till my flesh was raw again; my Child being even ready to depart this sorrowful world, they bade me carry it out to another Wigwam (I suppose because they would not be troubled with such spectacles) Whither I went with a very heavy heart, and down I sat with the picture of death in my lap. About two houres in the night, my sweet Babe like a Lambe departed this life, on Feb. 18, 1675. It being about six yeares, and five months old. It was nine dayes from the first wounding, in this miserable condition, without any refreshing of one nature or other, except a little cold water. I cannot, but take notice, how at another time I could not bear to be in the room where any dead person was, but now the case is changed; I must and could ly down by my dead Babe, side by side all the night after. I have thought since of the wonderfull goodness of God to me, in preserving me in the use of my reason and senses, in that distressed time, that I did not use wicked and violent means to end my own miserable life. In the morning, when they understood that my child was dead they sent for me home to my Masters Wigwam: (by my Master in this writing, must be understood Quanopin, who was a Saggamore, and married King Phillips wives Sister; not that he first took me, but I was sold to him by another Narrhaganset Indian, who took me when first I came out of the Garison). I went to take up my dead child in my arms to carry it with me, but they bid me let it alone: there was no resisting, but goe I must and leave it. When I had been at my masters wigwam, I took the first opportunity I could get, to go look after my dead child: when I came I askt them what they had done with it? then they told me it was upon the hill: then they went and shewed me where it was, where I saw the ground was newly digged, and there they told me they had buried it: There I left that Child in the Wilderness, and must commit it, and my self also in this Wilderness-condition, to him who is above all. God having taken away this dear Child, I went to see my daughter Mary, who was at this same Indian Town, at a Wigwam not very far off, though we had little liberty or opportunity to see one another. She was about ten years old, and taken from the door at first by a Praying Ind and afterward sold for a gun. When I came in sight, she would fall a weeping; at which they were provoked, and would not let me come near her, but bade me be gone; which was a heart-cutting word to me. I had one Child dead, another in the Wilderness, I knew not where, the third they would not let me come near to: *Me* (as he said) *have ye bereaved of my Children, Joseph is not, and*

Simeon is not, and ye will take Benjamin also, all these things are against me. I could not sit still in this condition, but kept walking from one place to another. And as I was going along, my heart was even overwhelm'd with the thoughts of my condition, and that I should have Children, and a Nation which I knew not ruled over them. Whereupon I earnestly entreated the Lord, that he would consider my low estate, and shew me a token for good, and if it were his blessed will, some sign and hope of some relief. And indeed quickly the Lord answered, in some measure, my poor prayers: for as I was going up and down mourning and lamenting my condition, my Son came to me, and asked me how I did; I had not seen him before, since the destruction of the Town, and I knew not where he was, till I was informed by himself, that he was amongst a smaller percel of Indians, whose place was about six miles off; with tears in his eyes, he asked me whether his Sister Sarah was dead; and told me he had seen his Sister Mary; and prayed me, that I would not be troubled in reference to himself. The occasion of his coming to see me at this time, was this: There was, as I said, about six miles from us, a smal Plantation of Indians, where it seems he had been during his Captivity: and at this time, there were some Forces of the Ind. gathered out of our company, and some also from them (among whom was my Sons master) to go to assault and burn Medfield: In this time of the absence of his master, his dame brought him to see me. I took this to be some gracious answer to my earnest and unfeigned desire. The next day, *viz:* to this, the Indians returned from Medfield, all the company, for those that belonged to the other small company came thorough the Town that now we were at. But before they came to us, Oh! the outragious roaring and hooping that there was: They began their din about a mile before they came to us. By their noise and hooping they signified how many they had destroyed (which was at that time twenty three.) Those that were with us at home, were gathered together as soon as they heard the hooping, and every time that the other went over their number, these at home gave a shout, that the very Earth rung again: And thus they continued till those that had been upon the expedition were come up to the Sagamores Wigwam; and then, Oh, the hideous insulting and triumphing that there was over some Englishmens scalps that they had taken (as their manner is) and brought with them. I cannot but take notice of the wonderfull mercy of God to me in those afflictions, in sending me a Bible. One of the Indians that came from Medfield fight, had brought some plunder, came to me, and asked me, if I would have a Bible, he had got one in his Basket. I was glad of it, and asked him, whether he thought the Indians would let me read? he answered, yes: So I took the Bible, and in that melancholy time, it came into my mind to read first the 28. Chap. of Deut., which I did, and when I had read it, my dark heart wrought on this manner, That there was no mercy for me, that the blessings were gone, and the curses come in their room, and that I had lost my opportunity. But the Lord helped me still to go on reading till I came to Chap. 30 the seven first verses, where I found, There was mercy promised again, if we would return to him by repentance; and though we were scatered from one end of the Earth to the other, yet the Lord would gather us together, and turn all those curses upon our Enemies. I do not desire to live to forget this Scripture, and what comfort it was to me.

Now the Ind. began to talk of removing from this place, some one way, and some another. There were now besides my self nine English Captives in this place (all of them Children, except one Woman). I got an opportunity to go and take my leave of them; they being to go one way, and I another, I asked them whether they were earnest with God for deliverance, they told me, they did as they were able, and it was some comfort to me, that the Lord stirred up Children to look to him. The Woman *viz.* Goodwife Joslin told me, she should never see me again, and that she could find in her heart to run away; I wisht her not to run away by any means, for we were near thirty miles from any English Town, and she very big with Child, and had but one week to reckon; and another Child in her Arms, two years old, and bad Rivers there were to go over, and we were feeble, with our poor and course entertainment. I had my Bible with me, I pulled it out, and asked her whether she would read; we opened the Bible and lighted in Psal. 27, in which Psalm we especially took notice of that, *ver. ult., Wait on the Lord, Be of good courage, and he shall strengthen thine Heart, wait I say on the Lord.*

4. PIERRE DE CHARLEVOIX, *JOURNAL OF A VOYAGE TO NORTH AMERICA*

The Jesuit Pierre de Charlevoix (1682–1761) traveled extensively in the Americas, and he wrote numerous descriptive accounts of his journeys, including *Journal of a Voyage to North America*. The following excerpt is interesting because Charlevoix describes the political role of women in Iroquois society. European settlers in North America usually viewed native treatment of women disparagingly because the women seemed to work harder than the men. What they often failed to realize, however, was that native communities in North America organized male and female labor differently than in Europe. Furthermore, because native women contributed significantly to the economic life of the community and frequently controlled the resources that they produced, they exercised comparatively greater political authority in their own society than did European women. Charlevoix's admiring account of Iroquois government shows that, though men still controlled high offices, informally women could organize to effect a change in policy and even a change in leadership. Women were respected and influential members of Iroquois society.

Journal of a Voyage to North America

It must be agreed, Madam, that the nearer we view our Indians, the more good qualities we discover in them: most of the principles which serve to regulate their conduct, the general maxims by which they govern themselves, and the essential part of their character, discover nothing of the barbarian. . . .

In the northern parts, and wherever the Algonquin tongue prevails, the dignity of chief is elective; and the whole ceremony of election and installation consists in some feasts, accompanied with dances and songs: the chief elect likewise never fails to make the panegyrick of his predecessor, and to invoke his genius. Amongst the Hurons, where this dignity is hereditary, the succession is continued through the women, so that at the death of a chief, it is not his own, but his sister's son who succeeds him; or, in default of which, his nearest relation in the female line. When the whole branch happens to be extinct, the noblest matron of the tribe or in the nation chuses the person she approves of most, and declares him chief. . . .

Nay more, each family has a right to chuse a counsellor of its own, and an assistant to the chief, who is to watch for their interest; and without whose consent the chief can undertake nothing. These counsellors are, above all things, to have an eye to the public treasaury; and it is properly they who determine the uses it is to be put to. They are invested with this character in a general council, but they do not acquaint their allies with it, as they do at the elections and installations of their chief. Amongst the Huron nations, the women name the counsellors, and often chuse persons of their own sex.

This body of counsellors or assistants is the highest of all; the next is that of the elders, consisting of all those who have come to the years of maturity. I have not been able to find exactly what this age is. The last of all is that of the warriors; this comprehends all who are able to bear arms. This body has often at its head, the chief of the nation or town; but he must first have distinguished himself by some signal action of bravery; if not, he is obliged to serve as a subaltern, that is, as a single centinel; there being no degrees in the militia of the Indians.

In fact, a large body may have several chiefs, this title being given to all who ever commanded; but they are not therefore the less subject to him who leads the party; a kind of general, without character or real authority, who has power neither to reward nor punish, whom his soldiers are at liberty to abandon at pleasure and with impunity, and whose orders notwithstanding are scarce ever disputed: so true it is, that amongst a people who are guided by reason, and inspired with sentiments of honour and love for their country, independence is not destructive of subordination; and, that a free and voluntary obedience is that on which we can always rely with the greatest certainty. Moreover, the qualities requisite are, that he be fortunate, of undoubted courage, and perfectly disinterested. It is no miracle, that a person possessed of such eminent qualities should be obeyed.

The women have the chief authority amongst all the nations of the Huron language; if we except the Iroquois canton of Onneyouth, in which it is in both sexes alternately. But if this be their lawful constitution, their practice is seldom agreeable to it. In fact, the men never tell the women any thing they would have to be kept secret; and rarely any affair of consequence is communicated to them, though all is done in their name, and the chiefs are no more than their lieutenants. What I have told your Grace of the grandmother of the hereditary chief of the Hurons of the Narrows, who could never obtain a missionary for her own town, is a convincing proof that the real authority of the women is very small: I have been however assured, that they always deliberate first on whatever is proposed in council; and that they afterwards give the result of their deliberation to the chiefs, who make the report of it to the general council, composed of the elders; but in all probability this is done only for form's sake, and with the restrictions I have already mentioned. The warriors likewise consult together, on what relates to their particular province, but can conclude nothing of importance which concerns the nation or town; all being subject to the examination and controul of the council of elders, who judge in the last resource.

It must be acknowledged, that proceedings are carried on in these assemblies with a wisdom and a coolness, and a knowledge of affairs, and I may add generally with a probity, which would have done honour to the areopagus of Athens, or to the senate of Rome, in the most glorious days of those republics: the reason of this is, that nothing is resolved upon with precipitation; and that those violent passions, which have so much disgraced the politics even of Christians, have never prevailed amongst the Indians over the public good. . . .

Each tribe has an orator in every town, which orators are the only persons who have a liberty to speak in the public councils and general assemblies: they always speak well and to the purpose. Besides this natural eloquence, and which none who are acquainted with them will dispute, they have a perfect knowledge of the interests of their employers, and an address in placing the best side of their own cause in the most advantageous light, which nothing can exceed. On some occasions, the women have an orator, who speaks in their name, or rather acts as their interpreter.

Figure 13.1 Preparing flax fiber for manufacture of linen. Courtesy of The Granger Collection.

Study Questions

1. Compare Doña Marina and Eva (Krotoa) from the *Journal of Van Riebeeck* (chapter 9). In what ways did their female gender influence/determine their role as interpreters? Their relations with the Dutch? With the native peoples?
2. What were the difficulties encountered by Marie de l'Incarnation during her time in New France?
3. What do the accounts of Mary Rowlandson and de Charlevoix tell us about the role of women in Amerindian society?
4. In what ways do these two accounts reflect European perceptions about gender roles?

Suggested Readings

Brown, Kathleen M. *Good Wives, Nasty Wenches and Anxious Patriarchs: Gender, Race, and Power in Colonial America.* Chapel Hill: Institute of Early American History and Culture, 1996.

Clinton, Catherine, and Michele Gillespie, eds. *The Devil's Lane. Sex and Race in the Early South.* New York and London: Oxford University Press, 1997.

Gaspar, David Barry, and Darlene Clark Hine, eds. *More Than Chattel: Black Women and Slavery in the Americas.* Bloomington: Indiana University Press, 1996.

Gutierrez, Ramon. *When Jesus Came, the Corn Mothers Went Away. Marriage, Sexuality and Power in New Mexico, 1500–1846.* Stanford, CA: Stanford University Press, 1992.

Web Sites

1. Margaret Brent

   http://women.eb.com/women/articles/Brent_Margaret. html

2. Iroquois Constitution

   www.law.ou.edu/hist/iroquois.html

3. Sexuality and the Invasion of America: 1492–1806

   http://www.virtualschool.edu/mon/SocialConstruction/SexualityAndInvasion.html

14

The Plantation Complex and the Slave Trade
1650–1800 A.D.

TEXTS

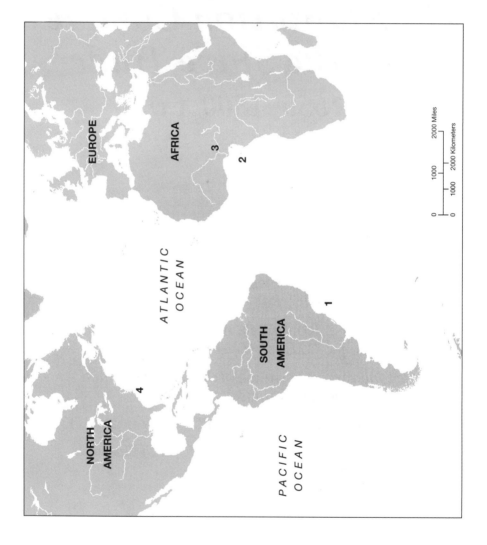

The discovery of the New World began a process that involved Europeans in important contacts with non-Europeans. Beginning almost as soon as Columbus returned to Spain, European powers established colonies throughout the Americas that provided an outlet for a wide variety of free migrants from Europe. This process of settlement meant, between 1500 and 1820, the movement of millions of people across the Atlantic. About 4 million of these came from European countries, as hidalgos, religious minorities, landless farmers, and impecunious artisans found their ways from the seacoasts of Europe across the ocean, sometimes as members of military expeditions founding settlements, at times as indentured servants bound to serve a master for several years to pay for their passage. Their arrival in the New World created constant contact between Europeans and the indigenous peoples of America. Virtually from the beginnings of European settlement, the colonists depended on Native Americans for food, advice about agriculture, and knowledge about rivers, streams, and paths through the forests of the continent. The increasing number of Europeans living in the New World opened the way for the creation of a series of economic, social, demographic, and political linkages across the Atlantic Ocean. The products of the North American and South American colonies found markets in Europe and in other colonies, and a set of trade relations developed across the Atlantic basin as Europeans increased their exploitation of the wealth of the New World. [1]

The inability of native populations or free migrants from Europe to provide an adequate labor supply for these plantations led to another form of exploitation, the import of slaves from Africa. The slave trade [2, 3, 4, 5] completed the formation of a plantation complex that involved the New World, Europe, and Africa in an intricate set of economic relationships, drawing timber, furs, and food from North America and Europe; slaves from Africa; and sugar, rum, indigo, coffee, and cotton from the slave plantations of the New World tropics. Geographically, it ran from the southern part of Brazil to the Mason-Dixon line in North America. Between the fifteenth century and the nineteenth, around 10 million slaves were brought across the Atlantic to provide the labor for this complex. Several more million Africans did not survive the trip across the infamous Middle Passage, dying en route.

The slave trade to the New World was therefore not only an aspect of European contact with the Western Hemisphere, but also one of the most significant causes of contact between Europeans and Africans in the years between 1500 and 1800. Portuguese and Spanish slavers moved slaves from Senegambia, Upper Guinea, and Angola to the Caribbean Islands, Brazil, Mexico, and Peru in a trade that began in the early sixteenth century and peaked in the seventeenth century. A larger cycle began in the seventeenth century with the expansion of trade between Europe and the Americas. This cycle principally involved English, Dutch, French, and Brazilian slave traders carrying their human cargoes from western Africa (the Bight of Benin, Angola, the Bight of Biafra, and the Gold Coast) to British and French territories in the Caribbean, Bahia, Brazil, and British North America. This cycle peaked in the eighteenth century. The slave trade was abolished by Great Britain and the United States in 1808, although the end of sales and emancipation of existing slaves did not take place until the middle of the nineteenth century. By this time, the plantation complex itself was in decline, undercut by the economic and social effects of industrialization, as well as the moral reservations of a growing number of Europeans and Americans about the slave trade and slavery itself.

1. WILLIAM DAMPIER, *A VOYAGE TO NEW-HOLLAND IN THE YEAR 1699*

Captain William Dampier (1651–1715) circumnavigated the globe three times, acquiring a reputation not only as a navigator but also as a hydrographer, naturalist, author, and even pirate. Dampier went to sea as a teenager, sailing on merchant ships to Newfoundland and Java before serving in the British Navy in a war with the Dutch in the 1670s. By the end of the 1670s, he had joined in the activities of the casual buccaneers of the Caribbean. In the late 1680s, he traveled on a series of ships that took him from the coast of Sierra Leone across the Pacific, to India, and around the Cape of Good Hope to England, a voyage recounted in his *A New Voyage Round the World* published in 1697.

In 1699, he commanded the *Roebuck* on a voyage to investigate New Holland, Terra Australis, and New Guinea. Dampier's *Voyage to New Holland* (1702) recounted the events of this voyage, including his stop on his way to the Pacific at Bahia in the Portuguese colony of Brazil. His account of the port describes the comings and goings of the ships that made up the sinews of the network of trade in goods and humans that bound North and South America across the Atlantic with Africa and Europe. It also shows the importance of African slavery in the life of this colonial settlement. Dampier's third major voyage was as captain of a privateer that left England in 1703, raided the South American coast, then proceeded across the Pacific to Java, where he was seized by Dutch authorities and only managed to return to England in 1707. He made one more voyage to the New World, as pilot and advisor of a privateering expedition that sailed in 1708.

Captain Dampier's Voyages

A great many Merchants always reside at Bahia; for 'tis a Place of great Trade: I found here above 30 great Ships from Europe, with 2 of the King of Portugal's Ships of War for their Convoy; beside 2 Ships that traded to Africa only, either to Angola, Gamba, or other

Places on the Coast of Guinea; and Abundance of small Craft, that only run to and fro on this Coast, carrying Commodities from one Part of Brazil to another.

The Merchants that live here are said to be rich, and to have many Negro-Slaves in their Houses, both of Men and Women. Themselves are chiefly Portugueze, Foreigners having but little Commerce with them; yet here was one Mr. Cock an English Merchant, a very civil Gentleman and of good Repute. He had a Patent to be our English Consul, but did not Care to take upon him any publick Character, because English Ships seldom come hither, here having been none in 11 or 12 Years before this Time. Here was also a Dane, and a French Merchant or two; but all have their Effects transported to and from Europe in Portugueze Ships, none of any other Nation being admitted to trade hither. There is a Custom-house by the Sea-side, where all Goods imported or exported are en-tred. And to prevent Abuses there are 5 or 6 Boats that take their Turns to row about the Harbour, searching any Boats they suspect to be running of Goods.

The chief Commodities that the European Ships bring hither, are Linnen-Cloaths, both coarse and fine; some Woollens also, as Bays, Searges, Perpetuana's, &c. Hats, Stock-ings, both of Silk and Thread, Bisket-bread, Wheatflower, Wine (chiefly Port), Oil-Olive, But-ter, Cheese, &c. and Salt-beef and Pork would there also be good Commodities. They bring hither also Iron, and all Sorts of Iron-Tools; Pewter-Vessels of all Sorts, as Dishes, Plates, Spoons, &c. Looking-glass, Beads, and other Toys; and the Ships that touch at St. Jago bring thence, as I said, Cotton-Cloath, which is afterwards sent to Angola.

The European Ships carry from hence Sugar, Tobacco, either in Roll or Snuff, never in Leaf, that I know of: These are the Staple Commodities. Besides which, here are Dye-woods, as Fustick, &c., with Woods for other Uses, as speckled Wood, Brazil, &c. They also carry home raw Hides, Tallow, Train-oil of Whales, &c. Here are also kept tame Monkeys, Parrots, Parrakites, &c. which the Seamen carry home.

The Sugar of this Country is much better than that which we bring home from our Plantations: For all the Sugar that is made here is clay'd, which makes it whiter and finer than our Muscovada, as we call our unrefin'd Sugar. Our Planters seldom refine any with Clay, unless sometimes a little to send Home as Presents for their Friends in England. Their way of doing it is by taking some of the whitest Clay and mixing it with Water, till 'tis like Cream. With this they fill up the Pans of Sugar, that are sunk 2 or 3 Inches below the Brim by the draining of the Molasses out of it: First scraping off the thin hard Crust of the Sugar that lies at the Top, and would hinder the Water of the Clay from soaking through the Sugar of the Pan. The refining is made by this Percolation. For 10 or 12 Days Time that the clayish Liquor lies soaking down the Pan, the white Water whitens the Sugar as it passes thro' it; and the gross Body of the Clay its self grows hard on the Top, and may be taken off at Pleasure; when scraping off with a Knife the very upper-part of the sugar, which will be a little sullied, that which is underneath will be white almost to the Bottom: And such as is called Brazil Sugar is thus whitened. When I was here this Sugar was sold for 50s. per 100 lb. And the Bottoms of the Pots, which is very coarse Sugar, for about 20s. per 100 lb. both Sorts being then scarce; for here was not enough to lade the Ships, and therefore some of them were to lye here till the next Season.

The European Ships commonly arrive here in February or March, and they have generally quick Passages; finding at that Time of the Year brisk Gales to bring them to the Line, little Trouble, then, in crossing it, and brisk E. N. E. Winds afterwards to bring them hither. They commonly return from hence about the latter End of May, or in June. 'Twas said when I was here that the Ships would sail hence the 20th Day of May; and therefore they were all very busy, some in taking in their Goods, others in careening and making themselves ready. The Ships that come hither usually careen at their first coming; here being a Hulk belonging to the King for that Purpose. This Hulk is under the Charge of the Superintendent I spoke of, who has a certain Sum of Money for every Ship that careens by her. He also provides Firing and other Necessaries for that Purpose: And the Ships do commonly hire of the Merchants here each 2 Cables to moor by all the Time they lye here, and so save their own Hempen Cables; for these are made of a Sort of Hair, that grows on a certain Kind of Trees, hanging down from the Top of their Bodies, and is very like the black Coyre in the East-Indies, if not the same. These Cables are strong and lasting: And so much for the European Ships.

The Ships that use the Guinea-Trade are small Vessels in comparison of the former. They carry out from hence Rum, Sugar, the Cotton-Cloaths of St. Jago, Beads, &c. and bring in Return, Gold, Ivory, and Slaves; making very good Returns.

The small Craft that belong to this Town are chiefly imployed in carrying European Goods from Bahia, the Center of the Brasilian Trade, to the other Places on this Coast; bringing back hither Sugar, Tobacco, &c. They are sailed chiefly with Negro-Slaves; and about Christmas these are mostly imployed in Whale-killing; For about that Time of the Year a Sort of Whales, as they call them, are very thick on this Coast. They come in also into the Harbours and inland Lakes, where the Seamen go out and kill them. The Fat of them is boiled to Oil; the Lean is eaten by the Slaves and poor People: And I was told by one that had frequently eaten of it, that the Flesh was very sweet and wholesome. These are said to be but small Whales; yet here are so many, and so easily killed, that they get a great deal of Money by it. Those that strike them buy their Licence for it of the King: And I was inform'd that he receives 30000 Dollars per Annum for this Fishery. All the small Vessels that use this Coasting Traffick are built here; and so are some Men of War also for the King's Service. There was one a building when I was here, a Ship of 40 or 50 Guns: And the Timber of this Country is very good and proper for this Purpose. I was told it was very strong, and more durable than any we have in Europe; and they have enough of it. As for their Ships that use the European Trade, some of them that I saw there were English built, taken from us by the French, during the late War, and sold by them to the Portugueze.

Besides Merchants and others that trade by Sea from this Port, here are other pretty wealthy Men, and several Artificers and Trades-men of most Sorts, who by Labour and Industry maintain themselves very well; especially such as can arrive at the Purchase of a Negro-Slave or two. And indeed, excepting people of the lowest Degree of all, here are scarce any but what keep Slaves in their Houses. The richer Sort, besides the Slaves of both Sexes whom they keep for servile Uses in their Houses, have Men Slaves who wait on them aboard, for State; either running by their Horse-sides when they ride out, or to carry them to and fro on their Shoulders in the Town when they make short Visits near Home. Every Gentleman or Merchant is provided with Things necessary for this Sort of Carriage. The main Thing is a pretty large Cotton Hammock of the West-India Fashion, but mostly dyed blue, with large Fringes of the same, hanging down on each Side. This is carried on the Negro's Shoulders by the help of a Bambo about 12 or 14 Foot long, to which the Hammock is hung; and a Covering comes over the Pole, hanging down on each Side like a Curtain: So that the Person so carry'd cannot be seen unless he pleases; but may either lye down, having pillows for his Head; or may sit up by being a little supported with these Pillows, and by letting both his Legs hang out over one side of the Hammock. When he hath a Mind to be seen he puts by his Curtain, and salutes every one of his Acquaintance whom he meets in the Streets; for they take a Piece of Pride in greeting one another from their Hammocks, and will hold long Conferences thus in the Street: But then their 2 Slaves who carry the Hammock have each a strong well-made Staff, with a fine Iron Fork at the upper End, and a sharp Iron below, like the Rest for a Musket, which they stick fast in the Ground, and let the Pole or Bambo of the Hammock rest upon them, till their Master's Business or the Complement is over. There is scarce a Man of any Fashion, especially a Woman, will pass the Streets but so carried in a Hammock. The Chief Mechanick Traders here, are Smiths, Hatters, Shoemakers, Tanners, Sawyers, Carpenters, Coopers, &c. Here are also Taylors, Butchers, &c. which last kill the Bullocks very dexterously, sticking them at one Blow with a sharp-pointed Knife in the Nape of the Neck, having first drawn them close to a Rail; but they dress them very slovenly. It being Lent when I came hither, there was no buying any Flesh till Easter-Eve, when a great Number of Bullocks were kill'd at once in the Slaughter-houses within the Town, Men, Women and Children flocking thither with great Joy to buy, and a Multitude of Dogs, almost starv'd, following them; for whom the Meat seem'd fittest, it was so lean. All these Trades-men buy Negroes, and train them up to their several Employments, which is a great Help to them; and they having so frequent Trade to Angola, and other Parts of Guinea, they have a constant Supply of Blacks both for their Plantations and Town. These Slaves are very useful in this Place for Carriage, as Porters; for as here is a great Trade by Sea, and the Landing-place is at the Foot of a Hill, too steep for drawing with Carts, so there is great need of Slaves to carry Goods up into the Town, especially for the inferiour Sort: But the Merchants have also the Convenience of a great Crane that goes with Ropes or Pullies, one End of which goes up while the other goes down. The House in which this Crane is, stands on the Brow of the Hill towards the Sea, hanging over the Precipice; and there are Planks set shelving against the Bank from thence to the Bottom, against which the Goods lean or slide as they are hoisted up or let down. The Negro-Slaves in this Town are so numerous, that they make up the greatest Part or Bulk of the Inhabitants: Every House, as I said, having some, both Men and Women, of them. Many of the Portugueze, who are Batchelors, keep of these black Women for Misses, tho' they know the Danger they are in of being poyson'd by them, if ever they give them any Occasion of Jealousy. A Gentleman of my Acquaintance, who had been familiar with his Cook-maid, lay under some such Apprehensions from her when I was there. These Slaves also of either Sex will easily be engaged to do any Sort of Mischief; even to Murder, if they are hired to do it, especially in the Night; for which Reason, I kept my Men on board as much as I could; for one of the French King's Ships being here, had several Men murther'd by them in the Night, as I was credibly inform'd.

2. ALEXANDER FALCONBRIDGE, AN ACCOUNT OF THE SLAVE TRADE ON THE COAST OF AFRICA

Alexander Falconbridge (?–1792) was a British surgeon who served on a number of slave ships during the 1780s on voyages from Bonny, Old and New Calabar, and Angola on the African coast to the West Indies. His experiences on these voyages formed the basis for this pamphlet, published in 1788. Although his position as surgeon on slavers allowed him to be critical of the slave trade, Falconbridge nonetheless was a participant in it, a position that affected his evaluation. His description is therefore different from that in the following selection by Olaudah Equiano.

An Account of the Slave Trade on the Coast of Africa

After permission has been obtained for *breaking trade*, as it is termed; the captains go ashore, from time to time, to examine the negroes that are exposed to sale, and to make their purchases. The unhappy wretches thus disposed of, are bought by the black traders at fairs, which are held for that purpose, at the distance of upwards of two hundred miles from the sea coast; and these fairs are said to be supplied from an interior part of the country. Many negroes, upon being questioned relative to the places of their nativity have asserted, that they have travelled during the revolution of several moons, (their usual method of calculating time) before they have reached the places where they were purchased by the black traders. At these fairs, which are held at uncertain periods, but generally every six weeks, several thousands are frequently exposed to sale, who had been collected from all parts of the country for a very considerable distance round. While I was upon the coast, during one of the voyages I made, the black traders brought down, in different canoes, from twelve to fifteen hundred negroes, which had been purchased at one fair. They consisted chiefly of men and boys, the women seldom exceeding a third of the whole number. From forty to two hundred negroes are generally purchased at a time by the black traders, according to the opulence of the buyer; and consist of those of all ages, from a month, to sixty years and upwards. Scarce any age or situation is deemed an exception, the price being proportionable. Women sometimes form a part of them, who happen to be so far advanced in their pregnancy, as to be delivered during their journey from the fairs to the coast; and I have frequently seen instances of deliveries on board ship. The slaves purchased at these fairs are only for the supply of the markets at Bonny, and Old and New Calabar.

There is great reason to believe, that most of the negroes shipped off from the coast of Africa, are *kidnapped*. But the extreme care taken by the black traders to prevent the Europeans from gaining any intelligence of their modes of proceeding; the great distance inland from whence the negroes are brought, and our ignorance of their language, (with which, very frequently, the black traders themselves are equally unacquainted) prevent our obtaining such information on this head as we could with. I have, however, by means of occasional inquiries, made through interpreters, procured some intelligence relative to the point, and such, as I think, puts the matter beyond a doubt.

From these I shall select the following striking instances:—While I was in employ on board one of the slave ships, a negroe informed me, that being one evening invited to drink with some of the black traders, upon his going away, they attempted to seize him. As he was very active, he evaded their design, and got out of their hands. He was however prevented from effecting his escape by a large dog, which laid hold of him, and compelled him to submit. These creatures are kept by many of the traders for that purpose; and being trained to the inhuman sport, they appear to be much pleased with it.

I was likewise told by a negroe woman, that as she was on her return home, one evening, from some neighbours, to whom she had been making a visit by invitation, she was kidnapped; and, notwithstanding she was big with child, sold for a slave. This transaction happened a considerable way up the country, and she had passed through the hands of several purchasers before she reached the ship. A man and his son, according to their own information, were seized by professed kidnappers, while they were planting yams, and sold for slaves. This likewise happened in the interior parts of the country, and after passing through several hands, they were purchased for the ship to which I belonged.

It frequently happens, that those who kidnap others, are themselves, in their turns, seized and sold. A negro in the West-Indies informed me, that after having been employed in kidnapping others, he had experienced this reverse. And he assured me, that it was a common incident among his countrymen.

Continual enmity is thus fostered among the negroes of Africa, and all social intercourse between them destroyed; which most assuredly would not be the case, had they not these opportunities of finding a ready sale for each other.

During my stay on the coast of Africa, I was an eye-witness of the following transaction:—A black trader invited a negroe, who resided a little way up the country, to come and see him. After the entertainment was over, the trader proposed to his guest, to treat him with a sight of one of the ships lying in the river. The unsuspicious countryman readily consented, and accompanied the trader in a canoe to the side of the ship, which he viewed with pleasure and astonishment. While he was thus employed, some black traders on board, who appeared to be in the secret, leaped into the canoe, seized the unfortunate man, and dragging him into the ship, immediately sold him.

Previous to my being in this employ, I entertained a belief, as many others have done, that the kings and principal men *breed* negroes for sale, as we do cattle. During the different times I was in the country, I took no little pains to satisfy myself in this particular; but notwithstanding I made many inquiries, I was not able to obtain the least intelligence of this being the case, which it is more than probable I should have done, had such a practice prevailed. All the information I could procure, confirms me in the belief, that to *kidnapping,* and to crimes, (and many of these fabricated as a pretext) the slave trade owes its chief support.

As soon as the wretched Africans, purchased at the fairs, fall into the hands of the black traders, they experience an earnest of those dreadful sufferings which they are doomed in future to undergo. And there is not the least room to doubt, but that even before they can reach the fairs, great numbers perish from cruel usage, want of food, travelling through inhospitable deserts, &c. They are brought from the places where they are purchased to Bonny, &c. in canoes; at the bottom of which they lie, having their hands tied with a kind of willow twigs, and a strict watch is kept over them. Their usage in other respects, during the time of the passage, which generally lasts several days, is equally cruel. Their allowance of food is so scanty, that it is barely sufficient to support nature. They are, besides, much exposed to the violent rains which frequently fall here, being covered only with mats that afford but a slight defence; and as there is usually water at the bottom of the canoes, from their leaking, they are scarcely ever dry.

Nor do these unhappy beings, after they become the property of the Europeans (from whom, as a more civilized people, more humanity might naturally be expected) find their situation in the least amended. Their treatment is no less rigorous. The men negroes, on being brought aboard the ship, are immediately fastened together, two and two, by hand-cuffs on their wrists, and by irons rivetted on their legs. They are then sent down between the decks, and placed in an apartment partitioned off for that purpose. The women likewise are placed in a separate apartment between decks, but without being ironed. And an adjoining room, on the same deck, is besides appointed for the boys. Thus are they all placed in different apartments.

But at the same time, they are frequently stowed so close, as to admit of no other posture than lying on their sides. Neither will the height between decks, unless directly under the grating, permit them the indulgence of an erect posture; especially where there are platforms, which is generally the case. These platforms are a kind of shelf, about eight or nine feet in breadth, extending from the side of the ship towards the centre. They are placed nearly midway between the decks, at the distance of two or three feet from each deck. Upon these the negroes are stowed in the same manner as they are on the deck underneath.

3. THE INTERESTING NARRATIVE OF THE LIFE OF OLAUDAH EQUIANO, WRITTEN BY HIMSELF

Olaudah Equiano (1745–1797) was born a member of the Nigerian Ibo tribe in Africa. When he was eleven years old, he was kidnapped by slave traders. Sold as a slave, he was shipped across the Middle Passage to plantations in the West Indies and Virginia. After gaining his freedom in 1766, Equiano lived in England; he died there in 1797. This account of his life was written in 1788 as a part of a protest campaign in England against the slave trade. His description of his abduction and passage to the Western Hemisphere conveys the brutality and disorientation of the slave trade as few other descriptions could.

The Life of Olaudah Equiano

I hope the reader will not think I have trespassed on his patience in introducing myself to him with some account of the manners and customs of my country. They had been implanted in me with great care, and made an impression on my mind, which time could not erase, and which all the adversity and variety of fortune I have since experienced served only to rivet and record; for, whether the love of one's country be real or imaginary, or a lesson of reason, or an instinct of nature, I still look back with pleasure on the first scenes of my life, though that pleasure has been for the most part mingled with sorrow.

I have already acquainted the reader with the time and place of my birth. My father, besides many slaves, had a numerous family, of which seven lived to grow up, including myself and a sister, who was the only daughter. As I was the youngest of the sons, I became, of course, the greatest favourite with my mother, and was always with her; and she used to take particular pains to form my mind. I was trained up from my earliest years in the art of war; my daily exercise was shooting and throwing javelins; and my mother adorned me with emblems, after the manner of our greatest warriors. In this way I grew up till I was turned the age of eleven, when an end was put to my happiness in the following manner:—Generally when the grown people in the neighbourhood were gone far in the fields to labour, the children assembled together in some of the neighbours' premises to play; and commonly some of us used to get up a tree to look out for any assailant, or kidnapper, that might come upon us; for they sometimes took those opportunities of our parents' absence to attack and carry off as many as they could seize. One day, as I was watching at the top of a tree in our yard, I saw one of those people come into the yard of our next neighbour but one, to kidnap, there being many stout young people in it. Immediately on this I gave the alarm of the rogue, and he was surrounded by the stoutest of them, who entangled him with cords, so that he could not escape till some of the grown people came and secured him. But alas! ere long it was my fate to be thus attacked, and to be carried off, when none of the grown people were nigh. One day, when all our people were gone out to their works as usual, and only I and my dear sister were left to mind the house, two men and a woman got over our walls, and in a moment seized us both, and, without giving us time to cry out, or make resistance, they stopped our mouths, and ran off with us into the nearest wood. Here they tied our hands, and continued to carry us as far as they could, till night came on, when we reached a small house, where the robbers halted for refreshment, and spent the night. We were then unbound, but were unable to take any food; and, being quite overpowered by fatigue and grief, our only relief was some sleep, which allayed our misfortune for a short time. The next morning we left the house, and continued travelling all the day. For a long time we had kept the woods, but at last we came into a road which I believed I knew. I had now some hopes of being delivered; for we had advanced but a little way before I discovered some people at a distance, on which I began to cry out for their assistance: but my cries had no other effect than to make them tie me faster and stop my mouth, and then they put me into a large sack. They also stopped my sister's mouth, and tied her hands; and in this manner we proceeded till we were out of the sight of these people. When we went to rest the following night they offered us some victuals; but we refused it; and the only comfort we had was in being in one another's arms all that night, and bathing each other with our tears. But alas! we were soon deprived of even the small comfort of weeping together. The next day proved a day of greater sorrow than I had yet experienced; for my sister and I were then separated, while we lay clasped in each other's arms. It was in vain that we besought them not to part us; she was torn from me, and immediately carried away, while I was left in a state of distraction not to be described. I cried and grieved continually; and for several days I did not eat any thing but what they forced into my mouth. At length, after many days travelling, during which I had often changed masters, I got into the hands of a chieftain, in a very pleasant country. This man had two wives and some children, and they all used me extremely well, and did all they could to comfort me; particularly the first wife, who was something like my mother. Although I was a great many days journey from my father's house, yet these people spoke exactly the same language with us. This first master of mine, as I may call him, was a smith, and my principal employment was working his bellows, which were the same kind as I had seen in my vicinity. They were in some respects not unlike the stoves here in gentlemen's kitchens; and were covered over with leather; and in the middle of that leather a stick was fixed, and a person stood up, and worked it, in the same manner as is done to pump water out of a cask with a hand pump. I believe it was gold he worked, for it was of a lovely bright yellow colour, and was worn by the women on their wrists and ankles. . . .

The first object which saluted my eyes when I arrived on the coast was the sea, and a slave ship, which was then riding at anchor, and waiting for its cargo. These filled me with astonishment, which was soon converted into terror when I was carried on board. I was immediately handled and tossed up to see if I were sound by some of the crew; and I was now persuaded that I had gotten into a world of bad spirits, and that they were going to kill me.

Their complexions too differing so much from ours, their long hair, and the language they spoke, (which was very different from any I had ever heard) united to confirm me in this belief. Indeed such were the horrors of my views and fears at the moment, that, if ten thousand worlds had been my own, I would have freely parted with them all to have exchanged my condition with that of the meanest slave in my own country. When I looked round the ship too and saw a large furnace or copper boiling, and a multitude of black people of every description chained together, every one of their countenances expressing dejection and sorrow, I no longer doubted of my fate; and, quite overpowered with horror and anguish, I fell motionless on the deck and fainted. When I recovered a little I found some black people about me, who I believed were some of those who brought me on board, and had been receiving their pay; they talked to me in order to cheer me, but all in vain. I asked them if we were not to be eaten by those white men with horrible looks, red faces, and loose hair. They told me I was not; and one of the crew brought me a small portion of spirituous liquor in a wine glass; but, being afraid of him, I would not take it out of his hand. One of the blacks therefore took it from him and gave it to me, and I took a little down my palate, which, instead of reviving me, as they thought it would, threw me into the greatest consternation at the strange feeling it produced, having never tasted any such liquor before. Soon after this the blacks who brought me on board went off, and left me abandoned to despair. I now saw myself deprived of all chance of returning to my native country, or even the least glimpse of hope of gaining the shore, which I now considered as friendly; and I even wished for my former slavery in preference to my present situation, which was filled with horrors of every kind, still heightened by my ignorance of what I was to undergo. I was not long suffered to indulge my grief; I was soon put down under the decks, and there I received such a salutation in my nostrils as I had never experienced in my life: so that, with the loathsomeness of the stench, and crying together, I became so sick and low that I was not able to eat, nor had I the least desire to taste any thing. I now wished for the last friend, death, to relieve me; but soon, to my grief, two of the white men offered me eatables; and, on my refusing to eat, one of them held me fast by the hands, and laid me across I think the windlass, and tied my feet, while the other flogged me severely. I had never experienced any thing of this kind before; and although, not being used to the water, I naturally feared that element the first time I saw it, yet nevertheless, could I have got over the nettings, I would have jumped over the side, but I could not; and, besides, the crew used to watch us very closely who were not chained down to the decks, lest we should leap into the water: and I have seen some of these poor African prisoners most severely cut for attempting to do so, and hourly whipped for not eating. This indeed was often the case with myself.

4. Communication to the *South Carolina Gazette*, 1738

Upon arrival in the Americas, slaves from Africa were distributed through the New World as commodities in a market. Through this process, their status as objects of investment was confirmed. The following letter, written in 1738 to the *South Carolina Gazette,* suggests the dehumanizing aspects of the slave system, as the writer discusses the variations in the market for slaves.

Communication to the *South Carolina Gazette,* 1738

March 9, 1738.

Mr. Timothy, I Was in hopes that the Complaint of bad Pay and Loss on Returns made for 2 years pass by the Gentlemen of London and Bristol, who are concerned in the Negro Trade to this Province, would have prevented so great an Importation for some Years to come, and the early Advices of our Crops being lost this Year, I also imagined would have induced those Gentlemen to have sent Orders to the West Indies for the Masters adressed for this Province with such Slaves, not to proceed. But the Arrival of Capt Power with above 300 Slaves, and by him Advice that several others may be expected, make me imagine, that either the former Complaints were groundless, or, that there must be an Extravagant Profit on that Trade in this Province, by selling the Negroes at a much greater Price here than in any other Port of America. The last Reason seems to be likeliest, for I have known many Slaves bought in the Barbadoes, etc. and sent here for sale, which have been sold with good Profit.

I cannot avoid observing on this Occasion, that altho' a few Negroes annually imported into this Province might be of advantage to most People; yet such large Importations of 2600 and 2800 Negroes every Year is not only a Loss to many, but in the end may prove the Ruin of the Province, as it most certainly does that of many poor industrious Planters, who unwarily engage in buying more than they have Occasion for, or are able to pay. It is for their Sakes only, I now take the trouble of writing this, that they may not further involve themselves in utter Ruin.

Negroes may be said to be the Bait proper for catching a Carolina Planter, as certain as Beef to catch a Shark. How many under the Notion Of 18 Months Credit, have been tempted to buy more Negroes than they could Possibly expect to pay in 3 Years! This is so notorious, that few Inhabitants I believe will doubt it. I have heard many declare their own Folly in this particular, with a Resolution never to do so again: Yet so great is the Infatuation, that the many Examples of their Neighbours Misfortunes and Danger by such Purchases do not hinder new Fools from bringing themselves into the same Difficulty.

Until about the Year 1733, the common Method of selling Negroes in this Province was, to be paid in Rice, whereby the Sellers knew to make above 10 per Cent per Annum Profits, by a Forbearance of Payment under the Title of commuting their Bonds. The Rice valued at about 37 *s.* 6 *d.* per C. and the Casks given for nothing: The Factors here were in general under no other Contract with their Employers at Home, than to remit the Rice when they had receiv'd it from the Planter. But now the Case is alter'd, the Sales and Contracts being now upon a new and quite different Footing, which I believe will in the End prove not only worse for the Merchants at Home, but also for the Factor Seller, and Planter Buyer here.

If I am rightly inform'd, the Negroes that are now sold in this Province are sent upon those Terms, *viz.* The Factors here to make good all bad Debts, to remit 2 thirds of the Value in 12 Months, the other one third in 2 Years after the Day of Sale. Now as they give Security in Great Britain to perform their Contracts, and as their further Business depends upon the doing thereof, it is no surprize to find them now more exact in requiring their Payments when it becomes due than they did 6 Years ago; and as our Currency is every Year decreasing in Value, so all others who have Remittances to make to Great Britain in Money, will be the more urgent to have their Payments.

It is so common for many Planters to buy Negroes and dry Goods for more Value than they can possibly expect to be able to pay for when due, that it may be called a general Distemper, which of late has very much encreased, by the two last bad Crops. In Case of failure of Payment they think they make full Satisfaction by giving Bond payable next Year, bearing 10 per Cent Interest. This is Sufficient, I must own, to those who lend Money at Interest, or who are only concern'd in our In-land Trade; but will not answer to those who must turn the Currency into Sterling. For suppose I had a Man's Bond for 700 £ two Years ago, that Money then would have purchase 100 £ Sterling, whereas I now give 770 £ for 100 £ Sterling. Now if the Debtor pays me with 10 per Cent Interest it is 840, so that altho' he pays me at the Rate of 10 per Cent. per Annum, yet I really receive but 5 per Cent: For the 840 £. he pays me, will only purchase 110 £. Sterling, which is but 10 £. upon the 100 £. for two Years. It's worse in Rice, for two Years ago 700 £. would have bought 65 or 70 Barrels of Rice, and now it won't buy above 40 Barrels, as Rice was then 40 s. and is now 71 s.

Those Reasons may be sufficient to excuse any trading Man for insisting upon punctual Payment, and also to warn those in Debt not to depend so much upon the Lenity of the Merchants in Town, besides as their is not one in 50 of those who sell Rice that will give 10 Days Credit, how can they expect the Buyers should be putt off with the Notion of paying Interest? Which it's well known will buy nothing at any Market, and Merchants can't support their Credit, or carry on Trade, without buying Produce.

My whole Design of this is only to warn the unthinking Part of our Planters against falling into the same Misfortunes next Year they have met with in this, *viz* being unable to pay their Debts. The common excuse is the Loss of Crop: But let many of those in Debt look into their Affairs, and they will find a good crop of Rice even suppos'd at 60 s. per C: not sufficient to pay all their Debts, nor will a good Crop next Year pay half the Debts now due to the trading Men in Town; and in Case a general good Crop should be made, depend upon, Rice will be under 40 s. per C.

If I may be so bold as to give my Advice in the Affair of Negroes, it would be this, that before any Planter offer to buy one more, or even to venture into a Negro Yard, he should first make up an Account of all he owes now to every Person, and then make a Calculation of what he may reasonably expect to make this Year. The most certain way to know this is, to sum up the Amounts of his last 4 Years Produce of the same Number of Hands a fourth Part of which he may expect to have this Year: For a wild Expectation of 10 Barrels per Negro only brings a Disappointment to the Owner, and in Time may prove his Ruin.

Suppose a Man has 20 Negroes, and for these 4 Years past has made in all 240 Barrels of Rice, he may expect to have 60 Barrels next Year, which at a Medium of Price will be about 700 £ Currency, now if that Person finds that he is in Debt 1000 £ or only 700 £ how can he engage for any further Payments Next Year, without exposing himself at the Mercy of his Creditors? But if the same Man finds he owes only 100 £ he may safely buy 2 Negroes and have a common Chance [to] pay [for] them besides his annual Charges. Would People take this prudent Method to think before they buy Negroes, it would in the End prove better for them. If they complain of the Merchants being pressing for Payments this Year, depend on it they will be worse next Year. Besides this Caution of those who are in Debt would make fewer Buyers and of Course cheaper Negroes, so that in Time they might be had here as cheap as in other Parts of America. But if any Person who can't pay his Debts now, encreases them by buying more Negroes, how can he desire any Person to have Patience 'till next Year? If his Slaves are then seized for Debt, who is to Blame? Is it not his own Act and Deed? Could he not have lived without these new Negroes? Buying the needful Apparel, Meat or Drink pleads for itself, as Mankind can't live without some Necessaries. Can any Man be certain of a better Crop next Year than he had last? If they can't they should not increase their Debts beyond absolute Necessity.

Were it possible to prevent any Negroes to be imported for 3 Years to come, I am persuaded it would be for the general Advantage of all the Inhabitants in this Province, and the only means to relieve us of the Load of Debts we are now owing to Great Britain, which I believe is equal to the Amount of 3 Years Produce.

5. SLAVE COFFLE IN AFRICA IN THE EIGHTEENTH CENTURY

The slave trade was a complicated activity that involved both Africans and Europeans. Africans remained in control of the coasts from Senegambia to the Niger, the point of interaction between European slave traders and the Africans who supplied them. Although some slaves were initially taken by Europeans on or near the coasts themselves, an organized trade soon developed. Individuals were sold into slavery either by native chiefs who wished to be rid of troublemakers, by their families, or by themselves in times of hardship. They were also kidnapped by other Africans and then sold, or had been taken as prisoners of war in domestic conflicts within West Africa. Slaves captured in the interior of West Africa were then moved to the coast in long marches that could last for weeks. In these coffles, slaves were bound hand and foot and kept together by wooden and rope braces linking one to another to make escape difficult. European traders who lived as permanent residents of the coast bought slaves when the coffles reached the ports, and kept on hand slaves to be purchased by slaving ships that set in at the port. The slaves were then placed on boats for the New World, primarily the West Indies, facing the perils of the Middle Passage and then transport from the West Indies to plantations throughout the New World.

Figure 14.1 An African slave coffle on its way to the coast. Courtesy of the National Museum of History and Technology, Smithsonian Institution.

Study Questions

1. Describe the principal features of the activity of the port of Bahia as Dampier saw them. What effects did the trade through the port have on the society of Bahia?
2. How does Alexander Falconbridge assess the consequences, for Africans and for Europeans, of the slave trade?
3. What were the effects of the enslavement of Equiano on him, other than the loss of liberty?
4. How does the author of the letter to the *South Carolina Gazette* approach the slave trade?
5. What impressions about the slave trade can you draw from the picture of the slave coffle?
6. What are the most important aspects of the Atlantic trading complex as portrayed in these documents?

Suggested Readings

Altman, Ida, and James Horn, eds. *"To Make America": European Emigration in the Early Modern Period.* Berkeley: University of California Press, 1991.

Bailyn, Bernard. *The Peopling of North America: An Introduction.* New York: Random House, 1986.

Curtin, Philip D. *The Rise and Fall of the Plantation Complex.* New York: Cambridge University Press, 1998.

Demos, John. *The Unredeemed Captive: A Family Story from Early America.* New York: Knopf, 1994.

Klein, Herbert S. *The Atlantic Slave Trade.* New York: Cambridge University Press, 1999.

Manning, Patrick, ed. *Slave Trades 1500–1800: Globalization of Forced Labor.* Brookfield, VT: Variorum, 1996.

McAlister, Lyle. *Spain and Portugal in the New World, 1492–1700.* Minneapolis: University of Minnesota Press, 1984.

Thornton, John. *Africa and Africans in the Making of the Atlantic World, 1400–1800,* 2d ed. New York: Cambridge University Press, 1998.

White, Richard. *The Middle Ground: Indians, Empires and Republics in the Great Lakes Region, 1650–1815.* New York: Cambridge University Press, 1991.

Web Sites

1. Chronology on the History of Slavery and Racism

    http://www.innercity.org/holt/slavechron.html

2. Excerpts from Slave Narratives

    http://vi.uh.edu/pages/mintz/primary.htm

3. Exploration and Settlement, 1675–1800

    http://lib.utexas.edu/Libs/PCL/Map_collection/united_states/Exploration_1675.jpg

4. The Jesuit Plantation Project

    http://www.georgetown.edu/departments/amer_studies/coverjpp.html

CREDITS

Africanus, John Leo. *Description de l'Africque tierce partie du Monde*, pp. 89–93. Volume 1. Paris: Ernest Leroux, 1896. Translated by Megan Armstrong.

Aquinas, Thomas. *The "Summa Theologica" of St. Thomas Aquinas*, III, pp. 22–28. London: Burns Oates and Washbourne, Ltd., 1894. Translated by the Fathers of the English Dominican Province.

Averroes, *On the harmony of Religion and Philosophy*, pp. 44–49. London: Messrs. Luzac & Co., 1961. Translated by George Hourani. Copyright © E. J. W. Gibb Memorial Trust. Reprinted by permission of the trustees of the E. J. W. Gibb Memorial Trust.

Battuta, Ibn. *The Travels of Ibn Battuta (1325–1354)*, pp. 74–80 (1829). Reprinted, London: Darf Publishers Ltd, 1984. Translated by Rev. Samuel Lee.

Biggar, H. P., ed. *The Voyages of Jacques Cartier*, pp. 85–91. Ottawa: F. A. Ackland, 1924.

Casas, Bartolomé de las. *The Tears of the Indians*, pp.1–8. London, 1656. Reprinted, Baarle-Nassau: SoMa, 1980, Translated by John Phillips.

Casas, Bartolomé de las. *The Journal of his First Voyage to America*, pp. 46–47, 62–68. London: Jarrolds, 1925 (?).

Castillo, Bernal Diaz del. *The True History of the Conquest of New Spain*, pp. 128–135. London: Hakluyt Society, 1808. Edited by Genaro Garcia. Translated by Alfred Percival Maudslay.

Charlevoix, Pierre de. *Journal of a Voyage to North America*, pp. 19–27, vol. 2. London: 1761. Reprinted, Chicago: Caxton Club, 1923.

Correa, Gaspar. *The Three Voyages of Vasco Da Gama*, pp. 326–334. London: Hakluyt Society, 1869. Translated by Henry E. J. Stanley.

Cortes, Hernan. *Letters of Cortes*, pp. 255–264. New York and London: G. P. Putnam's Sons, 1908. Translated by Francis August MacNutt.

Cyrano de Bergerac, Savinien. *A Voyage to the Moon* in *A Voyage to the Moon and Sun*, pp. 49–59. London, New York: George Routledge and Sons Ltd.; E. P. Dutton and Co., 1923. Translated by Richard Aldington.

Dampier, William. *Dampier's Voyages,* II, pp. 381–387. New York: E. P. Dutton, 1906. Edited by John Masefield.

Davenport, Frances Gardiner, ed. *European Treaties Bearing on the History of the United States and Its Dependencies to 1648,* pp. 75–78. Washington, DC: Carnegie Institution of Washington, 1917.

Egeria. *Egeria's Travels to the Holy Land,* pp. 141–147. Warminster: Aris & Philips, 1999. Reprinted with the permission of Aris and Philips. Edited by John Wilkinson.

Erasmus, Desiderius. *In Praise of Folly.* New York: Peter Eckler Publishing Co., 1922.

Falconbridge, Alexander. *An Account of the Slave Trade on the Coast of Africa,* pp. 12–15, 19–20. London: Phllips, 1788.

Galilei, Galileo. *Dialogues Concerning Two New Sciences* (1914), pp. 1–11. Reprinted, New York: MacMillan Press, 1933.

Gregory of Tours. *History of the Franks,* pp. 38–41. New York: Columbia University Press, 1916. Translated by Ernest Brehaut.

Hakluyt, Richard. *Voyages,* vol. 1 (1907), pp. 216–230. Reprinted, London and New York: Everyman's Library, 1962.

Hariot, Thomas. *Narrative of the First English Plantation of Virginia,* pp. 35–39. London: Bernard Quaritch, 1893.

Helps, Arthur. *The Spanish Conquest in America and Its Relation to the History of Slavery and to the Government of the Colonies,* pp. 358–361. London: J. W. Parker & Sons, 1855–1861.

Herodotus. *The History of Herodotus,* vol. 1 (1910), pp. 116–156. Reprinted, London and Toronto: J. M. Dent & Sons, 1927. Translated by George Rawlinson.

The Holy Bible, Authorized Version, pp. 702–705. New York: Thomas Nelson & Sons, 1901.

Homer. *The Odyssey of Homer,* pp. 158–166. New York: Anglican Book Exchange, 1880. Translated by Alexander Pope.

l'Incarnation, Marie de. *Lettres de la Révérend Mère Marie de l'Incarnation,* pp. 95–99. Tournai: Vve. H. Casterman, 1876. Edited by Abbé Richaudeau. Translated into English by Megan Armstrong.

The Interesting Narrative of Olaudah Equiano Written by Himself, pp. 45–52, 70–74. London: Printed by the Author, 1789.

Jacobsen, Thorkild, ed. *The Harps That Once . . . Sumerian Poetry in Translation,* pp. 298–303, 311–313. Copyright © Yale University Press (1987). Reprinted by permission of Yale University Press.

Friar Jordanus. *Wonders of the East,* pp. 26–33, 55–57. London: Printed for the Hakluyt Society, 1863.

Journal of Jan Van Riebeeck, 2, pp. 304–305, 328–329. Capetown: A. A. Balkema Publishing Company, 1954. Edited by H. B. Thom. Published by the Van Riebeeck Society. Reprinted by permission of A. A. Balkema Publishing Company.

Jubayr, Ibn. *The Travels of Ibn Jubayr,* pp. 318–325. London: Jonathan Cape, 1952. Translated by R. J. C. Broadhurst. Copyright © Random House, 1952. Reprinted by permission of Random House.

Kenton, Edna, ed. *The Jesuit Relations and Allied Documents. Travels and Explorations of the Jesuit Missionaries in North America (1610–1791),* pp. 211–218. New York: Albert & Charles Boni, 1925.

Laws of the Salian and Ripuarian Franks, pp. 39, 72–75, 86–87, 90–92. New York: AMS Press, 1986. Edited by Theodore John Rivers. Copyright © AMS Press. Reprinted by the permission of AMS Press, Inc.

Llull, Ramón. *Book of the Lover and Beloved,* pp. 23–27. London: Society for Promoting Christian Knowledge, 1923. Translated by Allison Peers.

Locke, John. *An Essay Concerning Human Understanding.* 1. pp. 25–45. Oxford: Clarendon Press, 1894.

Mercure de France IX (July–December 1725), pp. 2843–2853. Reprinted, Geneva: Slatkine Reprints, 1968. Translated by Megan Armstrong.

Monro, Charles Henry, ed. *The Digest of Justinian,* pp. 231–233, 239, 254–255, 259–260. Cambridge: Cambridge University Press, 1909. Translated by Charles Henry Monro.

Montaigne, Michel de. *The Essays of Montaigne,* pp. 271–286. Cambridge: Harvard University Press, 1925. Translated and edited by George B. Ives.

Moran, William L., ed. *The Amarna Letters,* pp. 1–2, 7, 16–17, 142–143. (Copyright holder). Reprinted with the permission of Johns Hopkins University Press, 1987.

More, Thomas. *Utopia,* pp. 77–90. London: M. S. Rickerby, 1852.

Morton, Thomas. *The New English Canaan* (1637), pp.123–129. Reprinted, New York: Burt Franklin, 1967. Published by the Prince Society.

Pico della Mirandola, Giovanni. "On the Dignity of Man," pp. 223–227. In *The Renaissance Philosophy of Man.* Chicago: University of Chicago Press, 1948, Edited by Ernst Cassirer, Paul Oskar Kristeller, and John Herman Randall Jr. Copyright © University of Chicago Press. Reprinted by permission of the University of Chicago Press.

Pliny. *The Natural History of Pliny,* vol. 2, pp. 117–122. London: Henry G. Bohn, 1855. Translated by John Bostock.

Pritchard, James B., ed. *The Ancient Near East. An Anthology of Texts and Pictures,* pp. 85–86. Copyright © 1969 by Princeton University Press. Reprinted by permission of Princeton University Press.

Ricci, Matteo. *China in the Sixteenth Century,* pp. 254–257. Translated by Louis J. Gallagher, S. J. Copyright © 1942, 1953, and renewed 1970 by Louis J. Gallagher, S. J. Reprinted by permission of Random House, Inc.

Bishop Rimbert. *Anskar, Apostle of the North, 801–865,* pp. 46–52. London: Society for the Propagation of the Gospel in Foreign Parts, 1921. Translated by Charles H. Robinson.

Roth, Martha, ed. *Law Collections from Mesopotamia and Asia Minor,* 2d ed., pp. 59–68. Atlanta, GA.: Scholars Press, 1997, Copyright © Society of

Biblical Literature. Reprinted by permission of the Society of Biblical Literature.

Rowlandson, Marie. *A Narrative of the Captivity and Restoration of Mrs. Mary Rowlandson.* Reprinted in *Narratives of the Indian Wars 1675–1699,* pp. 118–128. New York: Scribner's Sons, 1913. Edited by Charles H. Lincoln.

The Rule of Saint Benedict, pp. 7–9, 26–35, 54–60, 74–77. London: Chatto & Windus, 1925. Translated by Cardinal Gasquet.

Sahagùn, Bernardino de. *Florentine Codex* XII, pp. 117–119. Salt Lake City, UT, and Santa Fe, NM: University of Utah Press and the School of American Research, 1955. Edited by Arthur J. O. Anderson and Charles Dibble. Reprinted with the permission of the University of Utah Press.

Shakespeare, William. *The Tempest,* pp. 3–16. Boston: D. C. Heath & Co., 1905. Edited by Frederick S. Boas.

South Carolina Gazette, letter. In Donan, Elizabeth, ed. *Documents Illustrative of the History of the Slave Trade to America,* vol.4, pp. 291–294. Washington, DC: Carnegie Institution of Washington, 1935.

Strabo. *The Geography of Strabo,* 1. London, 1917; Reprinted, Cambridge: Harvard University Press, 1960.

Swift, Jonathon. *The Works of Jonathon Swift,* vol. 11, pp. 57–63. Boston: Houghton Mifflin and Company, 1883.

Tozzer, Alfred M., ed. *Landa's Relación de las Casas de Yucatan: A Translation.* Papers of the Peabody Museum of American Archaeology and Ethnology, Harvard University, vol. 18, 1941. Reprinted courtesy of The Peabody Museum, Harvard University.

The Travels of Sir John Mandeville, pp. 185–192. London: MacMillian and Co. Limited, 1900.

Vega, Garcilasso de la. *The Royal Commentaries of the Incas,* vol. 2, pp. 495–505. London: Hakluyt Society, 1871.

Villani, Giovanni. *Croniche Fiorentine,* pp. 160–163, 302–305. In *Selections from the Croniche Fiorentine of Villani.* Westminster: Archibald Constable & Co, 1897. Translated by Rose E. Selfe. Edited by H. Wicksteed.

Winthrop, John. *Winthrop Papers,* vol. 2. pp. 13–16. Reprinted with permission of the Massachusetts Historical Society. Edited by Stewart Mitchell.